Fiction's Inexhaustible Voice

Fiction's Inexhaustible Voice

SPEECH AND WRITING IN
FAULKNER

“ ”

STEPHEN M. ROSS

THE UNIVERSITY OF GEORGIA PRESS

ATHENS AND LONDON

© 1989 by the University of Georgia Press
Athens, Georgia 30602

Designed by Debby Jay
Set in Linotron 202 10 on 13 Plantin
The paper in this book meets the guidelines
for permanence and durability of the Committee on
Production Guidelines for Book Longevity of
the Council on Library Resources.

Printed in the United States of America

95 94 93 92 91   P   5 4 3 2 1

Library of Congress Cataloging in Publication Data
Ross, Stephen M.
Fiction's inexhaustible voice.

Bibliography: p.
Includes index.
1. Faulkner, William, 1897–1962—Criticism and interpretation.
2. Voice in literature.   3. Speech in literature.
4. Psychology in literature.   5. Oratory in literature.
I. Title.
PS3511.A86Z9625   1989   813'.52   88–4720
ISBN 0–8203–1045–X (alk. paper)
ISBN 0–8203–1375–0 (pbk.: alk. paper)

British Library Cataloging in Publication Data available

Dedicated to
Julian Lenhart Ross
and
Carol Moodey Ross

Contents

Contents

Preface

The experience of reading Faulkner has always been for me one of fascination with the expressive voice I hear in my reading. From my first acquaintance with a Faulkner novel, long before I began the professional study of literature, I was caught up by the power of his language in ways that I was not by the writing of any other author. I lost my sense of time; I would feel that I was reading rapidly only to discover I had completed just a few pages. My internal reading voice echoed words I could not understand in long and seemingly endless periods that I could not consciously absorb. Only in part did this effect derive from Faulkner's plots, for even when I was unable to follow the intricacies of a given novel (and in early high school I remember being hopelessly confused by my first attempt at *Absalom, Absalom!*), I was still mesmerized by the prose. I could not fully understand the effect Faulkner's prose exerted, but I knew it was powerful, and I knew I wanted to try to explain it.

I initially believed, with the naive mimeticism of a young reader, that Faulkner's prose affected me as it did because it captured and imitated the mind's movement, that he wrote the way we think. But that notion would not suffice for many novels, certainly not for *The Sound and the Fury* or *As I Lay Dying*, for there I was immersed in the way *others* thought—the movement of my mind was not "imitated" in Benjy's narrative, or in Quentin's, or Jason's, or Darl Bundren's. Later, in more formal studies, I rediscovered Faulkner as a complex artist whose novels readily lent themselves to close analysis. New Critical methodology led me to interpret his fiction, to uncover its symbols, myths, paradoxes, and ironies, and to locate those special scenes that, like fine short poems, have clearly demarcated parameters of meaning and effect. I looked also to structure as a

ix

wellspring for the power Faulkner's prose could exert, to architectonics of plot like the Christian parable that shapes *The Sound and the Fury*, the mythos of nature that permeates "The Bear," or the spiraling symmetries of narrative in *Light in August* and *Absalom, Absalom!* Later still I was led to Faulkner the Southerner. Reading about Faulkner as I reread the fiction, I believed that his compelling effect must derive from the context out of which his fiction emerges, both in the sense of historical circumstance and of literary tradition. I became enamored of Faulkner's *style*, believing that perhaps it was Faulkner's "Southernness" I was hearing in the prose, a modernist angst garbed in Southern oratory's flowing rhetoric.

Many readers of Faulkner and of the criticism he has inspired could probably recall a similar itinerary through differing ways of accounting for Faulkner. And the itinerary could, of course, be extended, for Faulkner studies have produced some of the best criticism in American and European scholarship, from narrative analysis to textual study to work grounded in myth, psychology, and philosophy. This superb critical literature has never quite solved the mystery of the power Faulkner's prose could exert over my reading. What was it about that voice that could charge reading with such strange, haunting power? I needed an inspiration to explain it to me. Embarrassingly trite as it might sound, I did experience a kind of epiphany in which I discovered what seemed at the time to be a "truth" about Faulkner. Sitting on a campus bench, unable to stay in my library carrel but needing to think of how to write about the Quentin section of *The Sound and the Fury*, I kept being disturbed by talking around me—on another bench nearby, on the grass behind me, among students walking by. I was not listening, but others' voices kept intruding; my thoughts were filled with voices. That bench may not have been a wisely chosen place to get work done, but it was a fortuitous one, for I thought to myself, "that's the trouble with Quentin—his head is full of talking. The whole book is full of talking." Not a brilliantly formulated or breathtaking thesis, to be sure, but new to me—and new as far as I then understood it to the criticism on Faulkner. I felt at the time that I had stumbled onto a crucial if fairly obvious fact that could lead to a greater comprehension of the effect Faulkner had on me. It was the effect of voice, both of a single Faulknerian voice and of voices heard within the fiction's world. Reading Faulkner generated a power that could mesmerize in the same way that listening intently could replace one's personal inner "self-voice" with another's voice or with others' voices over which one had no control.

I do not wish to claim that this discovery of voice in Faulkner solved the mystery of his power over my reading. Nonetheless, my thinking about Faulkner has never disentangled itself from the assumption that voice is in some way deeply implicated in the experience of Faulkner. I am quite sure I have not *accounted* for the impact Faulkner always made on me or on other readers, but I am convinced that a careful consideration of voice in his works touches upon a fundamental source of his fiction's power.

Literary theory has become so sophisticated and so intellectually rich (and to some so maddening) that personal testimonials like mine about Faulkner's literary power seem a bit trivial when offered as justification for yet another critical study, and I will not insist that my impressions provide sufficient reason for considering voice in his fiction. Nor do I claim that what this book offers is *the* way to read Faulkner. Recent theory has taught us, surely, that there are many more ways to cope with literary artifacts and with our reading than anyone thirty years ago could have begun to imagine. This book, simply put, is a set of four essays on voice in Faulkner that has the pragmatic goal of bringing such useful literary theory and theories of discourse to bear on Faulkner as will help explain the power of voice within his works and within our reading of him. I invoke many different approaches to literature in the course of my discussion because I have found in recent theory many ideas that take us further into the fiction than we have been able to go before. The four essays on voice therefore vary in their methodology, beginning with consideration of a phenomenology of voice manifested over the course of Faulkner's career (in chapter 1), turning to a more formal analysis of how speech and thought come to be represented in fiction (in chapters 2 and 3), and concluding with a discussion of the ideology of a discursive practice (chapter 4).

This mixture of approaches does not have as its primary goal new *interpretations* of particular Faulkner novels and stories—although I believe that fresh perspectives do indeed result from considering voice carefully. Like any reader, I care what the novels and stories might or might not mean, but I care more about *how* they express meaning, so our central questions will be: What is "voice" in Faulkner's fiction? and How does it function? Thus, the book does not proceed novel by novel, but rather voice by voice—in a sense that the Introduction's definition of modes of voice in Faulkner will initially spell out. Nor is this study of Faulkner's voice an attempt to offer new revelations into William Faulkner, the enigmatic Mississippian. I am intrigued by Faulkner the person (and I will talk about him occasionally in this book), but the voice my reading responds to comes from the pages of written texts and not from the mouth of a certain human speaker. Nor is this book a theoretical study of voice in literature that for convenience happens to borrow its examples from Faulkner's texts. I am interested in the possibilities of such a theory and hope to contribute to it, but my goal is to explore voice in Faulkner for the sake of better understanding his fiction. That is to say, the present book offers a *reading* of Faulkner, constructed within theoretically grounded notions of voice and aimed at changing how we experience his fiction and at adding to what we can discover in his texts.

Acknowledgments

I wish to thank Jill Faulkner Summers, the William Faulkner Foundation, and the University of Virginia for permission to examine the Faulkner manuscripts at the University of Virginia's Alderman Library. I also wish to thank Random House, Inc., for permission to quote from various novels and stories of William Faulkner published and copyrighted by Random House and its affiliates. I am indebted to various journals that published early versions of the ideas in this book: portions of chapter 1 appeared in the *Faulkner Journal*, of chapter 2 in *PMLA* and *Texas Studies in Literature and Language*, of chapter 3 in *Studies in the Novel*, and of chapter 4 in *Essays in Literature*. My debts to the many commentators on Faulkner and the theorists of literature who have influenced my thinking are noted throughout this study, but I owe special thanks, first, to André Bleikasten, who helped me with his insight and his kind encouragement at a critical stage in my work and, second, to those who have kindly read (or heard) and commented on pieces of this work over the course of many years: Albert Gelpi, Michel Gresset, Carol Kolmerten, Ilse Dusoir Lind, John Matthews, J. Hillis Miller, Thomas C. Moser, François Pitavy, Noel Polk, the late Claude Simpson, William T. Stafford, Karl Zender. My research has been supported generously by the resources and people of the National Endowment for the Humanities. I am also grateful for the professional administrative support I received at various times from Fred Fetrow, Michael Jasperson, Millie Kucher, Lawrence Mazzeno, and David Tomlinson, and I am grateful to Kenneth Kolson for (among other things) his willingness to relieve me of administrative pressures during the final stages of preparing the manuscript. I wish to thank also Karen Orchard, Madelaine Cooke, and Melinda Conner of the University of Georgia Press for their excellent editorial guidance. Many colleagues have helped, often without realizing it, by listening to me talk about Faulkner and by sharing their thoughts about literature: Harriet Bergmann, Neil Berman, Carol Burke, Jerome Christensen, William Epstein, Philip Jason, Dorothy Leland, David Miller, Charles Nolan, Molly Tinsley, Cully Wilcoxon. The patient indulgence of Aidan Ross, Derica Ross, and Laura McAfee warrants my particular gratitude. And, finally, I thank Carol Kolmerten, whose advice and warm encouragement have been utterly crucial.

Abbreviations and Texts

AA   *Absalom, Absalom!*. Quotations and the first page cited are from the corrected text. New York: Vintage-Random, 1987. The second page cited is from the first edition, New York: Random, 1936; Vintage, 1972.

AILD   *As I Lay Dying*. Quotations and the first page cited are from the corrected text. New York: Vintage-Random, 1987. The second page cited is from New York: Random, 1964; Vintage, 1964.

CS   *Collected Stories of William Faulkner*. New York: Random, 1950; Vintage, 1977.

ESPL   *Essays, Speeches & Public Letters*. Ed. James B. Meriwether. New York: Random, 1966.

FAB   *A Fable*. New York: Random, 1954; Modern Library, 1966.

FD   *Flags in the Dust*. Ed. Douglas Day. New York: Random, 1973.

FU   *Faulkner in the University: Class Conferences at the University of Virginia, 1957–1958*. Ed. Frederick L. Gwynn and Joseph L. Blotner. New York: Random-Vintage, 1965; orig. Charlottesville: University of Virginia Press, 1959.

GDM   *Go Down, Moses*. New York: Random–Modern Library, 1942.

H   *The Hamlet*. New York: Random, 1940; Vintage, 1973.

ID   *Intruder in the Dust*. New York: Random, 1948; Vintage, 1972.

LA   *Light in August*. Quotations and the first page cited are from the corrected text. New York: Vintage-Random, 1987. The second page cited is from the first edition, New York: Harrison Smith and Robert Haas, 1932; Vintage, 1972.

LG   *Lion in the Garden: Interviews with William Faulkner, 1926–1962*. Ed. James B. Meriwether and Michael Millgate. New York: Random, 1968.

M   *The Mansion.* New York: Random, 1964; Vintage, 1965.

MOS   *Mosquitoes.* New York: Boni and Liveright, 1927; Liveright, 1951.

NOS   *New Orleans Sketches.* Ed. Carvel Collins. New York: Random, 1968.

P   *Pylon.* New York: Harrison Smith and Robert Haas, 1935; Modern Library, 1967.

RN   *Requiem for a Nun.* New York: Random, 1951.

S   *Sanctuary.* Quotations and the first page cited are from the corrected text. New York: Vintage-Random, 1987. The second page cited is from the first edition, New York: Jonathan Cape and Harrison Smith, 1931; Random–Modern Library, 1932.

SAR   *Sartoris.* New York: Harcourt, 1929.

SF   *The Sound and the Fury.* Quotations and the first page cited are from the corrected text. New York: Vintage-Random, 1987. The second page cited is from the first edition, New York: Jonathan Cape and Harrison Smith, 1929.

SF Facsimile   *William Faulkner Manuscripts 6.* Vol. 1. *The Sound and the Fury,* Holograph Manuscript and Miscellaneous Pages. *The Sound and the Fury,* copyright 1986 by W. W. Norton and Company, Inc. Introduced and Arranged by Noel Polk. New York: Garland, 1987.

SFI (1)   "An Introduction for *The Sound and the Fury.*" Ed. James B. Meriwether. *Southern Review* 8 (October 1972): 705–10.

SFI (2)   "An Introduction to *The Sound and the Fury. A Faulkner Miscellany.* Ed. James B. Meriwether. Jackson: University Press of Mississippi, 1974. 156–61.

SL   *Selected Letters of William Faulkner.* Ed. Joseph L. Blotner. New York: Random, 1977; Vintage, 1978.

SO   *Sanctuary: The Original Text.* Ed. Noel Polk. New York: Random, 1981.

SP   *Soldiers' Pay.* New York: Boni and Liveright, 1926; Liveright, 1970.

T   *The Town.* New York: Random, 1957; Vintage, 1961.

U   *The Unvanquished.* New York: Random, 1938; Vintage, 1956.

US   *Uncollected Stories of William Faulkner.* Ed. Joseph L. Blotner. New York: Random, 1979; Vintage, 1981.

WP   *The Wild Palms.* New York: Random, 1939; Vintage, 1966.

Fiction's
Inexhaustible
Voice

Is it not wonderful how I remember the voices better than anything else? I think they must go deeper into us than other things. I have often fancied heaven might be made of voices.

—GEORGE ELIOT
Daniel Deronda

I made the strange discovery that I had never imagined [Kurtz] as doing, you know, but as discoursing. . . . The man presented himself as a voice.

—JOSEPH CONRAD
Heart of Darkness

Gradually the sense of hearing came to be my favorite sense; for just as the voice is the revelation of the external, incommensurable inwardness, so the ear is the instrument by which this inwardness is apprehended, hearing is the sense by which it is appropriated.

—SØREN KIERKEGAARD
Either-Or

The human voice . . . resounds out of one's own feeling and one's own spirit without any external impulse, just as the height of art in general consists in making the inner give shape to itself out of its own being.

—HEGEL
Aesthetics

Ye Voices, and ye Shadows
And Images of voice . . .
On with your pastime!

—WILLIAM WORDSWORTH
"On the Power of Sound"

[T]here are just too goddamn many of the human race and they talk too much.

—WILLIAM FAULKNER
Letter to H. L. Mencken

Introduction

‹‹‹ ›››

"VOICE" IN
LITERATURE—
VOICES IN FAULKNER

I listen to the voices, . . . and when I put down what the voices say,
it's right.

—WILLIAM FAULKNER TO MALCOLM COWLEY

William Faulkner's stories and novels resonate with living voices: voices
of characters, narrators, the author; voices quoted, mimicked, parodied,
and paraphrased; "liquid silver voices" and voices "harsh like tin and without heat like tin." Recordings of regional dialect ("Likely hit ain't fitten for
hawgs") harmonize, amazingly, with renderings of rhetorical floridity
"constant and inflectioned and ceaseless." Voices emanate from the heart
full of "frantic grief and despair"; voices call from without and around,
from "everywhere now . . . —the rapid and urgent beating of the urgent
and quiring heart of the late spring night." Once a man speaks words
"unprintable and vile, addressed to no one"; again he speaks in a "voice
almost pleasant, almost gentle." A story's central consciousness is one who
listens, one who "could not even see. . . . But he could hear"; one who
pauses in "those subsequent long seconds while there was absolutely no
sound," only to have "the fluid world [rush in] again, the voices coming to

I

him again." Fundamental to the experience in and of Faulkner's fiction is "listening to the voices."[1]

Listening was fundamental to Faulkner's own lived experience as well. In telling Malcolm Cowley that "I listen to the voices, and when I put down what the voices say, it's right" (Cowley 114), Faulkner surely meant in part that he listened to the voices of his Southern heritage: "The South's the place for a novelist to grow up because the folks there talk so much about the past. Why, when I was a little boy there'd be sometimes twenty or thirty people in the house, mostly relatives . . . swapping stories about the family and about the past, while I sat in a corner and listened. That's where I got my books" (Linscott 22). All his life Faulkner seems to have been a listener. His brothers mention occasions when the three boys were told stories by their father, grandfather, and especially their mammy, Callie Barr, who talked of slave days and the Civil War (J. Faulkner 49; Falkner 12–13, 16). Instead of playing with the others when the family visited their grandfather's farm, Faulkner would spend his time listening to the old blacksmith's tales (J. Faulkner 72–73). "At the stove in his father's office he watched and listened as his father's friends drank whiskey and swapped tales. At the courthouse he listened to old men tell stories about the War" (Minter 12). He emphasized listening in his description of his relationship to Sherwood Anderson: "We would meet in the evening, in the afternoons we'd walk and he'd talk and I'd listen, we'd meet in the evenings and we'd go to a drinking place and we'd sit around till one or two o'clock drinking, and still me listening to him talking."[2] In response to a question about his methods of "studying" the country people of his region, Faulkner described yet another kind of listening: "I don't go out with a notebook, but I like these people, that is, I like to listen to them, the way they talk or the things they talk about. . . . I would go around with [my uncle] and sit on the front galleries of country stores and listen to the talk."[3]

Faulkner read voraciously, we know, but listening fed his imagination's growth, as did reading, not simply because specific told tales became sources for his own, but because the very act of listening placed him in a certain relationship to the discourse of the world: "I was just saturated with [history] but never read about it," he claimed, and his image of saturation speaks accurately even if his denial of reading does not. Certainly the discovery of voice's power was a necessary step in the evolution of Faulkner's genius. As a poet, where he began, he had neither a voice of his own nor sources of speech—regional or personal—to draw on. David

Minter writes that Faulkner's problem as a poet "turned mainly on voice." "[Faulkner] needed to find a literary mode less haunted by giants and less bound by conventions. Only then could he discover voices that would encourage him to use not simply the books that he had read and the emotions that troubled him but the world he had observed and the old tales and talking that he had heard" (Minter 41). Needing to abandon the role of writer as creator of static, written, verbal constructs in order to achieve a writing infused with telling, Faulkner could not gain perspective on his own creative emotions until he discovered the "fluidity" of voice: "Unlike the poetry he had read, which seemed fixed because written, the stories he knew existed only in oral tradition" (Minter 82).[4]

The South's oral tradition exerted a profound effect on Faulkner's storytelling, from his admiration for the literary heritage of Twain and Southwest Humor, to his love of oratory, to his development of narrative techniques derived from an oral heritage's shared habits of gossip, swapping yarns, and telling and retelling stories about fellow humans. One gets the sense, too, from Faulkner's remark to Cowley, that he was haunted by the voices he heard. His comment, a response to Cowley's reference to "Hawthorne's complaint about the devil who got into his inkpot," is telling: "Sometimes I don't like what [the voices] say, but I don't change it" (Cowley 114). Although many writers have spoken of their characters taking on independent life once created, Faulkner's primary sign of independent life was speech.

"VOICE" IN LITERARY THEORY

The voices that concern us here are those *we* can listen to, those within the fictional discourse. As readers we can only read, of course, and we must thus keep under erasure terms like "listen" and "hear," which are necessarily figures of speech in reference to written fiction. Indeed, to speak of voice in written fiction is to speak from within the riddle of representation, for silent writing utters no "sound or the whole body of sounds made or produced by the vocal organs of man" (*Oxford English Dictionary* [*OED*]). Soundless print cannot embody "vocal sound as the vehicle of human utterance or expression" (*OED*). Yet I use such terms without bracketing them, for I would not abandon the figural and representational implications of *hearing* voice in fictional texts. As a critical concept "voice" can help us to straddle that gap between the represented world and the textual discourse that narrative analysis often falls into; while we always need to be aware of the concept's figurative origins, it is one intent of this study to speak simultaneously, and without apology, of voice as both a property of the discourse we read and as a part of the world we read about and imagine. Just as other phenomena that can be studied as aspects of both the represented world and the fictional discourse have been treated as fundamental to Faulkner's fiction—vision, or the gaze (Gresset, *Faulkner ou la fascination*), the "play" of language (Matthews), or tension and paradox (Slatoff)—so too does "voice" identify a range of concerns that bridges the gap between the text per se and its imagined events and characters. Faulkner's fictions and texts generate voice at every turn, immersing the reader in a polyphonic discourse where "the center of language is located in the voiced and heard sounding of the word" (Ihde 118).

To accept the figurative implications of "voice" and related terms does not entirely free one of definitional problems, however, for "voice" in literary criticism has a varied and inconsistent usage. The word "voice" has been employed traditionally as a metonymic designation for the human presence we hear or imagine whenever we read a poem or a story. In its commonsensical way "voice" signifies expressive "sound" in literary speech, those inscribed, perceivable differences among characters' talking, among narrators' story telling, and among authors' styles. The sound of *The Adventures of Huckleberry Finn* experientially differs from the sound of *Lord Jim* or *The Ambassadors*, just as Huck's talking sounds little like Marlow's or Lambert Strether's. Hearing imitated speech remains a deeply ingrained convention of reading that will persist despite such claimed exceptions as "concrete" poetry or the French New Novel which, as Stephen Heath put it, attempted to "dissimulate speech" in acts of pure *écriture* (Heath 26–27). Many writers have insisted that human speech is the fountainhead of written art: for Robert Frost, good writing must capture speakers' "sentence sounds"; for Yeats, literature should embody and amplify the "living . . . choir of voices" that are the true repository of any culture's recordable values; for Faulkner, getting his characters "right" meant "listen[ing] to the voices."[5] Voice for many critics pinpoints a basic analogy of literature with speech and grants an assumed priority to the latter; literature is seen as an imitation of speech, or a recording of a presumed (even if imaginary) oral discourse. Scholes and Kellogg, for example, derive a definition of narrative from the historical truism that oral storytelling and its performance antedate written art: "the traditional, oral narrative consists rhetorically of a teller, his story, and an implied audience. The non-traditional, written narrative consists rhetorically of the *imitation*, or *representation*, of a teller, his story, and an implied audience" (53).

As a category in poetics, voice has its roots in the distinction made in classical Greek aesthetics between *diegesis* and *mimesis*. Socrates (in *The Republic*) explains that a poet either speaks in his own voice or he imitates the voice of another (or he mixes the two modes). On this basis we can distinguish drama, epic, and lyric poetry: "Poetry and mythology are, in some cases, wholly imitative—instances of this are supplied by tragedy and comedy; there is likewise the opposite style, in which the poet is the only speaker—of this the dithyramb affords the best example; and the combination of both is found in epic, and in several other styles of poetry" (*Republic* 394B–C). When Homer tells us that Chryses, angry at Agamemnon, prayed against the Greeks, Homer speaks in his own voice without "lead[ing] us to suppose that he is any one else." The prayer itself, however, is rendered as Chryses said it, and in doing this Homer "takes the person of Chryses, and . . . does all that he can to make us believe that the speaker is not Homer, but the aged priest himself" (*Republic* 393A). The latter, the quoting, is *mimesis*, or an imitation of speech, while the former, the informing the reader that Chryses was angry and prayed, is *diegesis*, or simple narrative. The discourse that can be attributed to the poet (that is, the diegetic discourse) does not imitate any speech but it is still regarded as emanating from a speaker ("the poet is the only speaker"). The discourse that a poet attributes to someone else (that is, mimetic discourse) is always double voiced in the sense that the poet is still its origin, but we regard the speakers as personae other than the poet. Even in pure dramatic dialogue the author is responsible for the speech uttered by characters. Aristotle expanded the notion of mimesis by applying the term to both simple narrative and imitation, seeing all poetry as imitative of human actions. To Aristotle the crucial distinction was between more successful or less successful imitation—the dramatic being more imitative than the narrative (or diegetic)—whereas for Plato the crucial distinction was whether the poet spoke in his own voice or imitated another's voice. Thus, Aristotle makes the term "mimetic" one that expresses degree of imitation, not merely the name for the illusion of speech (*Poetics* 1448a).

T. S. Eliot, in "The Three Voices of Poetry," insists that readers will and indeed must read back through imitated voices to the poet's. He identifies three voices: "The first voice is the voice of the poet talking to himself—or to nobody. The second is the voice of the poet addressing an audience, whether large or small. The third is the voice of the poet when he attempts to create a dramatic character speaking" (96). The third, most imitative voice will fade back into the second, for the mimicry of character always depends upon our hearing the poet's own voice behind the character's: "Does not the point of mimicry lie in the recognition of the person mimicked and in the incompleteness of the illusion?" (104).

As Plato uses the distinction between the diegetic and the mimetic, and in its reworking by poets and critics like Eliot, speech is presumed to be the originating discourse of which the written version is essentially a script, a recording, a rendition. This traditional assumption that written literary discourse grows out of speech points to the crucial issue of human origin implicit in concepts of voice. References to "voice" would inherently seem to presume a speaker as origin for what a voice expresses. Plato simply took for granted that *someone* speaks in poetry; the puzzle Socrates explained to Adeimantus was "*who* speaks," not whether anyone speaks at all. As a term in literary theory, "voice" touches upon the whole range of problems clustered around ideas of human "presence": the question of intent, the sources of meaning, the ways an author's personality or cultural identity determines meaning, and the relation between real and represented personae. Notions of voice have often been advanced to mediate among conflicting theoretical solutions to the problem of author.[6]

For many critics voice means authorial distinctiveness or personality, serving as a metonymy for the person that readers sense behind every work. John Fowles insists that "the long evolution of fiction has been very much bound up with finding means to express the writer's 'voice'—his humors, his private opinions, his nature—by means of word manipulation and print alone" (113). To Douglas Fowler "the voice of a novel is its nervous system. . . . A novelist's voice involves his relationship with the material and his relationship with the reader" (103). Albert Guerard supplies the most usable definition of this "personal voice": "[A] voice that is the intimate and often unconscious expression of [every truly original writer's] temperament and unborrowed personality, a voice that in its structures and rhythms reflects the way his mind moves, and reflects too the particular needs and resistances of his spirit." (136). An author's authentic identity will be sounded out because he or she possesses a voice that, like fingerprints, cannot be disguised; it is the nature of personal voice to be discernible through the static interference from fictional events and characters, from intertextual interweavings of other writers' or the culture's texts. Valery calls this unique personal voice "timbre."[7]

6

Not all those who see in "voice" a name for human origin share Guerard's psychologist's faith in the presence of a unitary "unborrowed personality" that unmasks itself in voice. To some users of the term, "voice" identifies one of many possible verbal masks the "true" author can don for a given dramatic performance. Voice in this sense dissimulates the author's "unborrowed personality." Guerard himself recognizes (and carefully distinguishes from the "personal voice") those many voices that "though deeply felt, are clearly 'borrowed'" by an author (137). The novelist John Barth speaks of the "disembodied voice" in fiction, and in his *Lost in the Funhouse* plays hide-and-seek with characters, narrators, and "the disembodied authorial voice," all of whom, like his character Menelaus, equal "voice, no more . . . this voice *is* Menelaus, all there is of him" (131).

Structuralist and intertextual descriptions of discourse seek to disengage "voice" even further from the expressive individual consciousness. Structuralist theories do not locate the "presence" readers sense within a work in the figure of the author, real or implied, nor do they see voice as a disembodied authorial mask. Presence is revealed only within the linguistic and textual play of the discourse, for literary discourse does not imitate a prior speaker. Indeed, the word "voice" and its personal implications are often avoided in definitions of intertextuality, replaced by a notion of "text." Every individual text is traversed by other, prior texts, not as influences but as fields of discourse that cross and recross within each. "The *novel*, seen as a text, is a semiotic practice in which the synthesized patterns of several utterances can be read" (Kristeva 37). Roland Barthes, in *S/Z*, retains the *word* "voice," but primarily as a metaphor like "code," or "force." Literary discourse spins out a network of "forces that can take over [a single] text," a set of codes or "voices out of which the text is woven" (20–21). Voice is a function of grammar as well as the name for our vocal powers, and structuralists like Barthes found in the notion of voice as a linguistic relationship a convenient depersonalizing of its implications. Just as voice (or "diathesis") defines the grammatical relationship between the subject of an utterance and the action indicated by the verb, so in poetics voice can name one aspect of the "positional field of the subject" (Barthes's phrase) established by the arrangements negotiated between the narrative agent and the narrated action. Gérard Genette brings this grammatical analogy to fruition in his practical criticism of Proust. "Voice" does not define a medium of utterance, but rather a set of relationships among time of narration, implied or actual narrators, and diegetic levels of

7

the fiction's discourse. From this fundamental relationship Genette can derive subtle and elaborate configurations of narrative without pretending to solve the mystery of an author's (or implied author's) assumed presence behind voice and absence from discourse. Genette also expands the ancient distinction between diegesis and mimesis in order to define a series of narrative levels, such as "meta-diegetic" (stories told by a character inside the fictional world) or "extra-diegetic" (the author's writing of the book).[8]

Poststructuralist thought also disengages voice from person but offers no abstract structure as substitute. Jacques Derrida's writings interrogate voice as part of the logocentrism of Western philosophy (which includes structuralism) that must be deconstructed. In its struggle to discover an "origin" (or what Derrida more often calls "presence") that grounds life and thought in something unchangeable and underived from any prior source, philosophy has treated voice as the manifestation of that origin. Whether as God, or as consciousness, or even as abstract structure, philosophy's yearned-for presence has been expressed in figures of voice. Western philosophy is then, Derrida insists, a *phono*centrism wherein voice has been privileged "as a value of presence . . . presence of meaning to consciousness, self-presence" (*Positions* 5). Derrida argues that voice no more equals or expresses an "origin" than does any other manifest sign, for all discourse and all signs—indeed, all phenomena—are traces deposited in the play of *différance*. To choose voice as the "value of presence" only delays the inevitable realization that our entanglement in language renders our discursive universe originless. Theories of literary representation, like philosophy, can be deconstructed because they are similar gestures: the reading back through language to some origin—usually an author or a speaker—that serves as the source of representation and that is not itself represented. But in a Derridean poetics any author or speaker discerned in a work itself results from representation. Voice and speaker can be dissociated because both derive from the play of language; both are traces, neither is originary. Plato's distinction between diegetic and mimetic, for example, should not be regarded as a hierarchy wherein the diegetic discourse serves as origin for the mimetic, or where the fictional discourse imitates a prior and truer reality. Both are caught up in the representing enterprise, for there is no "reality" to be imitated other than representation. The poet's "own voice" that Socrates hears is every bit as much an imitation as any character's voice. So, too, is the written text a participant in the originless play of language; it is not simply a tool used by voice to express the reality of thought or event. Wherever one might be tempted to stop the play and assert "this is real, this is being imitated," Derrida would demonstrate that it, too, is a sign of yet another sign, for all we can perceive are signs. John T. Matthews, who offers a strong Derridean reading of Faulkner, concludes that "Faulkner's mature aesthetic" holds that "art cannot simply represent either its subject or its creator's mind."[9]

Many readers are reluctant to give up so entirely the representational implications of "voice," even as they acknowledge the inherent absence of a human speaker behind literary discourse. To many, poststructuralism has dissipated too thoroughly the idea of author or speaker into a rarified, humanless atmosphere where the structures and binary oppositions of literary discourse precipitate voicelessly like crystals in solution. Some of the more carefully elaborated uses of voice thus have served (deliberately or not) to balance the traditional sense of speaker with the free play of language apart from its human origin. Eric Rabkin, whose diagrammatic analyses of "diachronic structure" in narrative discourse are far removed from the kind of "personal voice" Guerard describes, still regards it as tautological that narratives have narrators and thus voice (59). Without an awareness of "voice as presence" there would be no narrative (just as, by analogy, there could be no drama for the theatergoer without an awareness of physical presence [140]). He defines voice as "an anthropomorphized notion of the continuing presence that keeps us within the narrative world and ameliorates the completeness" of any narrative segment except the last (186). For Gabriel Josipovici, voice emerges in fiction when we sense a disparity between the fiction's discourse and presumed truth, when an author like Chaucer seeks to dissociate himself from any claim to truth his fictions might imply, when a discrepancy opens up between the content of what is told and the tone, "when the tone [in 'The Nun's Priest's Tale'] is too high for the content [so that] the decorum is now seen as artifice and the *voice* of the narrator makes itself heard, struggling with the material" (84). Hugh Kenner, in *Joyce's Voices*, freely attaches the label "voice" to any imaginable origin for discourse: to the author James Joyce, to various characters, to distinguishable character-narrators and to unidentified narrators such as the "double narrator" with "one voice perhaps better informed about stage-management, the other a more accomplished lyrical technician" (67). Geoffrey Hartman uses voice as one of several concepts marshalled for the purpose of "reinvigorating the theory of art as mimesis or representation" (*The Fate of Reading* xii–xiii) and resisting that thrust of Derridean deconstruction that would "kill the voice" (*The Fate of Reading*

254). He argues that "to talk about writing as such or about language as such is too abstract, just as to talk about literary language per se is too isolating. At some point the affective power of voice, as well as the relation of particular words to that resonating field we call the psyche, must be considered" (*Saving the Text* xxii). Voice for Hartman is a kind of "ur-image" or origination of all a poem's images; it is not "character," though it can represent character; it is not author but a means for the movement of language from within a poem's representations outward toward the author, and further toward all literature.

From a broader cultural perspective "voice" can name the collection of ideologically derived identities that manifest themselves in fictional discourse. Voice need not reintroduce a personal author, with all the attendant theoretical problems of psychology and intent, if voice is expanded into an ideological phenomenon gathering to itself all the historical, cultural, and discursive currents that flow through the individual. Susan Lanser employs voice to evoke an image of a text's author as origin grounded in a social realm—including, of course, the institution of literature itself—that confers "diegetic authority" on the voice we sense in the discourse (122). Mikhail Bakhtin's theory of the novel as a complex web of many voices is the most famous, and to many the most attractive version of voice as having a human, yet nonpersonal referent. Bakhtin rejects the notion of a *single* authorial voice as an object of study in the novel. He stresses that the ideological multiplicity (which Lanser sees *behind* the textual voice) is, in the novel, foregrounded within the discourse itself. In "Discourse in the Novel" Bakhtin defines the novel as a "heteroglossic" genre, that is, a mode of discourse composed of many voices or languages in "dialogical" relationship to each other (*The Dialogical Imagination* 265–67). Each single voice has its own will, point of view, and consciousness, though its singularity is not so much personal as ideological. Voice is revealed through parody and caricature, through the presence of recognizable institutional discourse, through mere implication (in which a voice is "hidden" but still affects other voices), as well as, of course, through characters. For Bakhtin the concept of voice in prose fiction is inherently a culturally contingent mix within the fiction's discourse and constitutive of that discourse.

While I have touched only very lightly on some of the ways literary criticism has employed "voice," these brief samples can suggest how much complex and even abstruse weight the familiar term can be made to bear. But even if not consistently used, "voice" bears its weight of implication extremely well. The varied concepts it embraces in fact constitute its value, for differing theories of literary representation cannot escape each other when they employ "voice." Voice regarded as a personal expressive gesture of a consciousness, whether a character's or an author's, must confront the inevitable *absence*, in all writing but especially in fiction, of its own origin. Attempts to eject personal origin from the theater of voice's performance must likewise confront the inevitable practice of readers to read "back" from voice to person: even the use of voice (to quote Paul De Man) "in a grammatical terminology . . . is [still] a metaphor inferring by analogy the intent of the subject from the structure of the predicate" (139). However compelling Derrida's dismantling of the metaphysical assumptions drawn from such an "infer[ence] by analogy" may be, the very enterprise of deconstruction itself presumes that such inferences of origin have been and will be drawn.

From these comments it might seem that "voice" is a universal solvent of some sort by which conflicts in poetics might be dissolved. Perhaps it is, but to use a concept of voice to reconcile competing critical positions is far from the object of this study. The purpose here remains more pragmatic and more concrete: to uncover the nature—the "essence" if I may be allowed that outmoded term—of voice in Faulkner by examining various modes in which speech and writing are created and employed in his works. I do not seek to *define* voice in Faulkner so much as to explore it. To do so we will need to consider carefully the implications of voice and to organize them into a usable framework. My goal in terms of literary theory is such a workable taxonomy rather than an overall and abstract definition of voice.

My own use of the term "voice" will thus draw from various critical suppositions because I believe that, although representational and non-representational critical theories certainly teach us differently about literary discourse, they are not inherently contradictory. *Any* use of "voice" raises essential issues concerning a fiction's discourse and its implied human origin. Any use calls us to account for the private internal voice that resonates in the act of reading *and* the expressive speech acts we hear engendered in the fiction's world *and* the rules governing multiple features of the narrative text and its discourse. Whether we regard fiction's discourse as expressive of its author or as a supplement or trace of its absent originator; whether we insist that the grammatical and syntactical features that can be catalogued in a text's discourse express a narrator's psyche or define a particular arrangement on a bounded field of language's endless intertextual play, we can legitimately speak of voice. Despite, in other words, the vastly divergent critical predilections of, say, Guerard (and his impressionistic "personal voice") and Genette (and his structured *voix*), these issues are not mutually exclusive. "Voice" always retains its noncontradictory references to phenomena *in* the created world and to phenomena *of* the discourse. "Voice" must therefore be tied to the various forms of *represented* speech even as it should be studied as a textual and structural practice whose presented or implied human origin lies constantly under interrogation.

There is only one implication of "voice" often found in critical discussions that I will not adapt to my taxonomy of voice in Faulkner. That implication is (to use a convenient shorthand) the psychobiographical. I will not treat voice as revelatory of William Faulkner's innermost being, as an expressive stream that can be traced back into the composing author's psyche. To the extent that a representational theory of voice means that the author as biographical subject is "represented" in his fiction's voice, my use of the term is not representational. This is not to say that biographical information about Faulkner is irrelevant to voice in his fiction, but rather that voice in his fiction is irrelevant to his biography. The error of psychobiographical theories of voice lies not in connecting voice in written texts with speech, but in making the connection backward. Voice is always, to be sure, a mimetic concept in that it presumes speech as literature's primary representation, a phenomenon that comes to be embodied in literature's written discourse. Voice in literature always has its roots in the imaging of speech. Yet Faulkner repeatedly reminds us that speech is not a prior and more "real" phenomenon that writing imitates in a secondary enterprise. Nonrepresentational critical theory has taught us, correctly, that writing should not be regarded as merely subjected to the world it embodies. We should not seek the real speaker behind the written discourse; rather we should seek the original speech that the text itself generates. As a literary term, voice names the intangible relationship among quite tangible phenomena of reading—the speech we hear, the writing we see, the origins we discover. As the potential for sounded discourse embedded in the written text, voice is the expressive quality of the perceivable text that the cognitive (and internally vocal) act of reading must accommodate; thus, at the most fundamental level Faulkner's texts demand our response to voice.

FOUR VOICES IN FAULKNER

The chapters that follow propose four modes of voice in Faulkner's fiction. Each has an implied origin different from the others; each involves different speech acts or written objects in the fictional world; and each evinces different features of discourse in their varying relationships. But because the goal of this study is not an abstract definition of voice, but instead a framework that permits a concrete examination of voice in Faulkner, it would serve that goal best to introduce and begin to flesh out these four modes of voice by deriving them briefly from one manageable Faulkner story.

"Barn Burning," the story Faulkner placed first in his *Collected Stories* and from which come all the references quoted in my opening paragraph's invocation of voice, can serve as exemplar for the richness of voice in the fiction, and can serve, too, as a sounding board for my uses of "voice" as critical and analytical tools. Like many Faulkner stories, "Barn Burning" is rendered through the perspective of a young boy. Colonel Sartoris Snopes has watched his father, Ab Snopes, burn barns in county after county. Snopes does this as a gesture of pride, "as [his] one weapon for the preservation of integrity" (*CS* 8). As the story opens, Sarty's loyalty to his father is sorely tested by the possible need to lie for him. The story recounts Sarty's growing resistance to Ab's authority, culminating in the boy's flight—first to warn Major de Spain that Ab is about to burn his barn, and then fleeing his family for good.

Ab Snopes's voice, like his shaggy eyebrows and his heavy, limping tread, defines his relation to the world around him and to Sarty. Faulkner describes Ab's voice frequently: "cold and harsh, level, without emphasis," "harsh like tin," "calm, outrageous." The voice, to Sarty, comes from above him both literally and figuratively ("speaking above him," "the cold, dead voice speaking above him") holding him attached to Ab's principles of blood loyalty and rapacious revenge for his poverty. But Sarty hears other voices, as well. His world is full of voices, from the "flat loud" voices of his sisters to the kind, troubled voice of the Justice of the Peace who (almost) questions him about Harris's barn. Voice thus belongs among the sensations that make up Sarty's environment, along with "the smell of cheese and sealed meat" or the sight of Major de Spain's house "big as a courthouse." Faulkner images Sarty's flight after his rebellion as a movement into nature's peace and loneliness, figured in the stars, the dark trees, and the "liquid silver voices of the birds." Voice thus inserts itself into the phenomenal world experienced by Sarty in all the stages of his painful rejection of his father.

Faulkner records as well as describes the voices around Sarty. His skill at differentiating dialects shows in the talk of poor whites (like Sarty himself), blacks, white townspeople, and the gentry. Sarty's role as the filtering perspective through which talk is heard determines in large part how the talk is recorded. In two different scenes in stores, when Ab is being sued or is suing, the individual speeches of the Justice of the Peace and others lack identification (by speech tags) until the Justice directly speaks to Sarty, as if the text itself cannot record "he said" unless the "he" who speaks is immediately present to the central consciousness. The white farmer Harris accurately quotes the black dialect of the Negro who delivers Ab's threat (using "whut," for example, where he in his own speech uses "what"), as if fictional speakers possessed the author's skills and textual tools for rendering talk. Faulkner also makes speech acts the fundamental form of rebellion in the plot, both in that Sarty might refuse to tell the necessary lies for his father and in his final shouted warning to Major de Spain. His silence indicates his reluctant loyalty to his father, and his growing defiance shows in his courage to speak: "'Ain't you going to even send a nigger?' he cried. 'At least you sent a nigger before!'" (21). Ironically, it is a speech act by his father that makes Sarty aware of his helplessness as a child and thus brings him closer to rebellious self-consciousness: "His father had struck him before last night but never before had he paused afterward to explain why; it was as if the blow and the following calm, outrageous voice still rang, repercussed, divulging nothing to him save the terrible handicap of being young" (9). Talk and the acts that bring it forth form a crucial part of the story's mimetic world.

A private voice also is heard, in Sarty's mind. Faulkner records the boy's thoughts as direct quotations of appropriate internal language: "*our enemy* he thought in that despair; *ourn! mine and hisn both! He's my father!*" (3). When necessary Faulkner supplements Sarty's words in order to express emotions the boy cannot articulate: "*Hit's big as a courthouse* he thought quietly, with a surge of peace and joy whose reason he could not have thought into words, being too young for that: *They are safe from him*"(10). Sarty's inner conflict between love for his father and respect for what is right shows in various other forms of rendered and described inner speech. He fears to say aloud what he might have to tell the Justice: "*Maybe he's done satisfied now, now that he has* . . . stopping himself, not to say it aloud even to himself" (6, Faulkner's ellipses). He debates inwardly, telling himself he could run away, "*Only I can't. I can't*" (21). An inner voice of the psyche, often marked textually by italics, tracks the emotional fluctuations in the protagonist's agonized struggle against paternal authority.

Sarty's words, whether spoken or thought, must be supplemented by a more sophisticated discourse, for as is usually the case in Faulkner (even in first-person narration) no character's voice will wholly suffice to render experience. Only an authorial voice can provide information not available to Sarty, and explain that Ab Snopes (whom Sarty believes fought bravely in the Civil War) "had gone to that war as a private in the fine old European sense . . . as Malbrouck himself did: for booty" (24–25). Only a voice traversed by the "institutional" discourse of history, or of literature, can provide such allusions; only such a voice can evoke the presence of nature, "the slow constellations," and "the rapid and urgent beating of the urgent and quiring heart of the late spring night" (25). The authorial narrative voice here, though no match for the high rhetoric of, say, *Absalom, Absalom!* or *Go Down, Moses*, still has the figural and syntactical extravagance we label "Faulknerian."

The above paragraphs identify vocal registers in "Barn Burning," and it is these that will occupy us in the chapters to follow. Together they can provide a taxonomy of voice in Faulkner (and perhaps in fiction generally) that will allow us to explore systematically this special source of Faulkner's power. Each of the four deserves the name of "voice" in that each is a distinct mode of representing speech that functions expressively within the fictional world and within the discourse that evokes the world: a *phenomenal* voice depictive of speech (or writing) as an event or object in the fiction's world; a *mimetic* voice imitative of talk; a *psychic* voice expressive of the silent inner discourse of consciousness; an *intertextual* voice identifiably Faulknerian yet necessarily in touch with other texts, other discourses, and other discursive practices in the world at large.

I will take up each voice in turn, first in a general, definitional way, and then in relation to particular works. The four chapters are discrete essays in that, although the voices intermingle in each novel and story (as they do in "Barn Burning"), each will be disentangled and isolated for purposes of analysis. The phenomenon of speech when depicted implies, necessarily, the potential recording of words spoken, and inner, silent "speech" traverses the same language as speeches in dialogue heard by characters and recorded in the text. The four voices stand in a relation to each other that we can call (after Bakhtin) "dialogical," in the sense that each depends upon and converses with all the others within the total discourse.

Chapter 1 defines a phenomenology of voice, examining the qualities associated with voice that Faulkner draws upon for figurative effects. After exploring how Faulkner evokes the power of voice generally—in individual experience, in human communities, and in the world at large—the chapter focuses on *Flags in the Dust*, part 4 of *The Sound and the Fury*, *Sanctuary*, *Light in August* and, more briefly, on *Pylon*, *The Wild Palms*, and *The Mansion*. This is the only chapter of the four that proceeds chronologically, suggesting certain changes in the way Faulkner represented voice over the course of his career.

The second chapter, on "mimetic voice," examines in its first sections various theories of represented speech and proposes an analysis of "discursive functions" that Faulkner's texts fulfill in order to generate the illusion of speech. Various texts serve as illustrations for these functions, leading toward what I regard as Faulkner's most experimental and problematic creation of fictional speech, *As I Lay Dying*.

The discussion of "psychic voice" in chapter 3 focuses on Faulkner's habitual methods of depicting verbalized thought, methods again called discursive "functions," but less formally described. Of particular importance here is a concept of "textual voice," or the ways printed format (especially italics) serves to engender verbalized thought. I discuss the short story "Carcassonne" as a model for Faulkner's portrayal of thought, then turning to *Light in August*, *Go Down, Moses* and, most extensively, the three Compson monologues in *The Sound and the Fury*.

Chapter 4 treats only one special case of the "intertextual voice," oratory. I examine first the nature of Southern oratory as a discursive practice with definable consequences for a reader's relation to a text, as well as definable stylistic and structural traits. These consequences of oratorical practice are then followed out in Sutpen's monumental design as rendered in the narrative voices of *Absalom, Absalom!*. The choice of one kind of intertextual relation in no way gainsays the importance of others to understanding Faulkner's fiction, which is interwoven with other literary texts like those of Dickens, T. S. Eliot, Conrad, Joyce, Proust, and others. But a complete exploration of intertextuality in Faulkner is beyond the scope of this book.[10] I have chosen to focus on oratory, that discursive practice that has special importance to Faulkner as an American and a Southern writer and, more directly, is the practice in which voice is most fully implicated.

None of the four voices is limited in attribution to "character," "narrator," or "author." This most common way of answering the question "Who speaks?" possesses considerable utility, especially in identifying narrative voices, but such identification of speakers does not take us far toward understanding Faulkner's texts. For the "who" that "speaks" matters less in Faulkner than the "how" by which speech comes into the world and into the discourse. All four of the modes of voice identified in the four chapters are available to characters, to narrators, and to the implied author. A character or narrator, as well as the author, can describe the phenomenon of speech, and either can imitate another character's words. Only an omniscient author can, in principle, enter another's mind to record inner speech, but even here Faulkner allows the necessities of expression to overrule verisimilitude of source—and indeed, as we shall discover, the text as a written entity, more than an implied authorial speaker, becomes a source of psychic voice: in Faulkner the text "speaks." Oratorical Faulknerian prose rich in allusion and figuration can be spoken by anyone, by any narrator or character.

The direction of the analysis in each chapter leads toward a consideration of the relationship between speech and writing. Speech is by far the dominant discourse represented in Faulkner (and in fiction generally). But speech will not preclude considering the written—either the "writtenness" of Faulkner's texts or the presence of written documents within the fictional worlds. Voice intrudes into the written at every stage. Just as the printed fiction we identify as Faulknerian can legitimately be said to possess voice, so the written within the novels is placed always in some relationship to spoken discourse—relationships we again can call "dialogical." I follow Bakhtin in identifying "speaking persons" as requisite to the novel as a genre, but I also agree when he urges that "speaking person . . . need not necessarily be incarnated in a character" (*The Dialogical Imagination* 335). Indeed, one tendency we shall discover in the four modes of voice in Faulkner is that they always return to the written in some way: images of phenomenal speech in the early novels give way later in Faulkner's career to images of writing; mimetic voice depends upon manipulation of written signs to imitate speech; psychic voice revises inner "speech" into expressive textual signs; the oratorical voice derives power partly from its constant desire to create monumental texts lacking the impermanence of oral speech. Thus the final "voice," to be considered very briefly in the Conclusion, is Faulkner's *writer's* voice.[11]

Chapter One

PHENOMENAL VOICE

The Golden Dome (Beginning Was the Word)
—*Requiem for a Nun*

when the last ding-dong of doom has clanged and faded from the last
worthless rock hanging tideless in the last red and dying evening, . . .
even then there will still be one more sound: that of his puny inexhaustible voice, still talking

—NOBEL PRIZE ACCEPTANCE SPEECH

FAULKNER'S PHENOMENOLOGY
OF VOICE

Faulkner found voice at the beginning and the end of his world—the
"one Cap and one period" of his fictional sentence (*SL* 185; Cowley 14). As
the Gospel of St. John placed "the Word [that] was God" at the beginning
of existence, so Faulkner in his historical meditation in *Requiem for a Nun*
places "the Word" at the beginning of his Mississippi. And in his Nobel
Prize Acceptance Speech it is voice, not as evidence of God but as a sign of
the human spirit, that will echo from beyond time's horizon. Man is immortal "because he has a soul, a spirit," but voice manifests the human
capacity to endure beyond the "last ding-dong of doom" (*ESPL* 120). The
representations of voice's power—as sound, speech, thought, and textual

18

monument—differ from work to work, but whether merely in an isolated image or in repeated patterns of depiction and figuration, voice was clearly one phenomenon that mattered to Faulkner.

A consistent phenomenology of voice emerges in Faulkner's oeuvre. Voice engenders a certain experience, both in the fictional world and in the reader's engagement with the text. "Phenomenal voice" refers to voice as a depicted event or object within the represented world. When voice is named, described, commented upon, employed metaphorically, or in any way explicitly presented, phenomenal voice is created. Any depicted speech act implies the presence of voice: when a character speaks to another character, or (sometimes) to him- or herself, or (also sometimes) to the reader, that character is presumed, in the necessary illusions of fiction, to employ his or her voice to speak audibly. In this sense all dialogue implies voice as the accompaniment to any talking represented as part of a story's events. This resultant voice, however (which I will discuss in chapter 2 as "mimetic voice"), differs from phenomenal voice, for the latter is presented as such, in itself. Whereas voice in some sense always results incidentally from represented speech acts, *phenomenal* voice exists only when explicitly mentioned in the diegetic discourse as sound, act, gesture, or the power of speech irrespective of speech's semantic "content."

Voice images fill Faulkner's prose: direct references to and descriptions of characters' voices, notations of voices heard in the background, metaphors for voice comparing it to objects such as feathers, bees in a bucket, bubbles, boats, banners, guns, and more. The importance of phenomenal voice, however, does not derive simply from the manner in which Faulkner depicts voice, nor from any statistical frequency of vocal imagery, but rather from its implications of human presence, discursive power, and communion, and from the interchange it creates between the representing discourse and its represented world. Voice, the breath of life and speech, has always signified human presence—both the self-presence of the inner voice and the presence of the other or others embodied in the voices we hear. "If what is said is *in* sound, . . . *who* does the saying is also co-present in voice. . . . The sounding voice is both a penetration into my self-presence and the presence of *otherness*" (Ihde 174). Wordsworth evoked the capacity of voice to fill with harmonious "invisible Spirit" the void otherwise empty to our sight:

> The heavens, whose aspect makes our minds as still
> As they themselves appear to be,

Innumerable voices fill
With everlasting harmony.

("On the Power of Sound," ll. 181–84)

It is not merely language that distinguishes humans from animals, but voice, the capacity to utter language: Aristotle says that "voice is the sound produced by a creature possessing a soul" (*On the Soul* 420b6). Voice renders the spirit of humanness manifest in sound. Thus Kierkegaard came to prefer hearing to seeing for "the voice is the revelation of the external, incommensurable inwardness" of a human being (i). In its "essential and immediate proximity with the mind" voice is the central emblem of that presence that cannot be reduced to a sign of something else. Derrida, in *Of Grammatology*, defining what he sees as the logocentric yearning of Western philosophy for an absolute presence, or a signified that does not signify anything beyond itself, writes that "logocentrism . . . is also a phonocentrism: absolute proximity of voice and being, of voice and the meaning of being, of voice and the ideality of meaning."[1] The voice stood highest in Hegel's hierarchy of the senses because in conjoining sound and language it embraces both the subjective immediacy of sensation—as smell or touch do—and the representing function of signs and concepts. "The voice unites the anthropological naturalness of the natural sound to the psychic-semiotic ideality; therefore it articulates the philosophy of spirit with the philosophy of nature."[2] Any evocation of voice, then, implies both physical presence in a place and "presence" in the philosophical sense of unmediated existence. And because *phenomenal* voice exists outside of particular speech acts, residing in the world as object or event, it disseminates human presence throughout the world, infusing objects, places, sights, and sounds with implications of humanness. Although at times this effect can seem merely a version of the pathetic fallacy, phenomenal voice energizes Faulkner's universe by placing a uniquely human power at its very center.

Phenomenal voice embodies just that power itself. Voice signifies power to speak, communicate, think, and bring order to experience, even create—as well as power to harm, insult, condemn, or destroy. Whereas vision permits distance and precise location of experience, voice, like music, penetrates and "distributes [our experience] throughout space and carries it deep into our listening ear."[3] Voice is not simply the capacity to speak, but speech's power, associated always with God's omnipotence: "The voice of the Lord is powerful, the voice of the Lord is full of majesty," says Psalm 29. Divine authority can create by vocal fiat, can bring something into being by merely uttering "let there be . . ." Nearly all the permutations of voice described by Faulkner invoke its power. Never impotent and never innocent, phenomenal voice is always burdened with the power to affect and alter human life.[4]

Further, voice is efficacious in a universal or ultimate sense. That in his Nobel Prize speech Faulkner images voice as the last vestige of human life reflects the romantic's faith in voice that lies at the root of Faulkner's sense of its power. Wordsworth's "On the Power of Sound" closes with a depiction of the world's end that, like Faulkner's, locates in voice the only vestige of human existence after time has finally passed. Invoking the Gospel's creation story, in which time began when "A Voice to Light gave Being" (l. 209), Wordsworth's last stanza finds that voice shall also provide closure to human time, when

> A Voice shall finish doubt and dim foreseeing,
> And sweep away life's visionary stir
>
> (ll. 211–12)

"Silence," the void, will not erase and render meaningless "Man's noisy years" (l. 217) for

> though earth be dust
> And vanish, though the heavens dissolve, her stay
> Is in the Word, that shall not pass away
>
> (ll. 222–24)

In Faulkner's version the "heavens dissolving" becomes the "last ding-dong of doom," and what lasts beyond time is "man's puny, inexhaustible voice, still talking" instead of "the Word"; but it is still the resilience of voice that conquers ultimate silence. Voice's power endures even though the anchor of faith has shifted from divine "Harmony, blest queen of smiles and tears" (the "her" referred to in Wordsworth's line 223) to the human "soul" or "spirit" in Faulkner's speech.

Voice serves as one force, fundamental in Faulkner, of intersubjectivity.[5] Language as communication can bind people together, but beyond the talking, the gossip, and the story telling that cement a community like

Jefferson, Faulkner's discourse creates "in chanting measures beyond the need for words" a phenomenal voice such that it embodies the communal relation itself, in either the affirmative symbolic sense of communion and rejuvenating harmony or in the negative symbolic senses of entrapment, suffocation, and loss of individuality.

Phenomenal voice also marks one juncture where the fictional discourse and the represented world intersect and interrogate each other. Faulkner's texts often blur the distinction between *histoire* and *récit*, and his evocations of phenomenal voice contribute to this blurring. Faulkner's fiction derives its tremendous discursive energy—at every level of narration, text, mimetic representation, and even theme—from a dialogic mix of varied kinds of represented speech and writing. With phenomenal voice we can see how Faulkner tries to inject discourse into his imagined world and, conversely, how he tries to bring the created world into discourse—to capture and define life's inherently discursive quality. Faulkner, for all his modernist's skeptical reenvisioning of the romantic's faith in universal spirit, does seek a logocentric unity often figured most powerfully in evocations of phenomenal voice. Phenomenal voice invites us to perceive the world (and not merely a given persona) as empowered to speak and to be spoken. If voice is "the spirit of language" (Ihde 121), then phenomenal voice permits us to observe that spirit at play.

Three discursive gestures or habitual modes of expression generate the power of phenomenal voice in Faulkner's discourse, empowering written prose to evoke voice. First, Faulkner often sets voice and vision in some sort of contrasting arrangement, creating a movement in both figuration and depiction that culminates in a manifestation of voice's power. Some synesthetic figures for speech or listening allow people or objects to be "seen" as sound, voice, or speech; others have the inverse effect, turning voice into a visual object, as when Faulkner describes Temple Drake's scream as a "thin eeeeeeeeeeeeee sound like bubbles in a bottle" (*S* 104; 118), or when Temple and Ruby stand "face to face, their voices [are] like shadows upon two close blank walls" (*S* 64; 70). Faulkner captures the dichotomy between vision and voice in recurring metaphors of spoken words as printed or written: "His voice . . . was cold, implacable, like written or printed words" (*LA* 164; 139). In such figures, and also in extended passages, phenomenal voice replicates within the fictional world the reader's relation to the narrative discourse, for it is often out of voices that the imagination must construct its visions. Faulkner dramatizes entire scenes through voice. In *Absalom, Absalom!* Quentin Compson's grandfather comes upon Thomas Sutpen and Wash Jones during the first moments when Wash challenges Sutpen about his behavior toward Milly (Wash's granddaughter). "Grandfather couldn't see them . . . but he said he knew exactly how they would be" from their voices (*AA* 354; 283). Later, after Sutpen insults Milly (because her baby is a girl), Faulkner renders Wash's attack with the scythe as a dialogue overheard by the midwife (*AA* 356–57; 285–86). As Wash waits for the posse, Faulkner describes him hearing the voices of those who would ridicule him, hearing "all the voices, the murmuring of tomorrow and tomorrow and tomorrow beyond the immediate fury" (*AA* 362; 290). When the posse arrives they must imagine by listening to Wash and to his granddaughter's "fretful and querulous" voice as Wash cuts her and the baby's throats. Nothing is enacted directly here, nothing is seen except as filtered through voice. So, too, can the reader visualize only what the voices of the narrative discourse call forth.

Faulkner orchestrates visualized scenes and heard speech, as well as visual and vocal metaphors, so that voice can emerge and demonstrate its power. This is not to say that Faulkner's texts consistently affirm voice at vision's expense in some Manichean dichotomy of "good" and "bad" imagery. Destructive remembered voices haunt Quentin throughout his monologue, and the sound and fury of Benjy's voice is stilled only with the return of visually familiar patterns, "each in its ordered place." Gail Mortimer argues that in Faulkner both sight and hearing fail to discern truth: vision fails because it is deceptive and abstract; hearing, although it can convey "infallible truths" that sight cannot, yet is more threatening because it blurs boundaries and dissolves identity (37). Whatever their respective values in a given context, voice and vision seldom cohabit comfortably. Instead of reinforcing each other, speech and sight in all their manifest forms usually cluster into contrasting or alternating patterns governed by tension, opposition, and even mutual exclusion. Most simply, Faulkner alternates depiction of seen things with heard speech (as will be seen when we examine the Easter episode in *The Sound and the Fury*). Sights and sounds directly contrast with one another, as well, and patterns of metaphor and event oscillate between sight and voice.

The second gesture typical of Faulkner's rendering of voice is its insistent occurrence as a phenomenon in its own right, not merely as a vehicle for expression. Voice is called forth into the discourse of the fiction such that it escapes its subsidiary role as the incidental result of speech. Such evocation most usually and quite naturally emanates from the depiction of voice in sound imagery. Karl Zender has described the values associated with sound in Faulkner's fiction, in particular how those values changed over the course of Faulkner's career. Early in his career Faulkner tended to associate sound with annealing or inspiring powers of nature: "Almost from the beginning, what might be called positive images of sound—that is, images of annealment and reconciliation—can easily be found in his writings. Although these take a variety of forms, they usually depict an individual in a space bounded or defined by sound . . . a reciprocal relationship whose medium of expression is sound always exists between the individual and the surrounding scene" ("Power of Sound" 90). Like other sounds, voice is carried in the air and frequently is associated with air, wind, or breathing—all traditional icons for spirit, life, and soul.

Phenomenal voice in the early fiction evokes a communion of human life within a natural context. Images of voice in the early novels appear commingled with images of night and darkness, Negroes, trees and fields and woods—all indexes of Faulkner's early, romantically derived code of communion with nature. Background voices, especially singing voices, evoke in stereotypical ways the "natural" and "primitive" emotions associated with Negroes. Thadious Davis writes that "Faulkner uses the Negro to establish the basic rhythm of life . . . lost to the modern, postwar world. . . . [T]he sound of [Negroes'] voices is a musical accompaniment which is also the embodiment of feeling" (45). Typical of this are the final paragraphs of *Soldiers' Pay*, which describe the sounds of a Negro church service, a sound that reaches toward God: "From [the church] welled the crooning submerged passion of the dark race. It was nothing, it was everything; then it swelled to an ecstasy, taking the white man's words as readily as it took his remote God and made a personal Father of Him" (221). Even without language these natural voices can soothe, as does Louis Hatcher's voice, which, as Quentin remembers it, "sounded just like the horn he carried slung on his shoulder and never used, but clearer, mellower, as though his voice were a part of darkness and silence, coiling out of it, coiling into it again" (*SF* 132; 142).

While Zender is right that Faulkner's "meditation on the artist's power" (89) early in his career derived solace from positive images of voice, it is easy to overemphasize the "images of annealment and reconciliation." Voice, even in the early fiction, also sadly signals absence and death. Many of the early images of voice appear at funerals, refer to painful or at least nostalgic remembrances of lost times, evoke songs about the afterlife, and are heard when characters bemoan or threaten death. The Sartoris cook in

Flags in the Dust, Elnora, raises her song constantly in the background at the Sartoris house, singing of sinners and hell and *"All folks talkin' 'bout heaven aint gwine dere"* (*FD* 36). Vernon Tull remarks the voices of the women at Addie's funeral and Whitfield's voice preaching over her corpse (*AILD* 81; 86). Racist words and rumors in *Light in August* are "wind- or airengendered" like a fire. In *Sanctuary*, where voices and fire are also equated, and which at times figures nature itself as threatening, it is a murderer's voice that, "rich, sourceless," floats "out of the high darkness where the ragged shadow of the heaven-tree which snooded the street lamp at the corner fretted and mourned" (118; 135). Even avowedly positive images of voice often carry within them a sense of loss that, paradoxically conjoined with annealment and reconciliation, gives voice a haunting power.

In later fiction dehumanized voice more blatantly and mechanistically connotes death, or the absence at least of human presence. "Communion" changes to "immersion" and then to "intrusion" as the environment overwhelms the individual in a flood of unnatural phenomenal voices (Zender, "Power of Sound" 96–98). In *Pylon* the announcer's mechanized voice "harsh masculine and disembodied" replaces the natural voices heard in earlier works—but it still seems "as if the voice actually were that natural phenomenon against which all man-made sounds and noises blew and vanished like leaves" (*P* 27). The river in *The Wild Palms* makes "a profound deep whisper," or a "faint hissing sighing, almost a chuckling" (71, 170), and voices heard through megaphones, loudspeakers, or radios have become intrusive noises destructive of privacy and individual integrity, as "the county's hollow inverted air [becomes] one resonant boom and ululance of radio" (*RN* 244).

Voice is not merely sound, however, even when considered as a phenomenon separate from speech. More than other sounds voice humanizes the natural landscape, promising human participation in nature's beauty and peace. By humanizing the environment, voice's siren song lures one away from the confining universe of "mere" discourse; by becoming phenomenon, voice and the discourse it implies become event and act in the world outside of the enclosure of inner consciousness. If the personal voice originates the self's sense of its own existence, then a grounding of voice in the external world naturally links the world and the self, a conjunction uninterrupted by signs. The isolation of self-presence can be intruded upon only when voice is "exterior."

In weaving voice imagery into a novel's figurative texture, Faulkner calls forth into the discourse of his texts a phenomenon that is not merely incidental to the speech of characters. Indeed, the evocation of voice as phenomenon, which is usually figurative, permits the third, and perhaps most crucial discursive gesture in the rendering of phenomenal voice: the radical separation of voice from speaker, and sometimes from speech itself. As long as voice is mired in speech—either because its existence depends solely on speech acts or because it remains associated with individual speakers as unique to each—it cannot serve as a context or catalyst for communion. While the value of the connection with the world achievable through exteriorized voices certainly changed over the course of Faulkner's career, Faulkner's discourse habitually disengages voice from person so that individuals are taken out of themselves and implanted in a broader communal nexus defined in part by qualities given to voice "as such," that is, as separated from human speech as source.

Faulkner's novels exhibit various strategies for separating voice from speaker. The most straightforward denies voice its human origin: "Their voices seemed to materialize in the dusk between them, unsourced of either mouth, either still and fading face" ("There Was a Queen," *CS* 738–39). The short story "Mistral" renders a remarkable, concentrated series of figures for a priest's voice, all of which cut voice loose from speaker. The priest's voice first "filled the church, slow, steady, like wings beating against the cold stone" (*CS* 858). Then he becomes a composite of his body ("a shabby shapeless figure") and "a voice. It was as though neither of them was any part of the other" (862). His voice is "a sustained rush of indistinguishable words . . . muffled and sustained, like a machine might have been making it" (864–65). Finally, "the voice ceased, cut short off like a thread," but "it began again, abruptly, in full stride, as though silence were the thread this time" (866).

More frequently Faulkner displaces the speaker by employing voice as a metonymy. In the Nobel Prize address it is not "man" who will still be talking, but man's "voice," as if voice were the agent of the talking instead of its vehicle. This metonymic use of "voice" appears in virtually every Faulkner novel, and often with great regularity. "We could hear Father's voice, talking to Granny" (*U* 20); "from the group a voice spoke suddenly, loud" (*LA* 174; 148); " 'Kill him, kill the son,' a voice whispered" ("Dry September," *CS* 177). People become voices: Ratcliffe in *Requiem for a Nun* is "a single thin almost unheard voice crying thinly out of the roar of a mob" (31); the real estate agent who rents Charlotte and Harry the doctor's cottage is referred to (on the telephone) as "the voice" (*WP* 6–8);

Quentin Compson imagines a photograph of the Sutpens hanging "on the wall behind and above the voice" that Rosa Coldfield has become for him as he listens to her talk (*AA* 12; 14). Ike McCaslin's wife, when she turns away from him because he refuses to assume ownership of the McCaslin land, becomes just a voice "coming somewhere between the pillow and the cachinnation" (*GDM* 315). Sometimes a voice takes on volition, as when Mink Snopes in *The Mansion* drinks one bottle of soda and "in horror hear[s] his voice saying 'I'll have another one'" (*M* 260); Wilbourne in *The Wild Palms* "heard his own voice speaking out of an amazed and quiet incredulity," or he "heard his voice ask the question he did not want to ask and get the answer he did not want to hear" (57, 16–17). Of course, no isolated instance of such a metonymy significantly engenders voice's power, but clusters of figures embodying personae as voices can assume a density that defamiliarizes speech by extricating voice from speakers and calling attention to it in the discourse as well as in the fictional world of characters. Repeated voice qualifiers also contribute to this effect, such as those formulaic tags in *Sanctuary* that dehumanize characters like Popeye with his "cold, level voice." *Light in August* contains the highest density of such metonymies, repeatedly describing Bobbie, the waitress, as a "still, abject, downlooking voice"; she and Joe Christmas are referred to as voices (or their voices are described) some eighteen times in less than three pages of conversation (*LA* 198–200; 206–7; 168–70, 175–76).

In certain cases a vocal image of this kind does little more than delineate a personality trait, as in "between the voice and the face there were always two Ratliffs" (*T* 150); or a voice image dramatizes a state of mind, as when "Wilbourne could almost see [Rittenmeyer] struggling physically to keep his voice down . . . holding it on some sort of curb like a horse, yet forcing it on" (*WP* 56). Often, too, a person's voice becomes something else, figured as a different person or an object: Narcissa Benbow crouches "behind the screen of words her voice raised between [herself and Bayard Sartoris]" (*FD* 232); in *Light in August* the voice is "a shell . . . carried before [the] face" (234; 199). The banker in *Requiem for a Nun* kicks at Nancy Mannigoe's face "or anyway her voice which was still saying 'Where's my two dollars, white man?'" (121). Louvinia's "voice seemed to descend upon us [Bayard and Ringo] like an enormous hand, flattening the very dust which we had raised" (*U* 8). Tull, in *As I Lay Dying*, uses one of the more striking of these images: "Whitfield begins. His voice is bigger than him. It's like they are not the same. It's like he is one, and his voice is one, swimming on two horses side by side across the ford and coming into the house, the mud-splashed one and the one that never even got wet, triumphant and sad" (81; 86).

We find, too, what might be called "cosmic" versions of voice separated from its source in such a way as to place human life in a context of the infinite universe. In *Sanctuary* the "voice of the night" becomes "the friction of the earth on its axis, approaching that moment when it must decide to turn on or to remain forever still" (*S* 233; 267). A more mechanized version appears in *The Wild Palms*: "[the loudspeaker's] voice cavernous and sourceless . . . as if the listener (so enormous was the voice) were suspended in space watching the globy earth spin slowly out of its cradling cloud-wisps" (*WP* 135).

It is common in Faulkner to find both sounds and sights reified, sometimes grotesquely, by figurative language that disengages them from their sources. The separation of voice from speaker is not a unique kind of image in this respect: the fiction abounds with imagery in which sound or sight ceases to be a product of its source. A familiar example, often cited, is the sound of the Armstids' wagon as it mounts the hill toward Lena Grove early in *Light in August*. "At last, as though out of some trivial and unimportant region beyond even distance, the sound of it seems to come slow and terrific and without meaning, as though it were a ghost travelling a half mile ahead of its own shape" (*LA* 8; 6). But voice is not just another sound, nor is a speaker just another visualizable object; unlike a wagon and its terrific creaking, a speaker and voice are a signifying duality. To fracture the bond between vocal sound and its source shifts the perceived origin of meaning away from portrayed individual consciousness into a disseminated "consciousness" discernible only within the novel's overall texture. In this sense voice as signifying sound is a perceivable phenomenon superior to others—not morally superior, but superior in viably rendering a discernible universe outside the self. In her discussion of Faulkner's synesthetic imagery, Gail Mortimer shows how the mingling of senses can dissolve the boundaries that confer identity on the individual consciousness; thus, sound and smell are conducive of more intense experience than is sight, and at the same time are more threatening.[6] Yet voice can be understood as well as heard; it signifies, it possesses expressive symbolizing power. Voice's separation from other senses and from its sources may be more indicative of its place in Faulkner's cognitive universe than is the synesthetic union of sound and smell as intense but undiscriminating senses. Faulkner may be more in tune with Hegel's hierarchy of senses (especially if we speak of "voice" and not just of "hearing" or "sound") than his synesthetic imagery would imply, for the intelligible and the sensible reunite in voice outside of the individual consciousness. Speech becomes, as this discursive gesture repeats itself, a product of "voice"—no longer a discrete *medium* of human utterance but now a generalized *source* of all utterance.

Furthermore, this separation of voice from speech and speaker echoes the more fundamental rupture between author and text, a rift that readers conventionally heal by imagining an author's voice as an "ineffable presence within a novel, . . . its irreducible identity, . . . its nervous system . . . infinitely complex and ultimately mysterious."[7] No fiction's compelling voice can depend solely on an author's presence *as speaker*, for the author is necessarily absent from his text, at best an "implied" presence; yet a voice remains to haunt our reading, and we pay rightful homage to its power. So, too, does Faulkner's habitual gesture of separating voice from speaker permit the power of voice to be disseminated throughout a novel's discourse rather than remain merely derivative of depicted speakers and their speech acts.

NATURAL VOICES IN *FLAGS IN THE DUST*

Faulkner's return to take up more or less permanent residence in Oxford, Mississippi, after sojourns in New Orleans and Europe, has been cited by biographers and by Faulkner himself as a crucial focusing of his career. He came home in 1927 to discover that his "own little postage stamp of native soil was worth writing about" (*LG* 255). The first novel that resulted from this homecoming evokes place more overtly than any other Faulkner work, at least within traditional codes of verisimilitude. Lacking the rich figural resonance of mature Faulknerian discourse, *Flags in the Dust* pays more attention than do Faulkner's later novels to setting, to background literally conceived, to details offered simply because they "are there" as part of a conventionally "natural" world.

The world Faulkner elicits in *Flags* hearkens to a pastoral literary heritage. He depicts people and objects so that they emerge from nature; he places his world in painterly fashion within a landscape: "This was upland country, lying in tilted slopes against the unbroken blue of the hills, but soon the road dropped sheerly into a valley of good broad fields richly somnolent in the levelling afternoon" (9). The diegetic discourse notes voices again and again, along with natural sounds that figure as the "voice" of the world. Faulkner refers more directly to voice here than in any other novel, with the possible exception of *Light in August*. The discourse abounds with synesthetic clusters of sounds, sights, and odors that usually include some form of phenomenal voice: "A shrill monotone of crickets rose from the immediate grass, and further away, from among the trees, a fairy-like piping of young frogs like endless silver small bubbles rising, and a thin sourceless odor of locust drifted up intangible as fading tobacco-wraiths, and from the rear of the house, up the dark hall, Elnora's voice floated in meaningless and minor suspense" (36). Faulkner mixes light and sound, light and voice: "At the end of the hallway checkered sunlight fell in a long slant across the door and the world was drowsily monotonous without, and from somewhere beyond the bar of sunlight a voice rose and fell in a rapid preoccupied minor, like a chant" (10; see also 41).

Voices environ the listener, enveloping him or her in the annealing aura of maternal enclosure. Thus darkness, the distant sounds of dogs or of a hunting horn, and the voices of Negroes all contribute to immersing characters and reader within sound: "The dogs' voices welled out of the darkness mournful and chiming, swelled louder and nearer and swept invisibly past not half a mile away; faded diminishing and with a falling suspense, as of bells, into the darkness again" (323; see also 134, 275, 324). Negroes' voices in particular signal the blended voice of nature and community. Elnora's singing runs like a minor harmonic chord throughout the novel, sometimes quoted in a mixing of mimetic and phenomenal voice, more often merely mentioned for *vraisemblance*: "In the kitchen Elnora crooned mellowly as she labored; her voice came rich and plaintful and sad along the sunny reaches of the air" (205; see also 20, 21, 36, 102, 204, 232, 235, 362). Voices join persons with the community as well as with nature. Suratt's voice, as he talks to young Bayard after he has been thrown from the stallion, belongs to the peaceful, natural scenery: "[They] squatted in a small bowl of peacefulness remote from the world and its rumors, filled with the cool unceasing breathing of the spring and a seeping of sunlight among the elders and willows like a thinly diffused wine. . . . Suratt's voice went on affably, ceaselessly recapitulant" (125). Even life in town always includes notations of voices, such as Old Man Falls and Bayard shouting into each other's deafness in the bank, or Jenny and Bayard arguing, or the ladies at Narcissa's party ("a consonantless drone of female voices [on which Simon] rode into the kitchen" [22]), or Aunt Sally's "bland querulous interminability" (136), or Horace's "flaming verbal wings . . . chant[ing] in measured syllables" (154), or the "harsh wordless uproar of [Harry Mitchell's] voice" that punctuates every scene at Belle's (180, passim). If for nothing else, *Flags*'s discourse is remarkable for its sheer quantity of phenomenal voice.

In this early novel Faulkner solicits a characteristically romantic yearning for an originating natural community. The kind of "natural" community envisioned (or, it is better to say, bespoken) is one close to nature, a community in which free citizens participate in a social intercourse formed of direct person-to-person speech—conversation, storytelling, gossip, "visiting"—and its concomitant listening. It is an oral community where significant discourse requires the social and personal presence of speech, where the economy of language exchange is one based on events rather than on records, where living memory must actively recall a past not recorded in documents. The inherently social undertakings of communication and learning indelibly color knowledge with the living human beings who articulate it (see Goody and Watt 33; Ong 22). Faulkner seems to share with Rousseau the images of community that, as Derrida describes it, is perfect, originating whole and bound together by speech, "a community immediately self-present to itself, without difference, a community of speech where all the members are within earshot" (*Of Grammatology* 136).

In *Flags* the people of Faulkner's land possess or nostalgically seem to have once possessed a Rousseauvian oral community in which speech bonds each soul to each other and to the land. Even old Bayard's deafness does not bar him from this communal bonding (except, apparently, at convenient times), for he can hear Old Man Falls, Simon, even Jenny when he must: "Simon's voice was not particularly robust nor resonant, yet somehow he could talk to Bayard without difficulty. Others must shout in order to penetrate that wall of deafness beyond which Bayard lived" (8). Voice is all around, literally in the air, and even the near deaf live immersed within voice's ethereal embrace. Over and over the narrative discourse names and describes phenomenal voice. Other kinds of voice are heard within the novel, to be sure: the mimetic voice of dialogue (including some of Faulkner's most extreme dialect writing) and of storytelling by characters like Old Man Falls, Bayard, and Aunt Jenny; the recognizably Faulknerian oratorical voice hinted at in the paean to the mule (whose voice, we note, is "his own derision").[8] But the dialogical mix here favors the phenomenal, for voice is mentioned, referred to, or described in nearly every scene. Rarely again is Faulkner so *attentive* to voice as such.

In *Mosquitoes*, the novel that preceded *Flags in the Dust*, Faulkner was attentive not to voice but to *talk*, and the distinction is crucial to an understanding of how his discourse evokes a natural oral community yet often rejects speech, speakers, and even language as vehicles of truth. *Mosquitoes* satirizes the life Faulkner had been leading in New Orleans in the company of artists and writers like Spratling and Anderson. A motley group of artists and hangers-on fritters away in meaningless talk (ranging from silly chatter about grapefruit to discussions of aesthetics) any potential creativity the individuals may possess. Although many readers find the talk to be as successfully rendered and as interesting to read as the supposedly contrasting actions (such as the sculptor Gordon's taciturn posturing), Faulkner apparently wants to defame talk as a wasteful expenditure of creative energy: "Talk, talk, talk: the utter and heartbreaking stupidity of words. It seemed endless, as though it might go on forever. Ideas, thoughts, became mere sounds to be bandied about until they were dead" (186). The novel's discourse records talk, but that same discourse derides "voiceless talking" as hollow and sterile. Perhaps because his imagination had not yet returned to that postage stamp of native soil, Faulkner fails in *Mosquitoes* to provide voices to enrich, humanize, and energize the talk. *Mosquitoes* lacks a natural communal setting to nourish voice: there is no *place* for voice here. The characters gather into an artificially compressed conglomeration of relative strangers stranded on a yacht that has run aground, together only because they have no choice but to remain in each others' proximity. When their return to New Orleans releases the circumstantial pressure holding them together, the group dissipates, each member wandering off into his or her isolated life.

Throughout his career Faulkner raised objections to talk of this kind, and indeed he seems to have felt them personally. (He wrote to Hemingway, for example, that "I have believed for years that the human voice has caused all human ills and I thought I had broken myself of talking" [*SL* 251–52, also 234].) From such statements critics like Olga Vickery have demonstrated Faulkner's linguistic skepticism, his suspicions of the capacity of language to procure or express truth, his fear of too much verbiage, and his preference for a silence that brings one closer to a final pristine "presence" of the heart (see Vickery 266–81; see also Larsen; Lilly). Despite Faulkner's skepticism about language, however, especially language regarded as a container of meaning, voice as the natural vehicle of speech plays in Faulkner's discourse (in the early works especially) a privileged role potentially equivalent to the truth and beauty of nature itself. We recall that in Addie Bundren's monologue, perhaps the most famous statement of how "deeds" are better than "words," even Addie herself *"hear[s]* the land . . . and how terribly doing goes along the earth" (*AILD* 160; 165; my emphasis). Her meditation on words and deeds and her own sin is couched in images that, even as they are labeled "voiceless," evoke a version of nature's (and, ironically, of the Reverend Whitfield's) phenomenal voice: "I would lie by [Anse] in the dark, hearing the dark land talking of God's love and His beauty and His sin; hearing the dark voicelessness in which the words are the deeds, and the other words that are not deeds, that are just the gaps in people's lacks, coming down like the cries of the geese out of the wild darkness in the old terrible nights" (*AILD* 160; 166).

Not even the rich voice imagery of *Flags in the Dust* can overcome the suspicion that any true oral community is a chimera. The voices that shape the novel's world already grieve for a lost harmony. Like voice, which fades to nothing even as it comes into being, the natural community Faulkner evokes comes to us (like Elnora's voice) as a "dying fall."[9] The novel's discourse seems virtually enraptured of loss, of fading sounds that echo with the longing for a mythic harmonious past. Matthews has discussed this nuance of the novel as it reflects the absence inherent in language, which can only "represent what it cannot present" (57). The Rousseauvian dream of a past when speech unified all humanity in a social version of natural dialogue is recognized by *Flags* as only a dream.

Of all the characters, Narcissa Benbow most embodies the novel's mix of natural peace and chilling emptiness. Surrounding her is a "grave tranquillity like a visible presence or an odor or a sound" (94). She moves within yet remains exempt from the voices that constitute the world, her serenity a "walled and windless garden . . . while other women talked of their menfolks into her grave receptivity" (66). Yet her tranquillity is "grave" in a deathly sense, too, a walling out of speech and an ignoring of voices (even her own voice is a "grave contralto"). She ignores the women talking of their menfolks; she fetches shoes while Horace's "unintelligible" voice "soars into phrases which she did not herself recognize" (153–54), and after Bayard's death "she was serene again, . . . and Miss Jenny's voice was only a sound, comforting but without significance" (350). It is appropriate to her role in this closed oral community, where writing seems only an intrusion, that the important writings depicted in the novel, Byron's and Horace's letters, are all addressed to Narcissa. Reading, as Matthews points out, becomes a mode of sublimation for Narcissa, a way of hiding from her own desires. As she reads to Bayard she "crouch[es] behind the screen of words her voice raised between them" (232), and she takes "her book to bed, where she again held her consciousness deliberately submerged as you hold a puppy under water until its body ceases to resist."[10] This image of death captures perfectly Narcissa's role in the novel's dramatization of the loss of the natural communal presence of living voice, for she loses voice by denying it, by refusing to listen, just as she refuses to recognize the nature of her incestuous feelings for Horace (and her concomitant disgust at his affair with Belle Mitchell), just as she refuses to destroy the erotic anonymous letters from Byron Snopes and, finally, just as she tries to refuse to listen to young Bayard. Only Bayard's voice succeeds in penetrating her grave tranquillity, when he tells her his "brutal tale, without beginning, and crassly and uselessly violent and at times profane and gross" (251).

Young Bayard's talking itself denies the voiced natural community, as he seeks to find a death to clothe his Sartorial self-representations and the memory of his twin brother, John. His talking grates harshly amid the softer voices that fill the landscape. When he first arrives home and tells about John's death his strident voice clashes with the "locust [that] drifted up in sweet gusts upon the air, and the crickets and frogs . . . clear and monotonous as pipes blown drowsily by an idiot boy. From her silver casement the moon looked down upon the valley dissolving in opaline tranquillity into the serene mysterious infinitude of the hills, and young Bayard's voice went on and on, recounting violence and speed and death" (39). In town, when he talks, his voice garishly fills the little back room where Rafe MacCallum takes him to drink: "Bayard's voice went on, filling the cubby-hole of a room, surmounting the odor of cheap food too quickly cooked and of sharp spilt whiskey, with ghosts of a thing high-pitched as a hysteria, like a glare of fallen meteors on the dark retina of the world" (114).

The novel's primary story concerns Bayard's failed attempts to reimmerse himself in the community he has left. In farming and hunting he seeks the emotional peace he shared, or nostalgically believes he shared, with his brother John before the war. During the placid days after his first auto accident he marries Narcissa, runs the farm, and takes up former pastimes like possum hunting with Caspey. Here we have some of the most evocative presentations of phenomenal voice, as the very discourse seems to try to envelop Bayard in the plantation's life. Within the episodes dealing with Bayard come the hunting scenes with Caspey and the dogs, the oft-quoted paean to the mule, and the gathering of the Negroes at the cane press: "Sometimes they sang—quavering, wordless chords in which sad monotonous minors blent with mellow bass in passionless suspense and faded along the quivering golden air, to be renewed" (269).

The passage just quoted continues: "But when the white folks arrived the singing ceased, and they sat or lay about the crackling scented blaze," signaling in the change from song to talk Bayard's alienation from the natural voices. After each of his three violent accidents—his fall from the stallion and his two car accidents—he tries again to listen to the background voices; each mishap is followed by a period of calm associated in some way with the voiced land or community. Narcissa's lulling voice calms him as she reads to him after the first car accident; after the stallion throws him the itinerant salesman, V. K. Suratt, takes Bayard out to a farm to drink and talk—and he sits listening to Suratt's quiet country voice, which "seemed to fit easily into the still scene, speaking of earthy things" (125). Bayard's flight to the MacCallums after his grandfather dies in the car puts him again in the position of listener trying to discern in the voices and sounds around him the rhythms of peace.

Flags in the Dust, finally, attempts to hearken to a world long past, in a nostalgic listening to the voices constitutive of a dream that falls silent on awakening. Listening is indeed a common gesture of perception in *Flags*. Faulkner frequently adjusts perception (both a character's and the reader's) so that listening can take place and the world can be defined as heard. Over and over again the narrative describes a character's actions only to rearrange itself so that the same character's hearing becomes a medium of our perception. At times the gesture startles, as when old Bayard and Jenny leave Doc Peabody's office, still arguing, and the narrative places us with Peabody to listen: "[Doc Peabody] sat motionless and heard them quarrelling beyond it. Then the sound of their voices moved down the corridor toward the stairs, and still quarrelling loudly and on Bayard's part with profane emphasis, the voices died away" (92). Seldom does Faulkner seek to introduce Jenny's thoughts or perceptions; she is usually a character listened to or seen. But on occasion she, too, becomes a listener to the world's voices: "In her room, where she sat in a sunny window, she could still hear them—old Bayard's stormy rage, and Simon's bland and ready evasion rising and falling on the drowsy Sabbath air" (266; see also 362). Byron Snopes is employed in this listener's role as he hears Old Bayard's and Old Man Falls's voices behind the office wall. Even reading the bombastic inscription on the Sartoris tombstone is like listening to "a boastful voice in an empty church" (364).

Simon, Isom, Horace, Narcissa, Bayard (young and old, though the sounds around old Bayard are often unavailable to him)—all the characters attend to sounds and voices. Young Bayard's last hope is the listening he does at the MacCallums' farm, though it offers him nothing, finally: "The house was full of noises; to his [Bayard's] sharpened sense the silence was myriad" (315). And the novel ends appropriately with Narcissa in the *posture* of a listener, but not listening: "Narcissa played on as though she were not listening. Then she turned her head and without ceasing her hands, she smiled at Miss Jenny quietly, a little dreamily, with serene fond detachment. Beyond Miss Jenny's trim fading head the window curtains hung motionless without any wind; beyond the window evening was a windless lilac dream, foster-dam of quietude and peace" (370).

REV. SHEGOG'S POWERFUL VOICE

Nowhere in Faulkner's oeuvre is the presence and power of voice more beautifully conceived than in the fourth section of *The Sound and the Fury*, when Dilsey takes Benjy to her church's Easter service to hear Rev. Shegog's sermon. Contained within this one episode are all the strategies for creating phenomenal voice that Faulkner used throughout his fiction: contrasting figuration of vision and voice, attention to voice in itself, and separation of voice from speaker. Here, too, we find the full significance of voice as a phenomenon directly articulated.

However despairing or nihilistic a given reader may find *The Sound and the Fury*, the momentary ameliorative affirmation engendered by the Easter sermon is almost universally acknowledged. The sermon's power has been registered on a number of scales. Thematically, its depiction of Christ's resurrection envisions a salvation that will transcend the world's and the Compsons' degeneration: "the eloquent sermon [is] a vision of eternity which gives meaning to time and will wipe away all tears in a final vindication of goodness and in a full consolation of those who mourn" (C. Brooks, *Yoknapatawpha Country* 345). Structurally, the sermon provides closure for the "tragic-Christian" strands running through the novel (Hagopian 46–47). The sermon marks Dilsey as the novel's "ethical center" (Vickery 47–49). In social terms the church scene depicts a congregation of listeners sharing a communal moment in which their hearts speak each to each, an impossibility for the Compson family. The very content of the sermon ironically echoes and comments upon the variations of "Compson devilment" we have seen throughout the story (Matthews 108–10).

Rhetorically, the sermon testifies to Faulkner's mimetic skills in its faithful rendering of Southern black preaching (Rosenberg). André Bleikasten best expresses the overall significance of Shegog's performance: "The voice that takes hold of the preacher induces a vision, and this moment of vision, fully shared in by the congregation, is in fact the only experience of spiritual enlightenment recorded in the whole book. To Dilsey, in particular, the preacher's words bring the encompassing revelation of eternity, the mystical and prophetic vision of 'the beginning and the ending'" (*Most Splendid Failure* 201).

The movement from part 3 into part 4 of *The Sound and the Fury* has been described as an emergence from confining voice into clear sight. We escape from the novel's solopsistic monologues into highly visual description where objects and, most important, people can now be seen—if not objectively at least with striking clarity (Blanchard passim; Bleikasten, *Most Splendid Failure* 176–80). No longer buttonholed by Jason, we can watch Dilsey step out of her cabin door without feeling claustrophobic dependence upon what an obsessed or idiotic talker is telling us. Yet for all its visual clarity, the opening portion of section 4 mingles voice with vision in an orchestration of imagery that will culminate in Rev. Shegog's Easter sermon. Implanted within the visual imagery at the opening are sounds, voices, and moments of listening. Some sounds are described abstractly or even visually, dropped into the silent envisioned scene like pebbles dropped into water. The jaybirds' "harsh cries" are whipped away by the wind like "scraps of paper or of cloth" (*SF* 307; 331–32); Mrs Compson calls Dilsey's name "into the quiet stairwell that descended into complete darkness . . . with machinelike regularity" (308, 312; 333, 337); Dilsy sings "something without particular tune or words, repetitive, mournful and plaintive, austere" (312; 336); the clock ticktocks in "enigmatic profundity" (316; 341); and Luster plays a soundless tune with his fingers as he feeds Benjy (319–20; 345). The opening pages also contain a number of acts of listening, of one person listening not *to* others but *for* them. Dilsey listens for Luster and for Mrs Compson: "She ceased and tilted her head upward, listening. But there was no sound save the clock and the fire" (317; 342). We *see* Jason and his mother, in a description that emphasizes their eyes, as they *listen* to Dilsey "mount the final stair" to call Quentin:

When she called the first time Jason laid his knife and fork down and he and his mother appeared to wait across the table from one another in identical attitudes; the one cold and shrewd, with close-thatched

37

brown hair curled into two stubborn hooks, one on either side of his forehead like a bartender in caricature, and hazel eyes with black-ringed irises like marbles, the other cold and querulous, with perfectly white hair and eyes pouched and baffled and so dark as to appear to be all pupil or all iris. (323; 348)

When Quentin does not answer, Jason stands at her door "as if he were listening to something much further away than the dimensioned room beyond the door, and which he already heard. His attitude was that of one who goes through the motions of listening in order to deceive himself as to what he already hears. Behind him Mrs Compson mounted the stairs, calling his name" (324; 349–50).

The intrusion of sound into the Sunday morning silence, recorded both in images of sound and in acts of listening, predicts the more stately orchestration of vision and voice that begins when the Easter service episode itself gets under way. In this episode the three discursive gestures that engender voice's power—the contrast of vision and voice, the treatment of voice as a phenomenon separate from its function as a vehicle for speech, and the breaking of voice away from speaker and speech—come to fruition.

As Dilsey, Benjy, and Luster prepare to leave for the church, Faulkner describes Benjy's voice twice. Benjy's bellow has served, in the novel's earlier sections, as a palpable index of Caddy's loss. Now Faulkner renders Benjy's wailing as "hopeless and prolonged. It was nothing. Just sound. It might have been all time and injustice and sorrow become vocal for an instant by a conjunction of planets" (332–33; 359). The figurative meaning of the sound as "time and injustice and sorrow become vocal" is offered tentatively ("it *might* have been") as confirmation of the symbolic role Benjy's bellow has played earlier in the novel; yet the description emphasizes the voice's emptiness. It is voice as a hollow sound from which meaning has been extracted, now lacking its earlier significance as moral index. The second description, a few paragraphs later, even more explicitly empties Benjy's wailing of meaning as a "slow hoarse sound that ships make, that seems to begin before the sound itself has started, seems to cease before the sound itself has stopped" (333; 359). The voice is objectified as something present and hearable, and nothing more, separated from Benjy as a human source. A gap opens between the voice and its sound, for the one begins and ends before the other starts and stops. A visual counterpart to this aural image of Benjy's voice comes a few short paragraphs later. Luster has "a stiff new straw hat with a colored band" to wear to church.

A comically ill-fitting hat, it seems "to isolate Luster's skull in the be-
holder's eye as a spotlight would, in all its individual planes and an-
gles . . . the hat appeared to be on the head of someone standing immediately behind Luster" (334; 360).

The descriptions of Benjy's bellowing and of Luster's appearance begin
a narrative pattern in which aural and visual images alternate with one
another as contrasting strands in the texture of the discourse. The highly
descriptive narration maintains a rhythm of representation between moments dominated by voice and by images of objects seen. Under the sky
seen "broken now into scudding patches that dragged their swift shadows
up out of the shabby garden" we *hear* Benjy wailing and Dilsey soothing
him, " 'Hush,' Dilsey said. 'Hush, now. We be gone in a minute. Hush,
now' " (333; 360).

The alternation between vision and speech continues throughout the
stately procession to church. First comes talk. Luster and Dilsey fuss at
each other about Luster's hat and the umbrella, Benjy stops wailing as
they leave the drive, and Dilsey nags Frony about her dress getting wet
(" 'Mammy always talkin bout hit gwine rain,' Luster said" [335; 361]).
Then comes vision. We see the street's "quiet length" with "white people
in bright clumps mov[ing] churchward, under the windy bells, walking
now and then in the random and tentative sun" (335; 362). Talk returns in
Frony's complaint about Benjy because "folks talkin" (335; 362), a complaint Dilsey dismisses as coming from "trash white folks." Vision returns
as the street passes between small cabins "set in small grassless plots lit-
tered with broken things . . . [and] rank weeds [and] trees that partook
also of the foul desiccation which surrounded the houses" (336; 362–63).
Out of this visualized clutter voices emerge once again, as "from the doors
negroes spoke to them as they passed, to Dilsey usually:

> "Sis' Gibson! How you dis mawnin?"
> "I'm well. Is you well?"
> "I'm right well, I thank you." (336; 363)

Another visual description of the churchgoers follows, delineating their
dress and accoutrements. Then more voices, disembodied, written in
speakerless stychomythia as the children talk about Benjy:

> "I bet you wont go up en tech him."
> "How come I wont?"
> "I bet you wont. I bet you skeered to."
> "He wont hurt folks. He des a loony." (337; 364)

The discourse reverts to vision again in a striking picture of the church "like a painted church" instead of a real one: "the whole scene was as flat and without perspective as a painted cardboard set upon the ultimate edge of the flat earth, against the windy sunlight of space and April and a mid-morning filled with bells" (337; 364). The men converse against the back-drop of the church as the women and children enter, also to talk: "the women were gathered on one side of the room. They were talking" (338; 365). Sound and sight continue to alternate in the two paragraphs intro-ducing Rev. Shegog from "Saint Looey," who has come to preach the Easter service. Between the choir's singing and the children's singing in "frightened, tuneless whispers," the congregation watches Rev. Shegog with disappointment. He is "undersized," with "a wizened black face like a small, aged monkey." Faulkner often depicts the sound of a voice as physically affecting sight (or vice versa), an oxymoron that highlights the palpable solidity of sound's presence. Here the regular minister, himself a man of "imposing bulk," introduces Rev. Shegog "in rich, rolling tones whose very unction served to increase the visitor's insignificance" (339; 366). The journey to the Easter service ends as Dilsey again hushes Benjy, and Shegog's preaching begins.

Commentators on *The Sound and the Fury* have normally seen Shegog's sermon as divided into two parts, his "white" and his "black" rhetoric (see, for example, Davis 113–17). Important as the racial-phonetic distinc-tion is, the sermon is not bifurcated simply along these lines. Faulkner actually renders Shegog's sermon in *three* stages. The first is purely de-scriptive. The diegetic discourse informs about, but does not show, the qualities of Shegog's voice: "He sounded like a white man. His voice was level and cold. It sounded too big to have come from him" (339; 366). We find this vocal tag, "level and cold," employed frequently in Faulkner as a mark upon the discourse of any speaker not participating in a shared or sharable voice. To speak in a level and cold voice is to speak only for oneself, *at* but not *with* others. The congregation responds properly to this level and cold voice—that is, they respond visually, watching him and his voice as they would watch circus performers: "They listened at first through curiosity, as they would have to a monkey talking. They began to watch him as they would a man on a tight rope" (339; 366). The perfor-mance is a tour de force as Shegog "ran and poised and swooped upon the cold inflectionless wire of his voice." His performance depletes him and he stands "reft of all motion as a mummy or an emptied vessel"—visual im-ages of voiceless things. This first stage ends with the congregation unmoved (except to sigh and "move a little in its seats"). Dilsey comforts Ben, who apparently has moaned, by promising him that soothing voices will follow—"Dey fixin to sing in a minute" (340; 367).

Stage two of Shegog's sermon opens with a voice separate from its source, but a voice that can now *speak* instead of merely stretch like a wire to demonstrate a performer's verbal footwork: "Then a voice said, 'Brethren.'" For the first time the narrative depicts the voice distinctly as sound: "The voice died in sonorous echoes between the walls. It was as different as day and dark from his former tone, with a sad, timbrous quality like an alto horn" (340; 367). To this voice the congregation *listens*, as the sermon now sinks "into their hearts and speak[s] there again when it had ceased in fading and cumulate echoes." We "hear" Rev. Shegog in an oral performance: "I got the recollection and the blood of the Lamb!" The imagery reaches a crescendo of evocation here, as Shegog tramps back and forth behind the pulpit: "He was like a worn small rock whelmed by the successive waves of his voice. With his body he seemed to feed the voice that, succubus like, had fleshed its teeth in him. And the congregation seemed to watch with its own eyes while the voice consumed him, until he was nothing and they were nothing and there was not even a voice but instead their hearts were speaking to one another in chanting measures beyond the need for words" (340; 367). Now the congregation listens. Yet it still watches, too, as the voice "consumes" Shegog until he becomes "a serene, tortured crucifix that transcended its shabbiness and insignificance" (340–41; 368). The second stage of Shegog's sermon has transformed the visualized voice of the first stage into a voice powerful and sonorous—but a voice still "white," still that of a stranger. The congregation is caught, letting out a "long moaning expulsion of breath," and a "woman's single soprano" responds; but the total immersion in voice is yet to come.

A brief return to Dilsey again indicates a break between stages, as we see her sitting "bolt upright, her hand on Ben's knee." Ben, apparently, is no longer moaning. The third stage begins with Rev. Shegog shifting from white speech to black:

> "Brethren," the minister said in a harsh whisper, without moving.
> "Yes, Jesus!" the woman's voice said, hushed yet.
> "Breddren en sistuhn!" His voice rang again, with the horns. He removed his arm and stood erect and raised his hands. "I got de ricklickshun en de blood of de Lamb!" They did not mark just when

his intonation, his pronunciation, became negroid, they just sat swaying a little in their seats as the voice took them into itself. (341; 368)

The third stage *imitates* voice, re-creating the rhythms and sounds of Southern black preaching: "When de long, cold—Oh, I tells you bred-dren, when de long, cold. . . . I sees de light en I sees de word, po sinner!" (341; 368). Shegog's sermon is one of Faulkner's most sustained examples of black speech fully rendered and maintained in dialect writing. But now we see that the voice has more than imitated speech; it has been trans-formed into phenomenal voice, emerging as palpable and significant dis-course out of a carefully modulated narrative episode in which vision and voice alternate to evoke the presence of annealing voice in the world and human presence caught up in that voice.

The three stages have carried us from description to imitation, from visualized voice to heard voice recorded so that the reader, like the con-gregation, can be taken into its communal "chanting measures beyond the need for words." Bleikasten's insight that Shegog's voice "induces a vi-sion" aptly describes the paradoxical result of the sermon. Shegog ham-mers into the congregation what he has *seen*: "I sees de light en I sees de word, po sinner!" "I sees" punctuates his evocation of Christ's suffering. Thus within the represented world the power of voice is appropriately gauged by Dilsey's reaction to Shegog: "I seed de beginnin, en now I sees de endin" (344; 371). Furthermore, the dialect spelling produces power-fully "voiced" writing that marks the alteration from white to black into-nation. Faulkner makes us literally see so that we may hear: "breddren en sistuhn"; "ricklickshun"; "Ma'y settin in de do' wid Jesus on her lap." The dialect is, as usual in Faulkner, deftly controlled. Some of the dialect spellings mark phonetic differences between black and white speech, though others exaggerate those distinctions. (Many white Southerners would probably *say* "po" for "poor" just as black speakers would, but, as is necessarily true in dialect writing, the "standard" speech has virtually no unconventional phonetic markers [Ives, "Theory of Literary Dialect" 158–63].) Some of the spellings, too, are pure eye dialect, signifying dif-ferences they do not really render: "wus" for "was," or "whut" for "what." While the dialect is heavy, Faulkner carefully resists misspelling every word: we have "ricklick*shun*" but also "lamenta*tion*" and "resurrec*tion*." Only a visual analog this skillfully modulated can render voice's supreme triumph here.

The role of vision in Shegog's dialect is not a trivial matter of technique but an essential ingredient in that process by which Faulkner empowers written, visually accessible discourse to emerge as meaningful voice. Perhaps Faulkner gives us in this Easter service episode what Roland Barthes would have called an *erotics* of voice in narrative. Amidst a scene evoking divine love, this episode is a text of pleasure in which the discourse creates suspense through blockage and release of voice, through the alternating presence and absence of voice. We are led toward a climactic union with voice that, in promise at least, answers all questions and dispels all disappointments. Suspense results from the episode's steady movement toward something (a something that will turn out to be voice) that promises to overcome the disappointment of sight. What we see disappoints us, just as the sight of Rev. Shegog disappoints the congregation. What we seek at the narrative's end, then, is fulfillment and release from disappointment, or at the very least an explanation of our disappointment. We are disappointed by the weather, by the clutter of the Negro families' yards, by the church, which is "crazy," flat, perched on the precipice. Rev. Shegog disappoints by his small, wizened features that seem an insufficient vessel for the word of God—the word that is all encompassing, the word that is the world. The three stages of the sermon create tremendous suspense because we are led to believe that something crucial is imminent, as indeed it is. And the suspense maintains its rhythm, as it must, by forward movements blocked by delay. The metaphors themselves delay our hearing of Shegog: the authorial narrative *hides* Shegog's voice even as it describes it, offering instead verbal figures that reify the voice we want to hear. The image of the high-wire walker may delight with its inventiveness, but the reader does not want scenic ingenuity here; the reader wants to *hear* that voice. The pauses between stages delay our progress also, and may be the kind of passage that Barthes tells us is often skipped or read quickly (in the classic narrative) in the drive toward fulfillment of the story's promise, as we are "impel[led] to skim or to skip certain passages . . . in order to get more quickly to the warmer parts of the anecdote (which are always its articulations: whatever furthers the solution of the riddle, the revelation of fate)" (*Pleasure of the Text* 11).

The suspense ends when the denouement is reached in Shegog's actual words as quoted and thus as heard both by the reader and by the congregation. The immersion into voice, and the lull and peace such immersion provides, turn out to have been the narrative's goal all along. When we enter the dialect passage we cannot read blindly or even too quickly.

Shegog's heavy eye dialect is surely a "warmer part of the anecdote" that releases visionary voice by, in part, slowing our reading—even our literally measurable reading speed. And so the disappointment ends when the climactic union of heart and person has been achieved.

I would emphasize here that it is not the content of Shegog's sermon that provides this fulfillment, any more than the particular solution to a mystery provides pleasure. As long as a solution has been provided, the narrative has reached its goal. Critics who deduce a Christian "message" from Dilsey's tears or Shegog's retelling of the Easter story misconstrue the function of voice in this scene (and in much of Faulkner) as a function of communication, when voice truly functions to satisfy and fulfill. The sermon's power is not transferable to the world outside the church or, as an experience of reading, to the rest of the novel's text. Thadious Davis is right that "the church service occurs in isolation," and that we are not told "how the Negro's experience might have meaning or bearing on the white-centered world that is [Faulkner's] subject" (110). But I disagree with her assumption that the service's isolation constitutes a *failure* of "Faulkner's vision," for his "vision" is discoverable in the energetics of voice. Eric Sundquist, in the strongest denigration of the sermon's thematic value, cautions against being "taken in by [the sermon's] pose of cathartic naturalism." This pose leads only to "the eschatological sublime of *Uncle Tom's Cabin*," which in effect "declar[es] that, Negroes and idiots aside, it is of no real value whatsoever" (12–13). But even if thematically unsatisfying, the rendering of Shegog's voice still exerts "cathartic" force that is not fraudulent. John Matthews sees this force as authorial (if not necessarily authoritative) in that Shegog "complexly figures the role of the author in his work as he strives to deliver the word that will interpret experience truly and establish the communion of speaker and hearer" (108). But, ironically, for this communion to emerge, voice must be turned loose and separated from the author in order to enter the visual discourse of our reading. Whether such a turning loose is as Sundquist calls it "a pose of cathartic naturalism" may matter less to this novel than how the power of voice exerts itself.

Shegog embodies the role that phenomenal voice plays in this process. A soundful world in which voice moves like a presence, like God's voice upon the water, is a world in which the power of communion is efficacious. Although elsewhere Faulkner renders that power less positively, here, in the voice that for Dilsey affirms the tragic beauty of mourning, Faulkner perhaps sought to transcend the limiting dependence of fiction's voices

upon vision and to release voice to engender a communion not only beyond the need for words but beyond the site of fiction's written language.

INTRUSIVE VOICE IN *SANCTUARY*

Arthur Kinney has correctly argued that Faulkner creates his fictional
worlds in a manner best labeled "phenomenological." That is to say, he
orders the experience of the narrative through adjustments in perceiving
consciousness: "In so aligning one or more narrative consciousness with
our own consciousness of the work as a single unified aggregate,
Faulkner's novels are persistently phenomenological in origin and shape"
(5). Whereas Kinney's critical vocabulary articulates such alignment
nearly always in visual terms, the dying fall into "quietude and peace"
with which *Flags in the Dust* closes, or the "chanting measures" of
Shegog's sermon, accentuate the centrality of sound, of voice, and of listening in the novels' perceptual reenactment of community. Visual metaphors like "perspective" or "point of view," dominant in Anglo-American
critical vocabulary, may explain how "Faulkner shapes his work to reveal
the *visions* of his characters; their *visions* thus become his style" (Kinney 6;
my emphasis), but they do not adequately capture the effect of Faulkner's
descriptive prose, which creates more a gestalt cluster of named sensations
that saturate the fiction's world and its discourse with sound (and occasionally with odors and tactile sensations) as well as with visions. In *Flags
in the Dust* we have examined early versions of an often repeated rhetorical
strategy whereby Faulkner places a "consciousness" in the *attitude of listener*. Listening is a way of being in a phenomenal world. The reciprocal
implication between consciousness and "object" represented in Faulkner's
discourse is not always best defined as a perspective or a way of looking at
the world, but rather also as a *listening*, or a *hearkening* to the world. Not
only are intentional objects ("intentional" in the phenomenological sense
as those objects toward which consciousness is directed) often sounds or
sources of sound, especially human voices, but the consciousness that the
reader aligns with his or her own assumes the stance of a listener.[11] Criticism lacks any adequate term comparable to "perspective" but derived
from hearing or other senses. Kinney's terms, such as "align" or "shape,"
typically grow out of a visual presumption, as do theories of "point of
view" (especially after Henry James and Percy Lubbock). Possible substitute terms might be "hearkening" for "perspective," "attuning" for

45

"aligning," and "harmonizes" for "shapes." Given criticism's visually based vocabulary, it would sound odd—yet for Faulkner it might be more apt—to rewrite Kinney's statements in aurally derived terminology: "in so *attuning* one or more narrative consciousness with our own," or "Faulkner *harmonizes* his work to *amplify* the *hearkenings* of his characters."

The three novels that immediately followed *Flags in the Dust—The Sound and the Fury*, *As I Lay Dying*, and *Sanctuary*—all depict characters who are, in profound ways, listeners: Benjy, Quentin, Darl, Dewey Dell, and Vardaman are all portrayed as listeners, and their interior narrations are characterized by this stance vis-à-vis the phenomenal world. I will reserve discussion of *The Sound and the Fury* and *As I Lay Dying* for later chapters, and turn now to *Sanctuary*, a novel that employs phenomenal voice in ways similar to *Flags in the Dust*, but with strikingly different effects.

Sanctuary frequently describes Temple Drake as listening from within a confined space, usually a room, to the voices and other sounds of the world outside that space. As sounds penetrate walls and doors, so the world persistently invades wherever Temple tries to hide. Sounds, including voices, embody a threatful, intrusive world. At the old Frenchman place she listens to men's voices outside on the porch, or outside of the bedroom where she tries (or pretends) to sleep. The narrative mentions voices frequently, almost obsessively. From the breeze that draws through the "gaunt weather-stained ruin . . . with a sad, murmurous sound," to the "silence" Temple "hears" in the corncrib when Popeye is about to rape her, the discourse makes the reader attend to the voices and sounds Temple hears:

> She went on down the hall. Behind her she could hear Gowan's and the man's voices. (44; 48)

> [S]he could hear no sound save the voices from the front. (44; 49)

> From somewhere beyond the lamplit hall she could hear the voices. (56; 61)

> [S]he could hear the faint guttering the lamp made, and the meat in the skillet and the hissing of the kettle on the stove, and the voices, the harsh, abrupt, meaningless masculine sounds from the house. (58; 64)

> The men's voices grew louder. She heard a trampling of feet in the
> hall, a rasping of chairs, the voice of the man who had laughed above
> them, laughing again. (66; 73)

Popeye carries out the intrusive threat with which all voices in *Sanctuary*
seem imbued when he shoots Tommy and rapes Temple in the corncrib,
where sound suddenly condenses into a palpable, terrifying silence. Temple hears Popeye in the loft above her, then she follows him with her eyes
as "he cross[es] her field of vision, moving without a sound." The gunshot
makes a noise "no louder than the striking of a match: a short, minor
sound shutting down upon the scene, the instant, with a profound final-
ity." Popeye moves toward Temple silently, and the "released door yawned
and clapped against the jamb, but it made no sound either; it was as
though sound and silence had become inverted. She could hear silence in a
thick rustling as he moved toward her through it" (107; 121–22). Even
Temple's scream is silent ("Something is going to happen to me"), being
first rendered without quotation marks as a thought, and then with quotation marks when she imagines "saying it to the old man with the yellow
clots for eyes." She "void[s] the words like hot silent bubbles into the
bright silence about them" (107; 122).

Temple also listens from her room at Miss Reba's, where the sounds and
voices become less threatening as the cancer of her own corruption
blooms. If Popeye is a voyeur, impotent but aroused by watching Temple
and Red copulate, then Temple is an *écouteur* (a term proposed by Barthes
[*S/Z* 132]), one who listens, impotent but aroused by sounds from the
outside world. She "listen[s] to the hot minute seeping of her blood" (143;
163) riding to Memphis with Popeye, and when first in her room, "her ears
acute, her eyes a little blind with the strain of listening . . . [she] began to
hear a hundred conflicting sounds in a single converging threat" and "the
secret whisper of her blood" (155; 177). Sounds are catalogued: "The
house was full of sounds," people moving, doors banging, "a shrill
woman's voice," Miss Reba's voice "booming from somewhere," the dogs
"whimpering and scuffing" outside her door (see passim 149–67; 170–91
and 236–54; 269–90). Temple's Memphis world is indeed one of voices,
experienced as if through a closed door, as sounds penetrate into the range
of her awareness.

Temple's posture as listener invaded by a threatful world embodied as
sound, and especially as voice, makes her as much a victim as a genuinely

evil character, at least until her perjury at Goodwin's trial. Like Joe Christmas, Temple commits evil acts; yet, as in *Light in August*, readers share a character's perceptual condition so that they can share the character's estrangement from the phenomenal world—and that estrangement cannot be judged in simple moral terms. Temple is hideously raped, after all, invaded by Popeye and by the world outside whatever temporary sanctuary (a room, a corncrib) she flees to. When she tells Horace about the events at the old Frenchman place she cannot articulate the rape or the murder, but instead returns over and over to "the only part of the whole experience . . . which she had spent in comparative inviolation" when "she entered the room and tried to wedge the door with the chair . . . [and] herself sitting on the bed, listening to the men on the porch, or lying in the dark while they entered the room and came to the bed and stood there above her" (225; 257–58).

The discourse further attunes the reader's perceiving consciousness to that of a listener (sometimes a specific character like Temple, sometimes an implied listener) by providing voice qualifiers for speakers with the same attention and near obsessiveness that it notes the sounds Temple hears. Faulkner describes each speaker's voice in ways that, again, make voice threatening. Popeye has a "soft, cold voice," a descriptive tag repeated many times. Ruby's voice is "still, dispassionate," and she talks "as though she were reciting a formula for bread" (64; 71). Horace has a "dry, light voice" (191; 219), or, when Ruby hears him, a "quick, faintly outlandish voice"; Clarence Snopes has a "harsh, assertive voice" (184; 211), Miss Reba a "hoarse, fainting voice" (152; 173), or she roars in a "harsh, choking voice" (165; 189, 167; 191); Narcissa has a "cold unbending voice" (192; 220). Even the syntactic pattern of "[adjective], [adjective] voice" repeats itself in nearly every voice tag. Faulkner was always fond of such tags, but *Sanctuary* turns this discursive device into an objectification of the mechanical and threatening quality of the fictional world.

Phenomenal voice as an embodiment of the natural community figures much less extensively in *Sanctuary* than in *Flags in the Dust* but, especially in moments involving Horace Benbow, we do discover similar imagery evoked to blend the community with nature. The potential if unattainable annealing powers of sound and voice fade, however, behind *Sanctuary*'s desperately perverse and noisy world. In part this occurs because much of the story takes place in Memphis, with its city sounds of "threat and promise both." Even when the scene is Jefferson, however, the first of what in later Faulkner texts becomes a common image of mechanized

voices alters the quality of phenomenal voice: no longer is Elnora's crooning heard at the Sartoris house, instead there are "disembodied voices
blaring from imitation wood cabinets or pebble-grain horn-mouths above
the rapt faces, the gnarled slow hands long shaped to the imperious earth,
lugubrious, harsh, and sad" (116; 133).

Those figures that could evoke, at least by implication, a natural and
communal phenomenal voice in *Sanctuary* evoke death, crime, violence,
betrayal—all the threatening qualities inherent to this novel's world and
discourse. The only Negro voices we hear belong to a murderer and his
friends, singing at a jail window (in a passage that opened the original
version of the novel): "In it the negro murderer leaned; below along the
fence a row of heads hatted and bare above work-thickened shoulders, and
the blended voices swelled rich and sad into the soft, depthless evening,
singing of heaven and being tired . . . the singing followed them, dimmed
by the walls, the lights" (128–29; 146–47). The darkness out of which
voices emerge raises in Horace's mind nightmarish visions of sexual corruption. Figures of sight and sound blend in his thoughts of Little Belle
with her voice "like the murmur of the wild grape itself" (14); her secret
sexuality *sounds* in his imagination as he looks at her photograph and
thinks of "the grape arbor in Kinston, of summer twilight and the murmur
of voices darkening into silence as he approached, who meant them, her,
no harm; who meant her less than harm, good God; darkening into the
pale whisper of her white dress, of the delicate and urgent mammalian
whisper of that curious small flesh which he had not begot" (174–75; 199–
200). Horace vividly dreams, after hearing Temple's story, of Little Belle–
Temple "bound naked on her back on a flat car moving at speed through a
black tunnel"; the dream includes the sound of "the shucks [that] set up a
terrific uproar beneath her thighs" and a "darkness overhead now shred-
ded with parallel attenuations of living fire, toward a crescendo like a held
breath. . . . Far beneath her she could hear the faint, furious uproar of the
shucks" (234–35; 268). Horace's confrontation with a desire that literally
nauseates him transforms even the voice of the night itself (figured so
lovingly in *Flags in the Dust*) into proof of a cosmic entropy: "The voice of
the night—insects, whatever it was—had followed him into the house; he
knew suddenly that it was the friction of the earth on its axis, approaching
that moment when it must decide to turn on or to remain forever still: a
motionless ball in cooling space, across which a thick smell of honeysuckle
writhed like cold smoke" (234; 267).

A passage deleted from the original text of *Sanctuary* equates talking and corruption in a dream that grotesquely reverses and almost seems to parody the symbolic equation of voice with the maternal peace and tranquillity that characterized voice in *Flags*. Horace dreams that his mother sits at his bedside talking to him, "emanat[ing] that abounding serenity as of earth which his sister had done since her marriage and the birth of her child" (*SO* 60). But his mother "talks" without opening her mouth, and the dream then transforms her into Belle, Horace's mistress-become-wife "about to open her mouth and he tried to scream at her, to clap his hand to her mouth. But it was too late. He saw her mouth open; a thick, black liquid welled in a bursting bubble that splayed out upon her fading chin and the sun was shining on his face and he was thinking He smells black. He smells like that black stuff that ran out of Bovary's mouth when they raised her head."[12]

Horace's alienation from the natural sounds ("the voice of the night") has its counterpart in his estrangement from his community. His defense of Goodwin disqualifies Horace's voice as one the town listens to, and reduces him to another subject of the town's gossip and innuendo; indeed, Narcissa, who fears the gossip, turns informer to defeat her quixotic brother when she goes to the prosecutor with "gossip" about Temple. Voices heard in town form part of the community that Horace attends to even as he feels increasingly estranged from it. "The myriad noises of the square," which include "the footsteps and voices of people on the slow and unhurried pavement below the window; the people buying quiet things to take home and eat at quiet tables" (168, 172; 192–93, 197) are heard as background to Ruby's story when she tells Horace about Temple at the old Frenchman place. Not simply offered as part of "*l'effet de réel*," these voices later become part of the communal consciousness that will take Lee Goodwin from his cell and burn him: "Before he reached town he began to hear the sound, the voices" (307; 351). "It was not a sound Horace heard now; it was something in the air which the sound of the running feet died into" (310; 353). "He couldn't hear the fire, though it still swirled upward unabated, as though it were living upon itself, and soundless: a voice of fury like in a dream, roaring silently out of a peaceful void" (311; 355).

The "quietude and peace" that ended *Flags in the Dust* turns into a more threatening "peaceful void" in *Sanctuary* because the nostalgic phenomenal voice has become destructive. *Sanctuary* derives its unsettling effect from the way in which voice participates in the grotesque violence of the novel. One of voice's implications—power—is turned against its other implications—human presence and community. Voice's power within the discourse dehumanizes sound and erases communal potential: in the novel's discourse voices embody intrusive forces, the human voice is labeled mechanically (in repeated voice tags), and the community voices harbor only the threat of violent death.

VOICE AND ESTRANGEMENT IN *LIGHT IN AUGUST*

The "voice" of Jefferson that Horace hears in the running feet, the shouts, and the roar of the fire becomes in *Light in August* a central manifestation of the mentality—of individuals and of the community—that victimizes Joe Christmas. From the "thin, furious voice" of the dietitian who "hisse[s] 'You little nigger bastard,'" (135; 114), to Doc Hines's "mad voice" (140; 119), to McEachern's "voice . . . measured, harsh, without heat" (181; 155), to the people gathered at Joanna Burden's burning house whose words appear from nowhere, like anonymous sound, engendered "out of thin air" (315; 271), voices form the world in which Joe moves, the world that insists on defining him in its own terms. At the fire the people have gathered as at an "emotional barbecue, a Roman holiday almost," wanting to believe that "the flames, the blood, the body . . . cried out for vengeance." Voices are in and of the air: "The words that flew among them wind- or airengendered *Is that him? Is that the one that did it? Sheriff's got him. Sheriff has already caught him* . . . Behind them in turn the dying fire roared, filling the air though not louder than the voices and much more unsourceless *By God, if that's him, what are we doing, standing around here? Murdering a white woman the black son of a*" (319–20; 275).

These lines exemplify the novel's consistent depiction of Jefferson through its voices. The town comes alive in its talk. *Light in August* defines its characters—its "pariahs, defiant exiles, withdrawn quietists, or simply strangers" (C. Brooks, *Yoknapatawpha Country* 53) as creations of talk. We overhear Byron and the other workers at the lumber mill talking about Joe Christmas when he first arrives in Jefferson. Everyone talks about Lena, of course, and the "corridor" of her journey is "paved with unflagging and tranquil faith and peopled with kind and nameless faces and voices: *Lucas Burch? I dont know. I dont know of anybody by that name around here. This road? It goes to Pocahontas*" (7; 4). Voice objectifies the constant if "etheral" (Brooks's term) presence of the community. Faulkner likens Byron's attempt to keep Lena from hearing rumors (about Joe Brown and the fire) to trying to get out of the smoke that hangs in the air all around them: "It seemed to him that fate, circumstance, had set a warning in the sky all day long in that pillar of yellow smoke, and he too stupid to read it. And so he would not let them tell—the men whom they passed, the air that blew upon them full of it—lest she hear too" (90–91; 77). Hightower's history in Jefferson is like a play of voices everyone must act out until the gossip, "the whispering, . . . the idle word blown from mind to mind" could cease and "they could live quietly with one another" (65, 77, 78; 66, 67). The town's attitudes are figured in its talk, in a communal voice that carries with it the quality of something ineffably given, something literally "in the air," as integral a part of the environment as the buildings, roads, businesses, vehicles, and other trappings of communal life.

Talk becomes an objective correlative for the moral questions raised by the "pariahs" and "strangers" who live in or come into the townspeople's midst. Richard Godden has discussed the function of the talk most directly, calling the novel "a thriller whose villain is the word 'nigger'" (238). Whether that talk issues from the sourceless air of gossip or from a town spokesman like Gavin Stevens, it manifests an ideology in which, as Godden says, "decisions about identity are communal and collaborative; as such they issue from a debate whose nature is most apparent in vocal acts . . . at times it seems that every physiological quirk mutters with a social dimension" (Godden 236, 237). What Godden refers to as "physiological quirk" is often a version of phenomenal voice—references to and images of voice as a phenomenon present in the community. As the town's attitudes flow and thicken around the several characters, especially Joe Christmas, images of phenomenal voice help mold the town's condemnation or acceptance of outsiders.

Faulkner frequently employs all the various strategies discussed earlier for separating voice from person in order to raise individual verbal expression into a broader experiential realm of communal values. *Light in August* contains a high number of metonymic uses of voice, as when Joe as a teenager "strik[es] at the voice" of the Negro girl in outraged horror at female sexuality; or, in the same scene, one of his companions who taunts him is "a voice [that] spoke suddenly, loud" and "a second voice said quietly, carrying quietly, clear: 'See you tomorrow at church, Joe'" (173, 174; 147, 148). Voice is split away from speaker by metaphor as well as by metonymy, usually with the effect of making a voice seem both more palpable yet evanescent, like smoke, mist, or "a thistle bloom falling into silence without a sound, without any weight" (98; 83). The discourse defamiliarizes voice and the *act* of speech in order to make us perceive talk as paradoxically unnatural yet possessive of the implacable power of "natural" forces. One of the most striking images of voice separated from speaker in all of Faulkner is the extended portrayal of Doc and Mrs Hines telling Hightower Joe Christmas's history:

> [Hines's] voice ceases; his tone does not drop at all. His voice just stops, exactly like when the needle is lifted from a phonograph record by the hand of someone who is not listening to the record. . . . [Mrs Hines's voice] ceases. But hers is on a falling inflection, as if the machine had run down in mid-record. . . . [T]he two voices in monotonous strophe and antistrophe: two bodiless voices recounting dreamily something performed in a region without dimension by people without blood. . . . Then she begins to speak again, without moving, almost without lip movement, as if she were a puppet and the voice that of a ventriloquist in the next room. (409, 411, 414–15, 419; 350–51, 353, 355, 359)

As in *Flags in the Dust*, the sheer quantity of references to voice in *Light in August* indicates its important role in placing speakers within the context of community—though here the mythos is less that of the naturally derived land and village of *Flags* and more an ideological entity, ethereal yet pervasive, humanly created yet mechanical—"phonograph record," "machine," and "puppet."

Carolyn Porter argues that sound imagery in *Light in August* defines a realm of "sensuous human activity" and of "continuing life" from which all the main characters except Lena are alienated. In the novel's background sounds—the sounds of insects outside Hightower's window, the "voices, murmurs, whispers: of trees, darkness, earth; people" that Joe Christmas hears, and even in the sound of Armstid's wagon mounting the hill toward Lena ahead of the wagon itself—Porter discovers signs for a unified "natural, procreative realm" (very much like Rousseau's ideal community) in which humans are meaningfully joined to each other and to their environment and activity. Carefully distinguishing meaningful sounds from the voices that utter the town's "degenerate fiction," a fiction that worships death, Porter delineates the ideological implications of a type of figuration that places characters in relation to sound either as participants (as is Lena) or as observers (as is Hightower sitting at his window).

The portrayal of Hightower best supports Porter's reading, for in his estrangement he has overtly chosen to separate himself from community voice. He resisted the pressure of opinion and gossip to retain the fantasy of his grandfather's Civil War bravado, and as he sits each night at his window waiting for the precise moment when light will condense into vision and he can envision his grandfather's ride into Jefferson, he truly is the observer estranged from life, engaged in a deathwatch over "sensuous human activity." Meaningful activity, as Porter suggests, is figured (in the story) as the singing of the congregation that Hightower has abandoned to his vision:

> From a distance, quite faint though quite clear, he can hear the sonorous waves of massed voices from the church: a sound at once austere and rich, abject and proud, swelling and falling in the quiet summer darkness like a harmonic tide (82; 70).
>
> The organ strains come rich and resonant through the summer night, blended, sonorous, with the quality of abjectness and sublimation, as if the freed voices themselves were assuming the shapes and attitudes of crucifixions, ecstatic, solemn, and profound in gathering volume (404; 347).

The myriad sounds Hightower hears outside his window signify the continuing life he has opted out of: "The sound of music from the distant church has long since ceased. Now there is no sound in the room save the steady shrilling of insects and the monotonous sound of Byron's voice. . . . He ceases. Then there is no sound in the room save the insects. Beyond the open window the steady insects pulse and beat, drowsy and myriad" (98, 100; 83, 85). Hightower's listening posture reminds us of Temple, of young Bayard Sartoris, of Quentin Compson, and of Darl Bundren—listeners all estranged from soundful life either because it would intrude too profoundly into their secret selves or because they cannot or will not leave the safety of vision for active participation in sound.

Although the church music Hightower hears speaks to him of both hope and death, the sounds or voices that come from the town in its *social* function as creator of self-protective fictions are more associated with death than with life. Sound is not itself a sign of "the good" in Faulkner. Only when the sound allows or accompanies participation in life's "ongoing" or "procreative" activity does sound imagery refer to the "ordered fiction" the novel strives to become (or that the reader tries to make of the text). Thus Lena is at home in sound no matter what its source, even in the "gossip" of the furniture salesman in the book's last chapter, which renews her as a symbol of human time lived as ceaseless and amelioratory flow. And so for Hightower does all communal sound threaten to intrude into his dead grandfather's silent cavalry ride.

With Joe Christmas Faulkner represents a character not simply estranged from the community but from himself as well. Like Hightower, Joe stands outside the human community embodied as sound and as phenomenal voice. But Joe is not merely outside that realm as an observer, for he, more profoundly than Hightower, remains alien to it. What is the annealing voice of shared human presence in the Easter service in *The Sound and the Fury*, what in *Flags in the Dust* is a lost natural community of voice, or what Porter calls "sensuous human activity" is simply not available to Joe. The novel arranges events so as to immerse him as deeply in voice as are Dilsey, young Bayard, and Horace Benbow, but Joe is driven out of voice's midst as an air-filled balloon is forced from under water: voice comes to embody and exert the felt pressure of alienated existence. I have already noted how *Light in August* echoes *Sanctuary*'s images of threatening community voices; the novel also contains references to phenomenal voice that are qualitatively similar to those in *Flags*, and in one remarkable scene the novel virtually reenacts the journey toward the communion of voice of *The Sound and the Fury*'s Easter service episode. Yet, even though *Light in August* renders voice in the same code of figuration as do *Flags in the Dust* and *The Sound and the Fury*, it denies voice's positive power more intently even than *Sanctuary*. The novel's discourse rejects the dream of shared presence, not merely as long past or only momentarily obtainable (as for Dilsey in the Easter service), but as impossible and even inherently destructive. In *Light in August* Faulkner accepts fully the contingency of human existence by discovering that even the most cherished dream of presence—the soundful natural community of voice—is humanly and linguistically mediated.

The novel again places a perceiving consciousness within a particular sensuous context: Joe listens to the world, to the phenomenal voices not only of humans but of nature, the air itself, the land. The novel's discourse produces Joe out of the discourse of others. The dietitian labels him as the "little nigger bastard," Doc Hines, the children, McEachern call him abomination, nigger, and sinner. As a listener, Joe experiences more through hearing than through seeing. Those indicia of Joe's sexual education, for example, that make up the somewhat clumsy Freudian allegory delineating Joe's boyhood are events marked more by sound than by sight. He does not *see* the dietitian and the intern making love, he *hears* them from behind a curtain. He cannot see the Negro girl in the dark barn, as he "strik[es] at her voice," and he learns about menstruation by being told. In adulthood, too, Joe comprises voices he has heard. As François Pitavy notes, voices fill Joe's mind during the night he prepares to kill Joanna Burden (*Faulkner's* Light in August 17–18). Voice becomes the physical symptom of hated prayer that enrages Joe: Mceachern's voice rising in prayer from the kitchen below Joe's bedroom; Joanna's voice raised in begging forgiveness for their sexual sins. Phenomenal voice, in short, plays a crucial role in the very *creation* of Joe within the fictional world and within the fiction's discourse.

On the night and day before he kills Joanna Burden, Joe undertakes a passage into voice that echoes Dilsey's journey toward communion in the voice of Rev. Shegog, or young Bayard's nighttime visits to the cane making on the Sartoris plantation. One of the most powerful evocations of phenomenal voice in Faulkner, Joe's is a journey resonant with all the symbolic possibilities of voice: human presence, communion, and power. Joe does not find that communion, of course, and indeed his journey proves to be an attempt to escape voice: not simply the voices of gossip and rumor and deadly definition that we have seen embodied in the town's voices, but voice as natural flow of existence, as manifestation of that womblike communal place that Faulkner's discourse in *Flags* proposed as ideal presence.

Every moment of Joe's night walk enmeshes him in voice. The section (chapter 5) begins with his attempts to stifle the drunken Brown's voice ("The very longdrawn pitch of his voice seemed to smell of whiskey" [112; 95]). As he has done all his life, Joe tries to cut voice off, stop it sharply, as his presence at the spring near his foster father's farm would cut "the fluting of young frogs . . . like so many strings cut with simultaneous scissors" (174; 149). So he slaps Brown with those "hard, slow, measured blows" reminiscent of McEachern, while his own voice remains "level as whispering." Joe leaves the cabin in response to voices he hears: "Then it seemed to him, sitting on the cot in the dark room, that he was hearing a myriad sounds [*sic*] of no greater volume—voices, murmurs, whispers: of trees, darkness, earth; people: his own voice; other voices evocative of names and times and places—which he had been conscious of all his life without knowing it, which were his life" (115; 97–98). After standing beneath Joanna's window, "cursing her with slow and calculated obscenity" (117; 99), Joe stands naked in the headlights of a car, "[from which] a woman's shrill voice flew back, shrieking . . . [the car] sucking with it the white woman's fading cry" (118; 100). Joe returns to his cabin, only to be driven out again by the sound of Brown's snoring and "the intervals filled with the myriad voices, [which are] more than he could bear" (119; 101).

As the novel traces Joe's movements during the next daylight hours, it sets up alternating contrasts between voice and vision similar to those in the Easter service narrative in *The Sound and the Fury*. Unlike the night before, Joe seems at ease within the "yellow day opening peacefully on before him, like a corridor, an arras, into a still chiaroscuro without urgency" (122; 104). He reads, seeming "to watch the slow flowing of time beneath him, thinking *All I wanted was peace* thinking 'She ought not to started praying over me'" (123; 104). But the visual imagery is not offered as some symbolic representation of a meaningful existence Joe has missed in his victimization by the voices of others. For envisioned phenomena are empty just as they are voiceless, devoid of significance for Joe even as they are less threatening; indeed their very emptiness is their appeal, for Joe is trying to escape significance, definition, and articulation in the fictions of others. Thus, while the "slow constellations" that wheel overhead at night do not threaten Joe, they are devoid of even the usual commonplace significance of names: "not one . . . had any name to him or meant anything at all by shape or brightness or position" (116; 98). As he walks through the white neighborhood Joe moves in light, a figure to be seen, marked by light and shadow, an observer himself seeing. "He went on, passing still between the homes of white people, from street lamp to street lamp, the heavy shadows of oak and maple leaves sliding like scraps of black velvet across his white shirt" (125; 106). And when he emerges from Freedman Town he comes safely into light and silence:

> To his left lay the square, the clustered lights: low bright birds in stillwinged and tremulous suspension. To the right the street lights marched on, spaced, intermittent with bitten and unstirring branches. [He sees silent white people on their porches,] the white faces intent and sharp in the low light, the bare arms of the women glaring smooth and white above the trivial cards. . . . Then he could see the town, the glare, the individual lights where streets radiated from the square. (126–27; 107–8)

The white people are silently visible on their porches, whereas in Freedman Town the Negroes were "invisible." Freedman Town itself, and the black identity it represents to Joe, is depicted as lightless and voiced, defined by sound and odor instead of sight. Probably Faulkner's most striking image of "the original quarry, abyss itself," this passage marks the "denaturalization" of phenomenal voice. Whereas in *Flags in the Dust* darkness, Negroes, and voices clustered within a figuration of a *natural* communal unity, here the phenomenal voices become simply another version of an ideologically defined identity unacceptable to Joe. The voices, like black life in all its representations, threaten to engulf, drown, and asphyxiate him:

> Then he found himself . . . in Freedman Town, surrounded by the summer smell and the summer voices of invisible negroes. They seemed to enclose him like bodiless voices murmuring talking laughing in a language not his. As from the bottom of a thick black pit he saw himself enclosed by cabinshapes, vague, kerosenelit, so that the street lamps themselves seemed to be further spaced, as if the black life, the black breathing had compounded the substance of breath so that not only voices but moving bodies and light itself must become fluid and accrete slowly from particle to particle, of and with the now ponderable night inseparable and one. (125–26; 106–7)

Whether it is the "natural" voices of the night—insects, frogs, whippoorwills—or the human voices of Negroes, Joe is endangered by the very annealing and embracing qualities that offered hope to Dilsey and to Bayard in earlier texts. As in those texts, voice joins with other represented phenomena to take on significance in a figural code that defines a natural community at the heart of a yearned-for, peaceful existence "beyond the need for words." Nature will, of course, be romanticized in later Faulkner texts—most notably in *Go Down, Moses*—but *Light in August* signals the end of the dream of a natural community of voice that Faulkner's characters can sink into so as to escape the very discourse that creates them. The significance of voice changes such that it no longer can evoke or symbolize a dream of a natural community: more and more voice becomes talking, writing, or mechanically created sound. Listening becomes listening to others talk. To participate one must become a narrator or a talker oneself, instead of one in harmony with the voice of the phenomenal world.

MECHANICAL VOICES

Joe Christmas rises "soaring" into memory in the wake of a mechanical sound: "the scream of the siren mounted toward its unbelievable crescendo, passing out of the realm of hearing" (513; 440). His estrangement from the community of voices is marked by the aural streak of a siren smeared across the town's consciousness like paint smeared across a wall. The siren's sound also predicts, in the future of Faulkner's oeuvre, an increasing attention to mechanical sounds and mechanized voices. Phenomenal voice comes more and more to be heard over the radio, through loudspeakers and megaphones, or in the scratchy voices of a gramophone. *Sanctuary* takes note of the "disembodied voices blaring from imitation wood cabinets or pebble-grain horn-mouths" (116; 133), and by *Requiem for a Nun* the notation has become a serious, even a bit querulous, complaint: "And, now and at last, the last of silence too: the county's hollow inverted air one resonant boom and ululance of radio: and thus no more Yoknapatawpha's air nor even Mason and Dixon's air, but America's: the patter of comedians, the baritone screams of female vocalists, the babbling pressure to buy and buy and still buy arriving more instantaneous than light" (244).

Concomitant with the increased frequency of images of mechanized sound comes a decrease in direct references to or descriptions of the unaided human voice: fewer voice tags, fewer metonymies depicting persons as voices, less overall attention to voice as a phenomenon except as it comes through wires or over loudspeakers. The diminished presence of the "natural" voice does not mean that Faulkner paid less attention to talk; on the contrary he still used talk as narrative discourse, and even increased such uses. Elaborated figures for voice, however, more often are devoted to mechanized voices than to human speakers, with the result that phenomenal voice underwent crucial qualitative changes in the years after *Light in August*. Karl Zender, in his article "Faulkner and the Power of Sound," rightly emphasizes the change in values or concerns that the increased presence of mechanized sound signals over the course of Faulkner's career. Zender sees an alteration in the perceived relation between the artistic self and the world as Faulkner's images change from those that "displac[e] voice outward from his fictional characters [and thus] suggest that the tension between artist and culture . . . can be resolved" to images that "express, not reciprocity between the self and the other, but rather an invasion of the self *by* the other" (90). The images become more "negative," portraying "sound as an invasive force" (91). For Faulkner the "aural character of popular culture" threatened "the continued preeminence of reading as a cultural activity" (97). Faulkner's later works drift toward a despair—despite philosophically optimistic pronouncements—symbolized by the intrusion of mechanized sounds, until only silence can remain.

Greater attention to portrayed writing accompanies the increase in images of mechanized voice in many works. Those novels that depict the intrusion of artificial sounds evince an increased emphasis on the written over the spoken word. Phenomenal voice no longer figures as importantly in the interchange between the fiction's discourse and its created life as it did in the early fiction. A different phenomenon of language, the artificially created language of machines or print, replaces phenomenal voice in its role as a source of intersubjectivity. Letters, notes, books, and ledgers all appear in Faulkner's novels from the start of his career, to be sure, but the *relative* attention paid to writing as compared to spoken voice shifts in the middle and later fiction toward the former.

Two novels of the middle and late 1930s exemplify this change, for in both *Pylon* and *The Wild Palms* mechanized voices and written documents (or acts of writing) play concomitantly more important roles than do voice and speech acts. The famous depiction of the loudspeaker's voice in *Pylon* captures perfectly the mechanical qualities of a phenomenal voice that is omnipresent but no longer human or annealing. The announcer's enhanced voice, "brazen, metallic, and loud," is everywhere, "ghostlike and ubiquitous . . . possessed [of] some quality of omniscience beyond even vision" (27, 29–30). The characters move within it as within air itself:

> The announcer's voice harsh masculine and disembodied. . . . Then the band would begin to play again, though faint and almost trivial behind and below the voice, as if the voice actually were that natural phenomenon against which all man-made sounds and noises blew and vanished like leaves. . . . [T]he voice met them again . . . or rather it had never ceased; they had merely walked in it without hearing or feeling it, like in the sunshine; the voice almost as sourceless as light. (27, 29)

Aside from the "sourceless, inhuman" voice of the loudspeaker, *Pylon* pays little attention to the phenomenon of voice as something emanating from particular people, or (as in *Flags in the Dust*) from any community except the "steel-and-chrome mausoleum" represented by the loudspeaker. The image of cosmic entropy "heard" in the "voice of the night" in *Sanctuary* has its counterpart in *Pylon* in another artificial voice, that "heard" over dead telephone wires. This "bland machinevoice" of an operator and of the phone lines themselves "click fullvoiced before the avalanched, the undammed . . . the dead wirehum, as if the other end of it extended beyond atmosphere, into cold space; as though he listened now to the profound sound of infinity, of void itself filled with the cold unceasing murmur of aeonweary and unflagging stars" (75). *Pylon* contains few of the descriptive voice tags found in large numbers in *Sanctuary*, as if people's voices no longer matter. Instead of voices to hear there are headlines to read, in boldface, as the emblems of sterile or impotent language.[13]

What voices we do hear seem artificial, either because they are imaged as such or because they obscure speech and communication more than they enhance these powers of phenomenal voice. The Reporter speaks, of course, at great length, but except for the voice tag "he cried," which measures the Reporter's near hysteria, Faulkner makes little of voice as such. Indeed, the Reporter's speech confuses and befuddles those who perforce listen to him, especially his editor, Hagood, who usually is more outraged than attentive and who wants the Reporter to write his stories instead of talking them. Like the loudspeaker's, the Reporter's always-present voice fails to betoken human presence; the Reporter himself is ghostlike, an apparition, a haunt or scarecrow from whom words pour but—except perhaps in the final written story he throws away—who expresses the despair of sterile language more than the power of voice.

In "The Wild Palms" sections of *The Wild Palms* Faulkner replays images of artificial or incomprehensible voices as well as emphasizing writing over speech. Numerous written objects figure importantly in Charlotte's and Harry's love: the will that leaves Harry enough money for college, his medical textbook, his account books, the diploma, the railroad ticket, Rittenmeyer's check (for Charlotte to come home), Harry's stories, and the drawings Charlotte uses to communicate with the the Polish miners. Written or drawn objects clutter their lives. While "The Wild Palms" contains more numerous voice images than *Pylon*, the emphasis remains strongly negative. Like *Pylon*, "The Wild Palms" offers a striking image of a loud and intrusive mechanized voice, as heard over a loudspeaker in a train station. Again, as in *Sanctuary* and *Pylon*, sound reaches imaginatively into space to echo the void of emptiness:

> There was a loudspeaker in the bar too, synchronised too; at this moment a voice cavernous and sourceless roared deliberately, a sentence in which could be distinguished a word now and then— "train," then others which the mind two or three seconds afterward recognised to be the names of cities far flung about the continent,

cities seen rather than names heard, as if the listener (so enormous was the voice) were suspended in space watching the globy earth spin slowly out of its cradling cloud-wisps in fragmentary glimpses the evocative strange divisions of the sphere, spinning them on into fog and cloud again before vision and comprehension could quite grasp them. (135)

In both "The Wild Palms" and "Old Man" the protagonists must communicate with foreigners whose language they cannot speak. The convict lives and hunts alligators with a Cajun whose talk sounds like "gobble-gobble, whang, caw-caw-to-to," yet he communicates with little difficulty. Harry, far more alienated than the convict from any human community, fails to communicate with the Polish miners until Charlotte draws them pictures. To him the miners' voices are like "blind erratic birds" (187) or a "frenzied and incomprehensible human speech" that takes on palpable form "hanging batlike and perhaps head-down about the dead corridors until his presence startled them into flight" (207).

In Linda Snopes's deafness in *The Mansion* can perhaps be found Faulkner's most frightened image of the artist driven to silence by intrusive noise and waning creative powers. It is appropriate also to end this discussion of phenomenal voice with Linda's silent world because her silence and her speech are the last significant variation on the versions of phenomenal voice. Whether Faulkner engages in "a direct, almost brutal form of artistic control" (Zender, "Faulkner and the Power of Sound" 104) in depriving Linda of her hearing and thus of any normal voice, he does assert here a strange *value* in being freed from phenomenal voice, either as listener or speaker. As "a bride of silence," Linda has somehow escaped scot-free from evil—in which Faulkner includes "the human voice":

[She is] immured, inviolate in silence, invulnerable, serene.
That was it: silence. If there were no such thing as sound. If it only took place in silence, no evil man has invented could really harm him: explosion, treachery, the human voice. (*M* 203)

Linda's escape from the realm of sound fascinates both Chick Mallison and Gavin Stevens. Chick perceives her gain in sexual terms as an "immaculate chastity" in which she is "castrate of sound, circumcised from having to hear, of need too" (211); whereas Stevens sees her escape as one from time and "the entire dilemma of man's condition [which] is because of the ceaseless gabble with which he has surrounded himself, enclosed himself, insulated himself from the penalties of his own folly" (236). The gain lies in the conversion of necessary communication from sound to writing, a conversion embodied in Linda's ivory writing tablet. Here communication is returned to "the writer and the writer's art" (Zender 105). Only in written words can Linda communicate; only in read words can she be communicated with. Writing becomes a kind of speech, a kind of direct and immediate communication almost as fast as speech, as Linda reads "the words as [Stevens's] hand form[s] them, like speech, almost like hearing" (237).

Yet an appalling imagery of voice, Linda's "dry harsh quacking voice," counters the value Zender sees in Linda's writing, or in Stevens's newly found writer's communicative skills. Linda's deafness does not erase the phenomenon of voice; rather it makes voice ugly. Not artificial or mechanically amplified, Linda's is a human voice deformed into a sound "as penetrating and shocking almost as an old-time klaxon automobile horn" (241). This is Stevens's image for her voice when she tells him she loves him; he cannot respond to her love sexually or aurally and ultimately fails to enter her silent world where she plots Flem Snopes's death. Her voice evokes loss, which Chick sees again in sexual terms: "But it was still the duck's voice: dry, lifeless, dead. That was it: dead. There was no passion, no heat in it; and, what was worse, no hope. I mean, in bed together in the dark and to have more of love and excitement and ecstasy than just one can bear and so you must share it, murmur it, and to have only that dry and lifeless quack to murmur, whisper with" (217).

Finally, it seems fair to say that the alteration in the nature of phenomenal voice was a loss for Faulkner's novels, as it was for Linda Snopes. While no simple formula can be derived to measure affirmation versus negation in Faulkner's overall worldview, and no simple count of genuine and humanly present voice images versus loud and ugly sounds of mechanized voices can adequately chart the careerlong changes in Faulkner's perception of the world and of art, conclusions like Zender's about Faulkner's attitudes toward modern civilization and about art, as reflected in his portrayals of mechanical voices and silent writing, are by and large convincing. The distinction between "later" and "earlier" Faulkner may not be quite as clear-cut as Zender would have it, since mechanical images of sound as well as "invasive" and threatening images of voice appear as early as *Sanctuary*. And images of writing can be found that are imbued with the life of the voice, as are Celia Farmer's scratches in the jailhouse window (*RN* 255). More important, one cannot assume that mechanically reproduced sounds, especially voices, are inherently inferior to or more morally corrupt than the unamplified voice. A case could well be made, using the three fundamental implications with which this chapter began, that technology enriches rather than degrades phenomenal voice. Certainly a recording can imbue an absent person with presence in the form of his or her voice; certainly the power of voice is enhanced by electrical amplification; and indeed the intersubjectivity or community created by voice potentially expands as greater numbers of persons are reached by radio, telephone, and television. The "global community," as McLuhan called it, encouraged by technology, may well be ideologically a better community than the parochial and lost Rousseauvian village Faulkner's early novels nostalgically yearn for. One must, in other words, be careful not to raise Faulkner's own predilections to the status of "natural" absolutes. But according to the values dictated by the imagery in Faulkner's later works, voice in its mechanized form betokens absence at least of human source, leaving an abstract, "disembodied," and artificial—and thus undesirable—voice in its stead. Talking itself comes to be seen, in *The Town*, as alienated writing:

> It was like they were not even talking to one another but simply at the two empty reflections in the plate glass, like when you put the written idea into the anonymous and even interchangeable empty envelope, or maybe into the sealed empty bottle to be cast into the sea, or maybe two written thoughts sealed forever at the same moment into two bottles and cast into the sea to float and drift with the tides and the currents on to the cooling world's end itself, still immune, still intact and inviolate, still ideas and still true and even still facts whether any eye ever saw them again or any other idea ever responded and sprang to them, to be elated or validated or grieved. (*T* 199)

The power of voice changes from an annealing capacity to bind and nourish human life to an intrusive disruption of privacy and thought—only made worse by increased volume and range. Swallowed by the modern nation, the natural community of speakers within earshot of each other and of nature's sounds is silenced by the "hollow inverted air" that encloses individuals in a sterile collection of isolated listeners to "static or needle." The silent communion achieved through Rev. Shegog's voice, with its "chanting measures beyond the need for words," is a far cry from the silent void filled only by Linda Snopes's "lifeless quack."

Chapter 2

$$\text{《《《 》》}$$

MIMETIC VOICE

In the thick air it's like their voices come out of the air, flowing together and on.

—*As I Lay Dying*

The enigmatic title of Faulkner's fifth novel raises the issues we will consider under the rubric of "mimetic voice." Titles of novels usually carry
little implication that someone has spoken them, that the word or words
constituting the title have been uttered by a character, or by anyone else.
We may discover in reading the novel that its title is in fact spoken during
the course of events or narration: Conrad's Marlow, for example, tells his
listeners that he entered the "heart of darkness," but we do not perceive
the title *Heart of Darkness*, especially when first seen emblazoned on the
book's cover, as a spoken utterance. It is more a signpost, a marker, a
label, less spoken than stamped on the novel in order to identify it. Labels
carry little sense of being (or having been) uttered. If we see a sign that
reads BUCKINGHAM PALACE on the lawn in front of a building, or a sign
beside the highway with "ATHENS, GA., pop. 33,963" painted on it, we do
not imagine that someone has spoken these words to us. But if the signs
should say "I am Buckingham Palace," or "We are Athens, Ga., all 33,963
of us," the signs become propositions and sound more as if someone had
spoken the words. The self-referring "I" and "we" denominate both an

object of identification (the name of a place), and also the ones who name the place. The signs become more like speech; or more precisely, they have engendered the *illusion* of speech.

Titles, it is true, often communicate something about their works. *The Expedition of Humphrey Clinker* suggests that that book depicts an "expedition," *Jane Eyre* names a central character in the fiction, *Wuthering Heights* designates a place, and *Pride and Prejudice* announces a subject or theme of Austen's novel. The majority of titles name places or characters, or describe the fiction's world in some (usually oblique) way; others refer to the book itself, as in Smullyan's *What is the Name of this Book*, or Hoffman's *Steal this Book*. Faulkner's title is not enigmatic so much because it refers to a fictional world not yet created when we first perceive the title, but more because it carries the illusion of familiar speech in an unexpected place. *As I Lay Dying* "sounds" spoken because of "I," the self-denominator of the person uttering the words "as I lay dying," and because the title's phrase has the syntax of a proposition, albeit an incomplete one. We hear as spoken the words "as I lay dying" just as we "hear" Poe's speaker say "while I pondered, weak and weary . . . while I nodded, nearly napping . . ." in "The Raven." A title engenders the illusion of speech when it is a proposition (as in Flannery O'Conner's *A Good Man is Hard to Find*) or when it contains first-person reference (as in Cather's *My Antonia*). The strongest effect of speech derives from the combination (as in Horace Mc-Coy's *I Should Have Stayed Home*, or Jean Fleming's *Young Man, I Said, You are Dying*. This latter title is a quotation from a Scottish ballad, and thus doubly voiced like *As I Lay Dying*, a quotation from the eleventh book of *The Odyssey*.[1]

Although the intertextual reference to Agamemnon's shade may sufficiently account for the "I" in the title *As I Lay Dying*, we are also inclined to seek the "I" from within the novel itself by finding the character who "lies dying" and who speaks about doing so. We can naturalize the title by identifying who among the story's personae says "as I lay dying." The most likely candidate is Addie Bundren, who does indeed lie dying for much of the story and who, like Agamemnon, speaks from beyond death. But Addie never in fact says "as I lay dying," and her perspective (which we share for only one of the novel's fifty-five monologues) may not warrant treating her "I" as the titled focus for the entire book (as we can legitimately treat Jane Eyre as the central personage in *Jane Eyre*). Perhaps it is Darl Bundren who should be construed as saying "as I lay dying," at least in a figurative sense, since his is the most frequently heard voice in the novel, his mind the closest to a controlling consciousness, and he dies a kind of emotional death by the story's end.[2]

That we cannot say with certainty who begins but does not finish the proposition "as I lay dying" epitomizes how Faulkner manipulates our expectations about speech in the novel. From its title onward, *As I Lay Dying* interrogates the nature of represented speech in written prose narrative. Before turning to an exploration of represented speech in *As I Lay Dying*, however, we should consider in theoretical terms the status of speech in narrative and what conventions seem to govern its creation; we also need to examine Faulkner's general tendencies in employing the conventions of speech presentation. The experimental play of *As I Lay Dying* will be clearer if we establish the norms from which it purposefully deviates.

MIMETIC VOICE

The phrase "mimetic voice" refers to represented speech in fiction, to the illusion that a person—character, narrator, even sometimes author—is speaking. "Mimetic voice" is constituted by those features of a text's discourse that prompt readers to regard a particular portion of the text's total discourse as the utterance of an imagined person. A wide range of features contributes to mimetic voice, including grammatical forms (such as "shifters") that call attention to the fictive source, time, and place of enunciation; mechanics of written dialogue like punctuation or speech tags; techniques, both conventional and unique to a given author, for transcribing speech into nonstandard writing (phonetic spelling, colloquial phrasing, and the like); and, more broadly, any feature of the discourse governed by a *speaker's* identity, such as the word choice in dialogue or narration.

Plato gave the first dissertation on mimetic voice in *The Republic*, where he distinguished simple narrative from imitation in epic poetry. The crucial distinction between mimesis, or the imitation of speech, and diegesis, or simple narrative, has survived in modern narrative theory in such bipartite terminology as showing versus telling, drama versus narrative, and objective narration versus intrusive authorial discourse. Socrates' statement that Homer "does all that he can to make us believe that the speaker is . . . the aged priest himself" captures the essence of mimetic voice: the "doing" that creates the illusion that certain words in the narrative are the spoken words of someone. To many theorists the mimetic-diegetic distinction is the one on which all thinking about the nature of writing must turn, implicating, in Derrida's view, the whole of Western philosophy as it derives from Plato.[3]

The assumptions underlying the portrayal of speech in fiction are among the strongest, and thus the least questioned, that authors and readers share. So crucial is imagined speech to our sense of a fictional world that we seldom ask how it comes to be. Readers tend to treat quoted speech as a special kind of discourse that authors do not represent or imitate so much as lift directly from "life" into fiction. Gérard Genette demonstrates the strength of these assumptions by pushing the logical distinction between diegesis and mimesis to its inevitable conclusion that imitation "vanishes" entirely in the face of represented speech. In what he calls "narrative of words" as opposed to "narrative of events," imitation can be "absolute" because "there is no difference between the statement present in the text and the sentence purportedly spoken by the hero other than what derives from the transition from oral language to written. The narrator does not narrate the hero's sentence; one can scarcely say he imitates it: he *recopies* it, and in this sense one cannot speak here of narrative" (*Narrative Discourse* 169). Truly reported speech (Genette says elsewhere) would be "perfect" mimesis, "completely identical with [the character's] discourse." But the notion of "perfect mimesis" is an anomaly because a perfectly represented thing is no longer imitated, but must be "the thing itself": thus in represented discourse "the work of a re-presentation is nil" because discourses by characters can be reproduced "literally." Genette draws this analogy: if a painter were to glue an oyster shell onto his canvas, he would be inserting an actuality into an imitative medium; so, too, does direct speech "consist simply of interpolating in the middle of a text representing events another text drawn directly from these events" ("Frontiers of Narrative" 131–32). Genette's analysis, which articulates the usually unstated assumption that somehow exempts direct discourse from the manipulations of verbal imitation, reminds us how successfully writers can create the *illusion* of speech. We naturally and properly praise dialogue for its felt adherence to actual speech, but such praise only acknowledges the author's skill in *hiding* his "work" of overcoming mimetic imperfection: "Verisimilitude is the mask which is assumed by the laws of the text and which we are meant to take for a relation with reality" (Todorov 83). Critics' praise for dialogue often reflects the assumption that it is possible to imitate speech perfectly: "'consistently echoes the accepted speech of the day,' . . . 'there is no line of dialogue from a novel that could not easily be imagined proceeding from the mouth of an actual person'; and . . . 'the dialogues . . . could not reproduce actual speech more faithfully, and more unselectively, if they had been transcribed from a tape-recorder'" (Page 3).

But Genette himself makes the point that the transition from purported spoken words to written text, and the fictionality of "(re)produced" speech in a novel, render the perfection of the imitation only a dramatic illusion that rests on the illusory premise that it can be perfectly re-presented.[4] Genette is not the first, of course, to comment on the inherent and necessary imperfection at the heart of imitation. T. S. Eliot asked whether the "point of mimicry" did not rest on "the incompleteness of the illusion" (Eliot 104). Derrida writes that "imitation does not correspond to its essence, is not what it is—imitation—unless it is in some way at fault or rather in default. It is bad by nature. It is only good insofar as it is bad" (*Dissemination* 139).

Besides leading readers to accept the "reality" of an impossibly perfect imitation, fictional representation of speech also hides, more effectively than other illusions, the extent to which it is governed by convention and open to alteration. When transcribed on paper, oral speech (be it fictitious or reported) has been turned into writing, and is thus re-presented in a new expressive shape, just as other acts and events are "presented anew." We cannot reduce writing, even of direct discourse, to recorded talk, for the recording—the particular articulation of words—itself constitutes part of the narrative's aesthetic "work of representation." The textual and narrative context for dialogue always affects "what" is said just as the placing of an oyster shell—its position on the canvas, its size relative to the background, its texture and color in relation to the paint—transforms that "real" shell into a "re-presented" shell. An actual shell can be used to represent a shell just as can paint or plastic, and each means of reproduction will have its own appropriate effect on the viewer: a "real" shell used to represent a shell may be more *convincing* than a painted or plastic shell, but it is no less a representation. Discourse can likewise be used to represent discourse (in epistolary novels, for example, one kind of written discourse is used to represent another kind, letters). But any mimetic transformation of one "thing" (shell, written discourse) into another "thing" (image of a shell, the illusion of oral speech) is an act with aesthetic consequences, an act that springs from the artifice of representation.

We can also "use" discourse in another sense by reading a novel's speeches out loud (or vocalizing internally as we read), thus providing a "real" equivalent for the text's dramatic illusion of speech. Like the oyster shell borrowed from nature to represent an oyster shell, we can borrow our vocal powers to reproduce fictional speech. Yet even such a performance is a rendition, a version, and not the "thing itself" requiring no "work of representation." That represented speech can be "performed" and that audible speech and represented speech are both verbal certainly renders that work easier and seemingly more natural in dialogue than in other kinds of fictional events; and writers exploit different techniques and conventions to produce conversation than they exploit to depict a gunfight, say, or a sunset. The representation of speech, however, is no less grounded in convention. Readers share expectations about represented speech that range from knowledge of the rules of punctuation to acceptance of mannerisms (like phonetic spelling) unique to a given work, and these conventions are in principle as open to manipulation as any others. Semiotic theory stresses the conventionality of all reproductions. "A transformation does not suggest the idea of natural correspondence; it is rather the consequence of rules and artifice" (Eco 200). Eco offers an example of the outline of a horse: "thus even the continuous line tracing the profile of the horse . . . may be considered as the institution of a relation of similitude by a transformed correspondence. . . . [I]t is the . . . effect of a cultural decision and as such requires a trained eye in order to be detected as a horse's profile. . . . [S]imilarity does not concern the relationship between the image and its object but that between the image and a previously culturized content" (200, 204).

Even directly reported speech, with no apparent deviation from words as they were spoken, does not innocently duplicate some ideal semantic "content" of an original discourse. "Framing" always affects meaning: "The following must be kept in mind: that the speech of another, once enclosed in a context, is—no matter how accurately transmitted—always subject to certain semantic changes. . . . Given the appropriate methods for framing, one may bring about fundamental changes even in another's utterance accurately quoted" (Bakhtin, *The Dialogical Imagination* 340). As a pragmatic matter we accede to the necessary illusion of "literal" reproduction; but, as Genette comments, the term "reproduction" should not be used too strictly, for the "contract of literality" extends only to the "tenor" of a discourse (*Nouveau discours du récit* 34). More important, we should not let the "contract of literality" create the mistaken impression that represented speech is more "real," more "natural," and less artfully manipulable than other represented phenomena. "Literalness" itself,

Gérard Strauch concludes, is a mimetic trait that helps mark discourse as represented speech, especially in free, indirect discourse, common in fiction, where grammatical or syntactical markers for speech are absent.[5] All represented discourse, whether real or fictional, depends upon mimetic considerations, on the creation of the illusion that a prior discourse is being re-presented.[6]

In seeking to understand *how* an author generates the dramatic illusion of speech, we must not ignore its conventional, artificial nature. This is not to deny the effects of the illusion, however: the term "mimetic voice" acknowledges the power of Faulkner's imitation. As readers we rely on mimetic illusion. We need the conventional assumptions that permit us to naturalize represented discourse into the speech of characters, and we need the presumptions of truth and literalness that accompany the illusion. A powerful necessary convention governing direct discourse, for example, is the assumption of its accuracy, its truthful rendering. Words spoken by a character have been regarded frequently as more "real" than nonverbal phenomena represented in the same text; quoted speech possesses a kind of epistemological sanctity, a "facticity" seldom challenged even in a narrative that places all other represented "realities" under suspicion.

Quotation marks, the most common signals of direct discourse, create speech (and imply voice) by fiat, merely by asserting that we are to regard certain words as having been, or as now being, spoken; quotation marks also pledge a *true* rendering of just these words in the same order as spoken at some time by the person identified as the speaker.[7] Accustomed as we are to this usage, we should not forget that it is merely a contractual arrangement; we expect the words inside quotation marks to be truly recorded, but we can be disappointed. (Faulkner, as we shall see later, plays upon this expectation.) Until roughly the nineteenth century quotation marks were merely *citation* marks, employed exclusively for quoting another author's written words (Robertson 100, 147). The evolution of the practice (at least in English) of marking both spoken and written discourse with the same sign—a procedure that lent to reported speech the verifiability of cited documents—may be connected by more than temporal coincidence to the advent of the realistic novel and its supposed rendering of an "objectively" verifiable world. And we can ask, too, what the phrase "truly recorded" means. Actual speech proceeds haltingly, bumping along between hesitations, greased by meaningless sounds and vocal gestures that few novelists ever try to record.[8]

Another common and necessary tool of direct discourse, speaker identification, or speech tags (phrases like "he said" or "she asked" that attribute speech to appropriate characters), also brings with it a strong assumption of the real, for we almost never question the truthfulness of the narrative's attribution. The most untrustworthy narrator is assumed to remain a faithful recorder of other characters' speeches—direct discourse is, in fact, often the only certain occurrence in a story. Speech's reliability warns the reader of the narrator's unreliability. We see through Jason Compson's brutal tirades and cruel jokes partly because we can believe him when, acting as narrator, he reports someone else's words, and we can usually believe him when he tells us what he says to someone else. The contrast in values created between Jason's and others' words is a primary source of dramatic irony. We need the anchor to truth provided by conventional veracity of quotation and attribution to be able to read ironic narration. Along with Beckett's Molloy, we must assume that "the words were the same when I heard them as when first spoken," or literature would fall silent in confusion: "When I say I said, etc., all I mean is that I knew confusedly things were so, without knowing exactly what it was all about . . . [when I quote myself or others] I am merely complying with the convention that demands you either lie or hold your peace" (Beckett 40, 116).

FUNCTIONS OF REPRESENTED SPEECH

Faulkner's fiction, luckily, does not hold its peace. But because of the great variety of features that empower some portion of the fictional discourse to be regarded as spoken, it is not easy to analyze just how it lies so successfully in representing speech. The multiplicity of discursive features that contribute to mimetic voice can be organized into *functions* that are fulfilled, to greater or lesser degrees, in any rendition of speech. Five functions govern the conventional verbal transformations necessary to engender mimetic voice: description, communication, differentiation, identification, and transcription.[9] In even a brief snippet of recorded dialogue, such as the following from *Sanctuary,* these functions operate to create the illusion of speech:

> "Hush it, now," Popeye said.
> "I cant—I might—" she whimpered. "I'm hungry," she said. "I haven't eaten since . . ."
> "Ah, you aint hungry. Wait till we get to town." (*S* 145; 166; ellipses in original)

The verb "whimpering" *describes* the way Temple Drake utters the words "I cant—I might," and conveys a sense of how they would sound. We know the characters *communicate* because Popeye responds to Temple's assertion that she is hungry: she has vocalized her words. Punctuation, paragraphing, and speaker identification *differentiate* Popeye's speech acts from Temple's. Quotation marks and speech tags *identify* certain words as those to be regarded as uttered by certain speakers. And Faulkner directly *transcribes* words as spoken utterances by using contractions and the nonstandard form "aint." The term "function" is used here rather strictly: mimetic voice is a function of description, communication, and so on. As these collections of features vary, so will the qualities of speech in the fictional discourse. Authors employ many different techniques—most are conventional, some experimental—to fulfill the functions of mimetic voice; in any given text or part of a text the functions will vary as to how thoroughly they operate. A given feature of a printed text, or of a work's content and style, may serve more than one function (quotation marks, for example, both mark discourse as spoken and help to separate one speech from another), and the boundaries between them are not rigid. Each operates to a greater or lesser degree in every fictional and many nonfictional texts to transform certain written discourse into "natural" speech.

We will consider these functions in increasing order of their importance for Faulkner's fiction. Because it is the very nature of conventions to seem self-evident and unarguable, we will proceed slowly and risk at times stating the obvious so that we can better discern the special nature of Faulkner's portrayal of speech, especially how he varies conventional practices.

Description

"Description," the first function of mimetic voice, can be treated briefly here because the preceding chapter on phenomenal voice discussed Faulkner's most important method of describing speech, the description of voice. Speech within a fictional text is always characterized in some way, directly or by implication. Even the context in which a speech act occurs evokes cultural assumptions about appropriate speech: the anecdotal talk on the gallery of Varner's store in *The Hamlet* will not be identical to Gavin Stevens's courtroom summaries in *Knight's Gambit*. Description is inherent in punctuation marks that imply intonation, such as question marks and exclamation points, or in the verb used to attribute speech to a character; any variation from the neutral "said," for example, serves descriptive purposes. If we read that the Reporter in *Pylon* does not merely "say" words, but "cries" them (as he frequently does), then Faulkner has characterized his manner of talking. Speech can also be qualified directly through adverbs like "loudly," "mildly," or "harshly" (though adverbial qualifiers of this kind are not frequent in Faulkner), or speech can be qualified indirectly through accompanying gestures or portrayals of the speaker's place, attitude, or posture. Jody Varner's "suffused swollen face glar[ing] down at" Ratliff tells much about how Varner's talk will sound in their conversation about Ab Snopes (*H* 16). Doc Peabody's picture of Anse Bundren "standing by a post, not even leaning against it, his arms dangling, the hair pushed and matted up on his head like a dipped rooster. He turns his head, blinking at me" (*AILD* 40; 43) spills over into our sense of how Anse talks, even though Peabody has not explicitly described Anse's speech. Very few explicit instructions on how spoken words should sound are scattered among Faulkner's novels and stories, and these do not constitute an important or particularly effective tool for describing speech. In "My Grandmother Millard," for example, Faulkner describes dialect without rendering it: "He [General Forrest] said 'fit' for fought just as he said 'druv' for drove and 'drug' for dragged. But maybe when you fought battles like he did, even Granny didn't mind how you talked" (*CS* 692).

More often Faulkner describes voice rather than speech, often transforming speech into richly suggestive phenomenal voice. *The Hamlet,* for example, is filled with colloquial dialogue that is in most ways conventionally and effectively rendered. The opening pages introduce the first of those verbal confrontations (especially bargaining) that will play a crucial role in the novel by calling attention to voices:

> "You Varner?" the man [Ab Snopes] said, in a voice not harsh exactly, or not deliberately harsh so much as rusty from infrequent use.
>
> "I'm one Varner," Jody said, in his bland hard quite pleasant voice. "What can I do for you?" . . .
>
> "West." He did not speak shortly. He merely pronounced the one word with a complete inflectionless finality, as if he had closed a door behind himself . . .
>
> "Myself," the dead voice said . . .
>
> Now Varner's voice did not change either, still pleasant, still hard. (7–8)
>
> [Ratliff] spoke in a pleasant, lazy, equable voice which you did not discern at once to be even more shrewd than humorous . . . his voice pleasant and drawling and anecdotal. (13, 15–16)

Faulkner seems more concerned with typical speech habits than with how a particular utterance sounds: thus by saying that Will Varner's "*voice* was now sardonic, almost contemptuous" (*H* 27, my emphasis), Faulkner focuses our attention on the speaker as much as on the speech act, for descriptions of voice, like those of appearance, signify traits in a character, and ultimately traits of a group or entire region.[10]

Communication

To be taken as speech, discourse in written fiction must be "heard" or "hearable." Communication must be possible, or at least implied. Indications that certain words are spoken out loud contribute to the necessary illusion that the words are in fact uttered. Thus, if one character answers the question of another, the response implies that the question has been vocalized and heard—though fiction does not, of course, exclude the "unspoken" question or even mental telepathy. The communicative function can be served even in discourse that expresses a character's verbal thoughts that have all the indicia of speech but remain unvocalized, for there still exist a "sender" and a "receiver," now joined in one being (Segre 96). The auditor of speech in fiction may be only implied. Indications of communication range from direct evidence that a speech has been heard (as when a response is made), to overt depictions in the narrative (as in "she spoke loudly"), to verbal mannerisms or gestures that imply an audience (such as Jason Compson's frequent "like I say").

Communication becomes a significant factor in generating mimetic voice when a character narrates. A character may tell a story in the presence of other characters who hear the story and, perhaps, contribute or respond to it. In *The Hamlet* Ratliff tells Jody Varner the story of Ab Snopes burning Manfred De Spain's barn. Ratliff clearly vocalizes the tale, and Jody hears what Ratliff says. This kind of narration forms an integral part of all conversation, what speech-act theorists call "natural narrative" (Pratt 38–78). A character-narrator may relate a story to an implied audience, listeners presumed to be present though the diegetic discourse never explicitly names or describes them. Faulkner, especially in his short stories, employed such narrators and implied audiences with great frequency. In "A Bear Hunt" Ratliff tells how he, with some unplanned help from Old Ash, put a scare into Lucius Provine to rid him of hiccups. The sense of voice is strong here because most of the functions of mimetic voice operate: the story is attributed to Ratliff, the discourse transcribes his colloquialisms, and so forth. But the story does not portray listeners; no one responds to Ratliff and he addresses no one; no listeners are described or named, not even the original frame narrator who sets the stage for Ratliff and then vanishes entirely. Yet *implied* vocalization operates along with other mimetic functions to make the reader feel that Ratliff is telling the story out loud. Features of Ratliff's discourse typical of spoken storytelling imply listeners. Colloquial narration usually contains, early in the story, temporal or relational markers that establish a time and place of telling as well as the time and place the events occurred. We are told explicitly that "Ratliff is telling this" and that "Now Ratliff tells about Lucius Provine and his hiccup." The present-tense verbs enhance the immediacy of the telling—it is not a story once told now being transcribed for us, but rather a story being told as we read it. Colloquial narrators also vocalize how they came to know of the events, or how they participated in them, as well as what they think about them. The reader thus becomes Ratliff's narratee, listening to his audible tale.[11]

A framed tale, like "A Bear Hunt," generates mimetic voice by describing or implying a narrative circumstance in which storytelling is vocalized. Vocalization implies a "you" as addressee listening to the telling, and the presence of an addressee places discourse in a communication context more than does any other feature—even more than the present tense or first person (Banfield 171–73). This is a technique as old as literature, and certainly a common one in the Southwest Humor tradition within which Faulkner wrote. The narrator who "set[s] the stage for Ratliff" is part of a corporate narrating entity referred to in the first-person plural "we," denizens of the town who tell stories and listen to stories about their fellows. Self-reference always effects some sense of communication, and so in "A Bear Hunt" the narrator's references to "we" and "us" place the reader in the role of outsider to whom "we" must give sufficient background so that Ratliff's tale can be comprehensible. Such anonymous, communal voices are heard frequently in Faulkner—in "That Evening Sun," "A Rose for Emily," and "Hair," for example. Chick Mallison explicitly identifies this kind of community narrator in *The Town:* "So when I say 'we' and 'we thought' what I mean is Jefferson and what Jefferson thought" (3).

The Town is an interesting case because in it Faulkner consistently implies vocalization, and thus communication, as part of his creation of mimetic voices belonging to the named character-narrators Chick Mallison, Gavin Stevens, and Ratliff. Structurally, the narrators address only the reader, as no diegetic discourse depicts any storytelling scenes, and no "higher-level" narrator quotes them (except by labeling the chapters with their names). Yet our sense that the others do hear him is an important quality of each narrator's unique voice, as is the implication that the three narrate turn and turn about. The openings of many chapters pick up on and answer the preceding chapter's train of thought as if the characters were speaking in each other's presence, though technically their narrating remains purely diegetic discourse "heard" only by the reader. The novel's third chapter, for example, ends with Chick Mallison narrating "Gowan said you would even have thought she [Sally Parsons] was proud of it [a black eye her husband gave her]" (77). The fourth chapter, narrated by Ratliff, begins "She was. His aunt (not his two uncles nor his grandpaw, but any of his womenfolks) could have told him why: proud she still had a husband that would and could black her eye" (78).

Faulkner's stories show many possible permutations on how much communication can be implied. That the grammatical first person is not necessary can be seen in chapter 13 of *The Mansion,* where an anonymous narrator, who "sounds" like someone from the town and who collaborates with the named narrators, does not refer to him-, her-, or themselves and can quote thoughts like an omniscient author. In "Artist at Home" the anonymous narrative voice (which does not contain self-reference) introduces communicative and expressive elements typical of speech into narration by addressing an implied audience: "Now get this. This is where it starts" (*CS* 634). The most dramatic illustration of mimetic voice generated by implied communication (and one we will consider further in chapter 3), in what is strictly speaking pure and uncommunicated *interior* discourse, is Jason Compson's monologue in *The Sound and the Fury,* for many of Jason's characteristic verbal mannerisms (his frequent insertion of "what I say," for example) evoke a strong sense of communication, as if he were speaking out loud.

Differentiation

Differentiation is the principle by which separate utterances or speech acts are distinguished one from another. The manner in which the text divides spoken discourse into separate utterances, whether attributed to one character or to many, contributes to and affects the illusion that speech is occurring. All language, of course, functions on principles of differentiation, on our ability to distinguish among sounds, among graphic marks, and among words, clauses, sentences, and paragraphs. On this level the manner of differentiation can be said to characterize prose *style*. Every analyst of Faulkner's style notes his efforts to override differentiation with run-together words ("womanshenegro," "fecundmellow") and long sentences within which he tries "to say it all in one sentence, between one Cap and one Period" (*SL* 185; Cowley 14).

The reduction of differentiation normally interferes with the illusion of speech, lessening mimetic voice and concomitantly enhancing narrative discourse, or represented thought, or our awareness of the strictly written qualities of the text. For example, stream-of-consciousness writing often presumes to produce the effect of thought—as distinct from speech—by running words, sentences, or paragraphs together as well as by failing to designate different speech acts. Lack of differentiation contributes to the illusion that certain discourse represents the internal workings of the mind where, presumably, "utterances" are not distinguished one from another in coherent fashion. (Samuel Beckett's novels, for example, gain a strange reductive power—a power by which they seem to reduce all voice to silence—from the absence of separation among portions of discourse that in other ways possess strong mimetic voice.) Faulkner employed the stream-of-consciousness method as early as *Mosquitoes,* blurring differentiation by removing punctuation and capitalization and running clauses together to capture the unindividuated flow of the sculptor Gordon's thoughts as he gazes at New Orleans by night: "stars in my hair in my hair and beard i am crowned with stars christ by his own hand an autogethsemane carved darkly out of pure space but not rigid no no an unmuscled wallowing fecund and foul the placid tragic body of a woman who conceives without pleasure bears without pain" (*MOS* 47–48).

More important to our consideration of mimetic voice is differentiation of utterances and speech acts within discourse empowered by other mimetic functions to be regarded as speech. Conventional written dialogue separates one speaker's utterance from other utterances (by the same speaker or by other speakers) by distinct paragraphing, speaker identification, responses contained in other utterances—by any technique that isolates a certain portion of discourse as a single speech event. Just as an author's style grows in part out of differentiation within his or her prose, so an author will usually manifest habitual ways of verbally structuring and arranging speech acts in dialogue. Faulkner, for example, frequently creates transitions from one speaker's utterances to another's through some affirmative signal of comprehension. Words like "yes," "all right," "I see" often begin one character's answer to another's talk. These affirmative transitions appear in some speakers' dialogue so frequently as to become a kind of verbal tic or vocal punctuation, as for the title character in "Elly," where twelve such affirmative signals appear in a little over two pages of dialogue (*CS* 214–16). Faulkner's frequent use of affirmative transitions helps to vocalize dialogue and enhance the interchange between speakers, but it can also evoke a strange effect of nonverbal communication even as the speakers exchange words in dialogue. He has the second of two speakers affirm what the first has said even when the first has not fully articulated an assertion or question; or a speaker will use such affirmative transitions between his or her own utterances; or a character will answer "yes" to a question requiring a specific answer:

> "He was watching me!" Temple said . . .
> "Who was?" the woman said.
> "Yes," Temple said. "He was there . . . (*S* 97; 110)

Such nonverbal synchronization can occur either between characters who agree so fully as to make tacit understanding virtually automatic or, surprisingly, between characters who do not share the same values. In *The Unvanquished*, for example, Bayard answers "yes" to Uncle Buck, who is urging revenge on Grumby:

> "And then what you going to do with him?" Uncle Buck said. He was almost whispering now. "Hey? Hey?"
> "Yes," I said. "Yes."
> "Yes. That's what. Now you and Ringo stay back. I'll do this." (*U* 185)

In "An Odor of Verbena," however, Bayard also answers "yes" when he has abandoned the morality of revenge, communicating to Drusilla and George Wyatt that he is not going to kill Redmond, even though he has not said so explicitly (see *U* 275, 284).

Such verbal gestures, unremarkable in any single instance, contribute in the aggregate to a drift of Faulkner's dialogue writing toward monologue. The sense of dialogue's exchange gives way either to nonverbal understanding, or more often to one character monopolizing speech. Often one speaker in a dialogue remains virtually silent while the other talks at great length, even answering or correcting what he or she says as if the listener has responded. In any pair one character usually talks, one listens: Joe Brown and Joe Christmas in *Light in August*, the General and the Corporal in *A Fable*, the Reporter and his editor in *Pylon*, Rosa Coldfield and Quentin in *Absalom, Absalom!*. This last example points to what in Faulkner is certainly the most important speech act, narration itself. Storytelling often takes place within a context of dialogue. Many techniques of differentiation operate in his stories to distinguish and characterize narrative acts as speech acts—techniques as simple as implying a narrative scene by placing the words "Grandfather said" at the beginning of a 360–page novel (*The Reivers*), and as complex as the collaboration among narrators in *Absalom, Absalom!* or throughout the Snopes trilogy.

The more schematic the differentiation the more a narrative text approaches the status of a written dramatic script ("drama" being discourse all of which is spoken). A play's text separates speeches absolutely by naming the character assigned to speak particular lines in the drama's performance. At the opposite extreme is the essayistic monologue, in which we can regard all the discourse as one speech event essayed by one character or narrator. In prose fiction purely differentiated speech lies in the direction of drama, and purely unindividuated speech in the direction of the essay. From this perspective *Requiem for a Nun*, which Faulkner conceived of as a novel and as "an interesting experiment in form" (*SL* 305), constitutes his experiment with these differential extremes. *Requiem* is and is not a drama: it draws explicitly on conventions of the stage (or of dramatic scripts, at least) in depicting Gavin Stevens's attempt to force Temple Drake to reveal the truth about her sexual past. Numbered acts and scenes, stage directions, delineation of parts with characters' names isolated from the dialogue itself are all customary trappings of written drama capable of being performed. (The play was staged, after considerable adaptation, in New York in 1959.) *Requiem* also is and is not an essay: it contains three long prose sections that are highly monologic in their reduction of differentiation. Though called "prologues" by most critics, in keeping with the conventions of drama writing, these extended prose sections are more like essays on the history of Jefferson (and the world); indeed, parts of the second section are in fact modeled on an essay, the American Guide Series on Mississippi (Polk, *Faulkner's* Requiem for a Nun 100; McHaney). Reducing conventional differentiation almost to a nullity, each essay is a single sentence running for forty-five, ten, and fifty pages, respectively. Noel Polk urges us to treat the prologues as integral to the drama, perhaps even intended by Faulkner to be "heard." He found typescript evidence that the prologues were to be textually continuous with the scenes, so that "the intensity of the powerful closing lines of the [first] prologue [would] be ringing in [the] readers' ears as they began scene 1" (Polk, *Faulkner's* Requiem for a Nun 54–55). Polk is correct that the "prologues" are not extraneous, but it may be that we should see how the "dramatic" scenes can be accommodated to the monologues rather than how the monologues fit into the play. The term "dramatic narrative" applied to the book by Hugh Ruppersburg may better reflect its effort to straddle both ends of the dialogic-monologic continuum postulated above (Ruppersburg 133).

While the dramatic in Faulkner often drifts toward the monologic, dialogue that does remain truly *dia*logue in Faulkner tends to undergo a metamorphosis from *speech* act into some other mode of intense confrontation, usually violent in nature. Faulkner enhances the confrontational nature of dialogue, and by doing so turns dialogue into a symbolic verbal version of other events. Such scenes, which we can call "dialogic scenes," pit one character against another, as if speech is being transformed into other, more immediately violent acts. These have a dual effect: all dialogue becomes resonant with potential assault, even murder, and all violent confrontations partake of the nature of spoken exchange. Speech acts and violent confrontation impinge upon each other more in Faulkner than in most writers, and this mutual encroachment of speech and violence is central to the nature of conflict in his fiction. Two people with fearful or antagonistic motives confront one another through verbal gestures of exchange (question-answer, assertion-denial, challenge-response): "Their faces were not a foot apart: the one cold, dead white, fanatical, mad; the other parchmentcolored, the lip lifted into the shape of a soundless and rigid snarl. He said quietly: 'You're old . . .'" (*LA* 304, 262). "They faced one another, not close yet at slightly less than foils' distance, erect, their voices not raised, not impactive, just succinct" (*GDM* 275). Usually brief (extended dialogues in Faulkner inexorably turn into monologues), dialogic scenes distill speech into violence. Many contain imagery of weapons or blows: "Then they cursed each other, hard and brief and without emphasis, like blows or pistol-shots, both speaking at the same time and neither moving" (*H* 91–92).

In a densely figural novel like *Absalom, Absalom!* the dialogic scenes emerge with striking clarity out of the turgid monologic discourse: "The pistol lying yet across the saddle bow unaimed, the two faces calm, the voices not even raised: *Dont you pass the shadow of this post, this branch, Charles; and I am going to pass it, Henry*" (*AA* 165; 133). "The two of them, brother and sister . . . speaking to one another in short brief staccato sentences like slaps, as if they stood breast to breast striking one another in turn, neither making any attempt to guard against the blows" (*AA* 215; 172).

In *Go Down, Moses* the struggle between Lucas Beauchamp and Zack

Edmonds in Edmonds's bedroom combines dialogue with a literal physical struggle. Lucas has come to confront and kill the white man he believes has "taken" his wife Molly (as Old Carothers "took" Lucas's slave ancestors). The gulf between them, perfectly symbolized by the bed, is of course race itself:

> "You on one side, me on the other," the white man said. "We'll kneel down and grip hands. We wont need to count."
>
> "No!" Lucas said in a strangling voice. "For the last time. Take your pistol. I'm coming."
>
> "Come on then. Do you think I'm any less a McCaslin just because I was what you call woman-made to it? Or maybe you aint even a woman-made McCaslin but just a nigger that's got out of hand?"
>
> Then Lucas was beside the bed. He didn't remember moving at all. He was kneeling, their hands gripped, facing across the bed and the pistol the man whom he had known from infancy, with whom he had lived until they were both grown almost as brothers lived. (*GDM* 55)

A dialogic scene may have only imagined speech, as in Bayard Sartoris's confrontation with Redmond in *The Unvanquished*: "We didn't speak. It was as if we both knew what the passage of words would be and the futility of it; how he might have said, 'Go out, Bayard. Go away, boy' and then, 'Draw then. I will allow you to draw' and it would have been the same as if he had never said it. So we did not speak"(*U* 286).

Horace Benbow's meeting with evil in *Sanctuary* begins with his strange, and dialogical, meeting with Popeye at the spring near the old Frenchman place. This silence, as it consistently does with Popeye, communicates more than the exchange of words; Benbow's words, as is also consistently true throughout *Sanctuary*, have no effect on the evil he confronts:

> They squatted so, facing one another across the spring, for two hours. Now and then the bird sang back in the swamp, as though it were worked by a clock; twice more invisible automobiles passed along the highroad and died away. Again the bird sang.
>
> "And of course you dont know the name of it," the man across the spring said. . . . Popeye said nothing. He squatted in his tight black suit. (*S* 5; 3–4)

Mink Snopes, who can never cross the barriers that keep him from achieving self-sufficiency and self-respect, reenacts in *The Mansion* the confrontation with Jack Houston first told in *The Hamlet*, in a dialogic scene that literally is a prelude to murder: "It was tableau: Mink with one leg over the top rail, Houston standing inside the fence, the pistol hanging in one hand against his leg" (*M* 15). Mink's dialogic confrontations are usually one-sided, either because he is being told by Houston or Varner why he must pay more money for his cow, or because he can only stand helplessly and curse: "standing in the empty yard cursing the Negro and his family inside the blank house"; "cursing into the steamy vapor of his own breathing, cursing the Negro for his black skin inside the warmer garments than his, a white man's, cursing the rich feed devoted to cattle . . . cursing above all the unaware white man through or because of whose wealth such a condition could obtain, cursing . . ." (*M* 9, 11–12).

As these examples suggest, dialogic moments in Faulkner symbolically bring into sharp focus the differentiation necessary in the portrayal of speech as speakers face one another across some unbridgeable gulf of difference. Mimetic voice is intimately tied to those central moments when events reach a turning point, when characters discover and face their truest antagonists, when the fictional discourse reaches its thematic climax. Dialogue in Faulkner becomes emblematic of all differentiation.

Identification

Just as speeches need to be differentiated one from another, so must represented speech be identified. The text must identify speech by marking it in some way and by attributing it to a speaker. In answer to the puzzle of "who speaks" in fictional discourse, identification answers both "who *speaks*," by marking off certain discourse as speech in relation to other, nonspoken portions of the text, and "*who* speaks," by assigning speech to named or implied speakers. Mimetic voice is stronger—that is to say, the illusion of speech occurring in the fictional world is more convincingly established—the more clearly speech is marked and the more easily the reader can attribute it to an appropriate human origin. Various familiar conventions help fulfill this fourth function of mimetic voice. Formal speaker identification supplies the required attribution, as in "'I can pay you soon as I gin my cotton,' *Mink said*" (*M* 32; emphasis added). Internal indications such as self-references, style, and the substance of an utterance also identify speakers. A novelist can control the pace and rhythm of dialogue by the manner in which he or she identifies speakers. A given form of attribution, such as "she said," can appear with such regularity that it becomes like a punctuation mark devoid of semantic significance; or, conversely, constant changes from "said" to verbs such as "muttered," "cried," "mumbled," and so on, can serve descriptive and narrative purposes. Frequency, variation in the speech verb, punctuation, placement of the attributive speech tag—all such features of dialogue writing help mold characterization and plot, as well as the dialogue itself.

As with most formal devices for creating mimetic voice, Faulkner's texts manipulate speech tags, both exploiting and disrupting conventional usage. Faulkner employs speech tags frequently and often in the same position within a sentence, immediately after an initial spoken clause but seldom before or after the entire transcribed speech. Colloquial character narration tends to show a much higher incidence of speech tags than authorial discourse because the oral speaker cannot use textual signals such as paragraphing to mark a change in speaker:

> "Here's a place," *pa says.* . . . "We could get some water over yonder."
>
> "All right," *I say.* "You'll have to borrow a bucket from them, Dewey Dell."
>
> "God knows," *pa says.* "I wouldn't be beholden, God knows."
>
> "If you see a good-sized can, you might bring it," *I say.* (*AILD* 191; 196, emphasis added)

Even though Faulkner's choice of speech verb seldom varies from "said" or "says" (the use of "cried" for the Reporter's speeches in *Pylon* is exceptional), the frequency and positioning of attributive tags do characterize his narrators, as in Jason Compson's monologue where his incessant "I says" serves as one of many symptoms of egotistical self-assertiveness. Faulkner leaves speech tags out if a character serving as a story's central consciousness either does not know or does not directly confront the speaker (see, for example, "Barn Burning," *CS* 4, 18). For longer speeches he on occasion turns speech tags into more formal paragraph headings (see *M* 192–93). His most idiosyncratic practice places the speech tag at the end of the previous speech, as in this passage from *The Mansion*:

> . . . and I said to him:
> "Helen walked in light." And he says,
> "Helen was light. . . ." And I says,
> "What about all them others . . ." And he says . . . (133)

Part 4 of "The Bear," in *Go Down, Moses*, employs a version of this device in the extended debate between Ike McCaslin and his cousin, Cass

Edmonds. Each spoken passage ends with attribution for the next utterance, but without any verb, merely "and he" and "and McCaslin." The technique stylizes the debate, rendering it less a normal conversation and more a formal exchange of ideas. The variation from conventional dialogue form here diminishes mimetic voice somewhat, and the debate thus joins the ledgers as a permanent part of Ike's memory (marked also by the consistent reference to McCaslin by name and Ike by "he" in the speech tags). *The Sound and the Fury* contains an even more stylized version of this speech tag when Quentin remembers (or imagines) the long conversation with his father in which he tries to confess incest with Caddy. The speech tags blend with the spoken words as part of Quentin's barely controlled recollection: "no compson has ever disappointed a lady and i temporary it will be better for me for all of us and he every man is the arbiter of his own virtues . . . and i temporary and he was the saddest word of all" (*SF* 204–5; 221–22).

Identification plays an especially vital role in the interplay of mimetic with other kinds of voice because this function evokes the relationship between speech and character. At the level of mimetic voice, that is, at the level of the fiction's discourse where characters speak, conventions of appropriateness rule strongly. Readers apply deeply ingrained assumptions about "expressive identity," the appropriate correspondence between speech and speaker, to the speech heard in fiction. Quite naturally, readers are more inclined to regard a portion of a text's discourse as spoken if it is attributed to a character or narrator they believe capable of uttering it; characters are also expected to speak consistently throughout a story. Conventional expressive identity works in both directions to enforce verisimilitude of character through mimetic voice: character governs appropriate speech, and character in turn devolves from speech. Mimetic voice is an index of personal identity, and plausibility requires that a voice belong to someone and that the voice match other personal attributes such as socioeconomic class, level of education, probable mental powers, and so on. Any loosening of the bond between speech and person violates verisimilitude, making utterances sound "unnatural."

Faulkner willingly risks diminishing mimetic voice in order to fulfill narrative goals, especially to create psychic voice by attributing sophisticated, highly figural rhetoric to ordinary or even uneducated dialect speakers. As early as "The Cobbler," in the *New Orleans Sketches*, he imputes apparently verbalized thoughts to a speaker incapable of saying them. At times he reminds the reader that a character whose thoughts are being described could not say these things (see "Barn Burning," *CS* 10). Many characters and narrators speak at unnatural length and in ornate "Faulknerese": all the narrators in *Absalom, Absalom!*, Ike and Cass in part 4 of "The Bear," Gavin Stevens in *Intruder*, and the Old General in *A Fable* all discourse in extended rhetorical periods. Important as the dramatic illusion of speech is, it tends in Faulkner to play a subsidiary role to other discursive needs, especially the need to say as *much* as possible, to expand discourse until (as Faulkner wrote to Cowley) it embraces the whole world in each sentence, "to put it all, if possible, on one pinhead" (*SL* 185; Cowley 14).

DIRECT, INDIRECT, AND MINGLED SPEECH. Identification, particularly as it involves attribution, entails the issues much discussed in linguistics and literary theory under the heading of "free indirect discourse" or some related term like *style indirect libre, erlebte Rede,* "transposed discourse" (Genette), "free style" (Chatman), or "narrated monologue" (Cohn). The fundamental concept—fundamental to the mimetic problem if not to the purely grammatical one—is that of the relationship between speech and the discourse that reports speech, between (to return to Plato's basic distinction) mimetic speech and diegetic discourse.[12] The manner in which diegetic discourse reports a speaker's words varies according to how *direct* or *indirect* the rendering is. Temple Drake's dialogue, quoted from *Sanctuary*, is direct discourse and requires two expressions, the diegetic "she said" and the mimetic "I'm hungry . . . I haven't eaten since. . . ." Temple's expression is in quotation marks, includes contractions, and employs the first person and present tense: these features help identify her words as speech. If we were to rewrite the passage as indirect discourse it might read "Temple said that she was hungry, that she had not eaten since. . . ."

Considered mimetically, the terms "direct" and "indirect" suggest a spectrum of imitation from presumably exact reduplication of the words spoken in their proper order and with their expressive qualities intact, to a mere mention that speech has occurred. Between these extremes of directly quoted and indirectly rendered or narrated speech lie other means of fulfilling the function of identification, in which speech is variably marked and variably distinct from or merged with the reporting diegetic discourse. These intermediate forms of represented speech diverge from direct and indirect primarily in the way they mark or decline to mark speech as such.[13] These forms can be called "mingled speech" to emphasize their most salient trait in Faulkner's fiction: the mingling of identifiably diegetic discourse with mimetic speech. Mingled speech, like the directly quoted, can present a speaker's *expression* through elements not available to indirect reporting, rendering the distinction between diegetic and mimetic difficult to discern. A speaker's diction, syntax, even dialect pronunciation can be copied, yet mingled speech does not guarantee that any of the reported words or expressions were in fact vocalized (or even verbalized in the mind) by the speaker, or even that a speech act took place at all. Like indirect speech, the presented speech remains attributable, in certain respects, to the reporting diegetic discourse as much as to the purported speaker. Thus, an author can employ language that a character as a speaker would not or could not plausibly use in order to represent that character's consciousness without being restricted to quotation. Conversely, an author can employ language appropriate only to a certain character or type of character (but not appropriate to the authorial voice). Mimetic voice mingles with diegetic discourse without being clearly marked as different, so that expression can escape the obliqueness of paraphrase, on the one hand, and the inhibitions of accurate quotation, on the other. Rewritten as mingled speech, Temple's expression of her hunger (originally "'I cant—I might—' she whimpered. 'I'm hungry,' she said. 'I haven't eaten since . . .'" [*S* 166]) might be expressed as "She couldn't———. She might———. How hungry she was! She hadn't eaten since . . ." Because mingled speech is not overtly marked, it "hides" within other discourse we do not regard as spoken, and this dissimulation can infuse an entire narrative with a nonnarrating character's consciousness. Bakhtin refers to this mingling of voices as the essential and defining trait of the novel: "The speech of another [can be] introduced into the author's discourse (the story) in *concealed form*, that is, without any of the *formal* markers usually accompanying such speech, whether direct or indirect" (*The Dialogical Imagination* 303).[14]

While Faulkner does not rely as heavily as many novelists on mingled speech as a method of filtering his stories through a central consciousness, his works, like all written narrative since early in the nineteenth century (especially since Flaubert), exhibit many examples of mingled speech. Faulkner's overall fictional discourse tends, however, to move almost inexorably toward the *direct* presentation of speech. Not only does he frequently employ and collaborate with character-narrators, but when he does use mingled speech forms he establishes a discursive rhythm in which mingled speech transmutes into direct speech (or into thought couched as direct speech). Even when he "lends" sophisticated linguistic skills to a character, he often overtly marks that character's discourse as mimetic speech (either vocalized or verbalized inwardly).

Through the agency of mimetic voice, especially in the fulfillment of its identifying function in mingled speech, first-person point of view becomes in Faulkner a phenomenon of voice as well as of vision. As discussed in chapter 1, listening provides "perspective" just as seeing does. When a narrator embeds others' mimetic voices within his own he adjusts our "posture of hearkening" to his own, just as reporting what he sees focuses our vision. An excellent example is the story "That Will Be Fine." Seven-year-old Georgie's humorous narration of his Uncle Rodney's affairs and their serious consequences consists mostly of others' speech, but rendered in a fluid variety of direct, mingled, and indirect modes. In any given paragraph the direction of this prattle of voices generally tends to shift from the more indirect toward the more direct. Georgie's narration moves through various degrees of mingled speech, ending in direct quotation:

> So she went down to the door and it was Mr. Pruitt and the sheriff. And how Aunt Louisa begged Mr. Pruitt for Grandpa's sake and how she gave Mr. Pruitt her oath that Uncle Rodney would stay right there in the house until papa could get there, and Mr. Pruitt said how he hated it to happen at Christmas too and so for Grandpa's and Aunt Louisa's sake he would give them until the day after Christmas if Aunt Louisa would promise him that Uncle Rodney would not try to leave Mottstown. And how Mr. Pruitt showed her with her own eyes the check with Grandpa's name signed to it and how even Aunt Louisa could see that Grandpa's name had been—and then mamma said Louisa! Louisa! Remember Georgie! and that was me, and papa cussed too, hollering How in damnation do you expect to keep it from him? By hiding the newspapers? and Aunt Louisa cried again and said how everybody was bound to know it, that she didn't expect or hope that any of us could ever hold our heads up again, that all she hoped for was to keep it from Grandpa because it would kill him. She cried hard then and papa had to stop at a branch and get down and soak his handkerchief for mamma to wipe Aunt Louisa's face with it and then papa took the bottle of tonic out of the dash pocket and put a few drops on the handkerchief, and Aunt Louisa smelled it and then papa took a dose of the tonic out of the bottle and mamma

said George! and papa drank some more of the tonic and then made like he was handing the bottle back for mamma and Aunt Louisa to take a dose too and said, "I don't blame you. If I was a woman in this family I'd take a drink too. Now let me get this bond business straight." (*CS* 271–72)

The passage as a whole is Georgie's narration of Aunt Louisa's explanation to Georgie's parents of events the previous night. Georgie reports the conversation between Mr. Pruitt, the sheriff, and Aunt Louisa indirectly (we do not know how Aunt Louisa reported it to papa and mamma), in sentences beginning with "And how" (a variant of "that," the optional marker of indirect discourse). He shifts to more direct speech in "then mamma said Louisa!," which includes expressive punctuation but not quotation marks. Papa's cussing is even closer to direct discourse, being rendered in a sentence that also has expressive interrogative syntax, verb tense (indirect would use "expected" rather than "expect"), direct address ("you"), and punctuation, but still no quotation marks. The speech tag "cussed" further enhances the directly discursive qualities of Papa's words, as we rarely find indirectly rendered "cussing" (as, for example, in the ungrammatical "he cussed that he wondered how they expected to keep it from him"). The speech tag "hollering," however, could be used indirectly (as, for example, in "hollering how they expected to keep it from him"). Georgie's narrative then reverts to a more indirect mode in reporting what Aunt Louisa said (how everybody was bound to know about it and "that all she hoped for was to keep it from Grandpa"). The passage ends, as many do in Faulkner, by shifting into direct, quoted speech (including quotation marks) that comes as a climax to the accumulated mingled speech modes in Georgie's narration.

Faulkner's genius with mimetic voice is illustrated in the nuances of rendered speech, and also in the manner in which a young colloquial narrator exploits the full resources of the grammar of represented discourse. Georgie's own narrative speech sounds natural as he plausibly reports others' spoken words, and thus mimetic voice flows and ebbs complexly—far more complexly than the notion of point of view can account for. Our visual perceptions are always Georgie's, for we cannot be where he is not; but our "aural perceptions" eddy and swirl among various voices mingled within Georgie's own richly rendered narrative speech. It is these voices heard amidst Georgie's own that allow us to know more than the boy can know, and yet to remain within his narration. As the detailed examination of only one passage shows, voice is a far more precise compass than point of view to chart the currents of our experience of Georgie and of the events the boy tries to comprehend. Irony itself, that irony inherent in the child's innocent lack of full understanding, is best understood as a matter of voice.[15]

MINK IN *THE MANSION*. The various nuances of mingled speech are more than a collection of grammatical traits irrespective of semantic content. Mingled speech also invokes character, for when a given speech is attributed to a given character, the implications of that speech follow along. What a character says can be held against him or her, for speech serves as a primary source of value in fictional worlds. This truism has its obverse, as well, for the identity of a speaker colors the spoken word, giving it implications it might not carry from another origin. And because the spoken word is mingled with the narrative discourse, the speaker's identity also colors discourse for which he or she is not responsible. To put this another way, when Faulkner chooses not to quote a character, but to mingle his authorial discourse with a character's speech, he in effect grants to that character greater authority than he would give by merely quoting; in mingled speech a character-speaker cannot be merely the butt of irony.

The Mansion demonstrates the flexibility of mingled speech as author, character-narrators, and characters (especially Mink Snopes) move in and out of diegetic and mimetic roles in relation to reproduced speech. Mimetic voice, as affected by shifting relationships between diegetic and mimetic discourse and by degrees of directness in reported speech, becomes a field of implied values on which the reader's responses must play. In many ways a despicable person, Mink Snopes becomes an anti-Snopesian agent of retribution, not only because he kills Flem (with Linda's assistance), but even more because we share his perspective for much of the novel, seeing what Mink sees while he journeys inexorably from prison to Memphis to Jefferson. As always in Faulkner, "perspective" only in part means "point of view." "Perspective" also means voice, the "awareness" we are permitted to share as we hear Mink's thoughts and feelings in his speech, in the narrative discourse and, most important, in the mingled weave of these voices. Perspective derives from Mink's speech as it fades in and out of the discourse that creates the fictional world. Mink does not narrate, yet his actual or implied speech sets in motion the world revealed to us through the presence of his voice.[16]

Unreliable narrators are common in fiction, but in Mink's case Faulkner seems to have wanted to avoid that irony necessary for an unreliable narrator to reveal himself (unwittingly) for what he truly is. We do not "commune with Faulkner behind [Mink's] back" (as Wayne Booth describes the effect of Jason Compson's unreliability [*Rhetoric of Fiction* 307]). Mink is unlike Jason primarily because the novel's diegetic discourse takes up Mink's speech almost lovingly, even when we hear the story of his murder of Jack Houston. We may see the world through Mink's eyes, but we need not see through Mink, for he does not try to "fool" us by unreliable narration. Mink's speech mingles with authoritative diegetic discourse without always being overtly identified. Sometimes we know with certainty that a particular word or phrase is a "Mink-word," but often we do not, and so we are never free to dismiss *any* word as "merely" the character's, as merely belonging to "folks that hide in bushes and shoot other folks off their horses" (43).[17] Nor can we with certainty always determine that a given word is purely diegetic with nothing of Mink's idiom in it. Faulkner's method allows a morally questionable persona to serve as our perspective, but it also works the other way to tinge even the diegetic discourse with Mink's mimetic voice. What governs mingled speech in *The Mansion* is not simply the portrayal of events or of consciousness but the repeated discovery of values, a discovery required of the reader, who must account for the presence of Mink's "word" in the narrative; a discovery shared with Mink, who believes that Flem has failed to keep *his* "word"; and a discovery dramatized in Gavin Stevens's horrified realization that Linda has deliberately arranged to silence Flem forever.

From the novel's complex mingling of speech and narration we can extract three dominant strands. There is, first, mimetic voice associated with Mink Snopes, the lead character and contributor of words, phrases, turns of thought, and country images. In relation to Mink's mimetic speech we can identify a diegetic narrative discourse typical of communal, anonymous narrators found in many Faulkner stories and typical of Ratliff, Chick Mallison, and even Montgomery Ward Snopes in *The Mansion*; this discourse includes contractions, frequent fillers and transitional phrases like "in fact," "at first," "so," and "really," and colloquial syntax that hints at a listener, as in "It began in the spring. No, it began in the fall before. No, it began a long time before that even. It began . . ." These traits of colloquial diegetic narration become mimetic relative to a more "writerly" discourse, the recognizably Faulknerian diegetic prose, which employs long sentences, compound phrases, and sophisticated diction, as in "each subsequent daily manacled trip and transference." Samples extracted from the opening pages follow:

Mink's idiom (mimetic speech):
little wooden hammer
high desk
his and the damned law's both
yes, he admitted it
hurrah and hullabaloo
first hair on her bump
that durn McCarron boy was snuffing
a woods colt in his back yard next grass
had done already more or less eliminated
dropping a bastard
that damn girl
he had forgot that
Old Moster
aimed
a-tall
durn surly sullen son of a bitch

Anonymous colloquial idiom (diegetic discourse relative to Mink's idiom; mimetic voice relative to authorial prose):

didn't, wasn't, hadn't
in fact
hollering
really outrageous foolish interference
everybody in it knew everything about everybody
with his usual luck
All right, more than just luck then—

Faulknerian writerly prose (diegetic discourse):

into, against, across the wall of little wan faces hemming him in
each subsequent daily manacled trip and transference
grimed interstices of the barred window
imperious need
incarceration
extricate
the ancient immutable laws of simple blood kinship

Such phrases do not, of course, cluster neatly into lists as we read; indeed Faulkner's mingled speech in *The Mansion* constantly shifts among the various voices. Diegetic narrative becomes mimetic voice and vice versa in a continual dance among discursive levels. Only phonetic spelling signals Mink's mimetic voice with certainty since Faulkner's anonymous communal narrators may employ dialect usage, imagery, and even ungrammatical forms, but they virtually never use phonetic spelling (except in contractions). A phrase such as "little wooden hammer on the high desk" reflects Mink's perspective but not exclusively his language. Even more subtle are the shifts in syntax or diction within a sentence. "Hollering," a colloquial verb, immediately precedes one of Faulkner's noncolloquial writerly habits, the listing of grammatical function words (here prepositions): "himself hollering into, against, across the wall of little wan faces hemming him in." Besides pragmatic differences between words Mink could not use plausibly and the text's sophisticated diction, we also find grammatical features typical of mingled speech—expressive elements of direct speech rendered in the third person and past tense of indirect speech: "All right, if Houston was in too high and mighty a mood to be said much obliged to, he, Mink, for one wasn't going to break in on him uninvited. Not that he didn't owe a much obliged to something somewhere"(11). "Oh yes, Houston with the toddy of good red whiskey in his hand"(14). One sentence contains all three strands: formal authorial phrasing, colloquial misplacing of a clause in narration (the clause beginning "and each"), and Mink's diction:

> In fact, that whole first trip, handcuffed to the deputy, from his jail cell to the courtroom, had been a senseless, a really outrageously foolish interference with and interruption, and each subsequent daily manacled trip and transference, of the solution to both their problems—his and the damned law's both—if they had only waited and let him alone: the watching, his dirty hands gripping among the grimed interstices of the barred window above the street, which had been his one, his imperious need during the long months between his incarceration and the opening of the Court. (3)

A steady, accumulating movement toward direct speech, which characterizes all of Faulkner's versions of mingled speech, can be seen throughout the portions of *The Mansion* recounting Mink's actions. As in the passage from "That Will Be Fine" discussed earlier, many paragraphs in the novel progress toward more mimetically rendered speech. Mink's idiom increasingly intrudes as the discourse moves closer to direct expression of his

outrage and frustration: the density of identifiable "Mink words" increases; the rhythm of the syntax consistently drives toward Mink's voice
and a concomitant heightened intensity of frustrated complaint. The
novel's third paragraph modulates from a phrase like "extricate him from
its consequences" early in the paragraph into its final, almost direct quotation of Mink's sarcastic anger at all the trouble Eula brought: "They would
all have seen through that Texas trip even without the hurrah and
hullabaloo that Varner girl had been causing ever since she (or whoever
else it was) found the first hair on her bump, not to mention just this last
past spring and summer while that durn McCarron boy was snuffing and
fighting everybody else off exactly like a gang of rutting dogs" (4).

Diegetic discourse intermingled with unmarked speech often "breaks
out" into overtly recorded but uncommunicated direct speech, couched in
Mink's dialect and marked usually by italics and occasionally by quotation
marks, as if spoken out loud. These italicized thoughts, though they technically overstep the bounds of mingled speech into direct inner speech,
complete that rhythmic movement toward an increased presence of Mink's
idiom within a particular passage. The italicized thoughts appear most
frequently at the end of paragraphs, as if speakable thoughts had finally
broken free of the diegetic discourse and could now be heard (and seen in
italics), as if the presence of a character's implied speech had become
strong enough to demand identification.

Faulkner's writerly prose often supplements the voice of a character
(usually a character-narrator but sometimes a nonnarrating character)
whose idiom pervades large sections of a text. Mink's marked speech is at
one point literally confirmed by the diegetic discourse—in figural language Mink could not employ—when Mink describes the pistol he is
about to buy in Memphis: " 'Hit looks like a cooter,' he said. It did: snub-
nosed, short-barrelled, swollen of cylinder and rusted over, with its curved
butt and flat reptilian hammer it did resemble the fossil relic of some small
antediluvian terrapin"(291). On one occasion the authorial narrator points
out the word Mink would use for something ("now he was going to have to
do what he called 'figger' a little" [396]) and later adopts that word without
comment or identification ("But he could figger a mile whether he saw
mileposts or not" [404]).[18]

The novel achieves its closure through an inversion of the usual pattern
whereby mingled speech moves toward Mink's direct idiom. The final passage depicts Mink's death solely through the perceptible though formally
unmarked erasure of his voice from the discourse. Like a part of the text

being rubbed out, or a voice's volume slowly being turned down, discourse that is identifiably Mink's ("a fair active chance," "the folks that had the trouble," "skeers," and "wouldn't nobody even know") increasingly gives way as the final paragraph progresses to phrases that could not belong to Mink ("the justice and the injustice and the griefs," "being inextricable from, anonymous with all of them"), until the final phrasing loses Mink almost entirely in high Faulknerian rhetoric: "The beautiful, the splendid, the proud and the brave, right on up to the very top itself among the shining phantoms and dreams which are the milestones of the long human recording—Helen and the bishops, the kings and the unhomed angels, the scornful and graceless seraphim" (435–36).

"NEGRO"/"NIGGER".   One signal of mingled speech in *The Mansion*, and elsewhere in Faulkner, is the word "nigger." *The Mansion*'s authorial diegetic prose (as in other Faulkner novels) uses "Negro" (or "negro") to denominate a black person. The switch from "Negro" to "nigger" allows Faulkner to move into Mink's idiom without recourse to dialect, and often without moving significantly out of diegetic discourse. The two words frequently appear together in the same passage, with "Negro" appearing first in accord with the rhythm of the increasing presence of Mink's voice. The shift tracks Mink's growing frustration: "Negro" more objectively identifies the person in Mink's awareness, while the word "nigger" that follows emerges in conjunction with an expression of Mink's feelings. As he approaches Houston's lot to claim his cow, Mink knows that "only the Negro with his hayfork would be in the lot now." As he begins to speak to the man, Mink remains calm, "not having to fawn and cringe yet: just saying, level and white-man, to the nigger paused in the door to the feeding shed to look back at him: 'Hidy'" (*M* 13). In Memphis Mink is amazed to find that a store is run by a Negro: "A Negro man seemed to be running it or anyway serving the customers. Maybe he even owned it; maybe the new laws even said a nigger could even own a store" (290). Elsewhere the modulation from "Negro" to "nigger" occurs within the same sentence: "then a section all Negro homes . . . and then go even into a nigger house" (34), and "[the train] stopped, a Negro even more uppity than Houston's getting out with his footstool . . . the nigger with his footstool" (35). (Mink does, however, curse the "Negro" who owns a scrub breed bull [9].) As a sign of Mink's speech, "nigger" can be attributed to him, his vocabulary, his class and culture, his region and, most vitally, his values. We attribute the word "Negro" to the diegetic discourse rather than to Mink because we assume that Mink would consistently use "nigger," as that word is appropriate to him but not to a "well-spoken" narrator.[19]

Faulkner generally exercised caution with these words, limiting "nigger" to discourse that could be attributed in some way to a character rather than to an authorial narrator. In *The Wild Palms*, for example, Faulkner uses "nigger servant" in indirect discourse (19), but "negro maid" in a descriptive passage rendered from Harry Wilbourne's perspective but not as a direct or indirect report of his thoughts (42). In *Absalom, Absalom!*, that novel where perhaps more than any other the character-narrators speak in tune with the authorial diegetic discourse, Faulkner maintains the distinction: the diegetic narration contains "negro" in the first part of chapter 2, but when Mr Compson picks up the story he immediately uses "niggers" (50; 43). Characters can be "well spoken," too, of course: while Byron Bunch tells Hightower that Joe Christmas is "part nigger," Hightower echoes the words as "part negro," befitting his education and ministerial status (*LA* 97; 83). "Was," the first chapter of *Go Down, Moses*, is a story Cass Edmonds told Ike McCaslin at some unspecified time; Faulkner employs "nigger" consistently, perhaps because he renders the entire tale in indirect discourse attributable to Cass. Lucas Beauchamp's indirectly reported thoughts use "nigger" (*GDM* 34) because Lucas would use "nigger" in his speech, whereas the Northern black man who comes to marry Sophonsiba (in part 4 of "The Bear") is referred to as the "Negro" in a diegetic discourse aligned with Ike McCaslin's perspective (*GDM* 274).

This is not to say that Faulkner is always consistent in his choices between the two terms. The most puzzling usage occurs in *The Unvanquished*, where the first-person narration appears to ignore the usual principle governing attribution of "Negro" and "nigger." Sometimes the choice does seem to depend upon the narrating voice of Bayard Sartoris; at other times Faulkner may have had some semantic distinction in mind; other usages seem arbitrarily interchangeable. Bayard Sartoris narrates each story from a time later than the events, and thus we hear the voice of a man more mature than the child we see acting. Bayard uses both "Negro" and "nigger" to designate blacks. We might assume that "Negro" belongs to the mature (and well-spoken) narrating persona, and "nigger" to the child not yet aware of any special significance of that word. But no such pattern of attribution consistently obtains. The first appearances of each word do reflect a possible difference in Bayard's narrating voice: he uses "Negroes" (4) in the opening paragraph of "Ambuscade," a paragraph establishing setting and background; "nigger" appears when the boy seems to be speaking: "But I was just talking too, I knew that, because niggers know, they know things" (7). Ten lines later, however, Bayard uses "Negroes" again: "Because it was that urgent, since Negroes knew" (7). Then, five lines later, we read "But now it was that urgent even though Ringo was a nigger too" (7). When caught in the midst of the slaves moving northward Bayard uses "niggers" (94, 109, 120, 123), though Drusilla has referred to them as "Negroes" (105, 115), and while listening to her story Bayard says he is surrounded by the smell of "Negroes" (109). Uncle Buck's slaves are "niggers," befitting perhaps his pre–Civil War view, but even freed Blacks who come to the church where Granny distributes the proceeds of her mule trading are "niggers" (as were the slaves Bayard remembers in the gallery of the same church [153, 154]). A mature authorial voice can be heard clearly in "An Odor of Verbena" using "Negroes" (277), but "niggers" also appears. There may be a semantic difference implied on pages 256 and 257, where Bayard refers to carpetbaggers "organising the Negroes into an insurrection" and remembers "listen[ing] to the niggers passing in the road . . . the tide of crazed singing niggers"; no such difference in meaning is maintained throughout the novel, however, or within any separate story.

Connotative nuance may, in some instances, account for the shifts between the two words. In "The Old People" the authorial narrator refers to Sam Fathers, "who had been a negro for two generations" (*GDM* 164), as speaking in "negroid English" (172) but wearing "nigger clothes" (*GDM* 173). Faulkner offers two definitions of "nigger" that might distinguish it from "Negro": Quentin in *The Sound and the Fury* says that "a nigger is not a person so much as a form of behaviour" (98; 106), and in "The Fire and the Hearth" Lucas "became not Negro but nigger, not secret so much as impenetrable, not servile and not effacing, but enveloping himself in an aura of timeless and stupid impassivity almost like a smell" (*GDM* 60). But despite the inconsistencies in usage, the essential difference between the terms arises from attribution and its effects on the identification of mimetic voice; the crucial issue is not what "nigger" and "Negro" mean but who says these words, and when. If "nigger" is a "form of behaviour," it designates the behavior of those who employ the term more than those to whom it is applied. The variations in usage demonstrate that "nigger" is never innocent in Faulkner, even when not intended as a racial epithet, even when everyone in a given community uses that term, even when one black person applies it to another black person. Nor is mimetic voice in general ever innocent. The variance in Faulkner's usage of these two heavily value-laden words highlights the crucial role played by the identification of speakers in establishing *appropriate* mimetic voice.

The function of mimetic voice called "identification" gains its effect from the truism that speech emanates from some person; it does not simply appear on the horizon like a rainstorm. Humans talk in acts more or less willed, and the question of who speaks is always crucial to our sense of a fiction's people.[20]

Transcription

As the earlier discussion of *The Mansion* indicates, dialect usage and phonetic spelling mark the presence of a character's voice, for we do not normally find dialect in authorial diegetic discourse. Nonstandard spellings like "jest" for "just" or "hit" for "it" signal Mink's idiom as clearly as formal signs like quotation marks, italics, or speech tags. Such spelling brings us to the fifth function of mimetic voice, transcription: speech can be imitated in a graphic form that reinforces a reader's sense that certain discourse has been spoken. In a literal sense "transcribing" means putting down on paper whatever speakers say, but in fiction the word has literal meaning only as part of the dramatic illusion. Mimetic voice emerges as distinct from other voices when the novelist records variations on some standard discourse, be it a culturally defined standard language or a norm established within the text itself. Most striking, of course, are all the techniques of dialect writing: phonetic spelling of words, contractions, eye dialect, incorrect grammatical forms, and variations in word order or usage from a standard (i.e., written) language.

Paradoxically the most dependent of the mimetic functions on printed resources, transcription probably seems to many readers the least mediated way of creating mimetic voice. Except for borrowing the alphabetic conventions involved in phonetic representation, the writer merely "records" what he "hears" imagined characters say. "You've got to hear the voice speaking the speech that you put down," Faulkner once said. "You have to hear the vernacular he speaks in, rather than to think of the speech and then translate it into the vernacular" (*FU* 181). Ideally, transcription imitates without the intervening artifice of "translation," empowering written discourse to be regarded as spoken without any apparent (to use Genette's phrase again) "work of re-presentation."

Faulkner's comment, with its instruction that a writer transcribe speech as it is heard, restates the goal of transcription to generate a strong illusion of speech. In fact, however, transcription succeeds because of its reliance on conventions of writing and reading rather than on hearing, on a shared sense of *literary* appropriateness far more than on phonetic mimicry. Phonetic spelling, the most directly imitative form of transcription in its attempt to inscribe the different way a word sounds when spoken by a dialect speaker from the way it sounds in its standard spelling, depends for its mimetic effect on the reader's assumptions about conventionally *written* words, on what is as much or more a visual difference as an aural one. Some phonetic spellings do alter a word's implied sound, as in the case of two usages common in Faulkner, "jest" substituted for "just," and "hit" for "it." Other spellings, appropriately labeled "eye dialect" (which Pei defines as "the written form of a spoken dialect which purports to represent dialectical features or substandard language" [88]), often only appear to reproduce phonetic differences, but in fact register no change when actually enunciated. "Uv" for "of," "wuz" for "was," "wer" for "were" look like dialect but do not change the words' sounds. Excessive eye dialect can in fact hamper mimetic voice by interfering with the reader's "inner voice," with those automatic connections a reader makes between word sounds and graphic forms. Eye dialect calls self-conscious attention to the inherent textuality of transcribed speech, which as Genette points out is always a "risk [that] lies heavy over any too-perfect mimesis, which finally annuls itself in the circularity . . . of the link to its shadow" (*Narrative Discourse* 185). To imitate speech too intensely, too "perfectly," is to turn it into nonspeech, as mimetic voice gets swallowed in the visual gabble of the text. George Washington Harris's Sut Lovingood narrates in a dialect transcription that renders the prose so visually alien as to be unreadable until we become accustomed to the alphabetic conventions Harris employs. Here is Sut on "univarsal onregenerit human nater": "ef ever yu dus enything tu enybody wifout cause, yu hates em allers arterwards, an' sorter wants tu hurt em agin. an' yere's anuther human nater: ef enything happens sum feller, I don't keer ef he's yure bes' frien, an' I don't keer how sorry yu is fur him, thar's a streak ove satisfackshun 'bout like a sowin thread a-runnin' all thru yer sorrer" (Harris 245).[21]

Conventions of literary writing style within diegetic discourse also can encourage a translation of writing to speech. What Richard Bridgman calls the American colloquial style, for example, relies on general characteristics that bear a relation to some traits of spoken discourse: "stress on the individual verbal unit, a resulting fragmentation of syntax, and the use of repetition to bind and unify" (12). But speech can be characterized by other traits as well, that have the opposite effects to those Bridgman describes: vocal glides, for example, that keep syntax flowing rather than fragmented; fillers and shifters that lengthen syntactic units; or long, compound, additive sentences that lay stress on accumulation rather than on the "individual verbal unit." The features Bridgman names, and not incorrectly associates with colloquial discourse, are traits that some fictional prose styles share with spoken discourse, not necessarily as it "really" occurs but with spoken discourse as writers image it in American fiction; for the colloquial style Bridgman describes is, finally, a *literary* mode. A style like Henry James's (rightly included in the literary-historical tendencies Bridgman calls the colloquial style) sometimes does not evince strong mimetic voice and does not always generate a strong illusion that it is transcribing speech. Faulkner, on the other hand, surely qualifies as one of the most strongly "voiced," "oral," or "colloquial" writers in American fiction, yet as Bridgman admits, much of his prose hardly fits the three characteristics of colloquial style quoted above.[22]

Transcription does not turn on how accurately an author mimics a given dialect, but on the operation of literary conventions of written discourse. In the broadest sense, then, "transcription of speech" is a huge topic that transcends the boundaries of what is here called mimetic voice, spilling over on the historical side into broad trends in prose style, and on the formal side into the relationship of speech to writing inherent in our phonetic alphabet. Considered more narrowly, as one of the functions productive of mimetic voice, "transcription" refers to the process of enhancing the illusion of speech by *altering* alphabetical, lexical, grammatical, and syntactical norms to encourage readers to regard a certain portion of written discourse as spoken *and as sounding distinct from other discourse in the same text*. Transcription differentiates mimetic voice from other discourses within a text on the basis of its imaged sound. Transcribed speech may be distinct from other writing in the same text that we do not treat as speech, distinct from some other transcribed speech in the same text, as well as distinct from an implied standard speech. Faulkner's skill as a regional linguist in choosing the phonetic spellings through which he graphically renders nonstandard word sounds—that is, whether "jest" is a more aptly chosen phonetic spelling for the word "just" than, say, "jist"—is of far less concern for mimetic voice than how his choices function in relation to each other within the fiction's discourse. What matters is how consistent his choices are, how reflective of narrative needs and of implied social values, how transcription blends and contrasts differing voices into a dialogic mix.

When we consider transcription as more a matter of arranging verbal relationships within a text than of recording actual speakers, we discover how widely Faulkner varies his dialect renderings, constantly shifting the relationships his texts establish among represented speech acts, relationships that sometimes follow linguistic class lines, but sometimes do not, and in fact do not always accord with personal differences among characters. "The moment, the character, the rhythm of the speech, compels its own dialect," Faulkner said (*LG* 128). Faulkner did not feel a need to preface his novels with explanatory notes like the one Twain included in *Huckleberry Finn*, listing by region the types of dialect imitated in the book. Yet he, too, could claim that "the shadings [among dialects] have not been done in a hap-hazard fashion, or by guess-work; but pains-takingly" (Twain 9). The pains Faulkner took, however, were more internal to the fiction than external to his region's sociolinguistic configurations. Only in such a context can we comprehend his remarkable statement that "I doubt if I ever used any dialect" (*LG* 128). Faulkner explained his statement by saying that he was too "busy trying to create on paper living people . . . to bother too much about style or about dialect" (*LG* 128). Even if Faulkner did not deliberately try to write speech as he heard it in his region, and it is hard to believe he did not try to capture the differing voices of Mississippi's blacks, poor country whites, village folk, town storekeepers, and town and city professionals, or imitate the dialects he "heard" in other writers like Joel Chandler Harris, Mark Twain, or George Washington Harris, it is nonetheless in terms of "living people" in the fiction that we can categorize his transcribed speech types. The short story "A Bear Hunt" (1934) provides a conveniently compact collection of Faulkner's three main classes of portrayed speaker:

BLACK

"Never much happened," he [Ash] says. "Dey jest went down de road a piece en atter a while hyer he come a-hickin' en a-blumpin' up de road wid de lant'un en de gun. They took de lant'un en de gun away frum him en took him up pon topper de mound en talked de Injun language at him fer a while. Den dey piled up some wood en fixed him on hit so he could git loose in a minute, en den one of dem come up de hill wid de fire, en he done de rest" (*CS* 78).

COUNTRY WHITE

Hit sho stopped that poker game. Hit taken three or four of them to drag him offen me, with Major turned in his chair with a set of threes in his hand, a-hammering on the table and hollering cusses. Only a right smart of the helping they done was stepping on my face and hands and feet. Hit was like a fahr—the fellows with the water hose done the most part of the damage. (*CS* 67)

TOWN COLLOQUIAL

He was even at this bear hunt of which he speaks, at the annual hunting camp of Major de Spain in the river bottom twenty miles from town, even though there was no one there to whom he might possibly have sold a machine, since Mrs. de Spain doubtless already owned one, unless she had given it to one of her married daughters, and the other man—the man called Lucius Provine—with whom he became involved, to the violent detriment of his face and other members, could not have bought one for his wife even if he would, without Ratliff sold it to him on indefinite credit. (*CS* 63)

These passages contain the salient features that distinguish the dialect types: the black speech uses "d" for "th," "atter" for "after," "jest" for "just," some elimination of "r" sounds (lant'un), "en" for "and," and some eye dialect in "frum." (Other speeches by Ash contain "wuz" for "was," "fo'," "betwixt," and "gwine.") Ratliff's country white dialect contains some of the same features as Ash's, such as "hit" for "it," "skeered," and "hyer," and both employ incorrect verb forms (the most common grammatical variation in literary versions of American Southern dialect). Ratliff, however, does not substitute "d" for "th," and his speech contains more fillers and vocal glides like "I reckon," "so," "be dog it," and "ere." The density of phonetic spelling is greater in the black speech. While Ratliff's depends more on occasional misspellings of words like "druv" for "drove," "mizzable" for "miserable," or "fahr" for "fire," Ash's speech phonetically alters a significant proportion of words (forty-one out of ninety-five words in the passage quoted). The town narrator remains anonymous but refers to himself in the first person, and is thus identifiable as a speaker. His speech manifests no phonetic spellings or eye dialect, relying instead on colloquial repetitions, phrases, and one grammatical irregularity (in the final clause beginning "without").

It would be misleading to generalize too much from these samples, however, for dialects throughout Faulkner's works show wide variation. As I suggested earlier, the representational purposes Faulkner serves grow out of the needs of a given story, of a given speech, or even of a given expressive moment within a passage, rather than out of any apparent desire to depict a group's dialect accurately. His fidelity is not to speech but to the discursive relationships his fiction requires, so verisimilitude of dialect is always relative. Thus blacks sometimes use "d" instead of "th" and sometimes do not; within a given story some black characters will use "d" for "th," and others will not. A single dialect speaker within a story may manifest a certain trait at one moment, and at other times not: Ash says "they" (instead of "dey") in the second sentence of the passage quoted from "A Bear Hunt." Ratliff uses the standard "just" instead of the colloquial "jest," but in other works he and other country white speakers use "jest" frequently. Such alternate spellings occur side by side, in a few cases within the same sentence. The boundaries between the dialects are not rigid, especially between country white and town colloquial, for a number of town speakers employ occasional country idioms. It is not always easy to discern an "inconsistency" in Faulkner's dialect writing from a deliberate variation. If a black character's speech in the manuscript to *The Sound and the Fury* is transcribed by substituting an apostrophe for a dropped "-or" in "po'," did any principle of verisimilitude dictate leaving the apostrophe off "po" in the same passage (Manuscript 138; *SF* Facsimile 140), or was the difference simply an oversight? Tommy, a poor white in *Sanctuary*, leaves "g" off words sometimes but not always: "blocking," "comin," "coming," and "stoppin."

The most intriguing (and most common) unexplained variance is that between "hit" and "it," perhaps reflecting Faulkner's "ear" or instinct for what word seemed right at the moment. Ab Snopes in *The Unvanquished* uses "hit" and "it" in the same paragraph (140). "Hit" is not used in some heavy black dialect in "Was" from *Go Down, Moses*, but "hit" is used in "Fire and the Hearth" and "Pantaloon and Black." In "Barn Burning" Sarty's mother uses "hit" and "it," while Sarty's sisters use "hit" consistently; Ab Snopes himself uses "it." *The Mansion* exhibits both "hit" and "it" in Mink's and Ratliff's dialect; both appear in a single sentence attributed to Ratliff (*M* 113).

Faulkner clearly let "the moment, the character, the rhythm of the speech" govern his choices of dialect traits. He understood that the needs of the reader make extensive eye dialect undesirable, and that it is better to suggest irregularities with a few carefully chosen features than to try to render a character's speech entirely in dialect, thus some apparent inconsistencies are nothing more than wise restraint (see *FU* 181). His career shows some trend away from heavy dialect toward more subtle versions. Most of the short stories revised for inclusion in novels had much of the eye dialect removed and the phonetic spelling reduced. Tom-tom's speech in "Centaur in Brass," "I tends to my business . . . What Turl does wid hisn ain't no trouble of mine" (*CS* 155), becomes in *The Town*, "I tend to my business . . . What Turl does with his aint none of mine" (*T* 19).[23] Yet we must be guarded in making generalizations about changes in dialect over the course of Faulkner's career. *Flags in the Dust* (1929) manifests more phonetic spelling than most later novels, largely because of Faulkner's more extensive use of apostrophes ("jes'," "'ere," "yo'," "drinkin'"). But *Go Down, Moses* (1940) contains his heaviest black dialect (heavier in some features than even the very early "Sunset" [1925] from *New Orleans Sketches*), and Ratliff's dialect in *The Mansion* (1959) is still laden with "hit" and "jest" and "knowed." In that late novel, instead of phonetic spelling by means of apostrophes, Faulkner gives Ratliff humorous phonetic spellings of more sophisticated words like "dee-neweyment," "Grinnich Village," "showfer," or "a-teelyer."

However flexibly rendered, dialect transcriptions ultimately signify social classes. Dialect defines class relationships among speakers, between speakers and narrators, and between speakers, narrators, and readers. The paradigm is that an educated and literate author, using standard language, reports (or "records") the unsophisticated nonstandard dialects of speakers who are less educated, usually poorer, and often of "inferior" ethnic or racial background. In a study of dialect differences in Joel Chandler Harris, Ives generalizes that "an author employs dialect writing to identify a character as a member of some social group to which neither author nor reader is presumed to belong"; and the greater the density of dialect features, the lower the social class ("Dialect Differentiation" 91–92). Actual linguistic differences may be regional, but dialect in American *literature* invariably reflects other distinctions as well. Few authors record regional traits unless those also signal class differences: an educated Southerner like Joel Chandler Harris may have said "Ah" for "I," but only lower-class characters say "Ah" in his stories (Ives, "Theory of Literary Dialect" 163). Ives points out that the letter "r" is frequently a variable in American dialects. Harris probably said "poor" without pronouncing the "r," but in his stories he writes "poor" for standard speakers and "po'" only for substandard dialect speakers. "An author will fail to represent many features of his character's speech which may be regionally characteristic but which carry no implication of inferiority or 'difference' within those regions where they are formed" (163).

Although Faulkner was a modernist experimental writer responsive to the same cultural currents as the likes of Joyce, Eliot, Conrad, and Proust, he also inherited the American Southwest Humor tradition of transcribed vernacular story writing. Southwest Humor, beginning in the 1830s, employed devices for graphically imitating nonstandard speech sounds largely for comic and satiric effect. Originated by educated writers who wanted to entertain their primarily Eastern audiences by reporting the bizarre antics of American rustics, Southwest Humor reinforced class and regional stereotypes—though as the century progressed and Jacksonian democracy spread political power and respect somewhat more equitably among different regions, Southwest Humor increasingly took rustic figures seriously, even if it did not always depict them favorably. The vernacular speaker's talk encroached on the educated frame narration until, by George Washington Harris's *Sut Lovingood's Yarns* (1867), the Tennessee hillbilly was doing nearly all the narrating. With Twain's *The Adventures of Huckleberry Finn* vernacular style became high art, savoring rather than satirizing Huck's talk, itself created out of subtle turns of phrase, imagery, and syntactical rhythms rather than phonetic spelling or cumbersome eye dialect. Faulkner admired both Twain's Huck Finn and Harris's Sut Lovingood, though in his dialect writing he is closer to Twain than to Harris because he relies less on phonetic spelling or eye dialect and more on grammatical irregularities, imagery, and pacing.[24]

The evolution of Southwest Humor should remind us that the roots of dialect writing grow in parody; no matter how sympathetically an author portrays a colloquial speaker, he or she never merely records dialect. Speech rendered in dialect is always displayed and stylized, placed before the reader as *different* speech. And the differences are never innocent. The presence of dialect establishes discursive versions of cultural hierarchies that reflect upon each other, whether the "superior" standard speaker displays dialect in order to ridicule it, or whether the dialect turns back upon standard speech to expose and parody its pretensions. Genette argues that "'stylized' . . . 'imitation' is always a *caricature* through accumulation and accentuation of specific characteristics" (*Narrative Discourse* 184). Bakhtin makes the more inclusive claim that all representation of another's speech, whether stylized or not, is a parodic gesture (*The Dialogical Imagination* 51,

61, 322, 340). When Faulkner sets Rev. Shegog's two modes of speech side by side in *The Sound and the Fury* he is clearly leading us to value the "substandard" dialect over "correct" English. Shegog can speak either standard white or negroid dialect, but only the latter speaks to the hearts of his listeners. Yet the reversal of values in the novel works only because it is just that, a *reversal*. The parodic hierarchy created by stylized speech often challenges the norms that permit display of "rustic" speech; but the hierarchy never vanishes. It might be argued, in fact, that Faulkner (consciously or not) gave Rev. Shegog the power of standard speech to verify his credentials as a purveyor of the heart's truth: Shegog chooses to "descend" into "negroid . . . intonation, pronunciation" as a rhetorical ploy to win his listeners' attention; he condescends to speak their language.[25]

Go Down, Moses nicely illustrates the hierarchy of speech: Faulkner adjusts black dialect to match characters' self-perceptions and to play on white prejudices. In "The Fire and the Hearth" Lucas and Molly Beauchamp speak a dialect closer to town colloquial than to other black speech. Except for occasional phonetic spellings like "whar," their idiom relies mainly on nonstandard verb forms like "you needs to" for its transcribed effect. Lucas's daughter Nat, however, and her fiancé George Wilkins speak a dialect heavy with phonetic spelling and eye dialect: "uz" for "was," "shurfs" for "sheriffs," "ifn," "fotch," "shet," "fo," "leffin" for "let," and so on. Nat and especially George play clownish roles in a way the proud Lucas never could, even though the story of his whiskey and his search for gold is broadly comic; compared to Lucas, George is what the judge calls him, a "jimber-jawed clown" (*GDM* 74). As usual, however, the parody cuts both ways, for Nat and George play on Lucas the same kind of manipulative trick he has used successfully on whites like Roth Edmonds, and they get what they want from Lucas (married with "a cookstove. The back porch fixed. A well" [69]). Language thus defines roles among black characters, just as it does in more sinister fashion between blacks and whites, where the sign of an "uppity nigger" is the refusal to say "sir" or "mister." Lucas, to save his marriage, condescends in his own way to call Roth Edmonds "Mister" (129).

"Pantaloon in Black" dramatizes Faulkner's starkest parodic reversal of linguistic stereotyping. He gives to Rider and the other black characters the heaviest dialect in all his fiction (including "Ah" for "I," a borrowing, one suspects, from the Southwest tradition of Joel Chandler Harris that may itself deliberately parody that literary mode). " 'Dass awright, bossman,' he said, his voice equable . . . 'Ah aint drunk. Ah just cant wawk

straight fer dis yar money weighin me down'" (*GDM* 152). This is the
idiom of the stage darky, the minstrel-show clown, the "pantaloon." As
does Twain with Jim in *Huckleberry Finn*, Faulkner wants us to see
through the stereotype to the heroic man's universally human emotions;
indeed, Rider is more an American mythic figure than he is a clown, a Paul
Bunyan who can hoist monstrous logs singlehanded. Rider has lost his
wife and grieves with a hopeless intensity that "raises" him above the status of "nigger." Faulkner directs his parody at whites who remain blind to
the humanity in blacks, whites personified in the deputy, who despairs to
understand "them damn niggers" as he tells his own wife, "His [Rider's]
wife dies on him. All right. But does he grieve?" (154, 155). But the final
irony of the story, and it is an irony that no amount of reverse parody on
Faulkner's part could overcome, is that the reader remains "superior" to
Rider within that linguistic hierarchy that defines clownish *language* even
as we are instructed to discover the noble and grieving heart beneath the
clown's verbal mask.[26]

I am not suggesting that "Pantaloon in Black," any more than Shegog's
sermon in *The Sound and the Fury*, is poorly realized or insincere (although
Faulkner too easily sentimentalizes black speakers). We need not be cynical about the values inherent in rendered dialect to recognize its inevitably
parodic play, for parody need not be malicious; Shegog's dialect parodies
as it is parodied; speakers of heavy black dialect can be, as human beings,
jimber-jawed clowns or grief-stricken, tragic victims. And black characters "put on" dialect, of course, for the benefit of whites, as the Deacon
does in *The Sound and the Fury* (compare *SF* 111 with 112–13; 120 with
121–22). Faulkner clearly cherished the voices he recorded and in many
ways his oeuvre celebrates the value of his region's nonstandard common
speech. We saw in examining phenomenal voice that its most positive versions were dialect voices of blacks enriching the background against which
events occur. Elnora's songs from *Flags in the Dust* are the best examples
(see the discussion in chapter 1). When Faulkner nostalgically quotes
black speech that serves some ritualistic function in a milieu like the hunt,
he increases the density of dialect transcription. The Negro stable boys'
"short, mellow, meaningless cries" in the opening of "Fox Hunt" use
"ketch," while the groom's talk has "catch." Isham rouses the hunters in
"Delta Autumn" with "Raise up and get yo foa clock coffy" (*GDM* 354).

These speakers and narrators express more in their dialects than just
individual idioms. Every speaking person's unique discourse is also caught
up in an ideology of rhetoric that reflects implied social or cultural values

that may or may not be portrayed and commented on overtly in a story's thematic patterns. Class and racial assumptions are embedded in the way authorial, narrative, and mimetic voices blend with each other within a text as well as in the way an author draws character types from the world outside the fiction and displays their speech in mimetic transcription. Assumptions about where readers fit into the social hierarchies about which they are reading tend to rigidify discursive relationships. An author plays mimic in transcribing speech, and mimicry depends, as T. S. Eliot pointed out, upon the reader recognizing both the speech imitated and the speech imitating "in the *in*completeness of the illusion" (104). This is the "double-voiced" quality that Bakhtin finds at the heart of the novel as a genre: "A speaking person's discourse in the novel is not merely transmitted or reproduced; it is, precisely, *artistically represented* and thus—in contrast to drama—it is represented *by means of* (authorial) *discourse*" (*The Dialogical Imagination* 332). The mimic always remains in some sense superior to the speech (or gestures) imitated, for he or she possesses mastery of both the originating voice and the mimicked voice. Frame tales (like those in Southwest Humor) depend upon a conventional rhetorical hierarchy that never breaks down, even when the author intends to expose and ridicule the "superior" voice. As Myra Jehlen says of Lucas Beauchamp (of "The Fire and the Hearth"), "we and the white McCaslins [are always] talking over his head" (Jehlen 122). Readers of dialect fiction find themselves in the position of "the whites" vis à vis black speakers, a positioning that renders even internally vocalized enactment of dialect a kind of parody: the act of reading becomes in this sense a parodic performance regardless of thematic intent. Furthermore, dialect writing epitomizes a condition of all literature that evokes mimetic voice. Transcribed speech, the product of mimicry, always occupies an inferior position in relation to the diegetic discourse of its production. The mimetic voices we hear are always secondary, indulged and condescended to by the reader who shares (as an audience shares the mimic's knowledge) the author's power over all the voices.[27]

Faulkner always displays black dialect with a certain indulgent effect, even when the plot offers clear evidence of the speaker's moral superiority. Dialect voices are always heard from within a hierarchy, so that the place occupied by black idiom—though not always by black characters—is the "lowest"; there is no "inferior" dialect for a black narrator to mimic, unless it be another black's. Lucas Beauchamp could mimic George Wilkins because Lucas holds a special place as a McCaslin descendent in the social strata of Yoknapatawpha County; but George could mimic no one. It is thus no accident that black characters do not narrate significant portions of any story or novel in Faulkner, that even *Go Down, Moses* lacks "the personal validation of an independent black voice" (Jehlen 124).[28] Michael Grimwood attributes this absence of black narrators to the split between William Faulkner the artist, with "his sophisticated, analytical intelligence brooding upon what he regarded as simple customary spirits" and Bill Faulkner the man, who cared for the individual black persons he knew. Grimwood thus may be quite right to say that, for Faulkner (Grimwood writes here of "the mature Faulkner" of *Go Down, Moses*), "the most definitive characteristic of Negroes—certainly more definitive than any mere appearance or custom, and even more definitive than their capacity for 'endurance'—was their alienation from literary formulations of experience" (248). Faulkner wrote from within a deeply rooted stratification of imaged speech that, as it surely made itself felt in Faulkner's life, imposed itself on his fiction and prohibited certain voices from assuming certain roles.

Although many country white characters do narrate in Faulkner's stories and novels, their talk, too, is subject to the rhetorical hierarchy of imaged speech. The story "Wash" (which became part of *Absalom, Absalom!*) plays out its drama against the assumed status of poor whites and blacks. The blacks at Sutpen's plantation ridicule Wash as trash: "'Niggers?' they repeated; 'niggers?' laughing now. 'Who him, calling us niggers?'" They mock Wash as having "nothing else but dat shack down yon dat Cunnel wouldn't *let* none of us live in," and they bar him entry to Sutpen's house: "Stop right dar, white man. Stop right whar you is. You ain't never crossed dese steps whilst Cunnel here, and you ain't ghy' do hit now" (*CS* 537). Wash speaks a heavy country dialect filled with as much eye dialect as the black speech: "'Well, Kernel,' Wash said, 'they kilt us but they ein't whupped us yet, air they?'" (*CS* 539). "Ef Kernel wants to give hit to you, I hope you minded to thank him" (*CS* 541). Wash's speech must be heavily stylized to lower it to its appropriate level "beneath" black speech.

With some exceptions, narrators in Faulkner can transcribe speech in a dialect equal to or "inferior to" their own, but cannot transcribe speech from a higher level. Which is to say, of course, that what was discussed earlier as a *discursive* relationship between diegetic and mimetic levels is always also an implied ideological relationship, a difference in the power granted to possessors of the accepted standard language. Embedded narration can be less sophisticated than the discourse that contains it, but not more. A town narrator can "set the stage" for Ratliff and mimic him, but Ratliff never "sets the stage" for a town narrator. No story has as its frame narrator a "rustic" like Ratliff who then reports a story as told by a town narrator. In *The Town* and *The Mansion* Ratliff collaborates on more or less equal rhetorical footing with Gavin Stevens and Charles Mallison, but much is made of his heavy dialect (as of his visit to New York, where he is out of place yet proves to be a rustic master of urban sophistication). In Ratliff, Faulkner comes the closest to granting dialect speech the full and substantial credentials of narrative voice. What is missing, however, is indicative: Ratliff does not report more sophisticated narration without commenting upon it as being more sophisticated. He can tell us what Gavin Stevens said, and what words Stevens used, and he can gently mock Stevens, but he usually mispronounces "big" words ("dee-neweyment," "meelee," etc.). He uses his own dialect to record Stevens's talk or characters' thoughts, as when he imagines Chick thinking of Linda, *"Hell fire, she's durn nigh old as maw"* (*M* 113; see also Linda's imagined thoughts, *M* 144).

Faulkner enforces the hierarchy of imaged speech in other ways, too. When a character quotes another's speech, the quoting character may use an even more extreme dialect than the authorial discourse employs to transcribe the quoted speaker's words. In *Go Down, Moses*, for example, this technique emphasizes whites' perceptions of blacks as inferior subjects of their parody. The deputy quotes Rider as using "jest" when Rider's talk always shows "just" (157, 143); a deputy in "The Fire and the Hearth" quotes Lucas as having said, "Git the axe" (63) when Lucas, according to the diegetic narrator, actually said "Get the axe" (65); the editor quotes Molly Beauchamp as asking "Is you gonter to put hit in de paper" when her speech elsewhere in the story "Go Down, Moses" never substitutes "de" for "the" or "hit" for "it" (383).[29]

The reverse, however, does not obtain. A colloquial narrator virtually never quotes "superior" speech accurately or as more sophisticated than the speaker's already standard idiom. Standard speech is not mimicked. There are certain exceptions: child narrators in such stories as "Shingles for the Lord" and "Two Soldiers," and Vardaman in *As I Lay Dying*, are capable of reporting words beyond their educational level, though in the case of "Two Soldiers" the boy narrator mispronounces a word like "automatic" as "artermatic." Such child narrations are inherently ironic, for the child reveals more than he can know or understand about events and about himself. Certainly, too, Benjy Compson transcribes speech beyond his level—as any speech is beyond his level—but Benjy does not employ heavy dialect when reporting black speech, as do Quentin, Jason, and the authorial narrator of the novel's fourth section. Mimicry, collaboration, and irony are all possible treatments of colloquial dialect speech; but dialect speakers do not perform these rhetorical acts upon others. Faulkner could reverse the direction of parody on the levels of theme, character, and plot, but even he could not or did not easily alter the hardened destiny of characters manifested in their written speech.

AS I LAY DYING

As I Lay Dying is a virtual laboratory for experimentation with mimetic voice. Few texts interrogate so insistently—yet without abandoning—our shared expectations about the recording of speech. I suggested at the beginning of this chapter that the novel's title introduces speech into the text in an unusual way. Throughout its fifty-nine sections the novel employs, almost with a vengeance, the conventions of speech presentation to evoke truly "hearable" voices. The polyphonic sections, each headed by the name of one of the fifteen first-person narrators, exhibit striking variations in tone: we hear the dialect of poor white Mississippi farmers, the talk of small-town shopkeepers, tense and fast-paced narrative, richly metaphoric digression, and philosophically charged speculation burdened by Latinate diction and convoluted syntax. In narrative sections that range from one sentence ("My mother is a fish") to ten pages of elaborate Faulknerian rhetoric, *As I Lay Dying* forces us to treat unspeakable discourse as the speech of improbable characters—in one section a carpenter numbers his reasons for building a coffin "on the bevel," in another a decomposing corpse reminisces. The novel is fundamentally spoken; voices emerge from an eloquence of the spoken word that permits shifts into and out of differing registers of fictional discourse. Faulkner described *As I Lay Dying* as a tour de force, and from the perspective of mimetic voice it is truly that (*FU* 1).

André Bleikasten interprets the configuration that governs the novel's structure and themes as a "circular pattern." The characters, outsiders as well as family members, cluster around the remains of Addie Bundren in a "circle . . . made up of all those still alive who gather around the body, suddenly brought face to face with the enigma of death" (*Faulkner's* As I

Lay Dying 47). The circle, Bleikasten says, is one of "reciprocal illumina-
tion" wherein the differing narrative viewpoints shine like "little
lamps . . . illuminating one particular aspect of the central figure and sit-
uation" or like "reflecting mirrors . . . throwing an oblique and intermit-
tent light on Addie's personality [and] testify[ing] to the persistent effects
of her dark radiance" (47). Bleikasten's apt figure of the circular clustering
around Addie and his metaphors of lamps and mirrors fit well with the
novel's persistent visual imagery—its frequent descriptions of eyes, of
colors, of the day's fading light, of perspective created by distance and
movement. Voice, however, also plays a crucial role in orchestrating the
relationships among those who gather around Addie's corpse. Modulations
in voice existentially place each isolated character within that field of famil-
ial and communal consciousness focused around Addie. The mourners
cluster around Addie as might a chorus: besides existing as an actor in the
novel's drama, or more precisely in each other's fictions, every persona in
As I Lay Dying exists by virtue of his or her own voice; each character is
defined at any given moment by the modulations of his or her speech into
other registers of expression. The analog of a circle, with the void of death
at its center, reflects a static, symbolic significance created by the family
relations and the mythically cyclical funeral journey; but only a description such as "voices come out of the air, flowing together and on" (*AILD*
Tull 86) can capture the fluctuations of the novel's soundful language, the
play of voices that constitutes its discursive significance.

Nowhere is the truth of Barthes's emphatic assertion that "*the character
and the discourse are each other's accomplices*" (*S/Z* 178) more ingeniously
borne out than in *As I Lay Dying*. While this principle operates in all
fictional discourse, and particularly in the conventions of appropriate
speech that govern mimetic voice, the collaboration between voice and
character in *As I Lay Dying* takes a perverse form: consciousness emerges
not from appropriate speech, but from the *in*appropriate disruption of mimetic voice. In those moments when mimetic voice "breaks down," when
speech is dis-illusioned, we discover character. The illusion of speech un-
conventionally generated in a title, where some "I" speaks of lying and
dying, generates a power of voice that transcends mimesis.

As I Lay Dying constructs its verbal world, and its characters' expressive
identities, by first generating convincing mimetic voice and then either
heightening or disrupting the illusion of speech in a manner that articulates a given speaker's consciousness in its relation to others. Faulkner's
typical rhetorical gesture places the reader within imaged speech and then

disturbs the discursive illusion so that the mimetic voice we hear translates into another register, another mode of voice—the phenomenal, the psychic, even the oratorical. Faulkner makes speech an index to character not, as in conventional realistic fiction, by recording it "faithfully" and "consistently," but by disrupting such verisimilitude. The text renders identity as a felt and constantly changing verbal relationship to others. The fictional entities whose names we know (Darl, Cash, Tull) possess personalities distilled out of their speech; but because their speech defines them in relation to others, their talk escapes the gabble of idiolects to move into a shared, communal field of verbal expression, a not always harmonic choir of living voices.

The monologues differ greatly, especially on first reading, in the degree to which each experiments with conventional presentation of speech. Faulkner employs this strategy in virtually all the monologues, not merely in those most obviously imitative of a character's stream of consciousness. It is easy to see, for example, how he translates the illusion of speech into a more purely *written* discourse in Cash's first section, where he lists the reasons he built the coffin on the bevel. The numbered list transforms a potentially spoken explanation into a visual, documentary analog of Cash's orderly mental habits. To illustrate the play with mimetic voice, however, I will examine a less patently odd section, one that heightens rather than disrupts familiar conventions of mimetic voice, yet where individual expressive identity nonetheless emerges from within the text's field of verbal relationships.

By any standard of verisimilitude readers certainly hear Peabody and Anse Bundren speaking in Peabody's first section:

> He and Anse are on the porch when I come out, the boy sitting on the steps, Anse standing by a post, not even leaning against it, his arms dangling, the hair pushed and matted up on his head like a dipped rooster. He turns his head, blinking at me.
> "Why didn't you send for me sooner?" I say.
> "Hit was jest one thing and then another," he says. "That ere corn me and the boys was aimin to git up with, and Dewey Dell a-takin good keer of her, and folks comin in, a-offerin to help and sich, till I jest thought . . ."
> "Damn the money," I say. "Did you ever hear of me worrying a fellow before he was ready to pay?"
> "Hit aint begrudgin the money," he says. "I jest kept

a-thinkin . . . She's goin, is she?" The durn little tyke is sitting on
the top step, looking smaller than ever in the sulphur-colored light.
That's the one trouble with this country: everything, weather, all,
hangs on too long. Like our rivers, our land: opaque, slow, violent;
shaping and creating the life of man in its implacable and brooding
image. "I knowed hit," Anse says. "All the while I made sho. Her
mind is sot on hit." (*AILD*, Peabody 40–41; 43–44; ellipses in original)

All five functions for engendering mimetic voice in written prose operate
in the monologue. Peabody indirectly describes Anse's speech or manner
of talking in his image of Anse as a "dipped rooster . . . blinking at me,"
and he directly describes Addie's voice as "harsh and strong." We know
that Peabody and Anse communicate because they answer each other and
because the monologue as a whole possesses the implied vocalization common to Faulkner's first-person narratives. The section opens in a typically
colloquial manner with a temporal marker ("When Anse finally sent for
me . . .") plus Peabody's expressions of how he came to be involved and
what he thought and said about the events he relates to us. Peabody's
section itself, and different speech acts reported by Peabody, are differentiated and clearly identified by speech tags, paragraphing, and punctuation. The name "Peabody" at the section's beginning, and the colloquial
speech tags "I say" and "he says" within the monologue, attribute words
to the appropriate speakers. Peabody's discourse transcribes his own town
dialect (evincing rhythms of speech and an occasional "damn" or "durn,"
but virtually no phonetic spelling), and Peabody mimics Anse's country
white dialect: " 'Hit was jest one thing and then another,' he says. 'That
ere corn me and the boys was aimin to git up with, and Dewey Dell a-takin
good keer of her.' "

In most ways, then, this passage typifies Faulkner's methods of creating
mimetic voice, both characters' voices and those of character-narrators.
But certain oddities in Peabody's expression emphasize two identifying
traits in his relations with the Bundrens. When Peabody quotes Anse we
note the extreme version of country white dialect. Anse's talk has a high
density of phonetic spelling, higher than in most other speech in *As I Lay
Dying*; indeed, Anse in other sections does not exhibit much eye dialect at
all—no "hit," no "jest," and so on. "She'll want to start right away. I know
her. I promised her I'd keep the team here and ready, and she's counting
on it" (*AILD*, Darl 17). This technique of allowing the density of dialect to

vary in accord with the narrator who reports it was noted earlier. Peabody, as an educated town professional, reinforces the distinction between his own speech and Anse's by stylizing Anse's country pronunciation; other narrators, like Tull or Darl, transcribe "it" instead of "hit" in Anse's speech because they inhabit the same dialectic level as Anse, whereas Peabody is the "superior" speaker. In his frustration with Anse and his disdain for Anse's laziness, Peabody parodies (deliberately, we can assume) Anse's country talk. The mimetic consistency of imitated dialect here (as elsewhere in Faulkner) gives way to the need to establish a sociolinguistic hierarchy, which in turn helps define Peabody's expressive identity.

The illusion of speech is strong in Peabody's narrative partly because of its colloquial mannerisms. Faulkner simultaneously augments his voice with passages that contain hints of the allusive intertextual oratorical voice, either because of the diction or because they propound general ideas attributable to an authoritative "literary" presence more than to Dr. Peabody the fictional character. "Like our rivers, our land: opaque, slow, violent; shaping and creating the life of man in its implacable and brooding image." Such a description does not so much violate the verisimilitude of Peabody's verbal capabilities (as passages in Darl's and Vardaman's sections do) as it intensifies the expressive purpose Peabody must serve through his voice.

There are hints, too, of Peabody's internal, psychic voice. His colloquial narration turns subtly into interior monologue in two ways. First, past-tense narration switches to present tense in the course of the section. The recounting of events gives over to the recording of impressions as he experiences them. The opening recounts the past, as Peabody tells what he thought "when Anse finally sent for me." When he arrives at the Bundren farm ("When I reach the spring") the tense shifts in accord with his arrival in the family's presence. Not only does the present-tense narration indicate more immediate "mental" experience than does the conventional story-telling past tense, but also the *shift* in itself signifies Peabody's emergence from an objectively distant posture vis-à-vis the Bundrens into a concerned if frustrated sharing of their experience of Addie's death. (As we shall see, Tull's sections shift verb tenses even more subtly.) Peabody's narration also turns into psychic voice in his attention to Addie's eyes and to Vardaman, that "durn little tyke." Peabody notes, in highly impressionistic imagery, how Addie looks at him "like [her eyes] touch us, not with sight or sense, but like the stream from a hose touches you, the stream at the instant of impact as dissociated from the nozzle as though it had never been there" (39–40; 43). Peabody reacts to Vardaman through-out the section, always aware of him (though only once referring to him by name), always noting his whereabouts in each shift of scene, even though focusing his conscious attention elsewhere. "The boy overtakes us"; "She looks at me then at the boy"; "He and Anse are on the porch when I come out"; "The durn little tyke is sitting on the top step." Peabody senses what later sections will bear out, that Vardaman regards him with terrified loathing because he believes Peabody's arrival has caused his mother's death.

The transcription of excessive dialect, the hints of an augmenting or-atorical voice, and the record of interior impression all disturb the surface of mimetic voice in Peabody's section to place him appropriately within the cluster of voices weaving their self-referring discourse around the dying Addie. The novel sustains its strategy of mixing voices throughout, though the tactics vary considerably, depending always on a speaker's relation to the Bundrens and to Addie's death. Tull, for example, like Peabody, oc-cupies an intermediate position between the outside observers, who relate only one incident in the funeral journey, and the family members; his expressive identity reflects a shifting degree of closeness to the Bundrens, a modulating participation in their acts and emotions.

Unlike Peabody, Tull shares the Bundrens' country white dialect, both in his narration and when he quotes the Bundrens' speech. Though highly colloquial, Tull's speech shows little eye dialect, and only dialect words like "holp" or "mought" reflect a sound different from Peabody's more standard town speech. That Faulkner revised most of the extreme dialect out of the novel suggests his careful arrangement of relative dialect levels, as he reduced the stylizing effect of dialect and retained only words like "ere" or "a-hammering" that would be heard even by a speaker with the same speech habits.[30]

Tull's expressive identity, therefore, unlike Peabody's, does not differ from the Bundrens' in speech sounds or in the class distinctions implicit in dialect. His closeness to the family varies instead along a temporal axis reflected in verb tense. Faulkner manipulates the grammatical relationship between the time of enunciation and the time of the reported action in order to modulate Tull's physical and emotional involvement in Addie's death. Shifts between past and present narrative tenses signal concomitant changes in the intensity of Tull's involvement: when Tull is actually with the Bundrens, both physically and psychically, he employs present tense; when he is, or feels, separated from them, when he thinks about the family as from a distance, as an observer instead of a participant, he uses past tense. In his first section (beginning on page 25; 28) Tull sits on the Bundrens' porch waiting with Anse: he is present and involved, though like Anse he passively sits. In his second section (61; 65), however, when at home and thinking about Vardaman, he tries to comprehend the boy's actions more than he participates in them. He looks back on what happened the night Addie died, remembering and puzzling over the elemental injustice of Vardaman's grief. In this section Faulkner keeps Tull physically as well as temporally separated from events at the Bundren farm by bringing him back home ("It was long a-past midnight when we drove the last nail, and almost dust-dawn when I got back home and taken the team out and got back in bed" [65; 69]) before letting him tell us that Vardaman drilled holes in the coffin to let his mother breathe. None of the narration in this section occurs while Tull is at the Bundrens'. His thoughts, more than Vardaman's actions, constitute the real subject of his talk, so he renders these in a gnomic present ("Now and then a fellow gets to thinking. About all the sorrow and afflictions in this world" [63; 67]), while he recapitulates events in past tense.[31]

Some readers have regarded the shifts in verb tense in Tull's sections (and in others as well) as simple inconsistencies, assuming—quite wrongly, I believe—that Faulkner failed to engineer his experiments in tense with any credible skill. R. W. Franklin marshals the most complete case against the novel by arguing that Faulkner, when he began the story with present-tense stream of consciousness, failed to provide his reader with a "stable present" (which "traditionally . . . resides at the point of narration and is the present of the narrator") and so wrote himself into a corner that he could escape only by jumping out the window, by virtually abandoning the restrictive present tense. Franklin cites the manuscript as proof that in the twelfth section (Darl's fifth) Faulkner lost control of his present narrative tense and had to retreat to the more conventional past (Franklin 61). The first portion of the section, up to and including the first italics, was originally written in present tense. Faulkner then went through and wrote past forms above all the verbs in the first, roman-type portion without striking out the present forms. Faulkner was usually meticulous in crossing out whatever he changed in a manuscript. The roman portion after the first italics was written originally in past tense, but in the final published version all verbs throughout the section are in present tense. That this demonstrates Faulkner's confusion, as Franklin argues, is a highly speculative deduction. It is just as plausible that Faulkner did not cross out the present-tense verb forms because he was trying out the change, putting both tenses on paper to see which would sound more appropriate for Darl's voice at the moment. All of Darl's clairvoyant narrations are in present tense, so Faulkner's final decision is consistent. (Franklin fails to mention that the italicized portions in section 12 were never changed, as if Faulkner were considering putting roman type in one tense and italics in another—something he does in Darl's twelfth and sixteenth sections [127; 134 and 195; 202], as well as in Vardaman's fifth and eighth sections [136; 143 and 197; 204].)

Faulkner's careful experimentation allowed him to transcend the simple binary distinction of present time versus past time to make more subtle variations in verb tense that are integral to Tull's expressive voicing, for enunciatory questions matter here more than narrative ones. What is Tull's part in the choir of voices heard around Addie's death? Where is Tull when he speaks to us? In each of his monologues he assumes a different posture within the community and in relation to the family. The present-tense narration in his first section (25; 28), which quite simply reports the events he observes as they happen, differs considerably from the gnomic meditative tense in his second section (61; 65), when he generalizes on grief, God's justice, and Cora's useless piety. Tull's voice generates time in its own expressive terms, not in terms of the needs of the plot; time becomes a *product* of Tull's voice more than something external that his discourse reflects or imitates in his choice of tense. Tull's third section (75, 80), the funeral, begins with a brief exchange rendered in past tense with Armstid and Quick about Peabody's team, then shifts to present as Tull's attention focuses on Anse ("Anse meets us at the door"). Present narration continues until Tull describes the coffin, and how the women laid Addie in it backward; the drawing of the "clock-shape" calls sudden attention to Tull's account as retrospective and even as *written*, for one cannot say ⊂‾‾‾‾⊃.[32] When Tull's attention turns to Cash, and he tries to console him about the way the women have ruined his work, he continues to report the talk of the other men. His attention to Cash pushes that talk into the background, however, so Faulkner puts the voices in italics and removes speaker identification, as Tull is not listening closely enough to note who speaks which lines. Tull then reports the funeral itself, but only as it affects him, that is, as he feels the power of phenomenal voice:

> In the house *the women begin to sing*. . . . *The song ends*; the voices quaver away with a rich and dying fall. *Whitfield begins*. His

voice is bigger than him. It's like they are not the same. It's like he is one, and his voice is one. . . . *Somebody in the house begins to cry.* It sounds like her eyes and voice were turned back inside her. . . . *Whitfield stops at last. The women sing again.* In the thick air it's like their voices come out of the air, flowing together and on in the sad, comforting tunes. When they cease it's like they hadn't gone away. . . . *Then they finish.* . . .
    On the way home Cora is still singing. (81–82; 85–86; my italics)

This passage records movement through time marked by the voices Tull hears (the women singing, Whitfield eulogizing, Cora still singing) instead of by minutes and hours; time passes in the presence of voice. Tull's impression of the funeral becomes the time "span" here, with each change in voice (the sentences I have emphasized) serving as a temporal marker. Franklin faults Faulkner for jumping too abruptly from the funeral to the trip home, but the voices carry over into the trip ("Cora is still singing") so this, too, belongs to the voiced time period of the funeral itself. An external sequential time pattern gives way to time's expressive voicing.

The italicized portion that follows the description of the funeral (82; 86–87) has a detached quality similar to that of the italicized dialogue going on in the background when Tull talks to Cash. The attempt to persuade Anse to get started for Jefferson seems more half remembered than immediately experienced by Tull, as if only fragments remained in his awareness. The past tense helps create this impression, as does the jumbled sequence within the passage (Tull refers to Anse as still waiting after he tells us the boys have returned home and the family has started for Jefferson). Only bits and pieces have stuck in Tull's memory; these are all we get because these suffice to indicate the incident's importance to Tull. The past tense in the final portion of the funeral section, when the Tulls find Vardaman fishing at the slough, not only creates a slight mental distancing from the farm and funeral (the Tulls are now a mile away), but it also is consistent with the past-tense narration in Tull's second section (61; 65) in which he puzzles over Vardaman's behavior. Tull certainly experiences Vardaman in the immediacy of the moment, and thus we might expect present-tense narration, but the boy assumes a significance in the expressive voicing of Tull's consciousness almost always as someone pondered rather than someone faced in the present instant without time for speculation.

Peabody's section (37; 40) exhibits a change in tense from past to present concomitant with Peabody's arrival at the Bundren farm. Faulkner extends this tactic in Tull's fourth section (109; 117) when Tull joins the Bundrens at the river. By beginning with past and changing to present tense, Faulkner causes the past to continue into the present; what was and what is blend into a single progression of Tull's enunciation. The movement in enunciatory time tracks Tull's gradual passage from his own cotton field to the riverside, from the moments prior to his joining the family to his sharing their examination and crossing of the flood-swollen waters. The opening sentence states in simple, definite past tense that he rode from his field to the river: "After they passed I taken the mule out and looped up the trace chains and followed" (109; 117). When he arrives and first describes the Bundrens looking at the river, Tull uses more indefinite verb forms that depict a continuing past time: "was setting," "was watching," "was looking" (109–10; 117–18). And before talk commences in the present tense, Tull describes the river in a frequentative tense that refers to repeated action going on in the past and carrying on into the future: "Sometimes a log *would* get shoved over the jam and float on, rolling and turning, and we *could* watch it go on to where the ford used to be. It *would* slow up" (110; 118, my italics). Only then does true present-tense narration begin: " 'But that don't show nothing,' I say. . . . We watch the log. The gal is looking at me again" (110; 118–119).[33] The narrating discourse makes no simple jump from past to present but traces out a controlled progression in enunciation, in voiced experience, from past, through continuous past, to frequentative past, to present tense.

In his fifth section (123; 130) Tull crosses the submerged bridge with Anse, Dewey Dell, and Vardaman, and because of his direct participation in the action we might expect present-tense narration. But Tull vocalizes this moment more as an observer than as a participant: "Like it couldn't be me here, because I'd have had better sense than to done what I just done. And when I looked back and saw the other bank and saw my mule standing there where I used to be and knew that I'd have to get back there someway, I knew it just couldn't be. . . . When I looked back at my mule it was like he was one of these here spy-glasses and I could look at him standing there and see all the broad land and my house sweated outen it" (124–25; 131–32). Tull's last section (138; 145) brings Cora's judgment of Anse, plus Tull's rejection of that judgment, to bear on the events at the river. The Tulls look back on what Vernon has just been through, so they use past tense. The final portion of the section, after the brief dialogue with Cora, describes an action in a vivid, narrative past tense since this experience in Tull's memory demonstrates the irrelevance of Cora's contradictory explanation for the incredible scene Tull has witnessed—Jewel holding the wagon alone against the current, saving his mother (as she predicted) from the flood waters.

Like Tull, other speakers are existentially placed within the field of communal consciousness around Addie's death by the manner in which the text maintains or disrupts the illusion of their speech. As Tull's voiced relation with the Bundrens often has a spatial equivalent (depending on his physical place vis-à-vis the Bundrens), so the novel's imagery provides appropriate figural correlations between the speaker as character, the speaker's voice, and the speaker's place. For someone like Cash, or Cora Tull, "place" in this existential sense is as definite and secure as feet and inches, the number of eggs saved out for baking, or a numbered list of reasons for building a coffin on the bevel. Jewel expresses his place in the equally definite vision of himself on a hill protecting Addie, above the others, throwing rocks down upon them. Anse, who fills his talk with biblical rhetoric, sees himself stoically absorbing the bad luck that travels a road, and reasons that if men were meant to travel then God would have made them horizontal like snakes instead of vertical like trees. Images of space, of shape and direction, and of time fill the talk of every Bundren. The pregnant Dewey Dell feels trapped in time, which she perceives in terms of her body: *"That's what they mean by the womb of time: the agony and the despair of spreading bones, the hard girdle in which lie the outraged entrails of events"* (106; 114–15). Vardaman desires the impossible security of an eternal present because he cannot comprehend change and the passage of time. And to Darl, acutely sensitive to the uncertainty of human existence, time and space become inextricably one—"the space between us [is] time: an irrevocable quality" (132; 139).

Except for the section describing the funeral (75–83; 80–87), Tull's monologues uphold a verisimilitude of spoken narration despite the manipulations of verb tense. In Vardaman's and Darl's monologues, however, Faulkner violates conventional mimetic voice more daringly, and in a manner more unsettling to many readers. Not only does he shift narrating tense as in Tull's sections, to play upon the gap between time of enunciation and time of reported action in a way appropriate to the narrator's momentary position in relation to others, but he also manipulates the functions of mimetic voice to create differences in speech that echo nuances of felt experience.

As he does in Tull's monologues, Faulkner shifts the tense of narration in accord with the speaker's experience. In Vardaman's sections he modulates tense to emphasize the boy's confused obsession with his mother's death. Vardaman can comprehend the way things are in the present, but he cannot understand or accept emotionally time's passage. Addie continues to live for Vardaman, either in her coffin or as a fish he has caught. When Darl is taken away to Jackson, Vardaman in his last monologue (239) can recognize the action of going away as past, but he asserts what is still "present" to him: *"My brother is Darl. . . . Darl is my brother. Darl. Darl"* (234; 241–42). Three of Vardaman's sections contain past-tense narration that does not indicate remembered events as much as it signals the boy's psychological disengagement compared to events rendered in present tense. In his fifth section (136; 143), for example, he describes his brothers' struggle in the river in unpunctuated, run-on narrative in past tense, as if the description of action rushes through his mind involuntarily. But what vividly engages his attention is the instant when Darl, who Vardaman hopes has "caught" Addie, comes up out of the water: the run-on narration abruptly stops and the print switches to italics and the tense to present, focusing Vardaman's consciousness on this crucial moment: *"Then he comes up out of the water. He comes a long way up slow before his hands do but he's got to have her got to so I can bear it"* (137; 144). When Darl comes out empty-handed, the past-tense (nonitalicized) narrative resumes.[34] In Vardaman's eighth section (197; 204) tense changes and italics also modulate the immediacy of Vardaman's experience. In present tense the narrative tells of Darl and Vardaman "listening" to Addie in her coffin, and of Vardaman waiting to find out where the buzzards go at night. While these events are in the foreground of his consciousness, seeing Darl set fire to Gillespie's barn remains in the background, less important to the boy than the coffin or the buzzards. So seeing Darl is recorded as memory, separated from the rest of the section by italics and past tense: *"And I saw something Dewey Dell told me not to tell nobody"* (198; 205). Vardaman's dream about the train in the Jefferson store window shifts in tense, as well, as dream and reality blur in Vardaman's mind and talk.[35]

Darl's monologues, like his psychic states, are complex and otherworldly, not "eye to eye with other folks," as Cash puts it (216; 223). He narrates mostly in present tense, for he experiences the world around him with maddening intensity, and his talk strangely mixes controlled description, colloquial chat, and figural richness that moves at will in time and place. The few past-tense passages (other than those in which he clearly is remembering past incidents, such as the story about Jewel working nights to buy the horse "the summer when he was fifteen" [113–22; 121–29]) suggest a detachment from whatever he describes. He narrates his four-teenth section (167; 172), for example, in past tense until his attention turns to Jewel and the horse in a final italicized passage rendered in pres-ent tense (169; 174). His sixteenth section (195; 202) scatters references to Jewel (all in present tense) among narrative sentences (in past tense) tell-ing of Cash and of the coffin. Jewel, Addie's favored child, her "one pearl of great price," commands Darl's obsessive attention; he cannot find his "place" among the family's voices because Jewel has literally displaced him in Addie's affection.

Darl's mental acuity ranges eloquently but frantically through time and space, mixing his clairvoyance with a tenuous hold on his identity in the real world. The intensity of his present-tense narration simultaneously creates and overrides the greatest implausibility in narrative point of view, an implausibility that itself signifies his personal alienation. He can narrate Addie's death (in his fifth section, 43; 46) as if present in her bedroom, but his literal distance from her (on his trip with Jewel to get lumber) more accurately reflects his place in the family. Later, while still on the trip with Jewel, Darl struggles to declare the nature of his existence within the flux of time and language by playing with words, with the past and present tense of the verb of existence:

> And since sleep is is-not and rain and wind are *was*, it is not. Yet the wagon *is*, because when the wagon is *was*, Addie Bundren will not be. And Jewel *is*, so Addie Bundren must be. And then I must be, or I could not empty myself for sleep in a strange room. And so if I am not emptied yet, I am *is*.
>
> How often have I lain beneath rain on a strange roof, thinking of home. (72; 76)[36]

But words only leave Darl with the despair of not knowing the true nature of his existence. By the last section his voice has lost all cohesive identity, for there is no place in time or language for Darl. He becomes disengaged from himself, narrating in the past tense and the third person—except when his mind pictures (in present tense) his family waiting by the wagon in Jefferson. Darl's voice takes him anywhere, but nowhere that it takes him can remain his place—except a cage in Jackson.[37]

For many readers the most troublesome violation of conventional expec-tations about speech and identity is not Darl's clairvoyance but his and (even more) Vardaman's sophisticated rhetoric. Faulkner attributes to un-educated farmers, one a young boy, diction and imagery beyond the range of most educated speakers. Readers have found discourse they cannot believe: Vardaman speaks of his brother's horse as "an unrelated scattering of components—snuffings and stampings; smells of cooling flesh and ammoniac hair; an illusion of co-ordinated whole of splotched hide and strong bones within which, detached and secret and familiar, an *is* different from my *is*" (52; 55). The grammar of free indirect discourse (in represented speech or thought) permits rhetoric beyond a character's competence because the character's actual words are not, technically, being reported: the discourse implies no communicative function, only a representational one. But signs of communicative context, such as the presence of an identified speaker-narrator and the use of present tense, normally take grammatical priority and thus return discourse to a communicative posture. Faulkner, however, sidesteps the grammar of *both* indirect *and* direct discourse—a double maneuver that has contributed to complaints of his "mismanagement." So implausible is Vardaman's rhetoric felt to be that Faulkner has been accused of botching the first-person point of view by arbitrarily substituting "I" for "he" or "she." The objection raised here derives from conventions of expressive identity. Vardaman as a person could not talk this way; therefore he is poorly employed as a narrator.[38] The loosening of the expected bond between voice and person sounds "unnatural" to the reader's ear because readers accept the representation of the person as an actuality that voice must match. Violations of point of view—Darl's ability to describe distant events, Addie's posthumous reminiscence—bother us less than Vardaman's description of the horse because Darl and Addie *sound* natural—natural, at least, to the person constituted by our reading. The unquestioned assumptions about voice and identity are strong indeed. Vardaman's voice catches us on the horns of the paradox John Barth's character Menelaus (quoted in the Introduction) expressed when he asserted that he was nothing but his voice: "this isn't the voice of Vardaman; this voice *is* Vardaman, all there is of him." Faulkner's play here makes us realize how much a character emerges *from* his voice: voice, that is to say, constitutes the person that the voice must be appropriate to.

Faulkner manipulates the grammar of represented speech in order to symbolize consciousness—not merely to express it, but to constitute it out of voice. Faulkner maneuvers conventional mimetic voice into providing material for states of mind. This is particularly evident in how narrators report the speech of other characters: divergence from standard narrative practice in reporting dialogue signals a variance in the narrator's attitude, stance, and subliminal position vis-à-vis others. Not only does a character possess mimetic voice in his or her own right as a narrator, but each narrating character creates the illusion of others' speech in how he or she reports it. So the *creation* of the illusion of speech becomes an act undertaken by characters and indicative of each narrator's unique position in the verbal world—that verbal world analogous to the fictional world of the farm and Addie's death. This tactic constitutes another double disturbance of mimetic voice's verisimilitude: both the narrator's speech and the quoted speech sound (and sometimes look) unconventional.

Voice in *As I Lay Dying* also interrogates the metaphysics of *individual* consciousness, revealing characters' secret selves by immersing them in a *communal* discourse, making their private thoughts a function of how they hear, respond to, and render each other's speech. Ultimately, *As I Lay Dying* depicts a community of voices more than a series of isolated souls, a community like (as Ferrer nicely puts it) a series of "apparently closed wells joined by a subterranean stream" (Ferrer 17). Even as voices emerge from obsessed and grieving individual minds, they remain in crucial ways still a part of the Bundren family and the broader Yoknapatawpha region. This is not at all to deny that Faulkner in some sections conveys his characters' "secret obsessions, bringing into the light of language all the unspoken obscurity seething within [their] tortured mind[s]" (Bleikasten, *Faulkner's* As I Lay Dying 64). Rather it is to assert that the text expresses even the most private of concerns in the disharmony of a discourse shared with others. Voice is personal, yet also separated from person, to be heard always in relation to others: "When we speak our voices are quiet, detached" (*AILD*, Darl 128; 135). The text sets voices in playful oscillation, the way a painter sometimes plays with the figure and the background of a picture: if speech quoted in narrative is—to return again to Genette's analogy—like an oyster shell glued onto a canvas, then in *As I Lay Dying* we are not always certain whether the "oyster shell" is a shell, an ear, an outline of a face, or whatever. The illusion of speech eludes us, as one moment we hear a character named Darl saying "I reckon" in the idiom of his region, in another we hear a narrator named Darl comparing Addie's coffin to a "cubistic bug." Indeed, consciousness itself in *As I Lay Dying* often seems a matter more of communal awareness than of psychological idiosyncracies—and this is perhaps to say that, rather than being *revealed* by interior speech, consciousness *equals* speech used by and shared by the narrating figures. The sharing is evident at the level of dialect, as the closer the speaker is to Addie's death the fewer dialect distinctions his or her speech evinces in relation to others also close to Addie. The sharing is evident, too, on the level of imagery. Not only do the characters perceive the same phenomena, they employ the same metaphors to describe them: four different speakers liken the sound of Cash's sawing to snoring—though each couches the image in a slightly different manner: "It sounds like snoring" (*AILD*, Cora 7–8; 9); "Cash's saw snores steadily" (*AILD*, Peabody 42; 45); "the saw begins to snore again" (*AILD*, Darl 46; 49); "the saw sounds like it is asleep" (*AILD*, Vardaman 60; 63). The metaphor's articulation does not individualize the speaker's consciousness so much as it individualizes a manner of talking: mimetic voice moves gracefully between the ineffable uniqueness of individual consciousness and the communal language, "that meagre and fragile thread . . . by which . . . men's secret and solitary lives may be joined for an instant" (*AA* 313; 251). Often individuality manifests itself only in talk, in how one speaker expresses something, not in any content of the psyche. Tull's and Darl's descriptions of the flood-swollen river show a shared awareness rendered unique and appropriate to each only by mimetic voice, the illusion of the speech through which the image is expressed:

> The water was cold. It was thick, like slush ice. Only it kind of lived. One part of you knowed it·was just water, the same thing that had been running under this same bridge for a long time, yet when them logs would come spewing up outen it, you were not surprised, like they was a part of water, of the waiting and the threat. (*AILD*, Tull 124; 131)

> Before us the thick dark current runs. It talks up to us in a murmur become ceaseless and myriad, the yellow surface dimpled monstrously into fading swirls travelling along the surface for an instant, silent, impermanent and profoundly significant, as though just beneath the surface something huge and alive waked for a moment of lazy alertness out of and into light slumber again. (*AILD*, Darl 127; 134)

The verbal images of the river as alive and threatening, as well as some aspects of syntax, are all virtually the same here—yet how different the passages "sound." The differences can be isolated only with reference to imitated talk, to mimetic voice.[39]

The presence of public stories further enhances the sense of a shared communal discourse that serves to constitute character. The speakers farthest distant from the Bundrens narrate, appropriately, in conventional past tense with no incursion into present. Samson, Moseley, Armstid, and MacGowan sound like colloquial storytellers speaking in varieties of Yoknapatawpha dialect appropriate to their stations—the farmers Samson and Armstid speak in country white idiom ("durn," "sholy," "outen," etc.), while Moseley and MacGowan, the two druggists, are town colloquial speakers, the latter a nicely sardonic version of the typical Faulknerian town narrator. All four sections exhibit strong features of vocalization, as if told orally, without any trappings of interiorization except that no audience is explicitly dramatized. (Samson does use the vernacular "says" as speaker identification, rather than "said," creating that slight ambiguity of verb tense noted earlier. Otherwise his section contains past-tense verbs.) All begin in oral narrative fashion with phrases that establish the time and place of the events. Samson keeps trying to remember the name of the MacCallum twin he was talking to ("Rafe's twin; that one it was" [98; 106]), and Moseley accounts for how he learned part of the story ("It was Albert told me about the rest of it" [188; 193]). These anecdotal touches enhance the public quality of the outsiders' narratives, placing them at some remove from the family, expressing varieties of the community's accumulated oral lore. We can readily imagine their tales being told and retold, passed along from farmhouse to store to village throughout the county.

By both enhancing and challenging conventional illusions of speech, by defining "person" as participant in an ever-changing and hearable choir of voices, and yet by simultaneously disrupting expected correlations between voice and person, *As I Lay Dying* recalls us to the problematic status of verbal representation in general and of mimetic voice in particular. *As I Lay Dying* signifies the existential power of voice and its uncertainty and flux. Addie Bundren's central monologue, as Bleikasten explains, expresses the frustration of a life within language: "For whoever seeks in [language] the locus of truth, there can only be the disappointment of finding an empty shell. Yet in its very emptiness it exerts a coercive power from which none may escape. Man is born into language, just as he is born into time and mortality, and language is part of the intricate network of necessities that subject him to their law" (*Faulkner's* As I Lay Dying 136). To Addie, words are meaningless, empty sounds that the weak substitute for active confrontation with the forces of the real world. She has lived her life as a desperate struggle to unite her private self with the inaccessible outside world; she has sought to push herself into the elemental flux of life, to mingle her own life force with "the wild blood boiling along the earth." She has sought some ultimate and final acknowledgment from mankind and the universe itself, some recognition that she truly does exist. As a school teacher, before marrying Anse, Addie would whip her pupils to make them feel her in the most private reaches of their souls where her words could never reach: "And I would think with each blow of the switch: Now you are aware of me! Now I am something in your secret and selfish life, who have marked your blood with my own for ever and ever" (155; 162). It is this kind of intense recognition that Addie wants to give and to receive by accepting a man; she wants someone to batter his way (like Donne's three-personed God) into her soul, to break down the walls that keep her separated from "the terrible blood" she can feel at night in the spring when the geese fly overhead. When such a fusion with nature's vital forces or with some other human being fails to come to her, Addie grows bitter. Having married Anse in hopes of a violent commingling, she discovers, ironically, that the attempt to fuse herself with life has intruded on her own selfish privacy by causing her to bear a child.

Addie blames words for her dissatisfaction and for her failure to perceive, before she married and gave birth, the emptiness of Anse Bundren's version of life. She feels tricked into the sterile void between the desired mystical union with life and the violation of herself that such a union entails. Anse, instead of sweeping her headlong into the "doing," deceived her and made her feel "that living was terrible." She realizes that "words are no good; that words dont ever fit what they are trying to say at. When [Cash] was born I knew that motherhood was invented by someone who had to have a word for it because the ones that had the children didn't care whether there was a word for it or not" (157; 163). Although she accepts Cash as her punishment for ever believing in Anse, she cannot excuse Darl, the second child: "Then I found I had Darl. At first I would not believe it. Then I believed that I would kill Anse. It was as though he had tricked me, hidden within a word like within a paper screen and struck me in the back through it" (158; 164). Words (like "love," perhaps) have kept Addie from ever feeling genuinely alive: "I would think how words go straight up in a thin line, quick and harmless, and how terribly doing goes along the earth, clinging to it, so that after a while the two lines are too far apart for the same person to straddle from one to the other" (160; 165). And so Addie takes Rev. Whitfield as a lover because loving him is purely and simply a deed, without words, and through her action she and he can "shape and coerce the terrible blood to the forlorn echo of the dead word high in the air" (161; 167).

Addie's own harsh and urgent talking denies that language can help one deal with one's human condition, that words can ever bridge the gap between oneself and the world outside. Addie's *voice*, however, the voice of a corpse, demonstrates the irony of human existence in language, for by voicing her need and her deed Addie belies her own claim for "reality" over "words." Nowhere is Faulkner's comic-tragic irony stronger. In taking Rev. Whitfield, a master of the hypocritical word, as her lover, Addie gives in to language, to "hearing the dark land talking of God's love and his beauty and His sin; hearing the dark voicelessness in which the words are the deeds." For the novel bestows no identity outside of voice. The text mocks Addie's metaphor of "the land talking the voiceless speech" as she speaks it in her monologue bracketed between Cora Tull's and Whitfield's sanctimonious hypocrisy.

Speech betrays Addie Bundren doubly, and more than she could ever know or say, by enshrining her subjective "self" in a mere dead echo of a voice. The transcendent subject, that presence we call consciousness, is here, as it often is in Faulkner, deconstructed by its own verbal devices. Voice, imitated in expressive written speech, releases subjectivity for the reader's scrutiny and sympathy. Yet voice empties or drains consciousness as well, replacing its energy with the hardened shell of imitated discourse. Faulkner knew, of course, that voice creates character—the subject—but he also knew that voice erases transcendental subjectivity for the sake of its own production. For Addie Bundren, to speak is to fail to live or do; to speak is to fail to exist, to become an empty shape that cannot fill its own lack; it is to go mad, like the voluble Darl. By entering into the novel's discourse, Addie joins the chorus of voices "fumbling at the deeds like orphans," and thereby reveals that her deed, her "salvation" was itself "just words too." By giving Addie speech Faulkner at one and the same time creates her in voice and undercuts her voiced word. Dead as a person, speaking to us only from what Beckett's Molloy calls "the tranquility of decomposition" (Beckett 28–29), Addie is truly a "dead sound," ironically given life, as are all the fiction's characters, only in her voice. Dewey Dell unwittingly but aptly sums up her mother's fate when she says that Darl "told me ma is going to die without words" (24; 26).

Chapter 3

PSYCHIC VOICE

It was to isolate her out of the loud world . . .

—The Sound and the Fury

In *The Hamlet*, when Labove comes to Will Varner to apply for the schoolteacher's job, Faulkner provides a retrospective description of Labove's football playing at the University. It is not clear whether Labove actually tells Varner of his past, or whether Varner's questions merely evoke Labove's memories of playing. He stands before Varner, who is lying in his hammock, and is "forc[ed] . . . to spend time thinking about what he had never told anyone and did not intend to talk about since it did not matter now. It began . . ." (*H* 107). In the middle of the flashback the narrative returns to the present to say again, "He didn't tell this. He just stood beside the hammock, in the clean unmatching garments, composed and grave, answering Yes or No briefly and quietly to Varner's questions while it recapitulated, ran fast and smooth and without significance now in his memory . . . dreamlike and telescoped" (109). Yet, when the flashback ends, Varner acts as if he had *heard* the recapitulation, even picking up the last words in the narrated memory:

> the spurning earth, the shocks, the hard breathing and the grasping hands, the speed, the rocking roar of massed stands, his face even

then still wearing the expression of sardonic not-quite-belief. And the shoes. Varner was watching him, his hands beneath his head.

"Them shoes," Varner said. It was because I never did really believe it was going to last until the next Saturday, Labove could have answered. But he did not, he just stood, his hands quiet at his sides, looking at Varner. "I reckon they always had a plenty of them on hand," Varner said.

"They bought them in lots. They kept all sizes on hand." (109–10)

This minor confusion of realms blurs the distinction between speech and thought. We cannot know which discourse is spoken and which discourse remains in Labove's mind; we cannot be certain whether to regard the retrospection as speech, thought, or purely diegetic narrative discourse. What does Labove *say*? What does he *think*?

SPEECH AND THOUGHT

Questions about the relation between speech and thought arise frequently in Faulkner's novels. Does Temple Drake, when raped by Popeye, speak the words we are told she "was saying . . . to the old man with the yellow clots for eyes"? Or are the words "void[ed] . . . like bright silent bubbles into the bright silence" (*S* 107; 121–22)? Could Zach Edmonds in "The Fire and the Hearth" really be imagined as thinking such highly Faulknerian rhetoric as *"He is both heir and prototype simultaneously of all the geography and climate and biology which sired old Carothers and all the rest of us and our kind, myriad, countless, faceless, even nameless now except himself who fathered himself, intact and complete"* (*GDM* 118)? We have confronted such questions already in examining how mimetic voice becomes a tool for revealing consciousness in *As I Lay Dying*, where Faulkner attributes to the Bundrens discourse far beyond their capacities as speaking characters, and where Cash "thinks" in a list of numbered reasons for building the coffin on the bevel. We also considered the issue in examining mingled speech, when Faulkner uses an idiom phonetically and semantically appropriate to a character to signal that we are inside a character's mind and sharing a point of view, as in *The Mansion*, where words like "nigger" and "jest" express the unspoken yet central consciousness of Mink Snopes.

In this chapter we shall continue to address such questions more explicitly from the broader perspective of represented consciousness rather than just that of represented speech. We shall examine more directly the role that voice plays in Faulkner's portrayal of consciousness and attempt to define those special versions of represented consciousness that characterize his work. This chapter will define those techniques that constitute what is called here the "psychic voice" in Faulkner: the voice, that is, of and in the psyche, the silent voice of thought heard only in the mind and overheard only through fiction's omniscience.

Psychic voice gives verbal expression to voluntary thought and uncontrolled urge alike, to what William James summarized as "sensations of our bodies and of the objects around us, memories of past experiences and thoughts of distant things, feelings of satisfaction and dissatisfaction, desires and aversions, and other emotional conditions, together with determinations of the will, in every variety of permutation and combination" (17). The psychic voice turns the reader into a psychic, a mind reader: voices heard as from within another's consciousness permit us to enter a private realm from which, outside of fiction, we are barred.

Represented speech and represented thought in fiction are intimately related and often virtually identical; many theorists lump the two together and derive their models of consciousness from linguistic and narrative theories about represented speech. Derek Bickerton, for example, writes that "inner speech can only be rendered by one of the methods used for rendering spoken speech" (238), and he redefines Robert Humphrey's classification of interior monologues by showing their grammatical parallels with modes of reproducing speech. Thus, Bickerton says, there are four modes of interior monologue corresponding to four modes of represented speech: "(1) Soliloquy is inner speech rendered in direct speech. (2) Omniscient description is inner speech rendered in indirect speech. (3) Indirect interior monologue is inner speech rendered in free indirect speech. (4) Direct interior monologue is inner speech rendered in free direct speech" (238). Ann Banfield also joins represented speech and thought for grammatical analysis (35–36), and Brian McHale makes no distinction between speech and thought when he proposes a mimetically based scale for types of free indirect speech. He simply treats the "typical syntactical form of first-person interior monologue" as a variant of direct discourse, "shorn of its conventional orthographic cues" ("Free Indirect Discourse" 259). Seymour Chatman, though rightly insisting on certain commonsense differences between speech and thought, still treats those conventions that signal thought (like truncated syntax) as variations on represented speech conventions; his discussion of Leopold Bloom's thought as portrayed in a passage of free indirect style is essentially an analysis of speech attribution (182–84). In her extensive description of "narrative modes for presenting consciousness," Dorrit Cohn explicitly rejects a speech model (10–11), yet the three fundamental modes of represented consciousness she distinguishes still mirror modes of represented speech. What she calls "psycho-narration," or the presentation of consciousness by a narrator's description or commentary, is akin to speech presented indirectly by a reporting narrator. The second mode, "quoted monologue," matches direct discourse in that it purports to quote more or less verbatim the actual discourse—the words, the syntax, even the expressive nuances—of verbal thought. Cohn's third mode, "narrated monologue," mixes narration and quotation in much the way mingled speech does, by employing the person and tense of indirect discourse along with other expressive elements (diction, interrogatives, and so on) of the character's idiosyncratic and direct discourse.[1]

The theoretical similarities between represented speech and thought permit a method of analysis comparable to that employed in the previous chapter. As with mimetic voice, we can organize the discursive features that serve to represent thought into "functions"; that is to say, the psychic voice is a function of certain procedures that govern conventional verbal renditions of thought in fiction. We might simply adopt the functions of mimetic voice and apply them to represented thought: a text can describe thought just as it can speech; it can identify and transcribe thought, and can differentiate it from other discourse. Grammar governs the verb tags "said" and "thought" in identical ways, so that these and their many variants can serve equally well to mark discourse as speech or as thought without necessarily affecting the discourse itself. Temple Drake's statement to Popeye, quoted in chapter 2 to illustrate the five functions of mimetic voice (see above, pp. 72–73), has an exact analog earlier in *Sanctuary*: "[Temple] stood on tiptoe, listening, thinking I'm hungry. I haven't eaten all day" (*S* 59). Of the five functions of mimetic voice only "communication" could not apply, as it is the very nature of thought to remain uncommunicated, to remain within the mind's privacy. When one communicates one's thoughts they become speech, writing, or gesture.

Such an analysis would be too limiting, however, because it would not adequately track the full nature or range of psychic voice in Faulkner. It would restrict represented consciousness to nothing more than represented speech that happens to be unvocalized by the speaker-thinker. We need to consider instead the ways Faulkner *goes beyond speech* to represent thought. Although in Faulkner, as in other writers, the transformation of presumed "mental content" into communicable discourse often evokes processes similar to the representation of speech, neither consciousness nor even voluntary thought are simply internal or unheard speech. The history of stream-of-consciousness writing shows that novelists intuitively have assumed that thought cannot take the form of public speech. Writers disrupt the mimetic illusion of speech in various ways (truncated syntax, missing punctuation, run-together words, and so on) for the very purpose of rendering thought as *unlike* speech (what Faulkner called in *Absalom, Absalom!* "notlanguage" [5; 8]). They seek ways to enhance the reader's sense that certain discourse emanates *un*spoken and *un*articulated from a character's private consciousness. Furthermore, most novelistic depictions of consciousness embrace a wider range of mental experience than what is or can be verbalized in the mind, whether in conventional speech form or not.

It will be more informative, then, to propose separate functions for psychic voice, functions not identical to those that govern mimetic voice. No matter how closely represented thought follows represented speech, the differences between the two remain crucial. Furthermore, the techniques employed in representing thought vary more from author to author than do those employed in imitating speech, so that in isolating certain functions I am focusing more exclusively on Faulkner than was the case in proposing the five functions of mimetic voice. The functions of psychic voice discussed here are considerably less inclusive than the functions of mimetic voice discussed in chapter 2. Convention drives the portrayal of thought far less rigorously than it controls the imitation of speech, partly because the psychic voice often derives from an author's attempt to distinguish thought from speech (that is, to deliberately *violate* convention) and partly because the nature of thought is (or is felt to be by writers) less inherently verbal than is speech. The discussion is therefore limited to those functions of psychic voice appropriate to Faulkner but not necessarily applicable to other writers. In this examination we will explore how Faulkner brings voice to the service of portraying consciousness, and we will discover that his methods include but are not limited to mimetic representations of inner speech. We will consider the ways he narrates consciousness and the ways he uses textual conventions to enhance the expressive capabilities of written discourse. We shall also see that the term psychic *voice* is particularly apt for Faulkner because he fills the psyches of his characters with voices of many and varied kinds, such that a dominant mental experience for most Faulkner protagonists is one of voiced discourse.

FUNCTIONS OF PSYCHIC VOICE IN "CARCASSONNE"

"Carcassonne" can serve as an exemplary text to distill into manageable shape the multiplicity of discursive features that cause readers to regard certain portions of the fictional discourse as thought—that is, as in some way issuing from, occurring in, or verbalized by a character's consciousness, but not communicated to anyone outside the privacy of that character's mind. Written early in his career, probably in 1925 or 1926 (Blotner 502), "Carcassonne" is certainly one of the odder stories in Faulkner's oeuvre, unusual in its brevity, its minimal plot, and its abstraction. Faulkner admired the story for its fantastic and poetic qualities (*FU* 22), and he concluded both *These Thirteen* and *Collected Stories* with it, as if he had written it for the purpose of illustrating some fundamental version of the inner life. Michel Gresset (*Faulkner ou la fascination* 20) and David Minter (61–62), among others, convincingly argue for the story's special biographical significance in that it expresses the still unfulfilled hopes of the young novelist (*"I want to perform something bold and tragical and austere"* [*CS* 899])—though Michael Grimwood may push the biographical implications too far in reading the story's images of binding and suckling as being unconscious responses to Faulkner's mother and her constraints on his creativity (46–51). For Cleanth Brooks (*Toward Yoknapatawpha* 60–65) and others (Milum, Hamblin) "Carcassonne" celebrates the power of the imagination in conflict with mere physical existence. Noel Polk, however, finds in it less a celebration of art than a cry of despair, arguing that the imagery derived from such sources as Eliot's *The Waste Land*, along with the story's climactic position in *These Thirteen*, place "Carcassonne" squarely among Faulkner's early depictions of post–World War I alienation ("William Faulkner's 'Carcassonne'"). By any interpretation its "psychic" importance is crucial. More a contemplative set piece than a narrative, more a prose lyric evoking a state of mind than a tale relating events, "Carcassonne"'s only action is thinking. The protagonist's consciousness embraces a range of internal phenomena, from the deliberate formulation of discourse in the silence of the mind (as when the protagonist "shap[ed] his lips soundlessly in the darkness [and said] 'I would like to perform something'" [*CS* 898]) to automatic, uncontrolled, and (originally) non-verbal perceptions and sensations (as when the protagonist "tingled a little pleasantly . . . as he lay beneath the tarred paper bedclothing" [*CS* 895]).

We will consider in "Carcassonne" four functions typical of Faulkner's discursive modes of representing thought: the meditative, the dialogical, the psychoanalytical, and the expressive.

Meditation

The *meditative* function is the process of evoking a meditative scene and act: thought is a function of the narrated circumstance in which it occurs, the set of described conditions under which the act of thinking can be imagined as taking place, the conditions under which the presence, implied or actual, of a persona's consciousness is opened to the reader. Like the mimetic function of description, to which it is roughly parallel, meditation is the least-imitative method of evoking mental processes. A minimal meditative condition can be fulfilled by identifying tags like "he thought" or "she mused"—the internal equivalent of speech tags like "she said" or "he cried." Far broader are elaborated meditative scenes in which a thinking character is positioned, as it were, vis-à-vis the discourse of his or her mind. Here we can often discover those ways in which thought comes to be instituted in Faulkner's world, those boundaries where the objective and subjective meet, those stances the meditating subject assumes in relation to the world and in relation to his or her own psychic discourse.

In Faulkner meditation evinces a consistency well illustrated in "Carcassonne." This story depicts the quintessential Faulknerian contemplative moment: a man lies beneath a roof waiting for sleep or death. "Carcassonne" opens *in media cogitatio*, with italicized lines projected onto the screen of the protagonist's mind. The protagonist lies "beneath an unrolled strip of tarred roofing made of paper" under a "ceiling of [a] garret [that] slanted in a ruined pitch to the low eaves . . . groined with ribs of dying sunlight" (*CS* 895, 896, 899). Ruminating and imagining, yet aware of his body and of his environment, the protagonist "speaks" his mind, dreaming of performing something "*bold and tragical and austere*," though he does not know what. He muses and speculates, playing with various metaphors (the roll of tar paper is like "those glasses, reading glasses which old ladies used to wear"), conjuring up allusions to unidentified histories ("that riderless Norman steed which galloped against the Saracen

Emir"), commenting on an apparent patron "Mrs Widdrington" who "owns" him and "the rats too," debating with his skeleton about "the end of life," which he knows is "lying still." At the story's end we are not sure what has happened, for the protagonist merely reiterates his opening dream image of a *"buckskin pony with eyes like blue electricity."* Whether he has died, fallen asleep, or achieved some epiphany is not certain, though the wasteland imagery as well as the final image of "Earth . . . deep-breasted and grave of flank" do suggest death.

The most important meditative moments in Faulkner's fiction show remarkable similarities to that in "Carcassonne." Narrated meditation usually occurs while a character drifts into sleep or death, often lying down, seeking some insight that until at least the final moments of thinking, and sometimes forever, eludes him or her. Commonly a character lies beneath a roof, hearing rain and "thinking." Young Bayard Sartoris lies in the dark silence at the MacCallum farm the night after his reckless driving has killed his grandfather. He relives his brother's death and yearns for the peace that "comes to all." He hears rain on the roof and, while this permits sleep, it offers only momentary comfort: "It comes to all, it comes to all, his tired heart comforted him, and at last he slept" (*FD* 317). Darl Bundren tries to "empty" himself for sleep in a strange room by meditating on *is* and *was*, and on "how often have I lain beneath rain on a strange roof, thinking of home" (*AILD* 72; 76).[2] Again and again this kind of moment serves as Faulkner's typical narration of significant thought. Hightower broods in his window at twilight before his final vision of his grandfather's ride through Jefferson; the Confederate officer Weddel in "Mountain Victory" lies "in the dark, thinking of home" the night before his death (*CS* 766); Ike McCaslin lies in his tent in "Delta Autumn," reviewing his reasons for repudiating the land that was to be his heritage; Mink Snopes at the close of *The Mansion* lies down for one last time, risking the drag of the earth toward death. Horace Benbow imagines such a scene of meditation as relief: after he hears Temple Drake's hideous story of her rape, he is overwhelmed by a sense of the world's evil and yearns for "a gentle dark wind blowing in the long corridors of sleep: of lying beneath a low cozy roof under the long sound of the rain" (*S* 232; 265).

"Carcassonne" also illustrates another trait of Faulkner's meditative scenes: thought's movement from frustration and blockage toward release and revelation. As a character moves into sleep or death, he or she usually wrestles with some idea or insight that hovers just on the other side of full comprehension, some special awareness that might explain suffering or bring comfort. The poet-protagonist in "Carcassonne" muses on doing something "bold and tragical and austere"—but exactly what that something is eludes him. The story ends with a final release of his imagined "buckskin pony" soaring off into the imagined sky, free forever of the earth. What physical states the protagonist's musing leads from and into has been debated. Some see him as merely falling asleep, dreaming as he does so for some apotheosis of the imagination (C. Brooks, *Toward Yoknapatawpha*; Hamblin, Milum); Polk insists that the dreamer floats on the verge of death, that he is either "physically dead, or on the point of dying," or "in an artistically arrested moment right in the crack between living and dying" ("William Faulkner's 'Carcassonne'" 38). Other Faulkner characters experience similar psychic releases. Wilbourne in *The Wild Palms* teeters a number of times on the edge of understanding ("That was the second time he almost got it. But it escaped him again" [316]), only to have the final insight come as "no flash of comprehension" but "just a simple falling of a jumbled pattern" (*WP* 323). Wash Jones (in "Wash") thinks in this manner after he kills Sutpen: "Thinking went slowly and terrifically, fumbling, involved somehow with a sound of galloping hooves, until there broke suddenly free in mid-gallop the fine proud figure of the man on the fine proud stallion, galloping; and then that at which thinking fumbled, broke free too and quite clear, not in justification nor even explanation, but as the apotheosis, lonely, explicable, beyond all fouling by human touch" (*CS* 542).

This common imagery of "breaking free" characterizes even narrated consciousness that does not entail verbalization. When Joe Christmas envisions the cracked urns that symbolize his discovery of "womanfilth," or when Horace Benbow imagines Little Belle on the bed of corn shucks (in *Sanctuary*), both are sickened and both vomit, a physical expurgation of their imagining. Perhaps the most famous instance of such a meditative scene belongs to the penultimate chapter of *Light in August*, where the "wheel" of thought, "released, seems to rush on with a long sighing sound" toward Hightower's epiphany and perhaps death.

Polk is right, I think, that "Carcassonne" ends in the protagonist's death, not only because the internal evidence he describes is convincing, but because meditative scenes in Faulkner nearly always bear the symbolic weight of dying, of passing through the last instants of physical existence or of lying in the coffin, in the grave. Addie Bundren lies beneath the "roof" of her actual coffin—her monologue literalizes the symbolic relation between meditation, epiphany, and death. Throughout "Carcassonne" we return to the present context of the musing protagonist lying in his rat-infested garret, which has the feel of a coffin or a grave, and are thus reminded of the earthbound locus of his rumination. Self-awareness comes most powerfully in Faulkner to those passing from one mental state to another, from wakefulness to oblivion, from life into death. Those in Faulkner who meditate do so at the surface of oblivion, about to fall into its depths, "taking [their thoughts] into sleep with [them]" ("The Brooch," *CS* 654). For Darl Bundren or Bayard Sartoris the oblivion is that of sleep; for Gail Hightower, Mink Snopes, or Weddel it is the oblivion of death. The passage into oblivion in Faulkner is often an epiphanic moment when some insight bursts into a thinker's final instant of consciousness. Thought, or at least meditation, always entails a sinking or drifting into death, a "lying beneath" a roof, beneath life itself. The internal life for Faulkner seems, inevitably, to be fraught with fear and associated with the symbolic burial of the body and a yearning for an imaginative realm that tries but fails to transcend death.

Dialogic Thought

The second discursive practice governing the representation of thought is the *dialogical* function: by this is meant the extent to which, and the manner in which, thinking takes on the necessities of dialogue—its spirit if not its form. (Like its counterpart in mimetic voice, "differentiation," the dialogical function of psychic voice involves distinguishing one speaker's discourse from another.) The dialogical is the degree to which the discourse marks the presence of other voices, the covert or overt discourse of an Other or of the self as Other. Included here would be the self-reflexive awareness the thinking subject possesses that he or she *is* thinking, the ways in which thought is itself thought about. Features of the text split thought into varying voices (as when a thinker "thinks" the words of another) and indicate how aware the meditating character is of what transpires in his or her psyche. Especially important here is the act of responding to one's own thoughts or another's thoughts in one's own mind.

"Carcassonne" fulfills the dialogical function by explicitly projecting the protagonist's verbal thoughts as a dialogue between the protagonist's imaginative self and "his skeleton" (the "immortal part" in A. E. Housman's poem, which Faulkner may have had in mind [C. Brooks, *Toward Yoknapatawpha* 61–62]). The skeleton overtly speaks to the musing man in conversational, mimetically voiced form:

"All you know is what I tell you," he said.

"Not always," the skeleton said. "I know that the end of life is lying still. You haven't learned that yet. Or you haven't mentioned it to me, anyway."

"Oh, I've learned it," he said. (*CS* 899)

Some such splitting of the individual psyche occurs in most of Faulkner's meditative scenes. Rarely does a character think monologically, in a continuous stream-of-consciousness manner, but rather as Plato described thought, in an "unuttered conversation of the soul with herself" (*Sophist* 263E). In *Absalom, Absalom!* "two separate Quentins [talk] to one another in the long silence of notpeople, notlanguage," and what follows is a self-interrupting dialogue between the "two" Quentins (*AA* 5–6; 9). Thought answers thought, skeleton speaks to soul, soul to "body consciousness" ("Carcassonne," *CS* 896), the "top of his mind" to the deeper parts, the intelligence to emotions ("The Brooch," *CS* 654), the conscience ("the grim Moses") to desire (*WP* 35), "believing" to "knowing" (*LA* 131; 111). Faulkner objectifies in this way the Other with whom the "I" of a thinking character always communicates. Not merely a convenience of form, this doubling of internal voices reflects in Faulkner the same belief in the inherently dialogical nature of human consciousness that Bakhtin attributes to Dostoevsky: "The very being of man (both external and internal) is the *deepest communion. To be* means to communicate" (*Problems of Dostoevsky's Poetics* 287). For both writers consciousness is never singular, never "in the form of a sole and single *I*," though Faulkner conceived, I would argue, of an internal communication wherein the other's voice is less "socially alien" (as Bakhtin says it is in Dostoevsky) than an embodied "other of the self" (287). "Carcassonne" emphasizes the dialogical quality of consciousness through images of doubling that cleave the objects of thought, as well the mind's discourse, into symbolic dualities. The protagonist "thought of the Norman steed . . . thundering along in two halves and not knowing it." In the story's final image the "buckskin pony" leaves the earth as a "dying star upon the immensity of darkness," rising in apotheosis above "the dark and tragic figure of the Earth, his mother."

Psychoanalytic Layering

The third discursive practice that conventionally governs Faulkner's representation of thought is the *psychoanalytical* function, for it is based on Freudian notions of the layering of the psyche into realms more or less conscious. (This function is roughly parallel to the identifying function of mimetic voice, as it locates the source for interior discourse, attributing thought to some portion of the psyche.) It entails the notion that human consciousness varies in accord with degrees of control over and awareness of psychic content, control that is expressed analytically in a spatial metaphor of depth. Some thoughts we write legibly on the "surface" of our awareness, while other "thoughts" ooze from those "depths" of our being to which we have little voluntary access. The representation of thought is a function of the presumed entry into the "interior" (all our language here is perforce metaphorical) of a persona's psyche, and of the placement of the psyche's discourse within consciousness. Features of a text can signal how deeply we have plunged into a character's mind and, concomitantly, how much control the thinker can exercise over the act and content of his or her thoughts. The degree and form of *logic* is important here as well, as varying depths of the mind conventionally employ differing logical syntax— cause-and-effect reasoning at the conscious level, for example, as differentiated from the condensation and displacement typical of dreams. While the notion of "control" is perhaps more empirically accurate as a description of the psyche's activity than is the spatial metaphor of depth or level, the latter figure has considerable explanatory power and seems conventionally employed or implied in most fictive representations of consciousness.

In the Faulknerian geology of the mind, consciousness leaves its sediments at varied depths, each distinct from the other. Typeface, syntax, imagery, vocabulary—many formal features of discourse reveal these levels, from superficial awareness ("the top of his head") to deeper, more disjointed and perhaps unsayable musings. Thus in "Carcassonne" the quoted yet soundless thought, "I would like to perform something," presumably emanates from a different stratum of the protagonist's psyche than does the italicized "*I want to perform something bold and tragical and austere,*" even though the wording is essentially the same. *Light in August* employs the most consistent and extended formal system of layered consciousness, with its use of double quotes, single quotes, and italics (to be considered in the next section of this chapter). Some texts define the layers by verbal context as well as by formal markers: in "Carcassonne" the protagonist expresses his deeper emotions in a discourse filled with allusions to modern poetry—to Housman and Eliot, especially. *The Sound and the Fury* exhumes the past from the buried levels of Jason or Quentin Compson's psyches by increasingly frequent echoes of others' talk within their memories.

In Faulkner the unconscious is a highly intertextual weave of competing discourses, infused with remembered talk or with an allusive pastiche of other texts. Ironically, the more deeply Faulkner permits us to delve into the individual unconscious where the supposedly unique wellsprings of personality are to be discovered, the less original the discourse becomes, that is, the more it echoes other discourses. Subjectivity reverts to language the more intensely the text tries to evoke a private, noncontrolled, sublinguistic subjective realm. In this sense Faulkner's concept of the unconscious bears an affinity to Lacan's description of the unconscious as structured like a language wherein the interior life is instituted in language, not merely expressed by it.[3]

The psychoanalytic function incorporates all the methods of delimiting and marking portions of the text's discourse as being internal to some level of consciousness. Such representation varies in its degree of direct versus indirect, parallel with the varieties of direct and indirect imitated speech. Thought can be reported; thought can be quoted; thought can be freely expressed in forms that range between these extremes just as a character's speech can be embodied in mingled form. In "Carcassonne" Faulkner uses the tools of direct, indirect, and mingled discourse to allow thought to fluctuate from diegetic report to directly quoted silent speech, as seen in the following examples:

1. Narrated sensation. "He could see the shadowgirth" (*CS* 898)

2. Narrated act of thinking. "He mused for a time, while the beast thundered on" (*CS* 899)

3. Indirect report of a thought. "He thought of that Norman steed" (*CS* 898)

4. Free indirect internal discourse with uncertainty as to source. "It was like those glasses, reading glasses which old ladies used to wear . . . He lay still, savoring this" (*CS* 895)

5. Movement from narration into mingled discourse. "It was Mrs Widdrington's, the Standard Oil Company's wife's, darkness he was using to sleep in. She'd make a poet of you too, if you did not work anywhere" (*CS* 897)

6. Direct quotation. "'I would like to perform something,' he said, shaping his lips soundlessly" (*CS* 898)

7. Direct quotation, highly allusive. "Of a man, the worm should be lusty, lean, hairedover. Of women, of delicate girls briefly like heard music in tune, it should be suavely shaped, falling feeding into prettinesses, feeding" (*CS* 897)

8. Direct quotation marked by italics and absence of punctuation: *"what though to Me but as a seething of new milk Who am the Resurrection and the Life"* (CS 897)

Characteristic of Faulkner's reproduction and layering of internal discourse is his frequent distortion of clear boundaries between "internal" and "external" verbal realms, or between the various imagined levels of the psyche. The speech of the mind and the speech of the world notoriously intermingle in Faulkner, as he injects consciousness into the world and the world into consciousness. There is often some ambiguity about how to "assign" the words that represent thought: do they belong to the authorial diegetic discourse, as "reporter" of thought? Are they freely adapted versions of a discourse belonging to the thinker? Are they quotations of "internal" verbalization? In the fourth example given above we are uncertain as to source because we cannot with assurance assign the metaphor of the reading glasses to the authorial voice (which seems to first offer it) or to the character's voice (which seems to claim it). Is the protagonist "savoring" the metaphor itself, or is he savoring his ingenuity in making such a metaphor—and whose metaphor is it?

Expression

Example 8 in the list above, with its variations on conventional punctuation and typeface, illustrates how Faulkner (like many writers) also consistently tried to find modes of psychic expression more powerful than speech. The *expressive* function entails the transcendence of speech in the service of representing thought that will express more, or more powerfully, than speech can. Like transcription, its rough equivalent among the functions of mimetic voice, the expressive function reproduces in textual features qualities of discourse not expressible in conventional form. Sometimes Faulkner invokes a vocal trait—such as loudness—to demonstrate how thought is an enhanced mode of expression more powerful in some ways than speech. In *Absalom, Absalom!*, for example, he describes thinking as "louder" than speech, "filling the thunderous solitude of [Charles Etienne de Saint Velery Bon's] despair louder than speech could" (AA 248; 198), as "loud now, loud and fast too so [Bon] would not, could not, hear the thinking" (AA 411; 329). Images of "loud" thinking also define states of high excitement, as when Elly's blood is "aloud with desperation and exultation and vindication too, talking inside her at the very brink of surrender loud as a voice" ("Elly," *CS* 211), or when Sutpen as a boy comes to an understanding of why he was turned away by the Negro butler: "And then . . . all of a sudden it was not thinking, it was something shouting it almost loud enough for his sisters on the other pallet . . . to hear too . . . it too fast, too mixed up to be thinking, it all kind of shouting at him at once, boiling out and over him" (*AA* 296; 237). More commonly Faulkner seeks to make writing itself expressive of consciousness. Features of writing like print type, punctuation, syntactical irregularities, even on occasion drawings, all serve to distinguish thought from represented speech. Faulkner's textual techniques garner much of their expressive power in their very contrast to represented speech. He wants to generate differences between speech and thought in nonmimetic ways; the differences are nonmimetic because he seldom tries to imitate so much as to symbolize qualities of the mind. The psychic voice achieves a status of its own, distinguishable from narrative discourse or mimetic voice. The symbolic force in "Carcassonne" of "where fell *where fell where I was King of Kings but the woman with the woman with the dog's eyes to knock my bones together and together*" is enhanced by the garbled syntax, the associative logic, and the italics, all of which offer a discursive analog to consciousness without merely quoting verbalizable thought.

Faulkner sometimes treats thought explicitly as a form of writing, as visualizable words "appearing" silently in the mind. When the protagonist of "Carcassonne" "shap[es] his lips soundlessly in the darkness," he "says" "I would like to perform something" in that he expresses it and perhaps even moves his lips. But in another sense the words, which he never actually speaks, "shape" themselves on the screen or page of his imagination. A clearer example can be seen in "Mountain Victory," where Weddel "seem[s] to watch the words shape quietly in the darkness above his mouth" (*CS* 766). Mink Snopes also lets words "take shape in his mind" (*M* 42). The writer, too, produces a soundless discourse that shapes itself in silent reading. As an artist, Faulkner preferred words to music because "I prefer to read rather than listen. I prefer silence to sound, and the image produced by words occurs in silence. That is, the thunder and the music of the prose take place in silence."[4] The italics that, for us, flicker in and out of "Carcassonne"'s discourse repeat the "shadowy flickings from obscurity to obscurity" or the "pattering silence" created in the dark garret. The protagonist doesn't merely imagine the buckskin pony with eyes like blue electricity, he *sees* the words "*a buckskin pony with eyes like blue electricity.*"

A source of psychic voice, then, is the text itself, as a written object. Faulkner tried in various experimental ways to allow his texts to expand the semantic boundaries of language. "Voice" in its strictest primary meaning refers to sound in speech, to the signifying aspect of language embodied in sound. In speech the sounds of the voice—its accents, its pitch levels, its gestural rhythms—create meaning supplementary to the meaning of words or sentences; as the physical embodiment of discourse, sound signifies. The printed text, too, is a physical embodiment of discourse that can generate meaning. We can identify, as crucial to Faulkner's psychic voice, what might be called a "textual voice" through which physical features of print articulate visual differences that signify just as the speaking voice can articulate meaningful aural differences.[5]

Unfortunately, relatively few features of conventional print are expressive in and of themselves. Faulkner wished for more: he would have liked to have *The Sound and the Fury* printed in varied colored inks to signal time shifts, had such a technique been commercially feasible (*SL* 44). He includes drawings in *The Sound and the Fury* (the eye, 360; 388), in *As I Lay Dying* (Addie's coffin, 77; 82), and in *Go Down, Moses* (the delta, 343). He creates a monologue out of a numbered list; he invents runtogether words; he prints headlines in boldface, and signs (like roadsigns, or the sign in Hightower's front yard) are centered and printed either in boldface or italics.

Faulkner's most consistent play with print, however, and the one most directly relevant to psychic voice, is his use of italics. He employed italics more than most writers, and while the strictly binary alteration between italic and roman type would seem to offer minimal flexibility, he achieved remarkable effects aimed at suggesting varying states of consciousness or awareness. The subject of italics in Faulkner is a tricky one to generalize about, however, for, like his transcriptions of dialogue, italics depend for their significance on their immediate relation to other contiguous discourse more than on any consistent principles of their use over either entire works or over Faulkner's oeuvre. Italics, for example, seldom generate *semantic* differences; they are primarily a relational device. While italic type always enforces some distinction between itself and roman type, we can not easily measure what that difference signifies or assign a specific meaning to it.[6]

Clearly, however, by switching typeface Faulkner tries to express some change in the gestures of what Roman Ingarden called the "verbal body" of the literary work (20–21); the shift to italics seeks to encourage a change in texture, in the reader's perception of the events and the reader's sense of the discourse itself. Type changes contribute to the stratification of the psyche into deeper surface levels, with italics usually signaling less-controlled, deeper ranges of inner experience. Typeface changes can also mark shifts in awareness, without implying depth, as in the movement between the past and the present in Benjy and Quentin Compson's monologues; in these shifts Faulkner was not concerned with consistency so much as with nuance: "I purposely used italics for both actual scenes and remembered scenes for the reason, not to indicate the different dates of happenings, but merely to permit the reader to anticipate a thought-transference" (*SL* 45). Italics also help manipulate the discursive relationship between the given narrator's discourse and the events he or she reports (as we saw in *As I Lay Dying*, especially Tull's section [*AILD* 75–83; 80–87]).

Faulkner used italics to record written words—signs, letters, inscriptions, and so on. In *The Mansion* Gavin Stevens writes on a small tablet to the deaf Linda Snopes, and these words are italicized. Because of their frequent association with thought in Faulkner, italics used for writing can nudge written words in the direction of interior discourse, as if they were emanations of consciousness. Stevens's words addressed to Linda have the quality of thought more than of speech simply written down, partly because of the italics, partly because of the abbreviated syntax and informal or absent punctuation. Faulkner also employs italics in dialogical scenes, those intensely dramatic moments where two characters confront each other in a scene of conflict—scenes in which italics cannot be limited to any one character's thoughts, or even to thought alone as opposed to overt and mimetically realized speech (see chapter 2).

All of these varied uses bring the text into play to generate psychic voice, the expression of the inner life. One of Faulkner's more famous instances, the italicized fifth chapter of *Absalom, Absalom!*, which contains Rosa Coldfield's narration of her relations with Thomas Sutpen, creates a contrast with the novel's remaining eight chapters, engendering the sense that Rosa's narrative embroils Quentin and the reader more deeply in her frustration, anger, and fascination with Sutpen than does her opening narrative (in roman type) in the novel's first chapter. Albert Guerard writes that "generally in Faulkner, and I think here, extensive italics indicate a state different from that of normal consciousness or speech" (323), and that chapter 5 of *Absalom, Absalom!* "is of an interior voice, a stream flowing beneath full consciousness even, what the innermost spirit would say if it could" (308). But Guerard wisely does not assume that italics *imitate*

Rosa's inner speech. The fifth chapter's italics cannot be naturalized as reported thought—neither quoted inner speech nor a stream of consciousness—though they certainly encourage a felt difference, a heightening, an accenting of "not what was in Miss Rosa's mind but in her soul: what the whole personality would say if it could speak" (Guerard 323). Italics operate at a textual level and mark the heightened experience not only of a speaker but also of a perceiver (of Quentin as he listens to Rosa) or of the reader. The long italicized passage depicting the meeting between Henry Sutpen and his father at the bivouac as imagined by Shreve and Quentin depicts a state of mind explicitly announced as beyond speech and beyond thought, such that the two characters, we are told, are present in the world their imaginations create. Italics, while they do not simply equal thought in any mechanical or even imitative way, do return voice symbolically to the written, as happens with all the voices in Faulkner's discourse: the play of voices in the fictional world and in the representing discourse gives the expressive power of voice to the *written* language on the page.

PSYCHIC VOICE IN
LIGHT IN AUGUST

Like most Faulkner texts, *Light in August* crosses conventional boundaries between "internal" and "external" realms so as to intermingle consciousness and the world. As discussed in chapter 1, a richly figured phenomenal voice defines the Jefferson community and the protagonists' roles within it. An equally rich variety of mimetic voices records the rural and small-town talk of speakers as countrified as Lena Grove and Byron Bunch, and as educated as Gail Hightower and Gavin Stevens. One could well argue, however, that the phenomenal and mimetic voices ultimately serve voices emanating from within the inarticulate depths of the psyche, that for all its rich evocation of landscape, town, and event, *Light in August* is nonetheless one of Faulkner's most overtly psychological novels. It contains, certainly, his most blatantly Freudian depiction of the unconscious, chronicling with clinical thoroughness Joe Christmas's sexual experience from the primal scene at the orphanage, through his nausea when he learns about menstruation, to the associations between food and Joanna Burden's sexuality. In this and other ways *Light in August* seems more self-consciously concerned with the psyche than most Faulkner texts—even more than the first-person monologue novels.

No other Faulkner text so insistently *labels* thought as such, as if to instruct us how to read the disparate voices: signs everywhere alert the reader that this portion of the discourse expresses thought, that portion records speech, while still another remains apart from either speech or thought. No other Faulkner text more consistently isolates the psychic voice, to display it and distinguish it from other kinds of voice; no other novel seems so aware of, even preoccupied with, the mind's layering into levels of consciousness from its surface, where the mind articulates thought as silent speech, to the unconscious, where lie unspeakable desires. The authorial narrator often quotes thought as an internal speech sounding colloquially appropriate to the speaker. At the same time the authorial voice explicitly resorts to what one commentator nicely calls "epistemological incantations" to invoke levels of the unconscious inaccessible to speech (Taylor 48). Sometimes the novel's psychic voice merely echoes a silent mimetic voice: "Lena thinks, 'I have come from Alabama: a fur piece'" (3; I); at other times psychic voice is couched in a rhetoric no character would ever speak: "Memory believes before knowing remembers. Believes longer than recollects, longer than knowing even wonders. Knows remembers believes a corridor in a big long garbled cold echoing building" (131; 111).

The novel's opening pages establish a formal strategy of identifying and layering psychic voice. Double quotes with conventional punctuation bracket deliberate speech, uttered out loud. Verbalized thoughts—that is, words in the mind that the thinker could plausibly utter—appear in single quotes. Italics, without quotation marks and usually without final punctuation, represent thought drawn from deeper levels of consciousness less amenable to voluntary control, thought that perhaps the character could not utter. A striking example, in a passage that first renders the psychic voice indirectly, then in single quotes, then in italics, follows Varner's thinking as he watches Lena sitting on the store gallery waiting for the wagon to take her to Jefferson:

> The squatting men along the wall look at her still and placid face and they think as Armstid thought and as Varner thinks: that she is thinking of a scoundrel who deserted her in trouble and whom they believe that she will never see again, save his coattails perhaps already boardflat with running. 'Or maybe it's about that Sloane's or Bone's Mill she is thinking,' Varner thinks. 'I reckon that even a fool gal don't have to come as far as Mississippi to find out that whatever

place she run from aint going to be a whole lot different or worse than the place she is at. Even if it has got a brother in it that objects to his sister's nightprowling,' thinking *I would have done the same as the brother; the father would have done the same. She has no mother because fatherblood hates with love and pride, but motherblood with hate loves and cohabits*

  She is not thinking about this at all. (28; 22–23)

Although the italicized portions are often slightly more complex, formal, or "literary" in their rhetoric than those in single quotes, with fewer contractions and fewer colloquialisms like "I reckon," the differences are inconsistently upheld, and the italics only on occasion show rhetorical features we are likely to feel as too sophisticated for the character. Faulkner does not lend characters his most elaborate style, as he lent the Bundrens phrasing like "resolving him out of his integrity, into an unrelated scattering of components" (*AILD* 52; 55). He never seriously interferes with the mimetic illusion that a character is thinking in his or her own idiom.[7]

  As in the passage quoted above, single-quoted and italicized versions of a character's thoughts often occur together as if in virtual dialogue with each other—in almost a kind of "call and response" between levels of the psyche. In one instance italicized words appear *within* a single quoted sentence, as if the mind were representing or quoting its own thoughts from a deeper level (371; 319). Mimetic, authorial, and psychic voices mingle in the three levels of the psyche implied by the differing punctuation. Faulkner seems to seek here less a tripartite division than a continuum of discourse that moves freely between private and public articulation.

  Faulkner also takes pains to "locate" the discourse of consciousness within the psyche. For nearly every speaker-thinker, though most frequently for Joe Christmas, Faulkner tries to pinpoint the level of awareness represented by a given discourse marked as thought. He does this, as we have just seen, formalistically through punctuation and italics; he does this also by so frequently labeling passages with verbs of speech or thought that he creates an obsessive insistence on the discourse's status as thought. The verb tags "thinking" or "thinks" appear with nearly every single-quoted or italicized passage. Faulkner further locates the psyche's discourse through explicit descriptions like "the surface of thinking" (193; 165), or "at the top of [the] mind" (341; 293), or "between thinking and saying aloud" (14; 11), or "perhaps thinking would have suddenly flowed into a picture, shaping, shaped" (193; 165). Sometimes these descriptions equate thought and language, as when "it is like words spoken aloud now, reiterative, patient, justificative" (341; 293), or when "it seemed to [Joe] that he could actually hear the words inside him" (302–3; 261). Other descriptions, however, include a claim that what we are reading does not represent any *words* actually thought, either because they could not be verbalized or because even the omniscient narrator is uncertain about the content of a character's psyche. Some words appear in the consciousness "too fast and too complete to be thinking" (200; 170). Joe is described as "run[ning] far ahead of himself and his knowing" (235; 200), as giving a look "faster than thought" (235; 200), and even as "thinking too fast for even thought" (207; 176). Sentences sometimes appear in the mind visually, "like a printed sentence fullborn and already dead" (115; 98) or "fullsprung across his skull, behind his eyes" (541; 464). Faulkner also "quotes" words that he tells us the character does *not* think: "He was not thinking *Maybe she is not asleep either* tonight. He was not thinking at all now; thinking had not begun now; the voices had not begun now either" (130; 110). Just as the novel's voice imagery infuses the text with phenomenal voice, so the constant quoting and describing of verbal thought infuses it with psychic voice. Consciousness, the text implies, permeates the world, everywhere, whether localized deeply in someone's unconscious, at the "top of his mind," in articulated speech, or in communal voices.

Psychic voice does not merely represent thought in *Light in August*; it transcends the limits of any individual consciousness and comes to be a shared or at least a sharable discourse. Faulkner thus freely reports the thoughts of minor as well as major characters. Armstid's thoughts, or Varner's, figure as importantly as Lena's in the opening chapter not because their thoughts are in any way special, but for the very reason that they are common: each participates in a communal psychic voice in his response to this young, pregnant girl walking and riding her way from Alabama. The "gossip" of the mind plays a role equally important in the community's discourse as the gossip actually exchanged between neighbors. The novel consistently applies the same mechanics of depicting thought for all characters throughout the novel, causing psychic voice to pervade all the discourse, as if we were to regard consciousness as one feature of the broad discursive landscape that all characters traverse. Faulkner enhances this effect by recording anonymous speaking voices as well as characters' thoughts in italics without end punctuation, a technique he also uses to record thought. Thus thought and anonymous voices come to exert equivalent effects on the reader. Lena thinks of her journey as "filled with nameless kind faces and voices: *Lucas Burch? You say you tried in Pocahontas? This road? It goes to Springvale. You wait here. There will be a wagon passing soon that will take you as far as it goes* Thinking . . ." (9; 6). The voices of the mob at the fire, "wind- or air-engendered," are cast in the same form as thought: "*Is that him? Is that the one that did it? Sheriff's got him. Sheriff has already caught him* The sheriff looked at them" (319; 275; see also 459; 394).

Faulkner also blends psychic voice into the narrative discourse by techniques designed to establish the diegetic narrative as someone's "knowledge." Chapter 2 begins "Byron Bunch knows this:" so that the reader will treat what follows as "in" Byron's consciousness. Byron does not narrate this chapter, but his psychic voice pervades the rendering, for we hear frequently what Byron "knows," or "believes," or "thinks" as he listens to the stories about Hightower. His thoughts pick up the thread of narrative as if he were participating in the telling:

> [The doctor] also approved of Hightower's work, and the husband was satisfied too.
> 'But it was just too close to that other business,' Byron thought, 'even despite the fifteen years between them.' (80; 68)

A verbal object, the sign in Hightower's front yard, is rendered first as a sign, in roman type, centered and capitalized as it looks to any observer:

REV. GAIL HIGHTOWER, D.D.
Art Lessons
Handpainted Xmas & Anniversary Cards
Photographs Developed   (62; 53)

We then learn how the sign "looks" in Byron's awareness, rendered in his psychic voice, in italics, without end punctuation, and not identically quoted: "When Byron Bunch first came to Jefferson seven years ago and saw that little sign *Gail Hightower D.D. Art Lessons Christmas Cards Photographs Developed* he thought 'D.D. What is D.D.' and he asked . . ." (64; 55).

Faulkner also emphasizes the *present* consciousness of a character and the past events that impinge on that consciousness by shifts between present and past verb tenses. All the chapters except those dealing with Joe Christmas's past life (chapters 6–12) contain shifts in narrative verb tense. Like those in *As I Lay Dying*, the switches between past and present modulate the relation between a character's experience and the events described. Byron has learned of Hightower's history in Jefferson through many years of listening to people talk, and he retains in the present the knowledge so gained. This merely temporal difference, inherent in tense and in the chronology of Byron learning about Hightower, is also a quality in Byron's psychic voice, as his thoughts and knowledge move in and out of past and present experience. Faulkner manages the shifts (as he did in *As I Lay Dying*) with great flexibility: he always renders past events in past tense, but he may couch *thoughts* about those events in either past or present tense. To summarize only one example: the long passage describing how the town finally reconciled itself to Hightower's presence weaves Byron's psychic voice into the the depiction of events by representing both what he "thought" and what he "thinks":

> Then all of a sudden the whole thing *seemed* to blow away. . . . As though, Byron *thought*, the entire affair *had been* a lot of people performing a play and that *now* and at last they *had all played out* the parts which had been allotted them. . . . the neighbors *began* to send him dishes again . . . it was food, and wellmeant. Because, as Byron *thought*, people forget a lot in twenty years. 'Why,' he *thinks*, 'I dont reckon there is anybody in Jefferson that knows that he sits in that window from sundown to full dark every day that comes, except me. . . .' Because there *is* one other thing, which *came* into Byron's own knowledge and observation, in his own time since he came to Jefferson to live.
>
> Hightower read a great deal. That is, Byron *had examined* with a kind of musing . . . (78–79; 67, emphasis added)

The manuscript of *Light in August* reveals that the early chapters dealing with Byron, Lena, and Hightower were originally written as quoted colloquial narration. The manuscript contains many passages written in colloquial dialect, usually on sheets pasted onto the final manuscript pages. Some of the changes necessitated by third-person authorial narrative voice are made in the manuscript, others not until the final typescript. The manuscript also shows that Faulkner experimented with verb tense after he composed the original colloquial episode, for he made or indicated many such changes throughout the manuscript. Tenses on the pasted-on portions differ from those on the undersheets (onto which the original episode is attached). The revisions demonstrate, among other things, how surprisingly few major stylistic distinctions exist between the authorial voice and a town narrator. The revisions also suggest that Faulkner wanted to avoid relying on any single type of voice to render Byron's and the town's experience of Hightower: a pure exercise in colloquial narration could not so fluidly blend mimetic voice with authorial and psychic voice.

Like Byron's "knowledge" of Hightower, Joe's childhood experience is captioned as "memory" contained "within" his psyche. Phrases like "memory believes before knowing remembers" produce psychic voice by fiat. By themselves such pronouncements in the text create voice only in the weakest fashion, for the effect of a chapter's opening phrase diminishes over pages of narrative. As part of the novel's overall infusion of psychic voice into all other discourses, however, the power of such incantations enhances (and is enhanced by) the *attention* the text pays to consciousness. Though receiving no abstract explication, the distinctions between "memory" and "knowledge" nonetheless help evoke the varied levels of awareness created elsewhere, as we have seen, by the manner in which verbal thought is quoted, by the shifting verb tense, and by the direct descriptions of thought.

The psychic voice in *Light in August* reaches its profoundest expression in Gail Hightower's meditation in chapter 20, the novel's final view of the minister. In this superb example of a Faulknerian meditative scene in which a character struggles through painful thoughts toward a release into oblivion, Hightower sits once again at his window waiting for the vision of his grandfather to emerge from the twilight, from the "final copper light of afternoon." Hightower sits on the cusp between day and night, moving inexorably toward an apotheosis of moral comprehension. As he waits for the "dying yellow fall of trumpets" that always signals his recurring hallucination, he reaches a moment when "two instants [are] about to touch." That touching will this time spark another vision, one in which he simultaneously discovers his personal moral responsibility for his wife's death and for other human beings like Joe Christmas, and achieves the last visionary escape that leaves "his body empty and lighter than a forgotten leaf and even more trivial than flotsam lying spent and still upon the window ledge" (543; 466).[8]

In Hightower's meditation the movement from blockage to release, typical of the Faulknerian psychic voice, is brilliantly elaborated in the concluding figure of the wheel turning slowly in sand. After reviewing his childhood, his marriage, and his call to Jefferson's ministry, Hightower reaches a point of moral recognition—at least as an abstract discovery that "God cannot be accused by man and held responsible" for all his failings (538; 462). At this point Faulkner draws his metaphor: "Thinking begins to slow now. It slows like a wheel beginning to run in sand, the axle, the vehicle, the power which propels it not yet aware" (541; 462). The wheel turns slowly at first, grinding to a halt at Hightower's realization that he is culpable in his wife's death: "Thinking is running too heavily now . . . *I dont want to think this*" (464). What he thinks, horrible as it is to him, sets him free to pass into oblivion as the wheel of thinking is "released" in the final revelation that accompanies his last vision: "The wheel turns on. It spins now, fading, without progress" (543; 466). Hightower has finally entered into the realm of consciousness sharable within the human community as well as within the text's discourse; he is caught up in that psychic voice that all the characters share, and he is put in his place along the continuum that extends both "down" into the deepest unconscious and "up" into the communal memory that Joe Christmas's crucified spirit ascends into in chapter 19, riding the "unbelievable crescendo" of the siren, "passing out of the realm of hearing" (513; 440).

THE TEXT OF ISAAC McCASLIN'S CONSCIOUSNESS

Recalling the technique in *Light in August* by which Faulkner denominates whole portions of a text as a character's knowledge ("Byron Bunch knows this"), we can regard *Go Down, Moses* as a psychic text because it denominates its total discourse as being what one character, Isaac McCaslin, knows. Ike's consciousness, if not always his life and experience, pervades the novel, beginning with events that occur before his birth (in "Was") and ending (in "Go Down, Moses") with events after he dies. Ike's consciousness is coextensive with the text's discourse, beginning and ending not with his physical birth and death but with the text itself; Ike "lives" everywhere within the discourse. The psychic voice in *Go Down, Moses* creates a sense of the infinite nature of consciousness that cannot perceive its own death from within, as described by Bakhtin:

> Consciousness, by its very nature, cannot have a consciously perceived (that is, a consciousness-finalizing) beginning, nor can it have an end located in a sequence of consciousness at its ultimate link and made out of the same material as other elements of consciousness. A beginning and an end, a birth and a death are possessed by a person, a life, a fate, but not by consciousness, which by its very nature is

infinite, revealing itself only from within, that is only for consciousness itself. (*Problems of Dostoevsky's Poetics* 290)

We perceive the novel's events "only from within" Ike's consciousness,
even where those events are not shown to be perceived by Ike himself.
Thus even a story ("Go Down, Moses") whose events occur chronologically after Ike has died inhabits that consciousness the reader has come to
share. The verisimilitude of physical fact gives way (as it does with Darl
Bundren's clairvoyance or Addie's postmortem monologue) to the reader's
felt participation in Ike's psychic voice. In Ike's case "consciousness" no
longer refers only to what is inside the confining space of the mind, but
rather to a regional and moral heritage that exists in Ike's psyche and that
his psyche in turn inhabits. *Go Down, Moses* interrogates the distinction
between "inside" and "outside" in mental life as it makes consciousness in
this enlarged sense the fixed ground from which the reader's experience
derives.

Even at its most intensely vivid moments *Go Down, Moses* exudes an
aura of time long past, as if everything that happens has already happened
and exists or occurs only in Ike's awareness. Since the novel includes
events he has not necessarily witnessed or even heard about, and since the
novel ends after his death, the term "awareness" embraces all of Ike's heritage and region—all that his consciousness could absorb by virtue of who
he is and where he was born. Faulkner occasionally reminds us of this
quality of pastness by referring, within a scene of Ike's youth, to Ike as a
grown man: "1874 the boy; 1888 the man, repudiated denied and free;
1895 and husband but no father" (281). We know explicitly, in the fourth
part of "The Bear," that the ledgers Ike reads make up "a part of his
consciousness and would remain so forever" (271). In a scene in which the
boy Ike feels that he is metaphorically "witnessing his own birth," he
draws an image of stasis from his experience as a grown man: "The surrey
itself seemed to have ceased to move (this too to be completed later, years
later, after he had grown to a man and had seen the sea) as a solitary small
boat hangs in lonely immobility, merely tossing up and down" (195). The
prelude to the opening story, "Was," announces that Ike has heard but not
observed or acted in the events that follow, events that form part of his oral
heritage, "not something he had participated in or even remembered except from the hearing, the listening, come to him through and from his
cousin McCaslin" (4). Faulkner designates an unnamed "he" through
whose observation the story is filtered. "He" is literally Ike's cousin Mc-

Caslin Edmonds, but "he" stands as well for Ike as a vicarious central consciousness, as if consciousness itself, like knowledge of the family past, can be passed on from generation to generation. Different personae, including Ike himself, assume the position of "he"—Lucas in "The Fire and the Hearth," Rider in "Pantaloon in Black," Gavin Stevens in "Go Down, Moses"—but all are, in the crucial sense of *central* consciousness, foils for Isaac McCaslin. The prelude to "Was" hints, through familiar textual features of the Faulknerian psychic voice, that it does not simply frame a colloquial tale, but rather opens a window into a psyche. The incomplete syntax, the lack of an uppercase letter at the beginning of paragraphs, and the lack of punctuation at the end signal the representation (if not the direct quotation) of consciousness.

Although Faulkner does not dramatize the storytelling through which Ike has learned his heritage (as he dramatizes, for example, the scenes in *Absalom, Absalom!* in which Quentin listens to Rosa Coldfield and Mr Compson), the novel does trumpet the evocative power of an oral heritage to bring the past into the living present of Ike's knowledge and experience. The events come from "out of the old time, the old days," revivified and called forth into Ike's present awareness: "gradually to the boy those old times would cease to be old times and would become a part of the boy's present" ("The Old People" 171). So fully does the story telling shape Ike's experience that "the boy even at almost eighty would never be able to distinguish certainly between what he had seen and what had been told him" ("The Bear" 291). The tales that Ike hears do not transport him back into the past, but rather bring the past "forward" into his present awareness. What *is* present in Isaac McCaslin's consciousness, then, embraces two pasts, the past of event (chasing Tomey's Turl, hunting Old Ben) and the past of listening and learning about such events. There is a profound nostalgia in *Go Down, Moses*, but it is primarily a nostalgia for the second past, for the lost immediacy of listening, for "the best game of all, the best of all breathing and forever the best of all listening" ("The Bear" 192). This nostalgia constitutes yet another version of the yearning for the elusive presence of voice that pervades Faulkner's fiction.

To say that all the events in *Go Down, Moses* reside coextensively with Isaac McCaslin's psyche is not to say that this is in any conventional way a stream-of-consciousness or even a psychological novel, for its intent is not to reveal the inner workings of a character's mental life so much as it is to invoke that inner life as the groundwork for our reading experience. Much of what goes on in the various stories has so little to do with Ike that we must speak of his consciousness in the broad sense of background or heritage, a heritage he "knows" but that is not necessarily actively or portraya-bly present in his thoughts. After the prelude, in which discernible fea-tures of psychic voice seem to announce a psychic text, no significant features of the Faulknerian psychic voice (other than italicized, directly quoted thoughts) appear again until part 4 of "The Bear," some 250 pages later. Ike's point of view is ignored until "The Old People" (the novel's fourth story) and there, as well as in the first three parts of "The Bear," Ike serves as listener or participant in events, but Faulkner does not often represent his consciousness with those special features we associate with the Faulknerian psychic voice.

Faulkner collected previously written and in some cases previously pub-lished stories to form *Go Down, Moses*, and added as new material the crucial fourth part of "The Bear." A common criticism of part 4 is that it edges the novel away from dramatization toward exposition, and thus its addition to the previously written material marks a falling off in Faulkner's art. That Isaac in part 4 is "trying to explain to the head of my family something which I have got to do which I don't quite understand myself, not in justification of it but to explain it if I can" creates for many readers a serious flaw: the section expostulates on what is more effectively and viv-idly dramatized in "The Bear"'s hunting story. Joseph Gold typically com-plains of Faulkner's "pulpit tendency," and of the "long, sententious de-bate between Isaac and his cousin McCaslin which amounts to an analysis of the significance and meaning of what has passed before in the more convincing narrative part of the story" (5).

One way to answer this criticism is to point out, as John Matthews has, that talking is the fundamental act in not only "The Bear" but in all of *Go Down, Moses*. The novel ritualizes mourning: not only Ike but all the char-acters try to articulate their grief at the loss of a better world. The talking in *Go Down, Moses* stems not from Faulkner's desperate desire to explain, but from an act that allows "those who perform the ritual of the hunt [to speak] their grief over the loss of the wilderness, or big game, or a simpler, more heroic past" (Matthews 212–13). Matthews correctly contends that talk in part 4 is not excessive but essential; announced as a speech act in the section's second sentence, "Now he could say it," Ike's renunciation of the McCaslin land is also an enunciation of his moral knowledge (Matt-hews 257). Part 4 does gather around itself the discursive wilderness of the rest of *Go Down, Moses*, binding the disparate stories thematically in the context of Ike's moral values.

But to describe the section as speech distorts somewhat its fundamental role in turning the collection of stories into a psychic *text*. More important than what it expresses of Ike's moral education is what it embodies and represents of his consciousness. Or, to put this distinction in terms appropriate to this study of voice, part 4 is less fruitfully regarded as an instance of mimetic voice (though Ike does speak at great length) than as psychic voice—especially in its textual manifestations. Complaints like Gold's misconstrue the real aesthetic issue Faulkner raises here, for in this central section Faulkner not only "explains" the themes inherent in the novel's other narratives, and not only dramatizes attempts to articulate the significance of those themes but, more important, he subordinates these concerns to the textual representation of Isaac's consciousness. The creation of psychic voice in part 4 of "The Bear" demonstrates not a falling off of Faulkner's art but rather one of his more radical and arguably successful experiments in psychic voice.

The structure of part 4 reflects the moral knowledge that Ike gains and tries to explain to McCaslin. Interrupting the chronological sequence of "The Bear" by depicting events that begin when Ike is twenty-one (two years after part 5, in which he first returned to the woods after Old Ben had been killed), part 4 is a parenthetical text contained within a larger discourse. In order to explain and embody Ike's knowledge, Faulkner *inserted*—rather than added on—a text of psychic representation. As part 4 is itself bracketed by the rest of "The Bear" (and "The Bear" by the rest of *Go Down, Moses*), so its own structure builds on parenthetical insertions. The pages dealing with the ledgers interrupt the debate between Ike and Cass. In the middle of the debate Ike says, "'Yes. More men that [*sic*] Father and Uncle Buddy,' not even glancing toward the shelf above the desk" (261). The debate does not resume for twenty-one pages, when McCaslin repeats what Ike last said: "'More men than that one Buck and Buddy to fumbleheed that truth'" (282). The ledgers in their turn are interrupted by a parenthetical story (263–65) about Percival Brownlee, the one slave Uncle Buck and Uncle Buddy bought.[9] Like sets of brackets, the various discourses of *Go Down, Moses* surround and zero in on Ike's central discovery:

$$
\begin{array}{l}
Go \\
Down, \\
Moses
\end{array}
\left(
\begin{array}{l}
\text{``The} \\
\text{Bear''}
\end{array}
\left(
\begin{array}{l}
\text{part} \\
4
\end{array}
\left(
\begin{array}{l}
\text{the} \\
\text{de-} \\
\text{bate}
\end{array}
\left(
\begin{array}{l}
\text{the} \\
\text{led-} \\
\text{gers}
\end{array}
\left(\quad\right)
\begin{array}{l}
\text{the} \\
\text{led-} \\
\text{gers}
\end{array}
\right)
\begin{array}{l}
\text{the} \\
\text{de-} \\
\text{bate}
\end{array}
\right)
\begin{array}{l}
\text{part} \\
4
\end{array}
\right)
\begin{array}{l}
\text{``The} \\
\text{Bear''}
\end{array}
\right)
\begin{array}{l}
Go \\
Down, \\
Moses
\end{array}
$$

While short, parenthetical insertions are possible in speech, lengthy interruptions require written embodiment. The debate as written script, as text—not the debate as a mimetic speech act—best represents the nature of Ike's increasingly focused moral awareness, as each insertion narrows our attention toward the central discovery of the ledgers.

This pattern requires that each inserted text in some way differentiate itself from the texts that contain it, or that it contains. The three stories in which Ike is the protagonist are, for example, distinguished from the remaining stories in *Go Down, Moses* by the presence of Ike as the explicit central consciousness. The most important bracketing, however, is of part 4 itself, for with this insertion Faulkner seeks to coalesce the entire novel into a coherent whole. He differentiates part 4 from the remainder of "The Bear" (and from the rest of *Go Down, Moses* with the exception of the prelude to "Was") with the syntactical and textual features usual to his psychic voice. Parts 1–3 and 5 are punctuated conventionally, but in part 4 Faulkner deletes typographical signs for beginnings and endings of paragraphs: the section opens with lower case "then he was twenty-one," and subsequent narrative paragraphs (as distinct from paragraphs in dialogue) begin without upper-case letters; narrative paragraphs (including the section's last) also end without punctuation. The lack of beginning capitals and the missing end punctuation enhance the "run-on" effect of Faulkner's long, accretive sentences. Some paragraph breaks match syntactical shifts, but many continue a syntactical unit, picking up a previously unraveling thread of an idea that may have begun pages earlier: "a silver cup filled with gold pieces and wrapped in burlap and sealed with his godfather's ring in the hot wax, which (intact still) . . . had become not only a legend but one of the family lares" (301). "the cup, the sealed inscrutable burlap, sitting on the shelf in the locked closet" (304). Such prose establishes and maintains a consistent (and typically Faulknerian) rhythm in that most narrative paragraphs begin with a phrase that either repeats or is in logical (and often in grammatical) apposition to a previously mentioned noun. For example, Ike says the phrase "as a loan" one page (308) prior to its appearance at the beginning of a paragraph (309) in the diegetic discourse (see also 261, 262, 263). The rhythm creates a version of that continuous verbal flow we associate with conventional interior monologue writing, a convention based on the assumption that such a stream of consciousness echoes the processes of the mind and emotions, which have neither time nor inclination to honor grammatical or logical distinctions.

Faulkner, however, mitigates the "run-on" effect of the prose in various ways. The few sentence breaks within narrative paragraphs are marked conventionally: "not being the Nazarene, he would not have chosen it: and paid it back. He had forgotten the thirty dollars which McCaslin would put into the bank in his name each month" (310). The majority of paragraph breaks occur within the extended debate between Ike and McCaslin, and these are both logically and conventionally justified by the change in speaker and are punctuated normally. Here, as in all his novels, Faulkner's most ornate syntax, no matter how endlessly spun out into long sentences, follows grammatical rules. A relentless, accretive logic, in fact, drives these oratorical periods—they do not convey the sense of a mind lacking discursive controls so much as of a voice in too-complete command of its own rhetoric.[10]

While creating the effect of interior monologue by adopting certain conventions of stream-of-consciousness writing, Faulkner does not attempt to quote or *record* thought, or to represent a discourse that we are to regard as "flowing through" or "occurring in" Isaac McCaslin's mind. Merely by deleting beginning capitals and end punctuation, and by an accretive syntax, he succeeds in creating a discourse that is akin to quoted interior monologue yet still is his own clearly authorial rhetoric. Faulkner has it both ways: a psychic voice that moves us into the mind and a discourse not limited by imitative demands of a single idiosyncratic persona. As Albert Guerard has noted, with Isaac McCaslin (and other solitaries in Faulkner's fiction), the "rich rhetoric . . . has the effect of interior discourse" (37).

Other features of psychic voice that contribute to the effect of interior discourse are recognizable as such because they are familiar from other Faulkner texts. In the dialogue throughout part 4 Faulkner uses single quotation marks to bracket spoken words, instead of the double quotes used everywhere else in "The Bear" and in *Go Down, Moses*. Because elsewhere in Faulkner—as we saw most extensively in *Light in August*—single quotes mark a discourse derived from a deeper, less public realm of consciousness than words in double quotes, this otherwise unremarkable detail transforms the mimetic voices of part 4 into psychic voice, tinging them with Ike's overriding central consciousness in which all events in the novel symbolically reside. In *Light in August* the single quotes achieved their effect through immediate proximity to the double quotes and the italics in which differing levels of interior discourse were couched. In *Go Down, Moses* the contrast is among sections of a novel, making part 4 an insertion of interior discourse into the more public narrative sections with their "normal" double quotes. Faulkner here seeks a version of the layering of consciousness into variable "depths" or "intensities" that we saw in

Light in August, but without pretending that all the words are quotations from Ike's inner speech.

Two other techniques distinguish the debate between Ike and Cass from the rest of part 4: the use of capitals at the beginning of paragraphs, and a stylized speaker identification. Except for the first ("'Relinquish,' McCaslin said. 'Relinquish. You . . .'") and an occasional exception (as on 257), the speech tags are all of the form "and he" or "and McCaslin" attached to the end of paragraphs to identify the speaker who follows:

> 'or perhaps He would not see—perverse, impotent, or blind: which?' and he
> > 'Dispossessed.' and McCaslin
> > 'What?' and he
> > 'Dispossessed. Not impotent' (258)

Such identification stylizes the dialogue, turning it into an extended version of those dialogic confrontations discussed in chapter 2, in which two antagonists battle each other through the medium of words. Faulkner used this "and he" form (though in a passage without paragraph breaks) in *The Sound and the Fury* for the talk between Quentin and his father about Quentin's claimed incest with Caddy. The talk between father and son is highly charged emotionally and drawn from deep within Quentin's psyche. Ike's announcement and explanation of why he must renounce his inheritance is also a "son's" confession to a father figure ("I'm trying to explain to the head of my family something which I have got to do" [288]), and likewise probes deeply into a young man's psyche. But unlike Quentin's confused and chaotic memory, the rhetoric of the Ike-Cass debate is controlled and coherent, full of logical connectives like "for the reason that," "for which reason," "because," and of grammatical terms that draw parallels ("just as") or make distinctions ("not . . . but"); Isaac is not merely expressing, but explaining, trying to interpret the story of his family's past. Faulkner appropriately and ironically renders Ike's efforts to explain that past as an attempt to argue with a "father" because the significance of Ike's past lies in the silencing of the symbolic voice of the father. Ike's slave-owning grandfather, Carothers McCaslin, and all the McCaslins who follow have disqualified themselves to speak with the proper paternal authority—and Ike himself will always be just *Uncle* Ike." What Ike is trying to explain to his cousin is what he has discovered about his past and what he comes to harbor in his consciousness: proof of the moral failure of his patrimony.[11]

The proof is textual in nature. Ike discovers his heritage in the ledgers, themselves a parenthetical insertion within the Ike-Cass debate. The portion of part 4 that deals with the ledgers is distinguished from the debate, first, by a shift back to the uncapitalized or end-punctuated paragraphing that began part 4; second, by the direct citation of the ledger entries in set-off, italicized paragraphs; and, finally, by inclusion of brief digressions rendered in conventional capitalization, punctuation, and speaker identification (that is, the brief description of Ike at age sixteen going into the commissary to read the ledgers [268–69] and the passages chronicling Ike's efforts to give each descendent of Carothers McCaslin his or her legacy [273–81]).

At the heart of the ledgers is a gap, an empty space in the text (and in my representation, page 158) that perfectly symbolizes the failed patrimony Ike finds evidence for in the ledgers: "and the white man himself had travelled three hundred miles and better to New Orleans in a day when men travelled by horseback or steamboat, and bought the girl's mother as a wife for   and that was all. The old frail pages seemed to turn of their own accord even while he thought *His own daughter His own daughter. No No Not even him*" (270). At this moment Ike realizes that his grandfather has committed incest as well as miscegenation in fathering a child on his slave daughter Tomasina. The entire novel focuses on this parenthetical blank space that harbors the unspeakable (the word "incest" never appears in the ledgers) proof to Ike that the McCaslin heritage is corrupt.

Go Down, Moses, then, enfolds itself around a textual void, a silent point in a psychic text. But what are we to make of this gap, this silence? Perhaps it is not blank at all, for Ike's *knowledge* contains no gaps: he can answer the questions the ledgers raise with the unspoken taboo word "incest." He understands what act his grandfather committed, even though he can never justify the compassionless greed behind it. The facts of the case validate Ike's renunciation of his heritage. The McCaslin land *is* tainted, and Ike's refusal to taint himself makes both emotional and moral, though perhaps not pragmatic, sense. Many readers treat Ike's gesture as well intended but too idealistic, perhaps unmanly, or doomed certainly to failure because it can never match the spiritual wholeness of the experiences with Sam in the woods. (Faulkner himself seems to have felt that Ike's repudiation was justified but insufficient. Ike should have done "more than just repudiate. He should have been more affirmative instead of shunning people.")[12] One interesting version of this judgment on Ike, and one particularly relevant to our study of voice, rests on the diminished efficacy of a heritage that is preserved in writing instead of in orally told story. What Sam transmits is an *oral* heritage, superior culturally and even morally to the written, commercial record embodied in the ledgers. Wesley Morris argues that Faulkner demonstrates speech's purity, its grounding in a natural and spiritual wholeness unavailable to writing. Morris finds a parallel for the inadequacy of Ike's gesture in the very discursive form of the ledgers, arguing that the ledgers are history instead of myth, that they reduce time to chronology and make Ike "a slave to prose unable to transform it into an autobiographical narrative [or to] enter Sam's collective myth, which is spoken, not written" (74).

Admittedly, much in *Go Down, Moses* warrants treating Ike ironically. His great innocence shows when he loses his wife's sexual affection by refusing her request that he assume ownership of the farm, and his self-conscious imitation of "the Nazarene" has perhaps too much of pride and too little of humility in it. Certainly, also, "Delta Autumn" would appear to give the lie to Ike's heroic verbal defense (to Cass in their debate) of the black race, for he can only shout to himself *"Not now!"* in the face of the young black woman's suggestion that "miscegenation" is not a taboo at all, that lovers of even different races deserve their romantic place in the sun. But in other senses Isaac McCaslin should be taken quite seriously, with no irony, as Faulkner's most successful affirmative hero—the only one among his protagonists who refuses to be victimized by the discourses that have created him. For whatever the practical inadequacies of Ike's chosen action, he does fill the void at the heart of his psychic text, rather than succumb like Quentin to suicide's silence, or like Darl to insane laughter, or to the belated and empty self-discoveries of Gail Hightower. Ike is not destroyed by the voices he hearkens to; instead he learns to read and thus to master them. We should not denigrate the *value* of Ike's experience with the written.

It might be said that Faulkner created in Ike a listener born into an oral tradition, but one who matures beyond that heritage by learning to read a written text—and thereby to document the need for a moral response to the anomalies of his heritage. As a listener Ike experienced the revivifying power of his oral heritage under the tutelage of Sam Fathers. The paeans to told story that bring the old times into Ike's presence validate the discursive version of Sam's role as father, for Sam's is the voice of the father imbued with authority, dignity, and respect for life. Ike knows that no document can prove his "ownership" of the land Sam inhabits, "that although it had been his grandfather's and then his father's and uncle's and was now his cousin's and someday would be his own land which he and Sam hunted over, their hold upon it actually was as trivial and without reality as the now faded and archaic script in the chancery book in Jefferson which allocated it to them and that it was he, the boy, who was the guest here and Sam Father's voice the mouthpiece of the host" (171). The voice of the host, the forest's spirit, has the power to make Isaac (and McCaslin before him) *see* what may only be imaginary. The buck Sam addresses as "grandfather" comes into existence only when he has prepared the boy's imagination, only when Ike's listening fulfills itself through participation in the ritual hunt. Ike's initiation is a training of his power to imagine as well as to hunt: he learns to call into being what is not there.

Yet Ike's moral training cannot complete itself with mere listening. He must also become a reader, an active interpreter, and not simply a passive listener. His active participation begins when he tracks and sees Old Ben for the first time. An almost mystical conjoining of Ike with the spirit of nature (he must relinquish his gun, compass, and watch), this famous scene is also a scene of reading. For Ike has earned the right to see Old Ben by learning to read the "markless wilderness," by following the traces of the bear, "seeing as he sat down on the log the crooked print, the warped indentation in the wet ground which while he looked at it continued to fill with water. . . . Even as he looked up he saw the next one, and, moving, the one beyond it" (208–9). As Ike follows the prints the bear appears— whether to Ike's actual sight or to his imagination hardly matters, for he has demonstrated that he is worthy to read the wilderness.[13]

After this initiation—into nature and into man's claims on nature—it is not fanciful to say that Ike has also become worthy to read and interpret the ledgers. The opening of part 4 legitimately—not ironically—describes Ike's new authority: "then he was twenty-one. He could say it" (254). Ike, as Wyatt says, "celebrates his majority by wresting the narration of his life" from others and thus assuming the "authority and autonomy of voice" (83). It is an autonomy, however, that Ike gains from reading and interpreting; he has not merely grown from listener to speaker, but from listener to *auditor*—one who listens *and* also one who examines the books. The ledgers are, after all, commercial documents detailing credits and debits. Uncle Hubert also passes on a heritage that is a palpable and valued object that begins as a silver cup full of money and ends up as a series of IOUs to Ike (some, appropriately, written on ledger paper). It is appropriate, too, that Percival Brownlee, the one slave Buck ever bought, was purchased as a "cleark" and "Bookepper" (264). The consciousness Faulkner seeks to represent through the psychic voice in part 4 is the consciousness of an auditor trained to balance the books, to interpret and take an accounting.

This is not to say that the oral heritage learned from Sam must be abandoned or transcended; rather it must be assimilated and built upon. Ike must supplement his oral heritage with experience of the written word. The ledgers are brilliantly conceived as symbolic of *both* Ike's oral heritage and of his maturing powers as a reader. Written documents, the ledgers are nonetheless speechlike. "Long since past any oral intercourse" (263), Uncle Buck and Uncle Buddy "talk" to each other through the ledger entries. Faulkner's text reports the entries as it might report dialogue, as verbal exchanges with the "speakers" identified and in which the twins address questions and answers to each other:

> and this time it was the other, the hand which he now recognized as his uncle's . . .
> *Mar 23th 1856 Cant do that either Except one at a Time Get shut of him*
> then the first again:
> *24 Mar 1856 Who in hell would buy him*
> then the second:
> *19th of Apr 1856 Nobody You put yourself out of Market at Cold Water two months ago I never said sell him Free him*
> the first:
> *22 Apr 1856 Ill get it out of him.* (264)

But Faulkner also insists on the written quality of the ledgers, on their status as written text. The "yellow pages scrawled in fading ink" abide in ways that speech cannot. These ledgers will last, if not forever, at least until they can be "spread open on the desk or perhaps some apocryphal Bench or even altar or perhaps before the Throne itself" before fading back forever into the "anonymous communal original dust" (261). The ledgers create their own kind of textual voice in that their expressiveness derives in part from visual effects alone. Uncle Buck's and Uncle Buddy's handwriting is described, and certain features of their entries (such as abbreviations and odd spellings) are distinguishable only as written codes. The entry mentioning the "10acre peace" of land willed to the slave

Thucydus puns on the spelling as well as the sound of "piece" (266). Faulkner differentiates the two writers by how they date the entries, by how they inscribe dollar amounts—by traits that are primarily visual. The ledgers retain their status as written text just as much as they take on the immediate presence of speech in Ike's mind. Faulkner overrides the distinction between the written and the spoken to gain immediacy *and* permanence, bringing both qualities to the service of the psychic text that documents Ike's difficult moral maturation.

I would suggest that Faulkner included the qualities of the written in his representation of those discourses that comprise Ike's consciousness because he wanted the ledgers to serve as *evidence*: evidence in a way that stories told and retold cannot serve, evidence in the sense of information that can be discovered, analyzed, retained, and brought forward (as in court, appropriate to Ike's image of the "apocryphal Bench") to prove the nature of the McCaslin heritage. In this desire for evidence, as much as in what Gold called Faulkner's "pulpit tendency," we can see a desire for certainty characteristic of Faulkner's later novels. Ike does not speculate the way Quentin Compson speculates (and fictionalizes) in *Absalom, Absalom!*. He is not collecting versions of the past. Though he must interpret the ledgers, he believes that one correct interpretation exists. Ike knows because he has proof—he has read the tale of incest in the ledgers. They provide evidence that, unlike spoken story, can remain immutable, potentially nonambiguous once interpreted, and permanently recorded (and cannot be thrown out of court as mere hearsay evidence). Ike knows his grandfather bought a slave as a mistress for himself and then fathered a child on the daughter (his own) of that slave. Unlike the interpretations Quentin must recover in *Absalom, Absalom!*, the evidence here is not simply an oral heritage that Ike must reproduce every time he would try to understand it. "He would never need look at the ledgers again nor did he; the yellowed pages in their fading and implacable succession were as much a part of his consciousness and would remain so forever, as the fact of his own nativity" (271). The evidence is repeatable, exactly, fixed in its form. This is not to argue that what Ike discovers is free of moral ambiguity; like any "truth," well-intentioned humans can only "fumbleheed at it." But to the extent he can glean true evidence by reading and interpreting texts, Ike has achieved truth within his consciousness. Part 4 of "The Bear" brackets a certain kind of represented discourse and turns it into knowledge, not in a simple recording of thought but in a symbolic and evidential presentation of psychic voice in textual form.

THE COMPSON MONOLOGUES

Faulkner's greatest experiment in psychic voices is universally acknowledged as one of modern literature's masterful achievements in the representation of consciousness. "With the exception of Joyce's *Ulysses*, Faulkner's *The Sound and the Fury* . . . is probably the most important modern experiment in the use of narrative techniques to give form to individual structures of consciousness" (Iser 136). Even the brilliant *As I Lay Dying* seems fragmented by comparison in its versatile skipping across the surface of many speakers' voices. Nowhere else does Faulkner submerge us into psyche's discourse with the same intensity, duration, or tragic agony as in *The Sound and the Fury*.

Having already considered the role voice plays in the novel's fourth section (see chapter 1), we will consider here the method Faulkner employs for generating psychic voice in the three interior monologues by Benjy, Quentin, and Jason Compson. So strikingly different are the three characters—a congenital idiot, a suicidal Harvard freshman, and a Mississippi redneck bigot—that we could easily forget that Faulkner uses substantially the same procedure in each section. Each of the sections has as its foundation a conventional first-person narrative, as each brother tells a story of the events occurring on one particular day. The three accounts are *conventional* first-person narratives because, in telling of each day's happenings, the brothers fulfill the functions normally expected of narrators. They recount their days' events in chronological sequence. They describe things and actions. They quote dialogue and carefully identify speakers just as the authorial voice does in the fourth chapter. They employ the past tense, the most common narrative tense. By and large they remain faithful to their narrative duties when depicting what takes place on that one day.[14]

We can perhaps elucidate the narrative quality of Faulkner's technique by contrasting it briefly with two other methods of writing first-person interior monologue. Virginia Woolf, in *The Waves*, quotes the thoughts of six different characters, alternating among them as she traces their lives from school age to death. Her protagonists engage in explicit introspection: they consciously endeavor to express their own feelings and ideas, a process the reader overhears:

"The purple light," said Rhoda, "in Miss Lambert's ring passes to and fro across the black stain on the white page of the Prayer Book.

It is a vinous, it is an amorous light. . . . [H]ere I am nobody. I have no face. This great company, all dressed in brown serge, has robbed me of my identity. We are all callous, unfriended. I will seek out a face, a composed, a monumental face, and will endow it with omniscience, and wear it under my dress like a talisman and then (I promise this) I will find some dingle in a wood where I can display my assortment of curious treasures, I promise myself this. So I will not cry" (34).

The protagonists in *The Waves* narrate casually, giving us only those events or sensory perceptions that they can use in self-analysis, concentrating primarily on their private ruminations. Narration plays a secondary role to Rhoda's efforts to verbalize what the things she sees—the light, the other students—mean to her. "This great company, all dressed in brown serge, has robbed me of my identity." Though only of school age, Rhoda is a self-conscious and highly articulate critic of her own soul. None of the Compson brothers engages in this kind of introspection. They express but do not analyze their own thoughts or emotions. Rather than elucidating their own psyches, they narrate in modes of discourse that become unwittingly revelatory. Benjy is genetically incapable of self-analysis, and Jason's concern with superficial matters, plus his assumption that he already understands everything, preclude introspection; Quentin, while occasionally aware of his thoughts (he does identify two parts of his monologue as "thinking"), does not discuss them overtly, nor does he try to explain his feelings to us. Instead, he couches emotions in highly charged imagery or in dramatically remembered scenes. Quentin might *feel* (like Rhoda) "robbed" of his "identity," but he does not say so in such bald terms.

In *Ulysses* James Joyce imitates Molly Bloom's internal reverie by rendering her thoughts as a continuous flow of memories, images, and opinions: "hed like me to walk in all the horses dung I could find but of course hes not natural like the rest of the world that I what did he say I could give 9 points in 10 to Katty Lanner and beat her what does that mean I asked him I forget what he said because the stoppress edition just passed and the man with curly hair in the Lucan dairy thats so polite I think I saw his face before somewhere" (745). Joyce immerses us in a psychic voice that meanders through images and memories connected by Molly's subconscious associations. All narration is subordinated to the stream of Molly's consciousness. Joyce seeks the illusion of pure mental process that flows where it will without regard for story, and in which "person and event [serve] merely as a necessary scaffolding to present the abstraction of conscious-ness itself" (Friedman 8). Faulkner, in contrast, orders his characters' thoughts into the potentially public discourse of narration. By "public" I mean that the day's account on which each monologue is founded could be spoken to someone and followed fairly easily; the story becomes rumina-tion only as it departs from its narrative controls, whereas Molly's private voice evinces few conventional narrative controls at all.

Faulkner, unlike Woolf and Joyce, does not give us a narrating scene, what Cohn calls a "moment of locution." Nor does he place his characters in those familiar meditative circumstances ("lying beneath rain on a strange roof") that he employs in other works to generate psychic voice in third-person contexts. The monologues are not reveries in which charac-ters go back over events in moments of stasis. We do not know, nor does it matter, when the narrative discourse we hear occurs in the narrator's psyche. Yet readers have felt compelled to delineate when each section is thought (or "monologized"): Lawrence Thompson claims that Benjy's "reveries" take place as he falls asleep on the evening of his birthday, and that Quentin's monologue "occurs just before or during his act of suicide" (30, 38). Cohn wonders whether "the stream of memories springs up in the monologist's mind at the (indeterminate) moment of locution, or in the course of the generating episode itself." But this problem, as Cohn also says, is "vexing [only] on theoretical rather than on practical grounds" (250). We need not try to inject typical Faulknerian meditative scenes into the novel, for narration does not matter as an act in the fictional events but is only a discursive mode through which conventional narrative voice be-comes psychic voice. Faulkner distorts each brother's narrative in order to explore the depths of the speaker's mind not revealed through his straight-forward storytelling. While the distortions each brother's narration under-goes are appropriate to his psychological makeup, Faulkner's method is fundamentally the same with each: variances and disturbances in narrative voice and in the control of narrative conventions engender psychic voice.[15]

Of the three, Jason's monologue is the closest to conventional, public narration, echoing as it does colloquial storytelling of the Southwest Humor tradition.[16] Certainly one of Faulkner's best evocations of mimetic voice, Jason's idiom captures the rhythms of audible, colloquial speech with its fillers, its digressions and shifts in subject and logic, and its slight alterations in grammar, word order, or usage. We can easily imagine him spinning his "yarn" on the gallery of a store, suddenly starting up, banging his fist on the porch railing, and launching into "Once a bitch, always a bitch, what I say."

In fact, Jason's psychic voice grows out of the exaggerated conventionality of his discourse: the disruptions of convention in his case parody colloquial storytelling. We find none of the familiar textual signs of the Faulknerian psychic voice—no italics, no missing punctuation or capitalization. Thought is never even labeled as such, but is marked by some variant of "I say" as a silent version of Jason's speech. Faulkner modulates oral narration into psychic voice by transforming the jokes, complaints, and tirades that fill Jason's section into reveries on the past. All of Jason's memories begin as complaints against others (Quentin, his father, Uncle Maury). He then loses control of his "public" narration, willy-nilly reverting to the past. Tirades (common in Southwest Humor) turn into associative meditations as Jason begins in the present only to drift deeper and deeper into the past, losing narrative control as he talks. As Jason respeaks—and thus relives—his past, which emerges from his storytelling, the illusion of vernacular narration is never destroyed, though the mimetic voice blends into and finally becomes psychic. The loss of narrative control signaling Jason's immersion in memory takes the form of accelerated talking. Passages begin with controlled narrative statement, then build to a high pitch of memory as the sentences lengthen and run together, moving faster and faster through Jason's mind:

> I went on to the street, but they were out of sight. And there I was, without any hat, looking like I was crazy too. Like a man would naturally think, one of them is crazy and another one drowned himself and the other one was turned out into the street by her husband. . . . Selling land to send him to Harvard and paying taxes to support a state University all the time that I never saw except twice at a baseball game and not letting her daughter's name be spoken on the place until after a while Father wouldn't even come down town anymore but just sat there all day with the decanter I could see the bottom of this nightshirt and his bare legs and hear the decanter clinking until . . . (268; 290)

The longest reverie focuses on what might be called the moment of Jason's arrested development, when his hopes for a bank job vanish. The passage occurs while Jason is working in the store and complaining about having to wait on people for trivial items. He first complains generally about his lost "opportunities," moves to a specific memory about his father's funeral, then drifts further back in time to the arrival of Caddy's baby: "Well, they brought my job home tonight" (227; 246). He then reverts to the present, in Earl's store, for a brief complaint about Uncle Maury before once again returning to the funeral and the long conversation with Caddy at the cemetery (224–41; 243–61). Faulkner creates a private psychic voice out of the very stuff of public, colloquial discourse.

Benjy's monologue requires a far greater violation of narrative verisimilitude than does Jason's. Being a tale literally told by an idiot, Benjy's monologue imitates an impossible discourse. Faulkner, without warning or explanation, plunges us into a world created solely out of words uttered by a character physically and mentally incapable of speech. But because his section comes first in the novel, we respond initially to the "I" who speaks, and only second to the "Benjy" who cannot speak. By immersing us directly in Benjy's talk, Faulkner establishes the persona of the narrator, allowing us to respond first to a literary convention—that of first-person narration—and only later to the violation of that convention. By the time we fully realize who or what Benjy is, we are already listening to him talk.

Psychic voice always requires some such suspension of disbelief on the reader's part, for by definition interior discourse cannot be heard in the world. Benjy's inarticulateness objectifies the inevitable distance between all thought and all utterance. His literal verbal silence is emblematic of the more radical silence at the core of every consciousness that would speak itself. All are "idiots" in the face of the incommunicability of subjectivity. In order to communicate a speaker creates a persona, an "other" who "lives" in the voice, but who is never perfectly equivalent to the subjectivity of the speaker. "To hear oneself speak is to hear the voice of another. To be at one with one's words is the result of an effort made after the fact" (Carroll 82).[17] That Benjy cannot be at one with his words, even after the fact, emphasizes the always figurative nature of the Faulknerian psychic voice, which represents consciousness without simply reproducing it.

As he does with Jason, Faulkner parodies a recognizable kind of narration in Benjy's monologue. With its crisp, grammatically simple sentences and its recording of what can be seen and heard, Benjy's discourse seems to be that of a purely objective reporter, a neutral voice untainted by emotion. His is a voice saturated with fact: "We finished eating. T. P. took Quentin up and we went down to T. P.'s house. Luster was playing in the dirt. T. P. put Quentin down and she played in the dirt too. Luster had some spools and he and Quentin fought and Quentin had the spools. Luster cried and Frony came and gave Luster a tin can to play with, and then I had the spools and Quentin fought me and I cried" (34; 35).[18] We soon realize that Benjy is too objective, too literal in his descriptions. He can name those things that impinge directly on his senses, but nothing more. His labels make objects or events difficult to visualize because he isolates and names something a normal observer would not. In "the curling flower spaces" he objectifies spaces instead of flowers; he hears "the roof," not "the rain on the roof"; he "smells" the clothes flapping on the line. Benjy uses general words to point to specific objects: "the flowering tree" refers to one particular tree in Benjy's mind, but not in ours since we need generic names (like "magnolia") in order to be certain we are seeing the same thing. His discourse offers metonymies and metaphors as if they were facts, creating what is actually a richly figural prose in the guise of barren, "objective" speech. Benjy often cannot name sensations as such, but can only describe the movements that accompany a sensation. When he burns his hand on the stove, we are not told that it hurt or that it burned, only that "My hand jerked back and I put it in my mouth and Dilsey caught me" (67; 72).

At any given instant Benjy can respond to only a narrow range of phenomena, and he never connects events by any more sophisticated logic than juxtaposition: "It was red, flapping on the pasture. Then there was a bird slanting and tilting on it. Luster threw. The flag flapped on the bright grass and the trees. I held to the fence" (4; 2). Each utterance he makes tends to stand alone, side by side with other statements but not connected to them by the speaker himself—sentences are joined with "and" but never with "because" or "so," forcing the reader to translate the simple sequence of sentences into familiar causal relationships. That readers can accomplish the translation is just the point of Faulkner's method: such images and syntax retain the form of objective description but they arrange phenomena in odd patterns that the reader must "conventionalize."

The most obvious distortion in Benjy's narrative is the shifting back and forth in time. As a character, Benjy cannot distinguish past from present, living with equal immediacy in both. Faulkner modulates—as he does with Jason—narrative voice into psychic voice with the time shifts, but in Benjy's case the modulation has nothing to do with psychic "depth" or "intensity." The italics, for example, that mark time shifts cannot reflect, as they usually do in Faulkner, a layering of the psyche. Benjy's psyche is one-dimensional, without depth, immune to the psychoanalytic function of psychic voice. The mechanical association of one stimulus (an event, a place, a name) with another jerks his narration backward and forward in time without altering his awareness. So deceptively simple is the method—however chaotic the result for the reader—that here, too, Faulkner seems to be parodying convention—the convention of the flashback, or the modernist, Joycean convention of associative stream of consciousness.

In its associative logic Quentin's monologue is far more Joycean—in a *non*parodic sense—than Benjy's. As in Jason's and Benjy's monologues, but even more radically, Faulkner derives psychic voice from conventional narrative by moving Quentin's storytelling away from straightforward storytelling toward more spontaneous associative patterns. In Quentin's section we see techniques that in third-person contexts typify the Faulknerian psychic voice. Faulkner charts varying depths of Quentin's consciousness with changes in form—in syntax, punctuation, paragraphing, and printed type—but in this first-person context the variations signal degrees of control that Quentin possesses, as a narrator, over any given segment of the discourse. When Quentin has complete control over his words, he talks as an objective narrator does: he moves the action along chronologically, speaking in brief, lucid sentences; he fills in the background of people we meet, such as Gerald Bland or the Deacon; and he carefully identifies speakers when he quotes them. This last sign of control is especially important since most of Quentin's memories are of spoken words. Faulkner indicates Quentin's control by writing the prose in normal form. When Quentin narrates in this manner, he is not merely thinking out loud; he is telling a story, moving us through a day's events, and thus he is accomplishing a potentially public act of verbalization. Such talking reveals his private subjectivity, however, because Quentin cannot maintain his mastery over the objective narrative apparatus. Sometimes he seems able to choose what he will tell us, while at other times the words form in his mind whether he wants them to or not. Whenever he begins to lose control, whenever his talking turns from public articulation into private thought, his storytelling becomes distorted in form to "modulated narration":

> When it closed I crossed to the other side and leaned on the rail above the boathouses. The float was empty and the doors were closed. The crew just pulled in the late afternoon now, resting up before. The shadow of the bridge, the tiers of railing, my shadow

leaning flat upon the water, so easily had I tricked it that would not quit me. At least fifty feet it was, and if I only had something to blot it into the water, holding it until it was drowned, the shadow of the package like two shoes wrapped up lying on the water. Niggers say a drowned man's shadow was watching for him in the water all the time. It twinkled and glinted, like breathing, the float slow like breathing too, and debris half submerged, healing out to the sea and the caverns and the grottoes of the sea. The displacement of water is equal to the something of something. Reducto absurdum of all human experience, and two six-pound flat-irons weigh more than one tailor's goose. What a sinful waste Dilsey would say. Benjy knew it when Damuddy died. He cried. *He smell hit. He smell hit.* (102–3; 110–11)

Quentin's narration here steadily unravels. The fantasy about tricking his shadow is woven into the opening, controlled sentences, destroying their cohesion. A Negro folk saying, an allusion to Coleridge's "Kubla Khan," a half-remembered version of Archimedes' principle—these threads of past life randomly crisscross Quentin's irreproachably objective account of his last day as he drifts into brooding on the past, so that by the end of the passage he uncontrollably quotes words spoken far back in his Mississippi childhood.

The section's modulations defy strict categorization, as each captures a slightly different—and unique—level of subjectivity. It is not time that strictly governs narrative control, but pain. Standard narrative apparatus is not reserved for the day at Harvard, but for any moment in either the present or the past that Quentin seems able to face directly. He can deliberately remember and report, in proper form, some incidents from the past, as he does the anecdote about Louis Hatcher (131–32; 141–42). The day in school, however, when he counts the remaining minutes on his fingers (100; 108), is a bit more painful to recall, so the form of this episode is slightly unconventional—the speeches are not separately paragraphed. The more painful it is for Quentin to remember an event, the more unconventional the narrative form becomes, until words tumble uninhibited through his mind with only slight regard for punctuation, paragraphing, or speaker identification.[19]

It is possible that in writing Quentin's section Faulkner initiated his conception of psychic voice as a modulated version of mimetic narrative voice, for the revisions Faulkner made in the manuscript suggest that he began with Quentin's conscious talking and only later worked toward psychic voice through modulations in form. He initially cast the section as a standard first-person account. From page numbers that have been crossed out in the manuscript it appears that the conversation between Caddy and Quentin at the branch (171–87; 186–02) originally opened the section. In the manuscript this entire episode is written in normal form with quotation marks, internal punctuation, and speaker identification:

> "Is Benjy still crying?" she said without moving.
> "I don't know," I said. "He's gone to bed, I guess."
> "Poor Benjy," she said.
> I sat down on the bank. The grass was a little damp. I could feel that my shoes were damp.
> "Get out of that water," I said. "Are you crazy?"
> "All right," she said. But she didn't move. Her face was a white blur. Her hair framed it out of the sand.
> "Get out now," I said.[20]

In the typescript and final published versions Faulkner rewrote the dialogue to make it echo Quentin's uncontrolled memory:

> is Benjy still crying
> I dont know yes I dont know
> poor Benjy
> I sat down on the bank the grass was damp a little
> then I found that my shoes were wet
> get out of that water are you crazy
> but she didnt move her face was a white blur framed
> out of the sand by her hair
> get out now (172; 186).

Faulkner also enhanced the dramatic immediacy of this scene by eliminating many of Quentin's conscious thoughts and leaving only bare dialogue and frantic, run-on description. In the manuscript, for example, appears the following passage, which Faulkner considerably shortened (the lined-out portions are lined out in the manuscript):

> "Yes," I said. "Yes. Lots of times. With lots of girls." Then I was crying. Her hand came out and touched my head. I moved my head but her hand came again, and then I was crying against her wet

blouse and she was holding my head in her arms. Her blouse was still damp, but she was hard and warm under it, and she held me hard. Then she was lying on her back, looking up at the sky, and I bending over her. I could see her eyes looking past my head.

~~I had a little knife. The~~ I took my knife and opened it. ~~I thought about the knife Dilsey sliced meat with, and about Dilsey putting Benjy to bed, and about the night Damuddy died, when we all slept in the same room and the muddy bottom of Caddy's drawers in the pear tree. I held the point against Caddy's throat.~~ "Do you remember the day Damuddy died, when you sat down in the water in your underclothes?" I whispered.

"Yes," Caddy whispered. I held the point of the knife against her throat. (Manuscript 71; *SF* Facsimile 73)

The published version reads:

> yes yes lots of times with lots of girls
> then I was crying her hand touched me again and I was
> crying against her damp blouse then she lying on
> her back looking past my head into the sky I could see a
> rim of white under her irises I opened my knife
> do you remember the day damuddy died when you sat
> down in the water in your drawers
> yes
> I held the point of the knife at her throat. (174; 188)

The manuscript changes in Quentin's section highlight another feature of Faulkner's psychic voice in *The Sound and the Fury:* the roles dialogue and the voices of others play in each brother's monologue. In paring down the scene with Caddy, Faulkner removed portions of Quentin's description and memory, heightening the dramatic dialogical exchange between brother and sister. As revised, this scene is perhaps Faulkner's most intense dialogical confrontation (of the kind discussed in chapter 2) because even the textual apparatus for identifying speakers has been honed to the single feature of separate paragraphing. In all three monologues the dialogical function of psychic voice plays a crucial role. The amount and the manner of reported dialogue reflect back upon the Compson brothers as characters caught in webs of their own and others' discourse. The vast quantity of talking reported in each section is so great that it blends others' discourse into the very texture of each brother's psychic voice. Even formal elements in dialogue imposed by the text and not attributable to the narrator's control help engender a dialogic psychic voice appropriate to each brother.

The most aggressively self-centered of the three, Jason nonetheless expresses his entire monologue as if in response to others' words. His discourse fits perfectly Bakhtin's description of Dostoevsky's narrators who speak "in a style defined by the intense anticipation of another's words" (*Problems of Dostoevsky's Poetics* 205), whose words always cast a "sideward glance" at real or imagined interlocutors. Jason does not quote others so much as he paraphrases them, appropriating others' words to his own uses—a typical obsessive and self-centered gesture for him. "I says" punctuates his entire monologue, for even his thoughts are a kind of reported, self-justifying speech. He frequently recalls conversations with members of his family, especially exchanges in which he emerges (at least as he reports them) the victor by "topping" someone, saying something clever and insulting. The important interlocutor, the "other" against whose implied discourse Jason defines himself, is his mother. If Quentin is his father's son, Jason is clearly his mother's, for his adolescent perversity can be traced to his role as her favorite, her last hope among her lost brood, the only real Bascomb of all the children. It becomes evident, in fact, that Jason directs most of what he says and thinks *at* Mrs Compson. He not only reports present conversations with her, but much of what he appears to be merely stating turns out on closer examination to be something he has said or would like to say to Mrs Compson—the section's opening paragraph, for example, is addressed to her. His section is a dialogue masquerading as a monologue. Time and again a tirade that begins on some other subject reverts to Mrs Compson: "I might have been a stranger starving to death, and there wasn't a soul in sight to ask which way to town even. And she trying to get me to take aspirin. I says when I eat bread I'll do it at the table. I says . . ." (276; 298).

In one instance the remembered talking shifts from indirect to direct discourse. After a complaint against Benjy, Jason continues, "I says, you've done your duty by him; you've done all anybody can expect of you and more than most folks would do, so why not send him there and get that much benefit out of the taxes we pay. Then she says, 'I'll be gone soon. I know I'm just a burden to you' and I says 'You've been saying that so long that I'm beginning to believe you' only I says you'd better be sure and not let me know you're gone because I'll sure have him on number seventeen that night" (255; 276). But for all his tough talk to Mrs Compson, Jason spends his entire monologue, and we can assume his entire life, trying to prove himself a man in her eyes. Jason's psychic voice, with its childish self-justifications, its constant talking back to parental figures and to women, discursively echoes his truncated personality. He does not respect himself; he respects only what he believes he could become if the restraints on his life were removed. Arrested in emotional adolescence, his is the defensive self-centeredness of the child seeking proof of his own worth, of the teenager expecting to be scolded. He uses stridently childish phrases like "just for that" when he is angry; he drinks Coke all the time, and fantasizes about his manhood, even "if I don't drink"; he resents being sent on errands; he childishly will not take the medicine his mother wants him to; he hides from a barking dog.[21]

For Benjy the speech of others is just another sensation to be recorded, like sights or smells. His monologue treats each utterance by each character as a separate event of equal status with others like it, each worthy of unique but formally consistent representation. A speaker is carefully identified for each new line of dialogue. The identification, even in long conversations, is nearly always by name: "Father said" or "Jason said," not "He said." The constant repetition of "said" gives the dialogue a stilted, mechanical quality appropriate to Benjy's inability to gauge nuance or tone. A speaker identification does not include "said" when Benjy does not know the speaker or when he is not directly confronted by the person speaking. In such cases speech is merely sound from an unknown source, as if heard around a corner, out of sight and knowledge. When Mr Compson dies, a stranger opens the door of the sickroom to suggest that Benjy be taken out; Benjy does not know this man, so the words are not attributed:

> A door opened and I could smell it more than ever, and a head came out. It wasn't Father. Father was sick there.
> "Can you take him out of the house."
> "That's where we going." T. P. said. . . .
> "Better keep him there." It wasn't Father. (39; 41)[22]

Inflection conveys no meaning to Benjy. When he reports a question, Faulkner punctuates it with a period instead of a question mark ("'Shoot who, Father.' Quentin said") since to Benjy each utterance is equally a statement—or, more precisely, each statement has no logical or expressive status whatsoever. Periods, never commas, end quoted utterances, even when the speech tag follows the quoted words: "'Shut your mouth.' Quentin said. 'Are you going to get him away.'" Benjy's ears, like microphones, pick up all the talk around him, but he cannot respond to what the sounds mean—with the notable exception of the sound "caddy."[23]

A large portion of Benjy's monologue comprises dialogue among members of the Compson household. One remarkable feature of his section is that, while holding us to a confined perspective, it nonetheless opens up the life of the entire household, letting us hear the disharmonies of Compson family life through its talk. Though some of the talk, especially Luster's, is addressed to Benjy, most of it simply occurs in his presence. He records speech verbatim, like a tape recorder, whether or not he understands its meaning, never distorting a conversation to make it fit his linguistic abilities; he even quotes Mr Compson's Latin: "*'Et ego in arcadia* I have forgotten the latin for hay.' Father said" (50; 53). Benjy is a parody of an ideal narrator, a mere functionary of the text, fulfilling formal textual duties all too well.

Jason and Benjy stand at opposite ends of a continuum of narrative involvement. Jason imposes his own voice too much upon his world, distorting even the words of others; Benjy, who stands for a principle of excessive objectivity, imposes too little, embodying the inevitable distance between the story and its teller. Part of the pity Benjy evokes as a character comes, I think, from his helplessness as a narrator, for he cannot tell *us* more, any more than he can tell other characters what he wants: like his literal voice, which is only a moan or a bellow, his psychic voice is an emptiness, a voicelessness that isolates him from his story and from his family—the more so from this family, which seems trapped in the words they use against one another. Only the child Caddy tries to free Benjy into the realm of discourse: "'What is it, Benjy.' Caddy said. 'Tell Caddy. She'll do it. Try.'"[24] But of course Caddy can't do what Benjy would ask, for the stasis he would enforce on the world cannot be achieved or even articulated: Caddy cannot share her brother's innocence forever. Nor, finally, can Benjy say what he might wish to, either as a narrator or as a physically grown male "trying to say" to the little Burgess girl: "They came on. I opened the gate and they stopped, turning. I was trying to say, and I caught her, trying to say, and she screamed and I was trying to say and trying" (60; 63–64).[25]

Of the three Compson brothers, however, it is Quentin who is the most obsessed by voices. So much do voices dominate Quentin's consciousness that psychic voice in his section is a chorus made up of his sister's despairing indifference to his cherished ideals of Love and Honor ("*I've got to marry somebody*" [132; 143]), of his mother's "*voice weeping steadily and softly beyond the twilit door*" (108; 117), of his father's voice cynically proclaiming that "*women do have . . . an affinity for evil*" (110; 119), and, always in the background, Benjy's "*voice above the gabble*" (120; 130). The long passage quoted earlier, when Quentin is standing on the bridge watching his shadow in the water, is typical in content as well as technique. The major portion of Quentin's memories are either quotations or paraphrases of spoken words. In the quoted passage, besides alluding to Coleridge, Quentin thinks of what "Niggers say," he repeats his father's definition of time as the "reducto absurdum of all human experience," he thinks of what Dilsey would say about his suicide, and at his deepest immersion in the past he simply quotes spoken words in italics, without attribution: "*He smell hit.*" All of Quentin's major experiences, as remembered on this last day, take the form of dialogical confrontations: arguments between his mother and father, arguments with Caddy, with Herbert Head, with Dalton Ames, with his father. Quentin's experiences, as well as his memories, come fabricated out of dramatized discourse so that all phenomena in his consciousness take on the symbolic significance of language.

On his final day alive the words of others return to haunt his imagination. Quentin mentally objectifies his past as voices, reweaving the texture of his family's life out of their spoken words; people assume the shapes of their disembodied voices, distinguished by what they say or how they talk, not by what they do or how they look. Vocal imagery and references to voices and to talking occur throughout the monologue. The three boys Quentin meets on the bridge "all talked at once, their voices insistent and contradictory and impatient, making of unreality a possibility, then a probability, then an incontrovertible fact, as people will when their desires become words" (134; 145). Among Quentin's fondest memories of blacks is that of Louis Hatcher, whose "voice [was] a part of darkness and silence, coiling out of it, coiling into it again. WhoOoooo. WhoOoooo. WhoOooooooooo" (132; 142). He thinks of death "as a man something like Grandfather a friend of his" and he hears "the murmur of their voices from beyond the cedars they were always talking and Grandfather was always right" (201–202; 218–19). At Caddy's wedding Quentin expresses his hatred for Herbert Head and for all the relatives and guests by imagining someone saying over and over "*Quentin has shot Herbert he shot his voice through the floor of Caddy's room . . . Quentin has shot all of their voices through the floor of Caddy's room*" (120–21, 128; 130, 138). Benjy's bellowing hurts him as if it were "*hammering back and forth as though its own momentum would not let it stop as though there were no place for it in silence bellowing*" (143; 154). Even his broken leg, which had to be painfully re-broken and reset, speaks to him: "*told me the bone would have to be broken again and inside me it began to say Ah Ah Ah and I began to sweat*" (129; 140).

Among the many symbolic patterns in which Faulkner embodies Quentin's agony (patterns like Quentin's obsession with time, the imagery of water and of fire) the vocal imagery and the nature of remembered dialogue most clearly define the quality of Quentin's relationships with other people. Like a listener, Quentin allows others' words to formulate his subjective life for him, passively absorbing experiences that he should actively engage in. The sexual confusion and nausea that underlie much of his suffering have been enhanced by his tendency to transmute experience into a verbal form that he can listen to safely. Except for his preadolescent sex play with the "cow-faced" Natalie—a scene itself rendered primarily as a dialogue—Quentin has apparently had no direct sexual experience. He has discovered sex, like so much else, from what others have told him. Like Temple Drake, though in a far more linguistically oriented way, Quentin is what Barthes calls an "*écouteur*," one who experiences (and gratifies desire) by listening (*S/Z* 134). We can surely trace his romantic notions of honor and chastity to his mother's constant harping on respectability, while his father's words certainly abetted his contradictory obsession with physical sexuality. Mr Compson's imagery reinforces the disgust and fascination Quentin expresses as he thinks about Caddy and her lovers: "Because women so delicate so mysterious Father said. Delicate equilibrium of periodical filth between two moons balanced. Moons he said full and yellow as harvest moons her hips thighs" (147; 159).

Besides actually spying on Caddy, Quentin tries to get her to tell him about her lovemaking, for maybe he can understand sex if it is put into words. He demands to know if she loved her partners, being unable to imagine how she could have intercourse if she did not love them, but at the same time being unable to believe she could love a "cad," a "blackguard," or a "town squirt." He wants Caddy to admit her sin out loud, to put it into words so he can deal with it:

Why must you marry somebody Caddy
   Do you want me to say it do you think that if I say it it wont be. (140; 151)

His efforts to protect his sister's fragile honor deteriorate into purely verbal confrontations, as he can do no more than fling melodramatic lines at Dalton Ames—" Ill give you until sundown to leave town" (183; 198). Nor do his words have any more effect on Caddy, as she seems to ignore his attempts to threaten her with incest and murder. For the same reason he cannot cope with Caddy's surrogate at Harvard, the little Italian girl he calls "little sister," because she, too, refuses to comprehend or respond to his words. Quentin is helpless when words will not suffice, and for him they almost never do. Perhaps in reaction to guilt he feels over his incestuous desire for Caddy, Quentin's own sexuality so horrifies him that he dreams of being devoid of it altogether. One remarkable passage, beginning as so many of Quentin's memories do with something he has heard, sums up his own sexual fears and symbolizes the abstracted, secondhand, even linguistic nature of his feelings about sex:

> Versh told me about a man mutilated himself. He went into the woods and did it with a razor, sitting in a ditch. A broken razor flinging them backward over his shoulder the same motion complete the jerked skein of blood backward not looping. But that's not it. It's not not having them. It's never to have had them then I could say O That That's Chinese I dont know Chinese. And Father said it's because you are a virgin . . . and I said That's just words and he said So is virginity and I said you dont know. You cant know and he said Yes. On the instant when we come to realise that tragedy is secondhand. (132–33; 143)

Sex is indeed Chinese to Quentin—words he can hear but never understand.

The most frequent references to what another has said are to Mr Compson: "Father said" runs like an obsessive refrain through Quentin's thoughts. Nowhere is Quentin's role as listener more evident or more damaging than in his relationship with his father. Mr Compson appears in his son's memory as only a voice, never being described in any other way—by an action, a gesture, or by physical appearance. In his own thinking Quentin compulsively reiterates his father's cynical comments on sex, time, women, on life itself. In some ways Quentin's most traumatic memory, condensing into one painful episode all his impotent gestures at forcing truth into his own artificial mold, is the long debate he has with his father shortly after Caddy's wedding. Faulkner once stated that Quentin never actually told his father he had committed incest, that he only wished to make such a dramatic gesture (*FU* 262); but the debate with his father exerts its powerful effect whether remembered or only imagined. He wants to persuade his father (and himself) that things are not as they seem, that he has been Caddy's lover all along and that he intends to kill himself; he seeks to turn his own fantastic wishes into "incontrovertible fact, as people will when their desires become words." But, partly because he cannot convince his father of anything, only his suicide will become "incontrovertible."[26]

Quentin's tragedy, which we hear in *his* voice, is that he can never shut out the myriad voices whirling through his psyche. His psychic voice is really an *excess* of voice, a discourse that overflows the banks of his consciousness. In killing himself Quentin silences his intolerable psychic voice, finding a soundless void away from his loud world of voices: "it was to isolate her out of the loud world so that it would have to flee us of necessity and then the sound of it would be as though it had never been . . . if i could tell you we did it would have been so and then the others wouldnt be so and then the world would roar away" (203; 220).

Caddy, indeed, stands "isolated out of the loud world"—the loud world of the novel. Hers is the missing voice, she the character not permitted to speak except through the mouths of others. Perhaps this does constitute a kindness, as Faulkner said, given the plethora of voices that swirl within the troubled souls of her brothers.[27] This silence is proper, furthermore, because Caddy "functions" in the novel by being progressively written out of it. Each brother remains imprisoned within a lost dream embodied by Caddy as virginal child. To Benjy, Caddy embodies fulfillment in quite literal ways, as the nurturer who provides for his few delights of the spirit, the smell of trees and the bright shapes of firelight. In her loss he experiences the law of desire by which the absent other becomes only a sign to trigger grief. For Quentin, Caddy's silence fulfills a demand he makes upon her to remain the inviolate bride of quietude outside the "loud world" of time and sexuality. Though Caddy talks as much in Quentin's memories as anywhere else in the novel, he seems to hear her less than any other character does, asking naive sexual questions of her over and over: "*did you love them Caddy did you love them*" (171; 185); "*Why must you marry somebody Caddy*" (140; 151). Jason "idealizes" Caddy negatively, seeing her as Everywoman and thus as Bitch and Whore. Caddy's loss of virginity, besides verifying that all women are whores, means a lost bank job, and when Jason lost that chance he stopped maturing because the adult image he projected of himself collapsed; now he could not become a banker, now he could not become a man. Instead he remains stuck in what is a kind of "after-school" clerk's job, pretending to be a big financial wheeler and dealer, pulling off his petty thievery.

The figure of Caddy, whose loss measures the past for the Compson brothers, cannot answer her family's desire because as an idealized Other she "exists" only in her own effacement as the voiceless object of her brothers' desire. Caddy's silence permits other voices to be heard. If desire has been correctly described as "the revelation of a void, the presence of an absence of reality," then Caddy is desire's perfect sign.[28] Candace Compson the woman, the human being, deserves a voice, of course, and that Faulkner would not grant her one (as he grants significant voice to very few female characters in his fiction) may speak volumes about his ambivalent, even misogynist, attitude toward women. But in the context of *The Sound and the Fury* neither a narrative voice nor a resultant psychic voice would be proper for Caddy. She must remain mute, for she *is* Psyche, bereft, tortured by Venus, and abandoned to silence.

Chapter Four

‹‹‹‹‹‹‹‹‹‹‹‹‹‹‹‹‹‹‹‹‹‹‹‹‹‹‹‹‹‹‹‹ ››››››››››››››››››››››››››››››››››››

ORATORICAL VOICE

Oratory out of Solitude

—WILLIAM FAULKNER TO MALCOLM COWLEY

When Charles Etienne de Saint Velery Bon, Charles Bon's son, attacks a group of blacks for no apparent reason and is brought before justice of the peace Jim Hamblett, Hamblett "utiliz[es the] opportunity and audience to orate, his eyes already glazed with that cessation of vision of people who like to hear themselves talk in public." His speech has a familiar oratorical ring to it: "At this time, while our country is struggling to rise from beneath the iron heel of a tyrant oppressor, when the very future of the South as a place bearable for our women and children to live depends on the labor of our own hands, when the tools which we have to use, to depend on, are the pride and integrity and forbearance of black men and the pride and integrity and forbearance of white; that you, I say, a white man, a white—" (*AA* 254; 203). Such rhetoric was familiar in speech making about race in America in the early years of the twentieth century. It also sounds familiar because it sounds like Faulkner—not the speech-making William Faulkner but the authorial voice "Faulkner" heard throughout his oeuvre. This *ore rotundo*, this extended rhetorical period that accumulates parallel clauses as it rolls toward a climax, this accurate and parodic reproduction of Southern rhetoric's defensive celebratory appeal to regional

185

prejudices echoes the very discourse that parodies it, for Faulkner's style is notoriously oratorical.

Like other "people who like to hear themselves talk in public," Hamblett wants to celebrate his authoritative position in words. He evokes the shared assumptions behind his role as keeper of Southern peace and tries to erect a brief verbal monument to the necessary "pride and integrity and forbearance" of each race in the South's struggle against "a tyrant oppressor." What interrupts Hamblett, just as he launches into the duties of a white man ("that you, I say, a white man, a white—"), is his sudden confusion about Etienne Bon's race. Is the prisoner white, as he looks, or is he black? Nothing more quickly subdues the oratorical impulse than the loss of certainty or the loss at least of the appearance of certainty. Faced with what to him is a monstrosity—a figure whose race cannot be ascertained—Hamblett's public voice "die[s] away" into horrified query: *"what are you? Who and where did you come from?"* The breakdown of rhetorical certainty in this passage, the vanishing of voice in the wake of a monstrous (racial) truth, and the sudden shift from oratory into direct dialogue all perfectly illustrate the movement of discourse in *Absalom, Absalom!*. To be pulled up short in the face of racial uncertainty is, in a nutshell, Thomas Sutpen's fate in *Absalom, Absalom!*. For many readers the greatest of Faulkner's novels, *Absalom* derives its haunting power in part from an interrogation of the authority of its own rhetoric. This interrogation is conducted within and through perhaps the most distinctive of the voices we shall examine in Faulkner, the "oratorical voice."

The oratorical voice is more overtly intertextual than the three voices examined previously. It derives from a discursive practice—Southern oratory—recognizable outside the boundaries of any Faulkner text and identifiable as part of William Faulkner's biographical and regional heritage. Compared to the oratorical voice, the phenomenal, mimetic, and psychic voices are more *intra*textual in that the important features that define them are found within Faulkner's texts—though of course each gains effect by manipulation of (intertextual) conventions of depicting voice, spoken communication, and internal speech. Our definition and examination of oratorical voice, however, must include more explicit reference to an external discourse. As a set of expressive functions by which speech is represented, the oratorical voice integrates features of a cultural discourse into the fiction; furthermore, the manner in which this form of represented speech functions expressively within the fiction bears a strong (if often ironic or parodic) relationship to expressive functions of Southern oratory. After some preliminary remarks about Faulkner's relation to Southern oratory, this chapter will explore the nature of oratory as a discursive practice, and then examine the oratorical voice in *Absalom, Absalom!*, a Faulkner novel that not only manifests oratorical discourse but also explores its implications.

SOUTHERN ORATORY

Any discussion of the oratorical voice in Faulkner must negotiate its way through prejudice. Oratory in the twentieth century has a bad name: at best verbal ornamentation applied like a veneer over the "content" of discourse; at worst tasteless floridity deliberately designed to deceive the gullible, a smoke screen of words spewed out to obscure questionable motives. There is prejudice, too, in the associations between oratory and Faulkner's "Southernness," for the phrase "Southern oratory" has pejorative connotations associated with filibustering, racial invective, and political demagoguery.[1] Discussions of oratory in Faulkner formerly proceeded in this vein. Sean O'Faolain, for example, wondered whether Faulkner is "using, with care, the artist's meaningful language or the demagogue's careless, rhetorical and often meaningless language."[2] More typical than such a direct indictment is an embarrassed discomfiture that Faulkner has not shown proper restraint. Richard Bridgman wrote that Faulkner is "not embarrassed by the oratorical flourish," implying that he ought to be. Perhaps he was. In a letter to Malcolm Cowley, Faulkner described his style as the result of a regional curse: "I'll go further than you in the harsh criticism [of *Absalom's* style]. The style, as you divine, is a result of the solitude, and granted a bad one. It was further complicated by an inherited regional or geographical (Hawthorne would say, racial) curse. You might say, studbook style: 'by Southern Rhetoric out of Solitude' or 'Oratory out of Solitude'" (*SL* 215–16; Cowley 78). Considered merely as a set of stylistic mannerisms, the oratorical voice can be heard with more or less intensity throughout Faulkner's canon, from Shegog's sermon to "the kings and the unhomed angels, the scornful and graceless seraphim" that concludes *The Mansion*. But we should make no aesthetic evaluation based on this "Oratory out of Solitude." Faulkner's prose style is neither better nor worse because of oratory. His finest writing and his clumsiest show oratorical features, and his two most sustained performances in elevated rhetoric, *Absalom, Absalom!* and *A Fable*, are arguably his greatest and his weakest novels.[3] The later, post–World War II novels especially evince more patently oratorical mannerisms so that complaints about the quality of prose in later works have, not surprisingly, equated the oratorical with the undigested speculative discourse that in many readers' judgment mars the later fiction.

Such criticisms, even Faulkner's own, are beside the issue here. Nor is the issue one of "influence" in the causative sense. Whether Faulkner read or heard orations (though clearly he did), whether he consciously "aped" the verbal habits of Southern orators (though clearly he could parody these, as in Jim Hamblett's speech) matters less than the nature of oratory as a particular kind of discursive *practice*. Minter writes that "Faulkner associated with his own family . . . the elaborative, celebratory style [he heard when he] sat in Protestant churches, stood in front of political platforms, or attended local shows where 'Thomas C. Trueblood, A.M., Prof. of Elocution and Oratory. University of Michigan' recited soliloquies from Shakespeare and Henry Watterson, a regional specialist, recited 'Pickett's Charge' by Fred Emerson Brooks" (86; see also Blotner 101). Faulkner himself wrote of his "illimitable courage for rhetoric (personal pleasure in it, too: I admit it)" (*SL* 188). Far more important than Faulkner's sheepish comments to Cowley is his recognition that oratory was deeply embedded in the South's ideology, as a "style," yes, but also as a way of establishing and enforcing relationships among people, as a way of critiquing and commemorating assumed values, as a way of gaining and maintaining power. In the apologetic letter to Cowley quoted above, Faulkner called oratory the South's "first art": "They [the 'gentle folk' of the antebellum South] really did nothing: they slept or talked. They talked too much, I think. Oratory was the first art; Confederate generals would hold up attacks while they made speeches to their troops. . . . [E]ven these, if they had been writing men, would have written still more orations" (*SL* 216; Cowley 78–79). Oratory in this ideological sense designates certain ways of using language, and of being used by language. It is not just a matter of stylistic choice or habit, of choosing one way of saying something that could be just as well said in another. Faulkner knew better than this, and the "oratorical voice" that intersects other voices in his fiction is part of the essence of his "artistry" and his "Southernness," an essence that the fiction both demonstrates and interrogates.

Faulkner's claim that oratory was the "first art" of the South derives from the dominance of oratory in Southern public discourse, especially in the nineteenth century but also well into the twentieth. This "most serious of 19th century pastimes" appears—sometimes in a villainous role—in most accounts of Southern life. William Garrett Brown's 1902 history *The Lower South in American History* tells us substantially what Faulkner's letter to Cowley says: "It was the spoken word, not the printed page, that guided thought, aroused enthusiasm, made history. It is doubtful if there has ever been a society in which the orator counted for more than he did in the Cotton Kingdom. . . . The man who wished to lead or to teach must be able to speak. He could not touch the artistic sense of the people with pictures or statues or verses or plays; he must charm them with voice and gesture" (Brown 125–26, 127).

Orators, it is said, wielded "incalculable power" in molding opinion and in rousing the citizenry to action (Hergesheimer 38), and W. J. Cash's *The Mind of the South* emphasizes the special importance of "rhetoric" in the Southern character (Cash 53, 54, 82, 146, 225). Richard Weaver, one of the more restrained claimants for oratory's power, speaks of "the great prestige which the orator has traditionally enjoyed in the South, and not merely by those who have encountered Cicero and Quintilian in their education, but also by the masses. The kind of political folk hero who has proved incomprehensible to the rest of the nation finds the greatest source of his power in a widespread admiration of confidence and even bravura in the use of language" (Weaver 19).

Politics both before the Civil War and after naturally provided the central arena for oratorical performance, as the South struggled first to stave off the erosion of, and later to recover, its national power. Political candidates stumped their districts, battling each other first over nullification, then over secession, and later over Reconstruction. The Fourth of July celebration of 1831 in Charleston saw two rival meetings where speakers held forth for or against nullification.[4] Huge picnics and "oratorical feasts," where both food and rhetoric were served up in ample amounts, would go on for days at a time: one meeting at Indian Springs, Georgia, during the "hard-cider campaign" of 1840 lasted a full week, with speeches going continually both day and night (Brown 127). The Whigs, usually the minority party in the South, won elections in the years they most diligently carried on a campaign of stump oratory, that is, "when their leaders resorted to demagoguery, abandoning the defense of party platforms."[5] While in the North the abolitionist cause was advanced through journalism and belles lettres as well as through impassioned oratory, in the South the secessionists and unionists argued their cases almost exclusively on the public platform. Brown, as well as Cash and Weaver, attribute this difference between the North and the South to the Southerner's greater love of rhetoric. William Yancy, one of the secessionist "Fire-Eaters," was successful, according to Brown, because "he lived among a people peculiarly incapable of resisting any appeal that might be made to them as his was—a people over whom the power of a real orator was incalculable. An editor like Garrison, a poet like Whittier or Lowell, a novelist like Mrs. Stowe, could hardly have swayed the planters of Alabama as they swayed the people of new England; for it must be said of the lower South that its culture was not of books" (Brown 124).

After the Civil War the white South's powerlessness during Reconstruction enforced a more ceremonial, less deliberative political oratory. Celebration of the Old South and of Civil War heroes, in orations often delivered in dedicating Confederate war memorials, replaced campaign speeches. Reiterated social myths about the glory of the antebellum years and about the valor expended in a lost cause soothed and entertained as well as persuaded audiences. For orators in the postwar South, the only available option was "to strengthen attitudes and sentiments," not "to attempt the change of opinions or the implementation of courses of action" (Braden, "Repining Over an Irrevocable Past" 11). Defense of the "Anglo-Saxon" became common, turning in the 1890s and early twentieth century into the racial invective made notorious by demagogues like South Carolina's "Pitchfork Ben" Tillman and Mississippi's James K. Vardaman and Theodore Bilbo.

Some commentators have argued that Southern oratory was neither different from other oratory nor so unvaryingly "florid" as the stereotype portrays it. Residues of self-perpetuating myth do cling to the notion of a Southern oratory, especially in the choices historians make in depicting a special Southern mode of speech. Braden cites one early-twentieth-century historian of Southern literature who preferred the fiery eloquence of a William Yancy over the restrained reasoning of a John C. Calhoun, for the former reflects the "epitome of extremely Southern characteristics" in which the speaker "swept along with a rush that did not always permit his listeners to pause for thought, but instead, carried them away as willing captives" (Braden, "Emergence of the Concept of Southern Oratory" 178). W. J. Cash's famous generalizations on the "mind" of the South mix "rhetoric" into the blend of "romanticism and hedonism" unique to the South (53). The position of the South vis-à-vis the North as a defeated, occupied, and relatively impoverished "backward" region probably intensified the flamboyance of speaking styles. As deliberation gave way to celebration

and entertainment, oratory became more and more a "rhetoric of desperation" (Eubanks 21). Cultural values that must be buttressed against outside attack tend to be propped up, according to Kenneth Burke, with a
greater "profusion and vitality of the formal devices" evoking, without
debate, images of "the desirable" (57). However embellished accounts of
oratorical performance and efficacy may be, the evidence—which we need
not rehearse in more detail here—does establish oratory as at least a crucial part of the region's verbal life, if not "the most important folk art" of
the South. The South diverged from the North economically and socially
so that oratory as a discursive practice complexly entwined itself with the
fabric of a distinctive Southern ideology. Faulkner himself acknowledged
differences between North and South in terms that he applied to art generally: "We need to talk, to tell, since oratory is our heritage," he wrote in a
draft introduction to *The Sound and the Fury* (*SFI* [2] 158). Edmund Wil-
son connects differences in discursive practice—both in the sense of the
type of speech and writing, and their styles—to the Civil War's effect in
speeding up industrial development in the North. American prose before
the war was generally ornate and sermonistic (far more so than British),
but was replaced in the North (but not in the South) by a less florid prose
style that was "firmer," "quicker," more functional, and "efficient" (Wil-
son 635–54).[6]

ORATORY AS DISCURSIVE PRACTICE

Orators expressed power far more than they exerted power. A classical
rhetorical model of oratorical discourse portrays orators as wielding language like a tool or weapon with which they act upon listeners, persuading
them, *moving* them in some way. A better model is the concept of "discursive practice" in which both orator and audience participate, guided by
assumptions of appropriate behavior and "necessary improvisation." The
phrase is Pierre Bourdieu's, whose theory of social practice particularly
rejects static, structural explanations of behavior as proceeding according
to rules, as in a bounded game (like the communications model of oratory,
with its active speaker versus passive listener dichotomy), in favor of
"practice" seen as a dynamic process occurring over time and through
which individuals manipulate and maintain necessary material and symbolic power relationships.[7] While orators addressed their audiences with
persuasive intent, and while political candidates often disagreed and de-

bated with each other, the essential authority to which orators appealed was that of shared values; debate was possible only within a narrow context defined by ideological assumptions that it was oratory's purpose to express and vivify. Few orators changed anyone's mind. Those South Carolinians who favored nullification in 1831 attended the Fourth of July meeting where nullification was advocated; those opposed participated in another celebration.[8]

Orators thus expressed power—not the orator's own power but the power of the community—by speaking to the converted in discourse that was already internally persuasive. "Only those voices from without are effective which can speak in the language of a voice within" (Burke 39). Audience and orator alike were caught up in a ritualistic, discursive performance, a celebration not only of the participants' values, but also, it is better to say, a celebration of the *language* in which those values were couched. Indeed, the virtuosity of the rehearsal of communal ideology— that is, eloquence—came to be valued in and of itself. Eloquence became a criterion for judging a person's worth; like "liberty" or "honor," the very word "eloquence" turned into what one student of oratory has called a "value term to conjure with" (Eubanks 32). Anyone who had designs on power, leadership, or merely on respectability must perforce display proof of eloquence. By far the most popular handbook on rhetoric, Hugh Blair's *Lectures on Rhetoric and Belles Lettres*, equates eloquence (as did the classical models) with virtue and broad learning (Blair 2:230). Educated to be a public speaker, the Southern gentleman was taught the skills of rhetoric at an early age; some of the very first training a boy received was in elocution and declamation. Particularly in the Tidewater region of Virginia and the Mudsill region of South Carolina, students studied classical rhetoric in Latin: Hugh Legaré, the famous opponent of John C. Calhoun in the fight over nullification, was a scholar of high repute as well as an orator (see Christophersen 74, 77). Skillful orators played upon the myth of oratory itself. Mississippi's Vardaman won praise—and thus votes—for his flamboyant oratorical eloquence, even though at least one opponent tried, unsuccessfully, to draw forth prejudice against his "mere" oratory. "Vardaman's addresses resembled epideictic or ceremonial speeches rather than campaign or deliberative speeches, as whenever possible he avoided debate and used very little argumentation . . . deliver[ing] a ceremonial address in a deliberative speech setting" (Strickland 81–82). Usually, however, the eloquence of the average colloquial "stump orator" was a thin veneer over rough wood, having little to do with the restrained, balanced rhetoric of classical Ciceronian principles. Even in the pre–Civil War "Classical" era, the emphasis in speech training was less on the principles of classical rhetoric than on simple imitation; content and logic gave way to "pronuntiatio," and to the rote learning of mechanical rules for impressive declamation (Thomas 195). One learned to orate not by learning to argue well, but by committing famous purple passages to memory and by practicing forceful, dramatic delivery. Because eloquence was the mark of a good man—and I choose the gender-specific term deliberately because there were few women orators (see Shelby, "The Southern Lady Becomes an Advocate")—every speaker learned certain tricks of the trade, certain easily adopted, mechanical verbal forms to demonstrate his own eloquence.

The practice of oratory, then, in part commemorates the discursive authority of language in a self-reflexive performance or ritual that itself confers authority. Like the duelist who imputes honor to whomever he challenges merely by presuming that a "man of honor" will understand and respond appropriately, so orators conferred authority upon their audiences, themselves, and their discourse by the very act of performing eloquently.[9] Many discourses assume *semantic* authority and persuade by appealing to institutional or cultural sources of certainty. The scientific treatise invokes, either explicitly or implicitly, institutional procedures of controlled inquiry and investigation; the legal essay rests upon the authority of the law itself and on the interpretive enterprises through which courts apply law in particular cases.[10] What distinguishes oratory is its self-reflexive and celebratory assumption of its own certainty, making of the enunciatory act per se a source of semantic authority. Oratory's is the institutional authority inherent in ritual performed for reconfirmation of shared values—and thus performed for fun as well as for serious ends. Faulkner described the element of show endemic to oratorical practice and its institutional authority as a feature of all art in the South, and the bittersweet tone of his metaphors captures the ambivalence that descriptions of Southern oratory always seem to evoke: "But in the South art, to become visible at all, must become a ceremony, a spectacle; something between a gypsy encampment and a church bazaar given by a handful of alien mummers who must waste themselves in protest and active self-defense until there is nothing left with which to speak" (*SFI* [2] 157). Oratory's institutional appeal is also to the resources of language, to the cultural authority that language possesses within any linguistic community. While a given oration appeals to whatever evidence or values its immediate context requires, a fundamental principle of oratorical discourse is the (usually implied but sometimes explicit) appeal to the resources of language as a source of authority.

This is not to assert that oratory by its nature is devoid of content, "barren of thought" as the pejorative connotations of the word would have it.[11] Oratory is not "mere ornamentation." But there is always in oratory what Kenneth Burke calls "pure persuasion," which "involves the saying of something, not for an extraverbal advantage to be got by the saying, but because of a satisfaction intrinsic to the saying. It summons because it likes the feel of a summons. It would be nonplussed if the summons were answered. . . . It intuitively says, 'This is so,' purely and simply because this is so" (Burke 269). I would alter Burke's emphasis in his last sentence to say that pure persuasion says "this is so" not because of any referential truth to the "this" that is "so," but because the discursive gesture of the utterance "this is so" carries authority. The satisfaction Burke speaks of is, of course, not merely the speaker's, but the audience's as well, and that of the entire linguistic community.

Although the orator does not exert power in the sense of persuading his audience so much as he expresses the power of a discourse both orator and audience are caught up in, the orator still in some senses dominates the audience. Within the context of discursive celebration the orator exercises control over the audience, over the subject addressed, over even the language from which semantic authority derives. We can use a phrase like "the incalculable power" possessed by oratory if we see such power as an institutional authority taken up for the moment. Oratory's domination— which appears in the guise of semantic certainty—is a "possession" both in the sense that the orator possesses (and displays) his skills with rhetoric, and in the sense that the orator is possessed by the discourse of the celebratory moment, like a priest who dominates because he is possessed by the spirit of the ritual.

Southern demagogues, of course, knowing very well how to exploit their roles as shaman and showman, simply raised exponentially certain features inherent in all oratorical practice by orchestrating their often-festive campaign appearances, turning speech making into comic burlesque or a blend of "Fourth of July celebration and traveling tent revival" (Shelby, "Jeff Davis of Arkansas" 39; Logue 206). Gene Talmadge of Georgia used the "call and response" of revivalist preaching to bring his audience into his speeches (as one contemporary account put it, "all in all there were two speeches, one by the governor and another by the crowd" [Logue 220]);

yet his persistent message was his own infallibility, his own power and authority as savior of the common folk (Logue 221–22). By being both possessor of and possessed by authoritative discourse, the orator dominates this realm of discourse and its participants. Domination implies violence, so it is not surprising that oratorical performance could become violent. Not only were the language and gesturing of Southern orators frequently violent, but these men were also known to carry their messages physically into the audience. Lucius Q. C. Lamar, the famous political orator from Faulkner's own region of Mississippi, on several occasions drove home his points by more than mere words (Murphy 22–23, 41–42, 100–102).[12]

Faulkner's oratorical voice also manifests a mixture of participation and domination, whether embodied in characters' speech or in authorial discourse. Authority is always at issue within those speech scenes discussed earlier (in chapter 2, as a typical feature of Faulkner's mimetic voice) in which one speaker talks at such length as to turn ostensible dialogue into virtual monologue. Allen Tate's image of the Southern mode of discourse "presupposes somebody at the other end silently listening" (583): in Faulkner, as in oratory, the speaker dominates rhetorically and verbally, but in Faulkner that domination is always threatened from within, often by the silence of the speaker's auditor. Such scenes, which invariably are scenes of persuasion more than of mere narrative, usually involve relationships of authority, typically that of father and son. Byron Bunch and Gail Hightower in *Light in August*, Quentin Compson and Rosa Coldfield or Mr Compson in *Absalom, Absalom!*, the Reporter and his editor in *Pylon*, Isaac McCaslin and Cass Edmonds in *Go Down, Moses*, Gavin Stevens and Chick Mallison in *Intruder in the Dust*, Stevens (again) and Temple Drake in *Requiem for a Nun*, the Old General or the priest and the Corporal in *A Fable*—all these speaker-listener pairs set a figure of authority against someone ostensibly subservient to that authority. Ike wishes to "explain to the head of [his] family" (*GDM* 288) what he now understands about his heritage and God's will; Stevens would propound to Chick the correct interpretation of the civil rights issues raised by Lucas Beauchamp's near lynching; the Old General would persuade the Corporal (his son) to accept life instead of dying on his self-erected cross of mutiny.[13]

Individually complex as such scenes are in each novel, they always follow oratorical discursive practice in employing an elevated rhetorical style as sign and source of apparent authority. Even when the speaker speculates on uncertain information (as does Mr Compson in *Absalom, Absalom!*), he or she partakes of the power granted by possession and control of language. But such scenes also always parody oratorical practice in that the very elevated and persuasive style that engenders the speaker's authority at the same time undercuts it. Distanced from the truth by its excess, oratorical discourse possesses at best a contingent and supplemental authority. For true authority in Faulkner is more often associated with taciturnity than with loquaciousness, with a sparingly used creative power of speech that, like God's word, brings truth into being by simple utterance without explanation and without supplemental excesses of amplified speech making. (An excellent example of silent authority is Old Alec's "ordering the immediate return of this lock" in *Requiem for a Nun*: "It was not even an ultimatum, it was a simple instruction, a decree, impersonal . . . while Old Alec still smoked his pipe in front of his smoldering log" [17–18]. Appropriately, his instruction is never directly quoted or rendered.) Those who possess the discourse are nearly always undercut by irony. Edward Said describes "contingent authority" in a way that aptly captures the nature of oratory's authority in Faulkner:

> One aspect of authorship, then, is its contingent authority, its ability to initiate or build structures whose absolute authority is radically nil, but whose contingent authority is a quite satisfactory transitory alternative to the absolute truth. Therefore, the difference between Abraham's true authority in Kierkegaard's *Fear and Trembling* and the narrator's contingent authority is that Abraham is silent, whereas the narrator universalizes in language; the point is that any absolute truth cannot be expressed in words, for only diminished, flawed versions of the truth are available to language. This is as much as to say that *fiction alone speaks or is written*—for truth has no need of words—*and that all voices are assumed ones*.[14]

The particular nature of the irony that undercuts oratorical practice depends upon the circumstances of each Faulkner text (circumstances described for *Absalom, Absalom!* later in this chapter). Generally, the oratorical voice creates a special role for the listener. Joseph Reed describes the importance of hearing (as well as telling) stories about people in Faulkner's depiction of community, and Wyatt calls the kind of listening that entrances Ike McCaslin (when he hears the old tales from Sam Fathers) "the central human act in Faulkner" (Reed 19–31; Wyatt 83). But listening, especially in the face of a powerfully (if contingently) authoritative discourse, may also be a central *moral* act in Faulkner's thematics of humankind's complex relation to its own "puny inexhaustible voice." Like the demagogue's audience who gets too close to the stage or asks the unexpected embarrassing question, the listener can preempt discursive authority without necessarily usurping the discourse itself. In a manner that resembles the call-and-response pattern of revivalist preaching or of political oratory, Faulkner's listeners answer the orator—though, unlike the traditional audience, Faulkner's auditors utter repeated and cryptic phrases that puncture the balloons of the persuader's speech. Chick Mallison keeps repeating "They ran" despite Stevens's elaborate extrapolations from the townspeople's behavior. The Corporal responds "There are still ten" to the General's arguments that he (the Corporal) accept the offer of life, and he dismisses the priest's plea with the repeated "Tell him that." Listeners in Faulkner endure and reverse oratory's dominance; listening is seldom the passive, secondary version of experience it is for Quentin in *The Sound and the Fury*, because listeners seem in touch with some truth that need not, or cannot, be spoken—at least not at oratorical length.[15]

Faulkner had, it seems to me, a fundamental *trust* of listening, akin perhaps to what Erikson describes of Martin Luther: "The organ through which the word enters to replenish the heart is the ear, . . . for it is in the nature of the word that it should be heard. . . . [F]aith comes from listening, not from looking . . . and [one] succeeds [in faith] insofar as [one] develops [one's] own *passivity*" (207). Within the context of oratorical practice "passivity" is active participation insofar as silence resists the contingent authority of powerful rhetoric. It is not only speakers' authority that is "contingent," but the author's as well, for Faulkner's oratorical voice by no means confines itself to scenes of speech. Like an orator's enraptured audience and like Faulkner's many taciturn listening characters, his silent readers confront a dominant rhetoric that they must both accept and resist. If Said is right that a condition of narrative fiction is a "strong sense of doubt that the authority of any single voice, or group of voices, is sufficient unto itself" (88), then Faulkner's prose would seem to try to overpower or overwhelm doubt with its sheer prolixity.

THE ORATORICAL STYLE

In some measure the discursive authority of the authorial voice in Faulkner both gains and suffers from its affinities to a recognizable oratorical style, especially to colloquial (as opposed to formal Ciceronian) Southern oratory. A colloquial oratorical style permits endless amplification. Unlike the classical Ciceronian period, with its balanced movement toward a climax followed by a logical "rounding off" of thought and syntax, the colloquial oratorical sentence moves inexorably forward. For Aristotle the period had a beginning and an end, but the colloquial orator dares not admit (or permit) an end to what he can say: the most necessary skill was the ability to add to whatever had already been said. At camp meetings, political rallies, and "oratorical feasts" orators had to hold an audience's attention for hours on end. Syntactical patterns that permit addition of ever more information or qualification without apparent pause were pragmatically necessary as well as easily mastered.

Rather than being embedded within larger syntactical units, additions and necessary improvisations in colloquial oratory are usually tacked on to points in a phrase or sentence where the logic would permit an ending. Two samples follow:

> This is an appropriate place and time for the Democratic convention. The place is St. Louis, the chief city of the most populous state carved out of the Louisiana Territory acquired by the father of democracy. This time is the centennial anniversary celebration of the acquisition of that territory, a vast area of contiguous territory, whose possession was necessary for self-defense and which was fitted in climate and soil for home-making by the sons and daughters of the republic—the anniversary of the real and not pseudo-expansion—an expansion of our population, our industrial life, and our free institutions, over uninhabited lands, or lands sparsely settled by savages, whose tribal independence we recognized by trading with them, or settled in spots by white men easily and willingly assimilated; not a so-called expansion by mere superimposed force of our flag and our military authority. (Williams 3)

> Another leading reason why I have so earnestly favored the full and free coinage of silver is that it is gathered by the toil of man in the deep and dangerous mines; it is converted into coin by the highest art of the chemist; it is the gift of God, who made silver and gold alone for use as money in their functions of real value, and it is the reward in money, not in promises to pay, of the laborer; the reward of each day's work when the night shuts in. It is the fruit of the pick and the shovel, and it is not the product of some artful brain in a bank parlor that is busy with contrivances to deceive the world into

the belief that his credit is better for the people than this gift from heaven and that his wisdom has made a back number of the omniscience of God. (Morgan 5)

Williams, in the first sample, expands his description of the Louisiana Purchase by adding on to the third sentence, which could end with "that territory." He amplifies it by attaching an appositional phrase ("a vast area of contiguous territory") and two relative clauses ("whose possession . . ." and "which was fitted . . ."), by repeating "the anniversary" and "an expansion," and by adding to the definition of "anniversary" further description of proper "expansion." Senator Morgan's speech supporting free silver maintains its forward momentum through a basically *anaphoric* pattern. Anaphora, the repetition of a word or phrase at the beginning of successive clauses or sentences, is especially favored in colloquial oratory, both because it permits amplification and because its repetitive pattern is easily followed by auditors. Morgan begins each new definition of silver money with "it is" so that the phrase returns the listener's attention to the original referent, no matter how lengthened the sentences or how far adrift the definition of silver may go.

Amplification through anaphora permeates Faulkner's oratorical voice; here (condensed) is one example from *Absalom, Absalom!*, at the beginning of chapter 5, when Rosa relates for Quentin how Wash Jones came to tell her of Bon's murder:

So they will have told you doubtless already how I told *that Jones* to take that mule which was not his around to the barn and harness it to our buggy while I put on my hat and shawl and locked the house. That was all I needed to do . . . [to] traverse those twelve miles which I had not done since Ellen died, beside *that brute* who until Ellen died was not even permitted to approach the house from the front—*that brute* progenitor of brutes whose granddaughter was to supplant me . . .—*that brute who* (*brute* instrument of that justice which presides over human events . . . ruthless for appointed right and truth) *brute who* was not only to preside upon the various shapes and avatars of Thomas Sutpen's devil's fate but who was to provide at the last the female flesh in which his name and lineage should be sepulchered—*that brute who* . . . could not even tell me what happened. (*AA* 166–67; 134–35; emphasis added, original italics omitted)

Rosa is an emphatically oratorical speaker because she seeks to move Quentin Compson to action, to dominate him and persuade him to believe her version of Sutpen's history, and to accompany her to Sutpen's Hundred. But the repetition of "that brute" also serves the authorial discourse, and its authority, for the anaphoric pattern permits an amplification that embraces far more than the immediate referent, the "brutish" Wash Jones. The anaphoric series moves from the specific "brute" who could not approach Rosa's house to the more general statement about Jones as progenitor of brutes, to the broad definition of justice, back to Jones's role in Sutpen's fate, returning finally to Rosa's quite specific complaint about Jones's tobacco-chewing silence.[16]

Oratory seems to exhaust the possibilities of its subject and thus to assert its power through the excess of possible variation on a single theme or image. Barthes describes the excess of metaphor in Balzac's "Sarrasine" in this way, as not "logorrhea" ("the piling up [of] words for mere verbal pleasure") but as designed "to produce a constant model carried out to infinity, which is to constrain language as one wishes: whence the very pleasure of power" (*S/Z* 58, 59). In its demonstration of verbal mastery, in its total command of all nuance and all figuration, the oratorical voice creates rhetorical authority out of the whole cloth of exhausted discourse.[17]

Various rhetorical syntactical devices common to Southern oratory and to Faulkner support amplification and its power; I will mention only a few here by way of illustration. *Expeditio*, the rejection of all but the last of a series of alternatives (usually provided as a series of negatives followed by one positive) permits amplification as long as the orator can devise more negatives to accompany the final positive. *Expeditio* also reflects oratory's assumption that nothing be left unsaid, that all alternatives should be mentioned, that simple assertion is unauthoritative:

> Immediately after the close of the late war a gentleman of Northern birth, raising, and education, one who had been a brave and faithful soldier with the Northern army throughout the war, came to make his home in the South. He did not come to rob us in our helpless condition. He did not come to boast over the humiliation of our defeat. He did not come to breed strife between the races for the purpose of office and power. He came as a citizen, as a gentleman, as a patriot, to identify himself with us and with ours. (Hill 176)

> Ellen was dead two years now—the butterfly, the moth caught in a gale and blown against a wall and clinging there beating feebly, not

with any particular stubborn clinging to life, not in particular pain, since it was too light to have struck hard, nor even with very much rememberance [*sic*] of the bright vacuum before the gale, but just in bewildered and uncomprehending amazement. (*AA* 103; 85)

Antanagoge, the balancing of a single negative with a positive assertion (in "not A, but B" form), establishes an additive rhythm when used in series:

The mission, then, of the Anglo-Saxon is the mission of manhood—the mission of Christianizing and civilizing the world, *not* with a resort to oppression, *but* upon the platform of genuine, sterling manhood; the mission of justice, *not* of the cruel, harsh, relentless justice of Rome, *but* a justice beautifully tempered with love and mercy; the mission of war, *not* of greed or self-aggrandizement, *but* a war of principles, a war that is more noble and sublime because it is ever subservient to Anglo-Saxon manhood. (Weddington 3; emphasis added)

In fact, the sergeant had turned away, already in motion, when the voice, the murmur, stopped him—the murmur *not* so much gentle *as* just quiet, *not* so much tentative *as* bland, and possessing, for last of all the qualities, innocence: so that in the second, the instant of pause before he even began to turn back, he could see, feel all the quiet attentive faces watching, *not* him nor the speaker either, *but* as though looking at something intangible which the man's voice had created in the very air between them. Then the sergeant saw it too. It was the cloth he wore. Turning and looking back, *not only* at the man who had spoken *but* at all the faces surrounding him. (*FAB* 9; emphasis added)

In both *expeditio* and *antanagoge*, the mere mention of the negative alternatives brings them into the discourse as possibilities. The Northern gentleman who did not come south "to rob us in our helpless condition" reminds by contrast of the many Northerners who did. The mission of the Anglo-Saxon could be carried out with "a resort to oppression" or the "cruel, relentless justice of Rome," were the values the speaker upholds not those of civilized restraint. Faulkner's amplification gains persuasive effect from the ironic presentation of rejected alternatives: in the "briefs" Rosa Coldfield does *not* hold is given a complete list of the excuses she in fact does plead for agreeing to marry Sutpen: "No. I hold no brief for myself. I dont plead youth . . . I dont plead propinquity . . . I dont plead material necessity . . . And most of all, I do not plead myself" (*AA* 18–19). Rosa's list of excuses shows Faulkner's skill at adapting rhetorical devices to his own ends. Anaphora, *expeditio*, *antanagoge*, or any of a variety of such devices found in oratory persuade partly because they involve the listener or reader in what Burke calls "formal identification." Repetitive verbal patterns "awaken an attitude of collaborative expectancy in us . . . once you grasp the trend of the form, it invites participation regardless of the subject matter" (58). We await the positive conclusion of the series of negative alternatives, or we look automatically for the positive "but" element following the "not" in *antanagoge*. Faulkner sometimes withholds the positive element—Rosa never gives the alternative explanation she *would* plead—thus invoking "formal identification" without satisfying it.

We can see such disturbance of rhetorical expectation also in a third syntactical device common in oratory and Faulkner's prose, balanced compounds. Senator Morgan's speech on silver that was quoted above contains nine pairs of parallel words or phrases joined by "and," amplifying his subject with two synonyms instead of one word. Such pairs also create an illusion of rhetorical balance without the necessity of actually constructing elaborate Ciceronian periods: "In youth when boys are given to *mischief and frolic*, most providential is the suggestion of pleasing ideals to divert their *energy and animation* into some good channel, which otherwise might be squandered in *idleness and wantonness*, productive of *evil and remorse*" (Breitenbucher 3; emphasis added). Faulkner often pairs words of incongruent connotation as if they were synonymous: "visionary and alert," "tranquil and astonished," "wild and reposed."[18]

Faulkner's sophistication of verbal experiment certainly transcends the repetitive, habit-ridden verbosity of colloquial oratory at its worst. But we should not discount the importance of "mere" ornamentation here, of sheer pleasure in the fine phrase and the sparkling metaphor, in what Barthes calls "logorrhea," or what Robert Heilman has more elegantly termed the sense of the ornamental, "whatever comes from the feeling for rhythm, the sense of the incantatory, the awareness of style as integral in all kinds of communication; the intangible goods that lie beyond necessity; grace" (8). It is perhaps indicative of how deeply Faulkner's roots are embedded in oratory that the ornamental extravagance of his prose increased in those later novels that show, thematically, greater and greater distrust of talk; when he was writing in his letters about trying to "cure [him]self of the curse of human speech" (*SL* 234), he was beginning the series of his most highly oratorical late novels (*Intruder in the Dust*, *Requiem for a Nun*, and *A Fable*). Words may be, as Faulkner has Addie Bundren say, "just shapes to fill a lack," but Faulkner clearly preferred (or was compelled) to fill "lacks" to overflowing rather than leave them empty. His oratorical style, with its evocative patterns and constant improvisation, reveals the rhetorical energy that drives a discursive practice. Almost dreamlike at times, this oratorical voice chants to the rhythms of a desire for mastery over language.

MONUMENTAL RHETORIC

Rhetoric, as Burke reminds us, operates on the large discursive segments as well as on the small, on the structure of wholes as well as in the narrow devices of the rhetorical period (Burke 71). While some of the most flamboyant colloquial oratory pays little attention to form, classical rhetorical training always included attention to the argument in its structural completeness; the kind of oratory most likely to appear in written form—what Faulkner refers to in his letter to Cowley as common reading matter for the "gentle folk"—would be Ciceronian in its shape and tempo. The good oration balances opening and closing ploys around a substantive center and advances each argument at the properly prepared moment, moving from an introduction that captures attention through familiar matters to a climactic announcement of the central argument, tracing the claims for and against the argument in an order that connects the specific issue with general truths and leads toward an eloquently memorable conclusion. Mastery of oratorical language includes mastery of pace and order, and, I would argue, a mastery of verbal entities as *textual structures*. If the oratorical style produces a discourse that moves endlessly forward, oratorical architechtonics produces objects with demarcated beginnings, middles, and ends, with demonstrably functional arrangements of balanced parts.

Faulkner's texts manifest this structural sense of form predicated on rhetorical considerations. Few novelists concern themselves with parts—sections, chapters, divisions—more than Faulkner did. He *constructed* texts so that the components fit and support each other (his favorite figures for composition were building and carpentry metaphors).[19] Each text becomes a monument to its fictional world, placed before the reader, demanding to be confronted in a certain, controlled way. Faulkner regulated the tempo of revelation, seldom starting at the chronological beginning of a story but more often inserting sections or allowing images to emerge from the fictional discourse only when the reader has been properly prepared. The anachronistic placement of part 4 of "The Bear" and the odd placing of Addie Bundren's monologue in *As I Lay Dying* can both be explained in part by their presumed rhetorical effect on the reader. Faulkner had a sense of symmetry in constructing texts: *Light in August* opens with the three chapters on Lena, Joe Christmas, and Byron Bunch–Hightower, and ends with three chapters that again concentrate on Joe, Hightower, and Byron-Lena; the Snopes trilogy begins and ends with sections entitled *Flem.* He had a sense of counterpoint: *The Wild Palms* famously alternates unrelated stories in a thematic and figural dialectic. He borrowed and restructured biblical temporal patterns: *The Sound and the Fury* moves through an Easter weekend; *A Fable* rearranges Passion Week into rhetorically appropriate, nonchronological nights and days.

An orator from Faulkner's own Oxford, Mississippi, can provide us with an appropriate illustration of oratorical structuring. Lucius Quintus Cincinnatus Lamar was a fine practitioner of the Southern persuasive tradition in both its colloquial and classical forms. His not atypical education included training in Cicero, Quintilian, and Hugh Blair's *Lectures on Rhetoric and Belles Lettres*, and his school (in Georgia) combined manual labor with the requirement that the students "declaim, every week or two, such selections of prose or poetry as they might fancy" (Dickey and Streeter 185; see also Murphy 8–11). More "an orator and propagandist" than an "original thinker" (Murphy 45), Lamar and his speeches figured prominently in Mississippi and national politics before and after the Civil War. He was the first ex-Confederate elected to Congress (in 1873), and later served as a senator, cabinet member, and Supreme Court justice. He made his mark on the national consciousness with his "Eulogy on Charles Sumner," delivered in the House of Representatives in April 1874. For an ex-Confederate and "Fire-Eater" to eulogize the most vocal congressional abolitionist caused considerable stir in both the North and South, and helped plant the seeds of reconciliation—and of that sentimental fondness for things Southern that blossomed in the last twenty years of the nineteenth century.[20]

"Eulogy on Charles Sumner" (reprinted in the Appendix) shows the rhetorical imagination at work under difficult circumstances. Speaking to an overwhelmingly Northern Congress, Lamar carefully prepares his audience to accept his plea for national unity, a plea that could easily have aroused cries of betrayal from the South and of hypocrisy from the North. The eulogy begins with the startling statement that Mississippi regrets the death of her arch-abolitionist foe, Charles Sumner. After asserting this, and (we can well imagine) gaining his listeners' attention, Lamar backs off to the safe ground of Sumner's virtues. He reviews—by saying that he will *not* talk about them—those of Sumner's traits that everyone must admire. Lamar here fulfills his ceremonial duties as eulogist by praising the deceased, while the *expeditio* allows him to point toward the real subject of the address. He then elaborates on Sumner's greatest virtue, love of freedom, and displays the strength of that love by listing the rational obstacles Sumner had to wave aside in order to advance his abolitionist position so firmly. Sumner (we can again imagine) would have shuddered to hear the defense of the "peculiar institution" Lamar cleverly interjects here, but Lamar can get away with such irony because he slips the Southern arguments in as, of all things, proof that Sumner loved freedom.

About halfway through his address Lamar reaches his pivotal argument that Sumner showed no animosity toward the South, great as his abolitionist sentiments were. Now that he has led his listeners to renew their deep respect for Sumner, Lamar can urge upon them the idea that kindness toward the South was indigenous to Sumner's virtue. After an appeal to martial pride in both sections, Lamar moves to his perfectly rounded conclusion that, like Sumner the abolitionist, so should we all reconcile our differences: "My countrymen! *know* one another, and you will *love* one another." Tempo is crucial here. Lamar develops two emotionally charged images of Sumner (lover of freedom and compassionate patriot), and for his argument to work the audience must respond to the first before the second. The argument's rather simple logical basis (if the wildest abolitionist of them all can act graciously toward the South, so should you ordinary Northerners) lurks within a series of appeals to emotion: respect for Sumner's virtues, respect for his greatest virtue (conciliatory compassion), respect for martial glory, desire for national unity. Below is a structural outline of the eulogy's rhetoric:

Introduction: Mississippi regrets the death of Charles Sumner.
I. *First Exposition*: Sumner's high moral qualities (in general)
   A. Virtues not to be discussed: intellect, knowledge, retention, eloquence, logic, conversation
   B. Highest virtue: love of freedom
   C. Love of freedom so great that he abhorred slavery "despite weighty considerations to the contrary"
   Pivot: Good will toward the South (no animosity before the war, no desire for retribution after)

II. *Second Exposition*: Sumner's high moral qualities (in specific relation to the South)
   A. Love of freedom made him (perhaps mistakenly) a staunch defender of freedmen's rights
   B. Desire for unification equally strong: proposed removing reminders of the Civil War from national banners
   C. Speaker's misfortune of not knowing Sumner personally (offered as parallel for misfortune of sectional estrangement)
Conclusion: As death took Sumner before speaker could know him, so death takes us all; thus, before it is too late, we should *know* one another so we can *love* one another.

A rhetorical outline of *Absalom, Absalom!* shows interesting similarities:

Introduction: Chapter 1. Rosa creates for Quentin the "demon" image of Sutpen
  I. *First Exposition*: Detailed recounting of Sutpen's career in Jefferson
   A. Chapter 2. Sutpen's rise in Jefferson; marriage to Ellen Coldfield
   B. Chapter 3. Story of the Coldfields, especially Rosa and her childhood
   C. Chapter 4. First explanation of the mysterious murder of Charles Bon; emphasis on Charles-Henry relationship; fact of Negro blood (of Bon's morganatic wife) crucial to possible explanation
Pivot: Chapter 5. Rosa's confrontation with Sutpen
  II. *Second Exposition*: Sutpen's career again
   A. Chapter 6. Review of available information (by Shreve), account of Sutpen family after the war; Sutpen's death
   B. Chapter 7. Story of Sutpen's childhood; more detailed account of his death
   C. Chapter 8. Second explanation of the murder, again with emphasis on Charles and Henry; the fact of Negro blood is again crucial
Conclusion: Chapter 9. Rosa and Quentin visit Sutpen's Hundred; Quentin's cry that he does not hate the South.

Absalom, Absalom! is vastly more complex than any oration, but we can see here the novel's rhetorical symmetry in its return to and revision of

Sutpen's story. As Lamar does with the moral and personal qualities of Charles Sumner, Faulkner propels us through a series of images and explanations of Sutpen, presenting and rejecting alternatives (each in its proper time), revising the central image along the way, leading toward a conclusion that is discovered as the inevitable outcome of the rhetoric's own logic. The rhetoric shapes the text as a discursive object, balancing its parts into symmetry.

Itself very much an ironic "eulogy" on Thomas Sutpen, *Absalom* begins, as does Lamar's "Eulogy," with a startling image of its subject, an image that must be revised and explained because it cannot stand as proffered. Chapter 1 (which serves as a classical exordium) evokes a demon as protagonist, a "djinn," "fiend blackguard and devil"—figments of a clearly overwrought rhetoric, just as Lamar's image of a Mississippi grieving over Sumner's death seems initially farfetched. The demon image will be carried through to the end of the novel, revised and humanized but never fully rejected. Our succeeding responses to Sutpen depend on Rosa's demonology.

The novel's symmetry of rhetorical structure comes, like that of Lamar's "Eulogy," from the repetition and revision of descriptions of the eulogized figure. Lamar goes over the deceased's virtues in order to revise Sumner into a conciliatory standard of generosity toward the South. Faulkner revises Sutpen's demonic behavior until he can be seen as a person participating in demonic but not nonhuman acts. The second "exposition" repeats and elaborates the first: chapters 2 and 6 are both summaries of Sutpen and the Sutpen family's history (the first summary is prior to the murder of Charles Bon, the second is after); chapters 3 and 7 both explore a child's experience (first Rosa's and then Sutpen's) to clarify adult behavior; chapters 4 and 8 focus on the central mystery, Henry's murder of Bon, and both offer essentially similar clues, someone's Negro heritage. The results of each exposition are quite different, of course, for Mr Compson's analysis in Chapter 4 is "just incredible. It just does not explain" (100), while Quentin's and Shreve's imaginative reconstruction of events seems all too true. Quentin and Shreve do not reject Mr Compson's reasoning, however, for they repeat his portrayal of Henry as bewildered, showing him deciding whether to accept incest ("Yes. I have decided. Brother or not, I have decided. I will. I will" [354]), whereas Mr Compson showed Henry deciding whether to accept Bon's morganatic marriage. Lamar's initial explanation of why Mississippi mourns Sumner is "incredible," too, for mere personal virtues would not warrant forgiving Sumner's intense abolitionist sentiments. Not until the second exposition does Lamar make clear that "virtue" necessarily includes compassion for the defeated Confederacy.

I am not offering Lamar's "Eulogy" as in any sense a source for *Absalom's* structure; rather I am suggesting that the oratorical voice in Faulkner shares classical rhetoric's constructive impulse for symmetry and balance, for tempo and control, for leading the auditor-reader through explanations that require completion and "rounding off"—that provide, that is, the satisfaction of closure.

Rhetorical analysis like this requires a *text*. Unless auditors are uncannily perspicacious, they are not likely to perceive the persuasive and balanced stages an oration leads them through. But in a very real sense an oration, even though performed (or at least performable) as a speech act, always partakes of the shaped qualities of a written text. The oratorical voice in Faulkner—as did the phenomenal, the mimetic, and the psychic voices—returns us finally to the textual manifestations of discourse: oratorical voice in written fiction brings us full circle because it is a form of *re*-presented speech represented *in writing* of a certain form. The orator constructs (and performs) persuasive texts; Faulkner constructs (and the reader "performs") an ordered fictional text. I would call this quality of the oratorical voice (revising Heilman's phrase "the sense of the ornamental") the "sense of the monumental": a pressure within the discourse itself to coalesce into a temporal and spatial form that confronts the reader as a *monument* to be contemplated, accepted, and appreciated rather than as a *document* to be interpreted.

The distinction between "monument" and "document" is made by Michel Foucault in his meditation on historical method, *The Archaeology of Knowledge*. When we treat discourse as "document" we attempt to read through it, to translate it into the past event it might reveal. We use a document to reconstitute a past (real or fictional) from which the document emanates, treating it as the "language of a voice since reduced to silence, its fragile, but possibly decipherable trace" (*Archaeology of Knowledge* 6). Documents are signs of something else; they are ideally transparent, meant to be seen through to their meaning; they are allegorical and require interpretation. Discourse regarded as "monument," however, is taken "in its own volume." We can describe but not interpret monuments; we contemplate monuments for themselves, not for the "reality" they express, not for the truth they might reveal to us before the discourse vanishes in the wake of our interpretive enterprise. Oratory is monumental in that it does not initiate an interpretive process. Oratory answers no questions, for all its questions are rhetorical ones; it reveals no secrets, but rather invokes and confirms ideals, opinion, emotions. Orations are verbal constructs that are not, for the most part, meant to be understood so much as experienced. It is in Faulkner's oratorical voice, I would suggest, as much as in the narrative complexity of his plots, that we find his texts' resistance to the hermeneutic enterprise. The listener or reader contemplates oratorical discourse, the reader "gazes" upon it as upon a monument, but its very nature defies interpretation. An interpretive model of reading, by which the reader must "not merely . . . decipher the text but . . . revivify it [and] break free of imprisoning conventions and establish new forms of union with the world" cannot fully explain the effect of the oratorical voice (Zender, "Reading in 'The Bear'" 93, 97). Seldom does the listener or reader "break free of imprisoning conventions"—on the contrary, oratorical conventions are for the most part intended to imprison, to subjugate or mesmerize the reader-listener, and thus to inhibit interpretation, to enforce a union that is not new and is not a union with the world so much as with the discourse itself.[21]

The oratorical voice in its ceremonial domination of a shared discursive practice requires interpretation's antithesis, contemplation, an enraptured reading or listening. We see this phenomenon imaged in the many descriptions of enraptured readers or listeners throughout the novels. Some of Faulkner's most thoughtful characters—Quentin Compson, Ike McCaslin, Gail Hightower—even as they read or listen to and try to interpret some discourse, remain in exile outside interpretation's boundaries, barred from understanding and sometimes from revivification. In *Absalom, Absalom!* Quentin is inertly stuck in present meditation before verbal relics that he cannot read through into the past. He can virtually "see" Rosa's voice as a palpable thing as he listens to her; he contemplates the Sutpen tombstones in the rain "gray and solid and slow." The most striking example is of Quentin in his Harvard room contemplating but not reading his father's letter:

> He sat quite still, facing the table, his hands lying on either side of the open text book on which the letter rested: the rectangle of paper folded across the middle and now open, three quarters open, whose bulk had raised half itself by the leverage of the old crease in weightless and paradoxical levitation, lying at such an angle that he could not possibly have read it, deciphered it . . . yet he seemed to be

looking at it, or as near as Shreve could tell, he was, his face lowered a little, brooding, almost sullen . . . talking in that curious repressed calm voice as though to the table before him or the book upon it or the letter upon the book or his hands lying on either side of the book. (*AA* 271–72, 273; 217, 218)

Faulkner also frequently displays for us monuments to the past for which no interpretation is ever adequate, embodiments of a discourse (and they are most often letters, tombstones, ledgers—some form of discourse) that requires contemplation. I think, for example, of the ledgers Ike "leaned above . . . in the rank dead icy air" of the commissary (*GDM* 268); or of the bombastic Sartoris headstones in the Jefferson cemetery that Aunt Jenny visits at the end of *Flags in the Dust*, described as "like a boastful voice in an empty church" and "carven gestures of [Sartoris vainglory] in enduring stone" (*FD* 365, 367); or of Cecelia Farmer's name scratched in the jail's pane of glass in *Requiem for a Nun*—indeed, the interchapters in *Requiem* are themselves monuments, in the oratorical style, that in turn depict monumental objects (the lock, the dome, the jail) to Mississippi's vainglorious past. These are the occasions and sites of discursive relics that must be contemplated at some remove from interpretation.

From this perspective perhaps the quintessential Faulknerian listener-reader is not Quentin Compson in his struggle to unravel the Sutpen saga, or Ike McCaslin exhuming from the ledgers his ancestor's crimes, but rather Gail Hightower. Hightower's sin is that he so obsessively relives the past that he has denied the present. By re-creating in his frenzied imagination his grandfather's ride through Jefferson's streets, Hightower has irresponsibly insulated himself from human action. In his final meditation in *Light in August* he interprets his life for the first time and sees his moral blame for disregarding his wife's and his congregation's need for his care in their present lives. For most readers the novel's thematics compel the rejection on moral grounds of Hightower's monumental vision of the past because it forces him to hover outside of active, humanly meaningful life (see, for example, Porter 247–57). Nevertheless, his relation to the discourse of the world makes him *essentially* Faulknerian, turning the stories told him by his family's Negro cook and the relics discovered in an old trunk into a perfect monument to the past: its contemplated, imagined, but *unexamined* and *uninterpreted* reconstruction. Faulkner provides in *Light in August* a monument to Hightower's years in Jefferson in the sign in front of Hightower's house: "from the window he can also see the sign, which he calls his monument" (61; 52). Faulkner attends closely, as Foucault would urge the archaeologist to do, to this small icon of historical discourse, this sign that really says very little but serves as a monument to Hightower's life:

> Hence the sign, carpentered neatly by himself and by himself lettered, with bits of broken glass contrived cunningly into the paint, so that at night, when the corner street lamp shone upon it, the letters glittered with an effect as of Christmas:
>
> REV. GAIL HIGHTOWER, D.D.
> Art Lessons
> Handpainted Xmas & Anniversary Cards
> Photographs Developed
>
> . . . the paint and the shattered glass had weathered out of the fading letters. They were still readable, however; though, like Hightower himself, few of the townspeople needed to read them anymore. (*LA* 62; 53)

Hightower is dominated by his history and its discourses because, as he turns his face to it, it evokes in him the same passive inertia of enrapture as when he listened to the Negro cook's stories "with rapt, wide, half dread and half delight" (*LA* 526; 452). His life has not demanded that he interpret. As he sits in his window, or as he sits listening to Byron Bunch, "in the attitude of the eastern idol" (346; 298), his life itself becomes a relic of the past, "intact and on all sides complete and inviolable, like a classic and serene vase, where the spirit could be born anew sheltered from the harsh gale of living and die so, peacefully, with only the far sound of the circumvented wind, with scarce even a handful of rotting dust to be disposed of" (527–28; 453).

It is not surprising that in this discussion of Faulkner's oratorical voice we have moved from the highly oral tradition of colloquial Southern oratory to written forms of monument in the novels. Nor is it surprising that we find oratorical excess in Faulkner's later novels hand in hand with that rejection of talking and greater emphasis on writing that I discussed in chapter 1. Oratory is woven intertextually into Faulkner's texts, but not because it is the heritage of a residually oral society that has left its mark on a modern novelist. Rather, whether embodied orally or in writing, oratory as a discursive practice moves within Faulkner's texts as a generating force of a complex power: the power to move and to subjugate the reader-listener, the power to enchant and frustrate with an endlessly onrushing prose that coalesces into opaque, monumental *text*. That oratory's discursive authority is at best contingent and supplemental also makes it "arche-writing" in Derrida's sense of "writing" as the very principle of supplementarity in all discourse, oral or printed. All discourse to Derrida is "written" in that it stands in for that which can never be directly experienced but only represented—truth, presence, authority.

In summary terms, then, the salient features of Faulkner's oratorical voice are these: an intertextual relationship to Southern oratory, especially the oratory of the generations immediately preceding and following the Civil War; a discursive cultural practice, participated in by speaker (author) and listener (reader), that celebrates (sincerely or parodically) shared communal values; a struggle (often dramatized in a persuasive narrative scene) for dominance by the speaker, who possesses and uses language as a source of authority; an amplified, ornate, and anaphoric verbal style (employed either sincerely or parodically) that moves forward without pause, that tends to overwhelm and to inhibit possible response; and the creation of evocative textual monuments that articulate rhetorical tempo and construct symmetrically closed verbal patterns.

ABSALOM, ABSALOM!

To speak of the oratorical voice *in Absalom, Absalom!* may be misleading, for the novel *is* "oratorical" in every imaginable way. It portrays that Southern past in which—as Faulkner wrote to Cowley in a letter about *Absalom*—oratory was the dominant public discourse. The novel's overwhelmingly ornate verbal style, its density of metaphor and amplified repetition of event and scene, its scenes of persuasive storytelling, and its rhetorical structure all reflect (and sometimes parody) features of the oratorical mode. Most important, *Absalom* celebrates ironically the past and its monuments in order to interrogate the nature of authority and the discourse that represents it.

In many ways Sutpen seems the essence of the oratorical in his project to turn his very life into a monument to himself. His project begins with the realization of his own powerlessness as a poor white in a class- and race-structured society. After he goes to a plantation to deliver a message from his father, and is turned away at the front door by a "monkey-dressed nigger butler," the fourteen-year-old Sutpen debates with himself what to do. In a manner typical of the Faulknerian psychic voice, two boys ("debaters") inside his one mind talk out the possibilities, until active thinking gives way to a knowledge deeper than thought:

> Because he said how the terrible part of it had not occurred to him
> yet, he just lay there while the two of them argued inside of him,
> speaking in orderly turn, both calm. . . . [A]nd then he said that all
> of a sudden it was not thinking, it was something shouting it almost
> loud enough for [others] to hear too . . . it too fast, too mixed up to
> be thinking, it all kind of shouting at him at once, boiling out and
> over him like the nigger laughing: . . . *there aint any good or harm*
> *either in the living world that I can do to him.* (295–97; 237–38)

Sutpen passes here from self-questioning to a realm of presumed truth where debate and dialogue are no longer feasible.

Bakhtin's distinction between the *monologic* and the *dialogic* provides a convenient shorthand for the struggle enacted and reenacted throughout *Absalom, Absalom!*. By "monological" Bakhtin means discourse that is simply assertive of claimed truth; he means an object-oriented discourse uttered with no mind to any other speaker or responder, a discourse expressive of the full semantic authority of the speaker. By "dialogical" Bakhtin means discourse that by its nature takes other speech, other voices, other viewpoints into account. The dialogical is discourse that is "warped" or "bent" by the presence of another as light is bent by gravity (*Problems of Dostoevsky's Poetics* 181–204). The distinction is especially useful in considering *Absalom, Absalom!* because of the related distinction between monologue and dialogue. Oratory is inherently monological in both form and intent, for it articulates certainty. Certainty may be a disguise hiding confusion or ambiguity, but oratorical discourse appears possessed of Truth. The Negro butler spoke to the boy, but only to send him around back; he brooked no answer, "*he never even give me a chance to say it*" (296; 237). So the boy concludes that what and all he needs to combat those who would turn him away are the trappings of the plantation owners: "land and niggers and a fine house" (297; 238) and, he will realize later, a son.

This conviction, which Faulkner's narrators call Sutpen's "innocence," is also an attempt to participate in certainty, in monological truth that need only be fulfilled, but never questioned. The metaphor through which the young Sutpen's discovery is depicted, however, reveals the inherent oratorical mechanism that will doom the design. What the boy perceives as a truth for future living, the text offers as *already* a monument to a past: "It was like that, he said, like an explosion—a bright glare that vanished and left nothing, no ashes nor refuse: just a limitless flat plain with the severe shape of his intact innocence rising from it like a monument" (297; 238). And this monument "instructs" him, speaks to him in monologic certainty: "You got to have what they have that made them do what he did." To which Sutpen can only say "Yes."

Sutpen's design requires him to assume a certain position within the discursive practices of his community. Along with implements of economic and social power, he must take possession of the language in which power expresses itself; his word must become law. To some extent he succeeds. Especially in the early chapters of the novel, Sutpen seems to build his design in authoritative silence, needing and using speech only to bring his design into being, as Quentin imagines him, "pontific, creating the Sutpen's Hundred, the *Be Sutpen's Hundred* like the oldentime *Be Light*" (5; 9). He arrives in Jefferson silently "out of thin air," and he refuses dialogue with the town. "He would move gradually and steadily until his back came in contact with something—a post or a wall—and then stand there and tell them nothing whatever as pleasantly and courteously as a hotel clerk" (38; 34). Moving mysteriously about his business of establishing a dynasty, he appears to ignore the men who come to watch him build his house, and he is "contemptuous" of the town's opinion, silently "smiling behind his beard" at the community's outrage, or at most "talking to them [the vigilance committee] over his shoulder" (52; 43). His voice in some circumstances possesses genuine authority, as in his ability to control his slaves without raising his voice (41; 37). When he does talk his is not a discourse of communicative exchange but of proclamation: he literally proclaims his intended marriage to Rosa Coldfield by standing with his hand on her head, *"pronounc[ing] his own wild benediction on it"* (206; 165) just as he had "put his first wife aside like eleventh and twelfth century kings did" (300; 240). Even when Sutpen seeks advice by asking General Compson to help him find the flaw in his design, he "was not listening, did not expect an answer, who had not come for pity and there was no advice that he could have taken" (340; 273).

As in the description of Sutpen's innocence exploding his internal debate into monumental certainty, a monument image intrudes into the speech act in which Sutpen decrees that he will marry Rosa. Rosa tells Quentin that Sutpen looked at her once, one afternoon, and that night announced his intent. What began as a look is completed as phenomenal voice, for Sutpen is imaged through voice as Rosa perceives him: "*I do not know what he looked at while he spoke, save that by the sound of his voice it was not at us*" (204; 164). She listens "*to his voice as Ellen must have listened*" before her. But the proposal evokes nothing of voice's human presence and intimacy ("*he talking not about me or love or marriage, not even about himself*" [205; 165]), for Sutpen's is an oratorical voice that turns to stony monument: "*That was my courtship. That minute's exchanged look in a kitchen garden, that hand upon my head in his daughter's bedroom; a ukase, a decree, a serene and florid boast like a sentence (ay, and delivered in the same attitude) not to be spoken and heard but to be read carved in the bland stone which pediments a forgotten and nameless effigy*" (204–5; 164).

Sutpen would like to articulate himself in the world as a god or father absolute, whose word carries weight, whose word merely spoken brings the bespoken into being.[22] But like all the monuments he erects to himself—his house that was "an edifice bigger even than the courthouse," or the tombstones, those "bombastic and inert carven rocks" he miraculously procures in the middle of the war—Sutpen's univocality makes an empty gesture. Because he has confused the authority that validates a discursive practice with the superficial mannerisms that constitute its performance, Sutpen fails to articulate any but a dead monumental discourse. Other strands in *Absalom*'s figurative texture, interwoven with the images of monuments, show that what Sutpen desires as monuments he can produce only as show. "Swagger," "pompous arrogance," "bombastic," "florid," "forensic"—terms out of histories of Southern oratory depict in Sutpen that necessary and often superficial "eloquence" of speech and manner required of the gentry. He copies a manner of talking just as he acquires slaves and a plantation: "His head flung up a little in that attitude that nobody ever knew exactly who he had aped it from or if he did not perhaps learn it too from the same book out of which he taught himself the words, the bombastic phrases with which Grandfather said he even asked you for a match" (299; 240); "his gestures and the set of his shoulders forensic, oratorical" (344; 275). His storytelling to General Compson, which is the only extended direct representation of Sutpen's speech, sounds like legal oratory in the deceptively calm, reasoned, yet still florid tone in which he talks of choosing to "play my last trump card" and reveal Bon's Negro ancestry (341–42; 273–74). To Rosa the "bombast" is insane and devilish, as she listens to Sutpen "*talking that which sounded like the bombast of a madman who creates within his very coffin walls his fabulous immeasurable Camelots and Carcassonnes*" (199; 160).

Metaphors of drama, theater, and stage performance pervade the narrators' rehearsals of Sutpen's life. For all that he appears to ignore public opinion in his monomaniacal drive to fulfill his design, Sutpen is nonetheless a showman: "Destiny had fitted itself to him, to his innocence, his pristine aptitude for platform drama and childlike heroic simplicity, just as the fine broadcloth uniform . . . had fitted itself to the swaggering of all his gestures and to the forensic verbiage in which he stated calmly . . . the most simple and the most outrageous things" (307; 246). Building his house, fighting his slaves in his barn, his wedding, and the races to church are all performed for audiences. Faulkner gives each narrator some version of theater imagery. For Rosa, Sutpen's behavior is a "raree show" (17; 18); Mr Compson's fatalism sees Sutpen "still playing the scene to the audience [while] Fate, destiny, retribution, irony—the stage manager, call him what you will—was already striking the set" (87–88; 72–73); for Shreve the South is "better than the theatre, isn't it. It's better than Ben Hur, isn't it" (271; 217).[23]

As with his house and domain, Sutpen overplays his part, to be sure (Mr Compson calls him "underbred . . . like John L. Sullivan having taught himself painfully and tediously to do the schottische" [52–53; 46]), but he has not chosen the wrong script. These theatrical figurative patterns warrant a reading of Sutpen's career as a virtual allegory of oratorical posturing. But it would be a misreading to underestimate the seriousness of such posturing by seeing it as little more than an outward costume provided so that the reader can correctly judge Sutpen as "underbred," "not even a gentleman," as "this Faustus, this demon, this Beelzebub." Oratory and all its trappings imaged in *Absalom*'s discourse cannot be stripped away from the fictional world's total ideology any more than oratorical discursive practice could be isolated away from Southern life. Sutpen's oratorical discourse does carry the weight of authority (though certainly not the authority Sutpen himself would have wished). By mastering (or perhaps we should say by overpowering) the South's oratorical discursive practice, Sutpen inserts himself into realms of power. Tightly woven with the images of monuments, forensic manner, and platform performance are figures drawn directly from institutional sources of power—religion, law, economics. We can isolate these various figurative strands for analysis, but they are not really separate. That Sutpen's public speech sounds legalistic and economic when he pompously refers to his first marriage as an agreement between two parties; that Shreve invents a lawyer to machinate behind the scenes; that the narrators speak of "balanc[ing] the books" (406; 325) or "pay[ing] the check to which his wife, Nature, has signed his name" (82; 68); that Sutpen is described as *"a fine proud man [like] God Himself . . . come down [to] ride the natural earth"* (352; 282); that Sutpen's sole survivor is an idiot with a name that Luster says is "a lawyer word. Whut dey puts you under when de Law ketches you" (269; 215)—all these figurative patterns are caught up along with oratory in the discursive practices that constitute—not merely express—an ideology and its power. The oratorical voice functions in the fictional world to bring into the public domain versions of experience that otherwise remain unspoken. Part of the fascination Sutpen holds is that he tries to live out the dynastic patriarchy founded on slavery and rapacious economics that had been only implied in the South's self-imaging discourse. It is not so much that Sutpen honestly and frankly speaks what others have only thought, but more that he takes with absolute seriousness the implications of oratorical practice. Bourdieu, whose theory of practice was discussed earlier, describes the kind of process Sutpen initiates:

> "Private" experiences undergo nothing less than a *change of state* when they recognize themselves in the *public objectivity* of an already constituted discourse, the objective sign of recognition of their right to be spoken and to be spoken publicly: "Words wreck havoc," says Sartre, "when they find a name for what had up to then been lived namelessly." Because any language that can command attention is an "authorized language," invested with the authority of a group, the things it designates are not simply expressed but also authorized and legitimated. (170)

Regarding oratory as a discursive practice can help us see how it contributes to *Absalom*'s fictional world, which is haunted by the shades and avatars of Thomas Sutpen. But as the authorial narrator tells us early in the novel, Sutpen's ghost haunts a *voice* more than a place: "the ghost mused with shadowy docility as if it were the voice which he haunted where a more fortunate one would have had a house" (4; 8). Regarded as a *discursive* practice, oratory infuses *Absalom* with a distinctive rhythm of representation that derives from the somewhat paradoxical position of the orator as one caught up in a practice that confers power upon his discourse, and simultaneously as one employing discourse to assume dominance. For the dominant authority of the Faulknerian oratorical voice is both more problematical and more complete than that of the traditional orator. Like Southern rhetoric, Faulkner's oratorical voice gains authority from ornate language itself as a celebratory discursive practice; furthermore, it gains the even greater authority of the *author*, for whether assigned to a character or rendered as purely diegetic discourse, oratorical discourse gains legitimacy as being "Faulkner's," as deriving from a recognizable authorial source. At the same time, however, the oratorical voice is never adequate to the authority it exudes. The discursive authority of oratorical voice is persistently undercut in *Absalom, Absalom!*, either because the values it embodies are invalidated in the process of expressing them (as seen in Sutpen's case) or because the listener and reader are led to desire the end to oratory for the sake of "truth." The discursive ritual is never quite felicitously performed—or performable.

Absalom's representation depends upon the power of voice to evoke a world—the world of past events and people for the narrating characters, the fictional world for the reader. The evocation takes the form of a repeated calling forth of the past into the present, a process that is akin to the anaphoric patterns characteristic of oratorical prose style and rhetorical structures in which an idea or word or image is named and renamed so as to be elaborated and reelaborated again and again. The novel's discourse repeatedly evokes versions of the past and then seeks to elaborate these versions into textual *monuments* of various literal or symbolic kinds. The repetitive, almost syncopated movement, however, also includes as a final step a questioning of the power of the evocative oratorical voice on which it depends. Time and again the oratorical voice vanishes for the sake of living voices in dialogue. To use Bakhtin's terms again, the monological discourse so powerful throughout the novel gives way to dialogic scene. Just as Sutpen's failure to fulfill his design raises questions of morality and ideology, so the "failure" of oratorical voice to evoke a world raises questions about the nature of verbal representation, about the power of language to interrupt time's flow and erect permanent discursive "monuments."

The novel proposes a theory of memory—or more precisely of memorializing—when Mr Compson tells how Judith Sutpen delivered Charles Bon's letter to Quentin's grandmother. The crucial position occupied by "voice" as the finale in a series of metaphors proposed for memory can suggest the role that evocative oratorical voice plays in the full text. Judith does not deliver the letter for safekeeping, nor even to be read, but simply to make "an impression" on another's mind. Judith, whose own face is "absolutely impenetrable," wants to penetrate if only for an instant another person's life because, she says, we normally cannot make any impression. We struggle "all in one another's way like five or six people all

218

trying to make a rug on the same loom only each one wants to weave his own pattern into the rug" (157; 127). Since we cannot weave our own figure into the carpet, nothing remains except "a block of stone with scratches on it." Scratches abide but no one can read them, for "after a while [people] don't even remember the name and what the scratches were trying to tell" (158; 127). So Judith proposes an alternative. Go to any stranger and "give them something,"

> a scrap of paper—something, anything, it not to mean anything in itself and them not even to read it or keep it, not even bother to throw it away or destroy it, at least it would be something just because it would have happened, be remembered even if only from passing from one hand to another, one mind to another, and it would be at least a scratch, something, something that might make a mark on something that *was* once for the reason that it can die someday, while the block of stone cant be *is* because it never can become *was* because it cant ever die or perish. (158; 127–28)

By "scratching" a mark on another's consciousness, Judith would guarantee significance not, as we might think, by the permanence of the mark but by its very erasability. Only that can be remembered which can become *was*; only those can remember who can someday die. *Was* is necessary for *is*. A legitimate memorial is not something exempt from time's law but something that we can call forth (re-call) from within time.

Judith rejects (or perhaps it is Mr Compson, the narrator of these metaphors, who rejects) weaving as a suitable metaphor for memorializing because it is impossible to pattern life after one's own image. In doing so she rejects what her father has tried to create in his design—a life patterned after his own image and permanently extended through time "even after he would become dead . . . watching the fine grandsons and great-grandsons springing as far as eye could reach" (338–39; 271). But for Judith no pattern or structure, no edifice will suffice. For while she (who only a week earlier had laid Bon in his grave) acknowledges the need to engrave an "undying mark on the blank face of the oblivion to which we are all doomed" (159–60; 129), she also recognizes the paradox that to become a memorial the mark must be erasable; an inscription must be made that can become *was.* So she proffers as a monument another kind of inscription: a letter from Charles Bon. Judith places the letter into the community by giving it to Quentin's grandmother, but not as if she were putting up a tombstone in a public cemetery. Instead she proclaims this act a memorial superior to any erected block of stone because it is not a dead inscription but an act of inscribing, an impression that passes as it is made. No one even needs to read the letter, "it not to mean anything in itself and them not even to read or keep it."

The metaphors for memorializing the past move, in this passage, from weaving a final pattern to engraving a few scratches to writing a momentary impression on a mind. Each figure suggests greater fragility and thus greater value as a memorial. The authorial narrator extends the sequence of metaphors in the description of Quentin reading Bon's letter. When read the letter loses its inscribed hardness and takes on the evanescence of *was*: "[Quentin] read the faint spidery script not like something impressed upon the paper by a once-living hand but like a shadow cast upon it which had resolved on the paper the instant before he looked at it and which might fade, vanish, at any instant while he still did" (160; 129). The letter sloughs off its quality as inscription and becomes "a dead tongue speaking" (160; 129). The figurative progression culminates in the word "voice," given to us, ironically, in the first sentence of the letter itself. In effect, then, Judith delivers a written letter to preserve a trace of her lover's voice; the voice in turn will preserve a trace of herself "literally," by the letter. But in her act of passing the letter on, we are told that nothing but impermanent and evanescent voice—which in a written document can only be figurative and never literal—can remain as a monument to the past.

Absalom's narrative voices, repeatedly retracing the past, call forth lost events and people. The originating power of evocative voice is presumed as a defense against final silence. To tell and tell again, to listen and listen again, to hear and repeat—this anaphoric rhythm of the text reproduces an imagined past. The kind of voice necessary and sufficient for evocation, however, is not mimetic voice, not talking, but rather an oratorical voice figured throughout the novel as an almost palpable presence that contains the past. The novel's dense, figurative rhetoric often clouds the illusion that we are hearing characters narrate. It is an ornate and amplified style that Faulkner's own phrase, "oratory out of solitude," aptly designates as a prose whereby language becomes its own brooding celebration, gathering weight as if it were a monument to itself. Many commentators on the novel have emphasized differences among the narrators, finding each discourse to be motivated by the psychic needs of the storyteller.[24] The distinctions in tone, style, or type of metaphor, however, seem in the final analysis incidental compared to the overwhelming consistency of an oratorical Overvoice pervading the entire text. All speakers evince the features of the oratorical style discussed earlier. All the narrators more or less "sound like father"—and "father" names a principle of authority greater, of course, than Mr Compson. The Overvoice envelops the discourse, taking up into itself all subsidiary voices. Hyatt Waggoner's assertion that *"Absalom* has many voices but no official, sanctioned Voice" is correct only if we read "sanctioned Voice" to mean a standard of moral responsibility, only if we ignore the Voice of authority that sanctions the discourse we hear (Waggoner 148). This Overvoice becomes an entity unto itself, an extravagant and densely figured version of phenomenal voice, described again and again throughout the novel. The Overvoice seems excessively motivated, overdetermined in the Freudian sense, as if emanating from sources indefinable yet intensely felt. It is a Voice "level, curious, a little dreamy yet still with that overtone of sullen bemusement, of smoldering outrage" (272; 218). Voice is palpable, like "a stream, a trickle running from patch to patch of dried sand" (4; 8). Voice is a space one can occupy, as Sutpen "haunts" Rosa's voice, or as Quentin walks out of his "father's talking at last" (218; 174), or as Bon is "swamped and submerged in the bright unreal flood of Henry's speech" (397; 318).[25]

The function of the Overvoice is to evoke the past. Figures of evocation abound throughout the novel, especially in chapter 1, which announces the story-telling enterprise. Quentin sits listening to Rosa Coldfield "talking in that grim haggard amazed voice until at last listening would renege and hearing-sense self-confound and the long-dead object of her impotent yet indomitable frustration would appear, as though by outraged recapitulation evoked" (4; 8–9). Voice is presented as the source of a movement outside itself, an "appearing" out of and away from talking so the "voice would not cease, it would just vanish" (4; 8); "not ceasing but vanishing into and then out of the long intervals" (4; 8). Sutpen's "ghost" haunts the Voice only to "abrupt" onto the scene of Quentin's remembering and our reading. The Voice that calls this demon out of hell drifts in and out of Quentin's hearing so that the Sutpens, "in inverse ratio to the vanishing voice," can resolve themselves into pictorial stasis: "Quentin seemed to see them, the four of them arranged into the conventional family group of the period, with formal and lifeless decorum, and seen now as the fading and ancient photograph itself would have been seen enlarged and hung on the wall behind and above the voice" (12; 14). Sutpen "as though [he] had been created out of thin air" is called forth from some region beneath language by the tolling of his name "in steady strophe and antistrophe: *Sutpen. Sutpen. Sutpen. Sutpen*" (35; 32).

The subsequent listening scenes—and every chapter begins or ends with Quentin listening—remind us that the Voice we hear brings forth the dead and their antics. We are told frequently that "it seemed to Quentin that he could actually see them" (164, 237; 132, 189) as the past comes alive for him, more alive in some ways than if he had lived it: "He could see it; he might even have been there. Then he thought *No. If I had been there I could not have seen it this plain*" (238; 190). In the second half of the book Quentin and Shreve pass back and forth the duties of talker and listener until their imagining resurrects experience. They become, in their tomblike room at Harvard, the dead Henry and Bon, "two, four, now two again . . . the two the four the two still talking" (432; 346). Again and again *Absalom* sings its paeans to this triumph of the imagination whereby voice can evoke "out of the rag-tag and bob-ends of old tales and talking, people who perhaps never existed at all anywhere, shadows, quiet as the visible murmur of [Quentin's and Shreve's] vaporizing breath" (378–79; 303). In the climactic revelation of the reason for Bon's murder, they are said to become the past figures they create: "Because now neither of them was there. They were both in Carolina and the time was forty-six years ago . . . now both of them were Henry Sutpen and both of them were Bon, compounded each of both yet either neither, smelling the very smoke which had blown and faded away forty-six years ago" (438–39; 351). *Absalom, Absalom!* insists so strongly on this rhetoric of evocation that it is clearly more than simply another instance of Faulkner's often romantic commentary on art and the imagination, and the listening scenes do more than merely dramatize Quentin's struggle with his past. The novel instructs us how to read it by imaging its own discourse: *Absalom* presumes an energetics of oratorical voice through which language can be transcended and the past rescued. Through the elaborate recapitulation of past events the novel accumulates what seem to be versions of the imaginative real and the imaginative true, and creates thereby a textual monument to its own endeavor.

But evocative as it is, oratorical voice also creates the conditions for an interrogation of the novel's proposed aesthetics of evocation. Let us return for the moment to Charles Bon's letter. Judith wants his letter (or at least the act of transmitting the letter) to evoke the memory of Charles Bon. Yet the letter itself, like Bon's distant and rather cold love for Judith, in some ways counters her impulse by—like all oratorical discourse—making of itself a monumental text. When we read the letter we hear the same oratorical rhetoric that fills much of the novel, the rhetoric that Sutpen himself had learned to ape. The letter's tone is, as the narrator tells us, "gentle sardonic whimsical and incurably pessimistic" (160; 129) (much like Mr Compson); but the style is high rhetoric, with amplified periods, anaphoric constructions ("Imagine us. . . . And Imagine us . . . imagine, I say"), *expeditio* ("I wont say hungry . . . I wont say ragged. . . . So say we merely needed ammunition"), *antanagoge* ("not only must but do work"). This is the kind of voice that evokes in order to monumentalize; this is monological discourse that, even within the dialogical purpose of intimate communication with Judith, turns into proclamation ("we have waited long enough").

The letter's tone and style are appropriate in that Charles Bon in many ways repeats his father. He, too, has a "design," to win Sutpen's acknowledgment, and he, too, destroys the design by monomaniacally carrying it out. In Mr Compson's theorizing Bon is a clever persuader, carefully introducing Henry to New Orleans customs to get him to accept his morganatic wife as no barrier to marriage with Judith. He has mastered oratorical mannerisms more thoroughly and graciously even than Sutpen: "a man with an ease of manner and a swaggering gallant air in comparison with which Sutpen's pompous arrogance was clumsy bluff" (90; 74). Mr Compson imagines him waxing oratorical indeed as he discourses on why God, who "must have been young once," does not look askance at such relationships as his with the octoroon woman (143; 115–16). Bon's story repeats as well the image of a boy turned away at a plantation's front door just as Sutpen was. The most ironic repetition of Sutpen occurs when Mr Compson imagines Bon, in persuading Henry to forgive the morganatic marriage, playing the same "trump card" Sutpen will later play to persuade Henry that Bon cannot marry Judith. "The trump now, the voice gentle now: 'Have you forgot that this woman, this child, are niggers? You, Henry Sutpen of Sutpen's Hundred in Mississippi?' " (146; 118). Bon's similarities to Sutpen place him, and his letter, within the monological realm of oratorical practice.[26]

Faulkner also dramatizes the dominance of the oratorical voice in the narrative scenes in which Rosa, Mr Compson, and Quentin and Shreve recount the Sutpen saga. These are persuasive rhetorical scenes of the kind described earlier as typical of Faulkner's oratorical voice: a figure of authority assumes and exercises dominance over a listener. Rosa, who carries the social authority that Faulkner always gives to "undefeated spinster aunts" summons Quentin to her tomblike house so she can persuade him to accompany her to Sutpen's Hundred.[27] The note she sends him both presumes and establishes her position, "the quaint, stiffly formal request which was actually a summons, out of another world almost" (7; 10). She speaks an intensely oratorical, densely metaphorical rhetoric that mixes personal outrage and institutional condemnation; of all the narrators Rosa is at once the most individualized and the most representative of a public voice. Her imagery comes predominantly from that world of institutional authority to which she, presumptively, claims access by her status as an elderly and respected (if eccentric) citizen of Jefferson. She has a past here, she belongs to church and court and office, no matter that her own activities have been restricted and despite her father's antiwar sentiments. She also can claim authority as "the town's and the county's poetess laureate," writing an "official" verse—"ode eulogy and epitaph, out of some bitter and implacable reserve of undefeat" (8; 11). Her rhetoric, which condemns Sutpen, draws heavily on the social, religious, and legal language of judgment. "He wasn't even a gentleman"; "fiend blackguard and devil"; "I hold no brief for myself"; "I do not plead propinquity." Rosa also gains persuasive status by being a surviving eyewitness to Sutpen and a member by marriage of his family (though it turns out she actually witnessed only two important events, Sutpen's return from the war and his proposal to her).[28]

Mr Compson holds the ideally dominant, presumably persuasive position as Quentin's father. Though less personally frenzied than Rosa's, and more "sardonic whimsical and incurably pessimistic" (like Bon's letter), Mr Compson's rhetoric asserts its discursive authority over Quentin perhaps more directly than Rosa's. He does not try to move Quentin to a specific act, as Rosa does, but he instructs his son, fulfilling the role of mentor in the ways of the doomed world. He wants to transmit a heritage to his son, but it is also clear that Mr Compson wants Quentin to accede to his own authority in interpreting that heritage. Emblematic of this role is the moment when he brings Bon's letter out to the porch for Quentin to read. He does not give Quentin the letter right away but, after telling him he will need more light to read it, he tantalizingly withholds it so he can teach his son how to understand it. The moment shows Quentin's disappointed anticipation as he is forced to wait again and listen:

> [Quentin] rose from his chair as Mr Compson, carrying the letter, emerged from the house, snapping on the porch light as he passed.
> "You will probably have to go inside to read it," Mr Compson said.
> "Maybe I can read it here all right," Quentin said.
> "Perhaps you are right," Mr Compson said. . . . But he did not

give Quentin the letter at once. He sat again, Quentin sitting again too, and took up his cigar from the veranda rail, . . . raised his feet once more to the railing, the letter in his hand and the hand looking almost as dark as a negro's against his linen leg. (109–10; 89)

Both Irwin and Matthews tie Mr Compson's role here to that in *The Sound and the Fury* as the father figure who fails Quentin, but even without the earlier novel we can hear in his rhetoric the persuasive instruction of one anxious that his son realize how odd and intractable life is.[29] His imagery emphasizes the role of Fate in human events, and our inability to comprehend its workings. Mr Compson also has what might be considered "authorial" legitimacy, for to him are given many of the oft-quoted lines that comment on narrative art and history, on how little we can know about the past, how our information "just does not explain" and is like "a chemical formula [from which] something is missing" (124; 101), and how figures from the past seem "simpler" yet "larger, more heroic" than in our own day (109–10; 89). Mr Compson's account, especially in chapter 2, blends more smoothly with the authorial voice than the other narrators' accounts, picking up without missing a beat the story of Sutpen's arrival in Jefferson and his marriage (49; 43). The quotation marks signaling Mr Compson's assumption of narrative duties could be anywhere in the chapter, and, indeed, the manuscript shows that Faulkner moved the beginning mark without any other changes (in style, tone, or information) to differentiate the two voices. Matthews has argued that Mr Compson creates an image of himself in his portrayal of Charles Bon as a "passive, a little sardonic," and bemused observer of the human animal; we should supplement this with his role as a persuader with a "voice—the mentor, the guide standing aside now to watch the grave provincial face—casually and pleasantly anecdotal" (140; 113). Mr Compson's position as authoritative persuader of Quentin echoes Sutpen's relation to Henry when he forbids Judith's marriage to Bon. To the repeated pairings of father and son throughout the novel can be added another version, that of "persuader and persuadee," of orator and listener.

To such persuasion as Rosa's and his father's Quentin cannot respond directly except with a few questions and a "Yessum" or a "No, sir." He has been involved in an oratorical practice all his life, forced to listen to the town and his father talk about Sutpen; his is a "twenty years' heritage of breathing the same air . . . which the man himself had breathed" (9; 11)— and the image of breathing captures perfectly the listener's necessary taking in of an insistent communal discourse. "His childhood was full of them; his very body was an empty hall echoing with sonorous defeated names; he was not a being, an entity, he was a commonwealth" (9; 12). *Absalom* reminds us repeatedly of Quentin's role as listener.[30] And it is a debilitating role, for he is imaged as hypnotized in the presence of his heritage of voice. The telling partakes of "that logic- and reason-flouting quality of a dream" (22; 22). *"I have heard too much, I have been told too much; I have had to listen to too much, too long"* (259–60; 207. Also 243; 193; and 263; 211). Listening to Shreve, who "sounds like father," reinvolves Quentin in his heritage: *"Am I going to have to hear it all again* he thought *I am going to have to hear it all over again I am already hearing it all over again I am listening to it all over again I shall have to never listen to anything else but this again forever so apparently not only a man never outlives his father but not even his friends and acquaintances do"* (345–46; 277). The listening produces in Quentin a mesmerized, "downcast face, the relaxed body not moving except to breathe" (322; 258). He is utterly passive as he sits in his Harvard room staring at his father's letter, "his face lowered a little, brooding, almost sullen," and even his voice is a "repressed calm voice" (272; 218), a "flat curiously dead voice" (322; 258), "level, curious, a little dreamy yet still with that overtone of sullen bemusement, of smoldering outrage" (272; 218).

A great deal has been written about Quentin's participation in a storytelling act, or in an interpretive enterprise, a search for truth—in a process that self-reflexively depicts the narrative and hermeneutic processes of the text itself, and of all fiction texts.[31] That Quentin participates passively as listener in an oratorical discursive practice in no way interferes with his active struggle to interpret his heritage, but it does suggest that Quentin's position vis-à-vis the other narrators is one of a dominated audience or mesmerized listener, and in this role his consciousness permeates the novel's total discourse. In Quentin oratorical voice transmutes into a form of psychic voice. His consciousness does not govern all the text's discourse, as Ike McCaslin's perhaps does in *Go Down, Moses*; nor can we say that all the discourse is "in" Quentin's mind or heard only through him. Yet certain features of the Faulknerian psychic voice appear in the text in such a way as to mark all the discourse as colored by Quentin's listening. Some of these features appear in odd ways, as if to mark portions of the text as "partial" psychic voice, in touch with but not rendering Quentin's consciousness. Like the empty hall filled with sonorous names that Quentin is described as being, the novel's discourse echoes through Quentin's psyche without being equated with his thoughts. The psychic voice is seen first in the italicized summary of Sutpen's life given as a dialogue between "two separate Quentins" who talk in "the long silence of notpeople, in notlanguage" (5; 9). Quentin's psychic voice haunts the text like the ghost he is forced to be "since he was born and bred in the deep South."

Each of the scenes in which Quentin listens to Rosa and his father inculcates the narration with Quentin's psychic voice. Chapter 2 begins with a revision of the image of "breathing the same air" that Sutpen did, evoking twilight and the smell of Mr Compson's cigar carried into the room at Harvard; the same air in which the church bells rang in 1833. Chapter 3 has familiar textual features of psychic voice in the speaker identification, in which no quotation marks are used, no punctuation separates the speech tag from the mimetic voice, and the speech tags are italicized. (The speech tag for Mr Compson refers us, with the word "*again*," back to the conversation parenthetically inserted in chapter 1, pages 10–11; 12.) Chapter 4 returns to normal mimetic voice for Mr Compson's and Quentin's conversation, but it overtly describes what Quentin knows ("Quentin knew that"; "he knew that"; "he did know") about the upcoming journey with Rosa to Sutpen's Hundred. This, too, is a recognizable technique of psychic voice (reminiscent of *Light in August*). At the chapter's end we enter Quentin's mind (in a parenthetical passage interrupting Mr Compson's voice) directly as he imagines the scene at the gate between Charles and Henry.

The italics of chapter 5 also mark an interior voice, "a stream flowing beneath full consciousness even, what the innermost spirit would say if it could" (Guerard 308). The voice is also interior to Quentin, the one who *hears* what Rosa's "innermost spirit would say." Chapter 5 seems to be an interior discourse that both speaker and listener share, a stream both are immersed in. Quentin, we are told, is not actively listening because his imagination stops him at a door he cannot pass, the door to Judith's room when Henry bursts in after shooting Bon. Neither orator nor audience engages in an instance of oratorical practice, but rather both participate in an extended persuasive scene that becomes the shared discourse of consciousness.

Later chapters make more explicit Quentin's position as listening central consciousness. In Chapter 6 Shreve summarizes the Sutpen history, with Quentin answering "yes" a number of times as Shreve talks. Then Quentin thinks that Shreve sounds like his father, and an italicized passage records his "thinking" and continues Shreve's story: "*Just exactly like Father if Father had known as much about it the night before I went out* *there as he did the day after I came back* thinking *Mad impotent old man who* . . ." (227; 181). A few pages later Quentin answers "yes" again, literally to his own thoughts but actually to Shreve's talking as it has been transformed into Quentin's thinking. The italicized passage ends with parentheses in which Shreve is quoted normally—"('How was it?' Shreve said)" (234; 187).

These elements of psychic voice emphasize the passive, listening role Quentin plays in the novel's oratorical discourse. This is a listener's more than a teller's story, a reader's text more than a writer's. The oratorical voice attempts to impose its will on Quentin and on the reader and, I would argue, finally succeeds. Throughout the second half of the novel Quentin, along with Shreve, has taken over the duties of narrator-persuader. John Irwin may be right to see this as a son usurping the father's authority of heritage, information, and interpretation, supplanting Mr Compson as originator of the story (Irwin 113–14). The usurpation appears possible, however, only through Shreve as a father substitute in that we never hear Quentin telling his father what he learned at Sutpen's Hundred that night with Rosa. He tells Shreve that he provided Mr Compson with new information (332; 266), but Quentin is not permitted to assume the oratorical voice in a speech scene with his father. Only to Shreve can Quentin "sound like father" ("Dont say it's just me that sounds like your old man" [326; 261]). He and Shreve vie for the dominant role as persuader, each asserting his right to tell; neither entirely wins the oratorical role, however, though each can ape the oratorical style. The final chapter, where Quentin lies trembling and repeating "I dont hate it [the South]" over and over suggests that no catharsis will be available to him, for because of his listening he is "older at twenty than a lot of people who have died" (469; 377). Even in sharing the narrative with Shreve he is forced to *"hear it all over again because he sounds just like father"* (264; 211).

In reading Charles Bon's letter, Quentin escapes for a moment from his father's voice. Mr Compson may keep talking while Quentin reads ("meanwhile Mr Compson's voice speaking on") but Quentin can ignore it for the sake of the letter: "Quentin hearing without having to listen as he read the faint spidery script" (160; 129). But, as I have suggested, the letter's "dead tongue speaking" allows no escape because the letter's voice is the kind that must itself be made to vanish to do its evocative work. *Absalom, Absalom!* includes in its aesthetics of evocation the *erasure* of oratorical voice as a necessary gesture within the process of reconstituting the past, just as Judith insisted on the necessity of her act's *was*.

It is not that Charles Bon's voice, in particular, must vanish, but that any manifestation of the oratorical voice must be reduced to silence so that the past, imaginatively evoked, can come forth. This seems to occur, after Bon's letter, to Mr Compson's narrating oratory: the text interrupts Mr Compson with a long parenthetical passage in which "it seemed to Quentin that he could actually see them [Charles and Henry] facing one another at the gate" (164; 132). But there is still a voice of the authorial narrator, and it, too, is oratorical, amplified, ornate in style. Only when the narrating voice turns into a dialogical scene does the monological, evocative oratory vanish and the past momentarily emerge—now as mimetic voice: "The two faces calm, the voices not even raised: *Dont you pass the shadow of this post, this branch, Charles*; and *I am going to pass it, Henry*" (165; 133).

The only feasible catharsis for Quentin would seem to come from the self-banishing evocative power of that very oratorical voice which dominates his listening and telling. Evocation, if complete, entails the cessation of voice. Voice must vanish—that is its role and its power. For an imagined past to appear in its full, living truth, the voice that calls it forth must be silenced. Derrida writes, "In the truth, language is to be filled, achieved, actualized, to the point of erasing itself, without any possible play, before the (thought) thing which is properly manifested in the truth" (*Margins of Philosophy* 241). If Quentin, or here we should say Quentin and Shreve, discover truth even of an imaginative rather than a factual kind, then they will escape from voice into their own telling's creation. All along Quentin has tried to elude the voices he must listen to—by refusing to listen so he can imagine instead. To brood as Quentin must on Sutpen requires an escape "behind and above voice," an escape from the very voice that prompts and permits the brooding. "Quentin was not listening" to Rosa (in chapter 5) "because there was . . . something which he . . . could not pass," a something that appears to him as the vividly imagined confrontation between Judith and Henry after Henry shoots Bon. That same scene is in his mind on "that very September evening when Mr Compson stopped talking at last, he (Quentin) walked out of his father's talking at last because it was now time to go, not because he had heard it all because he had not been listening" (218; 174). The final escape, that best of all ratiocination, the happy marriage of speaking and hearing when Quentin and Shreve think as "one, the voice which happened to be speaking the thought only the thinking become audible, vocal" (378; 303), culminates at the moment when Quentin and Shreve succeed in empathically merging with their ghostly counterparts in a vivid scenario untold by any voice: "Shreve ceased again. It was just as well, since he had no listener. Perhaps he was aware of it. Then suddenly he had no talker either, though possibly he was not aware of this" (438; 351). The scene evoked crystalizes in the text without being narrated, emanating directly from Quentin's and Shreve's imagination. Italics, unconventional punctuation, and present verb tense give the scene a texture of heightened immediacy typical of Faulkner's psychic voice. Even the imagined characters' talking is quiet, almost silent, *"their voices are not much louder than the silent dawn itself"* (445; 356). Donald Kartiganer says that at this moment we have an identification of creator and created so complete as to be "beyond the ordinary uses of metaphor . . . it is the candor of knowing the self through its perfect image in the imagined past" (Kartiganer 98).

But the "candor" of this scene lies in the struggle it reveals between discourse and evoked world, for what the scene renders is the secret diabolic power of the word when wielded in a monological manner. The dialogic richness of the scene runs headlong into the thematics of the oratorical practice that has surrounded Thomas Sutpen throughout the novel. He alone, among all the personae, has resisted participation in the dialogic world. Rebuffed at the plantation door, where he was not even allowed to deliver his message, Sutpen built his fantastic design in silence from that moment on. He arrives in Jefferson silently, "out of thin air," and he refuses dialogue with the town, choosing instead "platform drama." And, indeed, his design is safest when he remains silent, for it is in dialogical moments that Sutpen always falters; he possesses no instinct for saying the right thing—in either the tactful or moral sense of "right." Mr Compson imagines the scene at Christmas in the Sutpen library when Sutpen tells Henry about Bon, "the father and the brother, percussion and repercussion like a thunderclap and its echo and as close; the statement and the giving of the lie" (111; 90). After successfully ordaining his engagement to Rosa, he *"suggested what he suggested to her, and she did what he should have known she would do and would have known probably if he had not bogged himself again in his morality"* (348; 279). He insults Milly Jones so outrageously that even Wash Jones, his "faithful retainer," rises up and kills him. (It is appropriate that Sutpen's death is a dialogic scene overheard by the midwife: *"The old negress squatted there and heard them, the voices, he and Jones: 'Stand back. Dont you touch me, Wash'—'I'm going to tech you, Kernel'"* [232; 185].)

Most important, Sutpen has withheld his word of recognition from his son Charles Bon. To protect his monumental design he has refused that word or gesture which (according to Quentin and Shreve, at least) would actually save it. Bon comes home with Henry and "saw face to face the man who might be his father, and nothing happened—no shock, no hot communicated flesh that speech would have been too slow even to impede—nothing" (400; 320). This is what we might call a "voided" dialogical scene, a refusal to speak when the moment demands speech. Bon, Quentin and Shreve surmise, would settle for any sign—a nod, a fingernail paring, anything. In the scene with Henry at the bivouac Sutpen does finally "recognize" Bon—by telling Henry that Bon is black. He utters a word, "negro," and death follows. This word explains everything. That it is only a word and that it is spoken constitute the horror this moment engenders. Sutpen, the very principle of silent death building an immortal design, sterile and lifeless, suddenly speaks to his son—but only to pronounce a word that will lead to death of another son. What compounds the horror is that the word is an interpretation, a guess even by Sutpen about Bon. He says he knows Bon is black but we never know how he knows, only that it was "a fact which I did not learn until after my son was born" (329; 264).[32] Sutpen is given voice in a dialogue, only to evoke through the power of the word the death of his son. And the irony is compounded still further by Sutpen speaking to Henry in words that echo King David's cry at the death of Absalom:

—*Henry . . . his father holds his face between both hands, looking at it.*
—*Henry, Sutpen says—My son.*[33]

Thus, in this most vividly realized moment, the demonic symbol of the oratorical voice paradoxically steps into that dialogical, mimetic discourse that speaks the title of the novel *Absalom, Absalom!*. The verisimilitude of this moment demands Sutpen's humanization through speech, and thereby speech itself assumes an awesome and silent power.

This scene, like nearly all the vividly imagined moments in *Absalom, Absalom!*, is a dialogic scene of mimetic voice, which I described in chapter 2 as common in Faulkner. Here our vision of the Sutpen past is the clearest, the outlines of the past are the sharpest. The visual implications of "clearest" and "sharpest" are appropriate, for the dialogic scenes offer moments of visualized clarity that the narrators wrest from the turgid past like bits of glass plucked out of clay. As we listen to oratorical narrative voice, it vanishes and speech appears in a represented dialogic confrontation often italicized to mark its emergence from the narrative and its place in the listening consciousness. At the close of chapter 5 Rosa's long tirade ends ("Quentin was not listening") and Quentin imagines the confrontation between Henry and Judith:

Now you cant marry him.
Why cant I marry him?
Because he's dead.
Dead?
Yes. I killed him. (215; 172)

Like this one, dialogic scenes throughout the novel constitute scenes of assault, violence, even murder. Judith and Henry speak "in short brief staccato sentences like slaps, as if they stood breast to breast striking one another in turn neither making any attempt to guard against the blows" (215; 172). Dialogue does not merely accompany assault, it is assault ("the two of them slashing at one another with twelve or fourteen words" [219; 174]) paradigmatic of all confrontations, and of all the violence underlying the Sutpen design. Chapter 1 coalesces into the scene in Sutpen's barn where he fights with his slaves, "both naked to the waist gouging at one another" (31; 29), a scene that includes the only dialogue between Sutpen and Ellen, a dialogue in which (according to Rosa) the true horror of the marriage is spoken. Chapter 4 ends with Quentin imagining Bon's murder, a confrontation of ultimate violence.

Thus the imagination is no haven for Quentin from his voiced oratorical heritage. The return to the dialogic that usually effects Quentin's escape into an imagined realm may free him from the monological discourse but it does not free him from its consequences—from the violent and deadly word. A second concluding attempt to escape voice occurs in chapter 9, when Quentin becomes a direct participant in the Sutpen story. Here his possible escape, his "walking out of his father's talking" is not imaginative, but literal and strikingly physical. In the most gothic scenes in the novel Quentin passes through the door he could not pass in his imagination, steps over the sill at Sutpen's Hundred, and comes face to face with Henry Sutpen. Dialogue would seem essential in this scene, for this conversation is the apparent source of Quentin's knowledge. But we get, instead of mimetic communication, a kind of deathly dialogue precipitated out of the narrative like a crystal out of solution:

And you are——?
Henry Sutpen.
And you have been here——?
Four years.
And you came home——?
To die. Yes.
To die?
Yes. To die.
And you have been here——?
Four years.
And you are——?
Henry Sutpen. (464–65; 373)

The phrases form a palindrome, turning on the words "*To die?*" Talk, voices, language all freeze symmetrically above the flesh of the dying Henry Sutpen. No discourse will suffice here except that which is removed from speech and voice and is transformed into symbolic object. Kartiganer sees this moment as the purest possible evoked experience where language vanishes; it is, he says, "fact stripped of art . . . emptied of metaphor" (Kartiganer 105). While I agree that the moment is "just this side of silence," I cannot agree that it is silent because it is emptied of metaphor. On the contrary, this is a metaphor of speech itself, a virtual hieroglyph for all speech in its struggle with silence and death.

The text erects the strange silence of writing as a memorial to talking itself, engraving the power of *was* in the silence of voices. We return to still another version of the oratorical—to discourse as monument. This most literal of Quentin's escapes turns into an unspeakable meeting with death, with the dying scion of Sutpen grandeur, his "wasted hands crossed on the breast as if he were already a corpse" (464; 373). The horrific experience reminds us of Marlow's meeting with Kurtz: Marlow had imagined Kurtz as "a voice"; what he found was "an animated image of death carved out of old ivory" (Conrad 48, 60). Quentin's meeting with Henry brings him, too, only the terror of voice, not its catharsis.

Conclusion

THE WRITER'S VOICE

What the hell can I do? Goddamn it I've spent almost fifty years trying
to cure myself of the curse of human speech, all for nothing.

—WILLIAM FAULKNER TO MALCOLM COWLEY

The four voices explored in the preceding chapters constitute an array of
strategies for overcoming the silence that threatens all writing. Writing, as
Geoffrey Hartman puts it, "*orphans* words by depriving them of a voice
that is alive and present" (*Saving the Text* 119). More than most writers,
Faulkner sought to reunite the written, orphaned word with its lost but
authorizing voice. If nothing else, the sheer amount of voice imagery, of
represented talking, of verbalized thought, of oratorical rhetoric and posturing justify the conclusion—experienced, I believe, by every attentive
reader of Faulkner—that Faulkner's written texts are fundamentally
voiced, deriving their energy from the play of voices on the imaginative
field of written language.

By evoking voice's affective power Faulkner, the writer, seeks to induce
the reader to forget the originless and silent nature of written fiction. With
phenomenal voice he tries to reinfuse the world—in an often romantic
gesture—with the originating and annealing power of voice. He gave voice
to nature, to the lowly, to the chanting measures of faith. His fiction's
discourse locates voice in the background sounds of talking, singing, the
"quiring" of natural objects, exuding voice in rich, often synesthetic figur-

234

ation that evokes the embracing, soothing qualities of sound as opposed to the starker, more rigid and isolating implications of sight. Characters' perceptual postures as listeners surrounded by sound and speech, though even in the earliest works tinged with yearning for a lost communal wholeness, nonetheless dramatize voice as "Word" in the biblical sense of originating power, the logos: humankind's umbilical link with the world and with others outside the self. Nostalgic even in its earliest versions in the early fiction, phenomenal voice can embody loss, threat, and alienation as well as communal wholeness. As Faulkner's career progressed, his fiction interrogated its own nostalgic voice. For Temple Drake or Joe Christmas the act of listening, which was in *Flags in the Dust* a hearkening to communal voices, becomes in *Sanctuary* and *Light in August* more a defensive cowering from an intrusive, sound-filled environment. In the later fiction nature's crooning turns to mechanical noise, or to barren silence; the maternal singing of Elnora gives way to the ducklike quacking of Linda Snopes.

Mimetic voice, most obviously of the four, invigorates the written with the sense of the spoken, for it comprises various tactics of inscribing the speech of fictional personae. Here, too, Faulkner asks his readers to forget his books' writing for the sake of imagined talk. The verbal gestures of written discourse function to transcribe speech into readable dialogue and dialect. In trying to delineate the formal properties of these gestures, we found that the techniques Faulkner employs to create speech carry implications for event and character that always seem to disrupt the illusion of speech being played out on the fictions' stage—especially in *As I Lay Dying*, where Faulkner experiments with all the discursive functions that generate speech and character. Dialogic scenes take on the patterns of exchanged talk, and yet also the necessities of silent assault and violence. Dialect transcription, which in the illusion of speech mimics supposedly absolute differences in talking, actually imposes them as relative differences dictated by the needs of the fiction text and by complex ideological assumptions.

In creating the third voice, the psychic, Faulkner depicts verbalized thought by both employing and disrupting represented speech; the result is an interior discourse that is expressive more than imitative. He attempts to take the reader "beneath" speech into the psychic origin of fiction's discourse, not so much by recording thought (as a form of speech) but more by transforming the "ordinarily" spoken into stylized consciousness: the stylized meditative moment, for example, in which the thinker lies beneath a roof waiting for sleep or death; or the stylized layering of the mind into depths from which emerge differently articulated versions of speech/thought. The way each Compson brother fulfills his narrative responsibilities, especially the rendering of others' speech, defines his character and produces a psychically evocative voice as origin for the written monologue.

The fourth mode, the oratorical, derives its power from a discursive practice historically identifiable in Southern oratory, by which written fiction comes to be invested simultaneously with the vigor of performance and the structured permanence of monument, as the time-bound process of story telling is paradoxically brought to the service of eliminating temporality and process. Ornate and evocative stylistics, contained within closed, often symmetrically patterned verbal designs, evoke a public, formal—and to some extent a regional—speech as origin for the written novel. The silence of writing is to be overcome by the pronouncements of the figure invested with the manipulative authority of rhetoric, with the orator's manufactured authority over audience.

To say, as I have, that his novels and stories seem exercises in *overcoming* writing for the sake of living voices is not to diminish the importance of writing to Faulkner. Along with the conclusion that Faulkner's written texts are fundamentally voiced I would draw another, namely that Faulkner's voice is always that of a writer. At every point in this study we have seen how voice and writing are in constant tension, how the tools of writing can be used to generate voice, and also how the voices of fiction constantly lead us back to the written nature of literature. We have not examined voice as simply part of the world represented in the fiction, but also as a product of the text itself. Voice emanates from the imagined world, *and* it resides in the reader's experience of the printed text. If we began this study with the assumption that voice is fundamental to Faulkner's writing, we should end with the awareness that writing is fundamental to Faulkner's voice. Faulkner's strategies of voice themselves never abandon the written. His success, indeed, is the fusion—a forced, paradoxical fusion—of speech and writing. The four vocal registers that pervade Faulkner's work are not naive strategies that try to hide the written behind illusions of speech; rather they are provisional practices that exploit fiction's textual nature in order to invigorate the written with living voice. Although our attention has been largely on permutations of represented speech, one current we have charted frequently in Faulkner's modes of voice is how voice always returns us to the written in some way.

Our consideration of speech has not precluded us from noting the written—either the "writtenness" of Faulkner's texts or the presence of written documents (letters, signs, headlines, and so on) within the fictional worlds. Voice, we discovered, impinges upon the written at every stage, and vice versa. Images of phenomenal speech in the early novels give way later in Faulkner's career to images of writing. Mimetic voice depends, we saw, on manipulation of written signs to imitate and distinguish speech acts and speakers, and most of Faulkner's experiments with represented speech—such as those in *As I Lay Dying*—produce a drift away from speech's illusion toward a self-reflexive depiction of written objects. Psychic voice revises inner "speech" into expressive textual mapping of the psyche, disrupting speech so as to cloud the transparency of prose with the psyche's unspeakable syntax or print: the speech of the mind becomes possible when the mind's discourse "writes" without punctuation or in italics. And the oratorical voice gains power from its yearning, dramatized in Sutpen's design, toward the monumental text safe from the impermanence of passing speech.

We began, too, with the knowledge that the discovery (or rediscovery) of "voice" was crucial to the development of Faulkner's novelistic art; we should conclude with the knowledge that Faulkner was nonetheless always a writer. Certainly he had to learn to "listen to the voices" and, as David Minter correctly says, to put aside the literary, written conventions of poetry to recuperate his heritage of regional and childhood voice. Yet there remained in Faulkner some regret for this necessary transformation. He often spoke of himself as "a failed poet" as much as a successful novelist (*LG* 19, 217, 238), a mere storyteller whose "prose is really poetry" (*LG* 56), a "decrepit gaffer telling stories [more than] an old master producing jewels" (*SL* 203–4). Faulkner said that he listened to the voices when he created his fictions, but he also sought a purity of writing. When he described his most important creative experience, writing *The Sound and the Fury*, he used images of static art, of "the yet unmarred sheet beneath my hand," and of "a vase like that which the old Roman kept at his bedside and wore the rim slowly away with kissing it" (*SFI* [1] 709, 710). Faulkner, I think, always harbored a suspicion that "real" art was poetic, not prosaic, so the prose writer must always be a failed poet in some sense. When the young Faulkner wrote something beautiful in prose, he described it as "poetry though written in prose form" (Sensibar 221). Voice, Faulkner seems to imply in some of his self-deprecating remarks, intrudes on ideal art, sullying its purity with mere talk, with "the curse of human speech." It is one of the ironies of Faulkner's career that his writer's voice was never quite the one he wanted it to be. Only when voice invigorates the written does Faulkner's writer's voice find expression, for only in written form could his writer's voice be heard.

What "pure" artistic writing must sacrifice for the sake of becoming voiced is illustrated in a short story that has always seemed to me an allegory of both the success and the regret Faulkner experienced in giving up poetry for prose fiction. "Artist at Home" depicts a writer who must symbolically kill off the poet within himself in order to tell/write a story. This story can also articulate for us the necessary conjoining of telling and writing that characterizes voice in Faulkner and that marks all of Faulkner's work.

Roger Howes is a onetime "advertisement writer" turned novelist. He moved from New York to his brick house in the Virginia Valley to live out his commercial success in the guise of a country squire who also writes. His artist friends from New York come, usually unannounced, to visit him and to obtain free advice, apparently not so much about their art as about their careers as artists because Roger knows what sells. The story turns into what James Carothers calls "a wry parable of the process of creative inspiration" (72) when John Blair, a young, eccentric poet, comes to visit. During his stay he, like the others, asks Roger where his poems might sell, but Roger knows that despite his cavalier attitudes Blair is a genuine poet, a "Shelley" who's got "good stuff" in his work: "He's got it in him. It may not be but one poem. But it's there. Maybe if he can just stop talking long enough to get it out" (*CS* 632). Typically for Faulkner, a requirement for an artist, at least for a poet, is to "stop talking" so he can write.

Blair becomes infatuated with Anne, Roger's wife, and manages to turn his "doping" after her into a strongly felt love affair. One product of the affair's intense emotion is a poem that Howes realizes is the great poem Blair has had buried within him, the "shot . . . that Roger had always claimed to be waiting for" (*CS* 643). In the form of an artifact written on a fly-spattered café menu, the poem arrives after Anne has ended the affair and sent Blair away, ill from pneumonia caught while standing in the rain outside Anne's window. Blair dies from the pneumonia before the poem can be published and thus never shares in his own fame or fortune. Part of what must be "sacrificed or cannibalized" for artistic creation is one's own emotional stability—and by implication one's very life—for Blair could write only under the impress of strong emotion. That these same emotions lead to Blair's death only reinforces the special pathos and beauty of inspiration.

The theme of creative inspiration really involves Roger Howes himself, however, more than John Blair. Howes has not written much for some time, but is moved to write by the pressure of the affair's emotions, specifically Anne's rejection. He acts the gentleman by not interfering between Anne and Blair, but he also wants her back. More important, he starts to write. When Anne locks him out of their bedroom, "he came back down to the office and put some paper into the typewriter and began to write . . . [B]y daylight he was sounding like forty hens in a sheet-iron corn-crib, and the written sheets on the desk were piling up" (*CS* 638). By the end of the story Howes, like Blair, has written a significant piece, a story publishers want. It, too, like Blair's poem, was inspired by the affair that is its subject. "What was it he had been writing? Him, and Anne, and the poet. Word for word, between the waiting spells to find out what to write down next" (644).

In one sense Howes's success with his story is the target of Faulkner's irony. His production, which after all is just "gossip," just an exploitation of everybody's feelings, makes money Howes can enjoy, whereas the more inspired artistic creation Blair writes for Anne grants the poet only posthumous success. Within the boundaries of the romantic image of the perishing young artist dying of unrequited love and in pursuit of self-expression, the story affirms Blair's art and mocks Roger's. Like Roger's original success—his money, his house, his "earn[ing] enough food to need a cupboard to put it in"—his second success with the story of the love affair seems cheapened by its exploitative nature, perfectly symbolized by the fur coat Roger buys Anne with the proceeds. She, in a gesture of affirmation toward Blair's memory, refuses the coat, saying she "got it under false pretenses." "That he . . . to dress me in the skins of little slain beasts" (645; ellipses in original). Such an allegory of cheapened art is not surprising, for Faulkner in 1931, when he composed the story, still believed himself a failed poet and yet was trying desperately to earn his way by writing and peddling short stories. Faulkner surely felt the tension between art as pure inspired object and art as commercial product. (Ironically, "Artist at Home," which he sold for $25 in 1933 to *Story* magazine, "brought in as little money as a short story sale possibly could" [Skei 69].) As much about two differing projections of himself as about Sherwood Anderson (whom Blotner identifies as the model for Howes [688]), "Artist at Home" overtly contrasts Howes, the "rural plute," the "bald husband with next week's flour and meat actually in sight," and Blair, "the home-wrecker that needs a haircut," this "dashing blade," this "home-wrecking poet" (637, 642). As the bohemian poet gave way to the "fattish, mild, nondescript man of forty" Faulkner perhaps feared he might become, he resisted at some level of his artist's soul the literary success that must be gained through "gossip" and mere storytelling. The last word on the theme would seem, in fact, to belong to Anne when she insists that even though Howes has written a story about Blair, he could not "finish it" because he wrote it before he could know about her sacrifice of the coat, the ill-gotten gains from Roger's gossipy exploitation of her emotions and Blair's love. "You put him in a book, but you didn't finish it. You didn't know about that coat, did you? God beat you, that time, Roger" (645).

The story's narrative voice introduces still deeper ironies, however, that undercut the allegory's implied preference for "genuine" creative art (Blair's poetry) over commercially successful gossip (Howes's fiction). The narrative voice sounds very much like other of Faulkner's folksy gossips who tell stories about their fellow townspeople in a colloquial, somewhat sophisticatedly wry sort of way. Capable as many of Faulkner's narrators are of a wide range of idioms, this narrator can describe the artists who visit Howes as "those gaunt and eager and carnivorous tymbesteres of Art," as well as liken Howes's typing to "forty hens in a sheet-iron corn-crib." The narrator, too, collars the audience, addressing us directly: "Now get this. This is where it starts." "Now get this. This is it." "Anyway, here's the rest of it, what they did next." He generalizes the way town narrators do, mouthing a communal wisdom "we" all (that is, all males) supposedly share: "When you see a woman sitting half dressed before a dressing table with a mirror and not even watching herself talk in the mirror, it's time to smell smoke in the wind" (632–33). The story's tone, then, is highly "voiced" in the sense of the *mimetic* renderings examined in chapter 2: a strong illusion of talking makes us feel the presence of a story-teller even though no such teller identifies, characterizes, or even refers to himself (or herself) in the first person.

This narrator, however, quite clearly differs from other Faulkner community spokesmen in that he does not assume the standpoint of one who remains on the outside, looking in at private events only as these could be told by someone uninvolved or at most only peripherally involved. Instead he speaks from the inside, being present at private conversations, for example, in the couple's bedroom. He possesses, in fact, the limited omniscience of a central consciousness implicated in events even while sounding as if he were an outsider merely reporting what any observer could see. From this disparity of perspective we can deduce that Roger Howes himself is the story's narrative voice: Roger is present wherever the narrating perspective is; when he is not physically present he is listening in (as he does to Anne and Blair's conversation in the garden when he "happens to come out from behind this bush" [636]) or he reports what likely happened because it has happened before (as when he reports what the station agent says to Blair when the poet arrives in town [628]). Despite the third-person references to "Roger," and despite the descriptions of him, the narrating perspective must be Roger himself.

Joseph Reed extends this equation of the implied narrating persona with Roger Howes one step further to argue that what we are hearing is the very story Howes has written (41–42). That is, we read the story that Roger sends off to be published, that he reads aloud to Anne, the story that is about "Him, and Anne, and the poet," that is, importantly, "word for word." As he tells, so has he written; or, as he has told, so he writes. Depicted telling and writing are mingled in a metanarration that becomes a self-image of the literary artist at work. "Artist at Home" thus becomes a piece of writing imitating a told story that itself represents a piece of writing of itself. The written version of Howes's story of the love triangle is the version we "hear" in the narrator's voice, and the narrator, our teller, is in fact only a writer who has produced a text of telling. This story may well qualify as Faulkner's most circular, most self-reflexive, most self-implicative text.

Only such a reading can adequately account for one of the oddest features of this story, the narrative verb tense. The narrating discourse switches tense frequently, and seemingly at random: "The market *held* steady for three or four days, without closing at night, even after Pinkie *told* him how the telephone *was* out of fix and he *found* where the wires were cut and *knows* where he *can find* the scissors that did it when he *wants* to. He doesn't go to the village at all, even when he *had* a free ride. He *would spend* half a morning sitting by the road" (640; emphasis added). The present tense invokes, in colloquial narration at least, an immediacy of telling, while the past tense is the conventional tense of written narrative. That both are at work here suggests a movement into and out of telling and writing, an oscillation appropriate to Howes's role as writer and teller, as artist and gossip. Howes at will moves us into the time of telling, and then past it to a later time when he can look back upon events. The telegram Howes goes to the station to pay for nicely objectifies this play with time, as it tells "him how his guests would arrive two days ago."

If Howes is indeed telling us the story that he is writing/has written, then "Artist at Home" resonates with still greater ironies, both in theme and in how it illustrates the relation between speech and writing that, I am arguing, characterizes Faulkner's *writer's* voice. For if we in fact do read the story that Howes writes, then Howes has the last word, literally. He does know all the story that Anne says he could not finish; he does know about the coat; God does not "beat" him this time. And if this is true, the whole hierarchy of value is shaken. The degradation of true art into gossip is reversed, as "mere" gossip is transformed into written art in which the artist does understand himself. The story dramatizes the triumph of the written text, which contains *both* the told story itself and the claims for a superior or more pure art as emotionally generated artifact (Blair's poem). The story becomes profoundly self-reflexive in that what seems to be an allegory expressing Faulkner's discomfort at his change from "poet" to "decrepit gaffer telling stories" is actually a story in which written fiction—the act of writing by Roger Howes and the written text of "Artist at Home"—asserts its own valid status as art. By a paradoxical, spiraling play between telling and writing, Faulkner articulates his commitment to written telling, and to his own voiced art.

Any ambivalence Faulkner felt about turning away from poetry resolved itself in the voices of his fiction. Only in such voiced writing could his writer's voice be heard. Despite cynical references to speech and talking in his letters, in which he described human speech as a curse, or the source of all human ills (*SL* 235, 251–52), Faulkner wanted his voice to be heard. He wanted to know "that if you just keep on trying to say a thing long enough and hard enough, it will emerge; someone will hear it" (*SL* 296). While he generally hated giving speeches or interviews ("I dont think I know anything to talk about worth 200 dollars" [*SL* 271]), he came late in his career to have opportunities to be heard.

At that moment in his career when he had virtually the whole world as his audience, on December 10, 1950, when he rose to accept the Nobel Prize for literature, Faulkner said that he would like to "us[e] this moment as a pinnacle from which I might be listened to by the young men and women already dedicated to the same anguish and travail" that he himself had endured and was enduring as a writer. He wished to deliver words of inspiration so that young writers would learn what he had learned, that certain fundamental human verities—"love and honor and pity and pride and compassion and sacrifice"—must inform all art, or it will succumb to "a general and universal physical fear" that drains the human spirit. Even as he imagined the end of time, he envisioned—or rather *heard*—the "puny inexhaustible voice" of humankind surviving beyond the "last ding-dong of doom." Voice, which in itself cannot give man the capacity to endure, betokens the "soul, a spirit capable of compassion and sacrifice and endurance." Thus Faulkner's peroration is appropriately an appeal to voice: "the poet's voice need not merely be the record of man, it can be one of the props, the pillars to help him endure and prevail."

Ironically, however, the occasion of the Nobel Prize Acceptance Speech marks for us, again and finally, that paradox of voice in written art that the previous chapters have explored. For virtually no one heard Faulkner. Notoriously shy and quiet of voice, uncomfortable before audiences, not at all at home with his public speaking voice, more anxious to hide behind his usual public reticence than to declaim from even such an august "pinnacle," Faulkner stood too far from the microphone, hurried through his address, and left even those in close proximity to the podium at a loss to know what he said. To many "his voice was totally inaudible" (Blotner 1365–66). Indeed, not until his speech became a piece of writing could it express what Faulkner hoped to convey to the world. "We did not know what he had said until the next morning," one listener remembered (Blotner 1366). William Faulkner's voice could be heard only in the silence of his writing. And perhaps this is the final conclusion we should draw from our examination of voice in Faulkner: only in the silence of the written text can an author make voice heard; only from the paradoxical disunity of telling within writing could Faulkner's, the writer's, voice emerge.

Only the most hardened cynic could doubt Faulkner's sincerity in this brief oration. Despite his diffidence in presentation, and regardless of the speech's difference in tone from so much of his best fiction—which offers only occasional and usually comic relief from a dark vision of human existence—Faulkner clearly wanted in his Nobel Prize speech to affirm the meaning of his "life's work in the agony and sweat of the human spirit." As a testimonial of an artist's faith in his art, the speech raised the value of "voice" to its highest reach, for it is through the poet's voice speaking of the "heart in conflict with itself" that writing takes on significance beyond mere "lust" or "the glands." The "poet's voice" becomes a monument to the human spirit.

APPENDIX
"Eulogy on Charles Sumner,"
by Lucius Q. C. Lamar

Presented in the U.S. House of Representatives, April 28, 1874.
(Quoted here from Mayes 184–87.)

Mr. Speaker: In rising to second the resolutions just offered, I desire to add a few remarks which have occurred to me as appropriate to the occasion. I believe that they express a sentiment which pervades the hearts of all the people whose representatives are here assembled. Strange as, in looking back upon the past, the assertion may seem, impossible as it would have been ten years ago to make it, it is not the less true that to-day Mississippi regrets the death of Charles Sumner, and sincerely unites in paying honors to his memory. Not because of the splendor of his intellect, though in him was extinguished one of the brightest of the lights which have illustrated the councils of the government for nearly a quarter of a century; not because of the high culture, the elegant scholarship, and the varied learning which revealed themselves so clearly in all his public efforts as to justify the application to him of Johnson's felicitous expression, "he touched nothing which he did not adorn"; not this, though these are qualities by no means, it is to be feared, so common in public places as to make their disappearance, in even a single instance, a matter of indifference; but because of those peculiar and strongly marked moral traits of his character which gave the coloring to the whole tenor of his singularly dramatic public career; traits which made him for a long period to a large portion of his countrymen the object of as deep and passionate a hostility as to another he was one of enthusiastic admiration, and which are not the less the cause that now unites all these parties, ever so widely differing, in a common sorrow over his lifeless remains.

It is of these high moral qualities which I wish to speak; for these have been the traits which in after years, as I have considered the successive acts and utterances of this remarkable man, fastened most strongly my attention, and impressed themselves most forcibly upon my imagination, my sensibilities, my heart. I leave to others to speak of his intellectual superiority, of those rare gifts with which nature had so lavishly endowed him, and of the power to use them which he had acquired by education. I say nothing of his vast and varied stores of historical knowledge, or of the wide extent of his reading in the elegant literature of ancient and modern times, or of his wonderful power of retaining what he read, or of his readiness in drawing upon these fertile resources to illustrate his own arguments. I say nothing of his eloquence as an orator, of his skill as a logician, or of his powers of fascination in the unrestrained freedom of the social circle, which last it was my misfortune not to have experienced. These, indeed, were the qualities which gave him eminence not only in our country, but throughout the world; and which have made the name of Charles Sumner an integral part of our nation's glory. They were the qualities which gave to those moral traits of which I have spoken the power to impress themselves upon the history of the age and of civilization itself; and without which those traits, however intensely developed, would have exerted no influence beyond the personal circle immediately surrounding their possessor. More eloquent tongues than mine will do them justice. Let me speak of the characteristics which brought the illustrious Senator who has just passed away into direct and bitter antagonism for years with my own State and her sister States of the South.

Charles Sumner was born with an instinctive love of freedom, and was educated from his earliest infancy to the belief that freedom is the natural and indefeasible right of every intelligent being having the outward form of man. In him, in fact, this creed seems to have been something more than a doctrine imbibed from teachers, or a result of education. To him it was a grand intuitive truth, inscribed in blazing letters upon the tablet of his inner consciousness, to deny which would have been for him to deny that he himself existed. And along with this all-controlling love of freedom he possessed a moral sensibility keenly intense and vivid, a conscientiousness which would never permit him to swerve by the breadth of a hair from what he pictured to himself as the path of duty. Thus were combined in him the characteristics which have in all ages given to religion her martyrs, and to patriotism her self-sacrificing heroes.

To a man thoroughly permeated and imbued with such a creed, and animated and constantly actuated by such a spirit of devotion, to behold a human being or a race of human beings restrained of the natural right to liberty, for no crime by him or them committed, was to feel all the belligerent instincts of his nature roused to combat. The fact was to him a wrong which no logic could justify. It mattered not how humble in the scale of rational existence the subject of this restraint might be, how dark his skin, or how dense his ignorance. Behind all that lay for him the great principle that liberty is the birthright of all humanity, and that every individual of every race who has a soul to save is entitled to the freedom which may enable him to work out his salvation. It mattered not that the slave might be contented with his lot; that his actual condition might be immeasurably more desirable than that from which it had transplanted him; that it gave him physical comfort, mental and moral elevation, and religious culture not possessed by his race in any other condition; that his bonds had not been placed upon his hands by the living generation; that the mixed social system of which he formed an element had been regarded by the fathers of the republic, and by the ablest statesmen who had risen up after them, as too complicated to be broken up without danger to society itself, or even to civilization; or, finally, that the actual state of things had been recognized and explicitly sanctioned by the very organic law of the republic. Weighty as these considerations might be, formidable as were the difficulties in the way of the practical enforcement of his great principle, he held none the less that it must sooner or later be enforced, though institutions and constitutions should have to give way alike before it. But here let me do this great man the justice which, amid the excitement of the struggle between the sections—now past—I may have been disposed to deny him. In this fiery zeal, and this earnest warfare against the wrong, as he viewed it, there entered no enduring personal animosity toward the men whose lot it was to be born to the system which he denounced.

It has been the kindness of the sympathy which in these later years he has displayed toward the impoverished and suffering people of the Southern States that has unveiled to me the generous and tender heart which beat beneath the bosom of the zealot, and has forced me to yield him the tribute of my respect—I might even say of my admiration. Nor in the manifestation of this has there been anything which a proud and sensitive people, smarting under a sense of recent discomfiture and present suffering, might not frankly accept, or which would give them just cause to suspect its sincerity. For though he raised his voice, as soon as he believed the momentous issues of this great military conflict were decided, in behalf of amnesty to the vanquished; and though he stood forward, ready to welcome back as brothers, and to re-establish in their rights as citizens, those whose valor had nearly riven asunder the Union which he loved; yet he always insisted that the most ample protections and the largest safeguards should be thrown around the liberties of the newly enfranchised African race. Though he knew very well that of his conquered fellow-citizens of the South by far the larger portion, even those who most heartily acquiesced in and desired the abolition of slavery, seriously questioned the expediency of investing, in a single day, and without any preliminary tutelage, so vast a body of inexperienced and uninstructed men with the full rights of freemen and voters, he would tolerate no halfway measures upon a point to him so vital.

Indeed, immediately after the war, while other minds were occupying themselves with different theories of reconstruction, he did not hesitate to impress most emphatically upon the administration, not only in public, but in the confidence of private intercourse, his uncompromising resolution to oppose to the last any and every scheme which should fail to provide the surest guarantees for the personal freedom and political rights of the race which he had undertaken to protect. Whether his measures to secure this result showed him to be a practical statesman or a theoretical enthusiast, is a question on which any decision we may pronounce to-day must await the inevitable revision of posterity. The spirit of magnanimity, therefore, which breathes in his utterances and manifests itself in all his acts affecting the South during the last two years of his life, was evidently honest as it was grateful to the feelings of those toward whom it was displayed.

It was certainly a gracious act toward the South—though unhappily it jarred upon the sensibilities of the people at the other extreme of the Union, and estranged from him the great body of his political friends—to propose to erase from the banners of the national army the mementos of the bloody internecine struggle, which might be regarded as assailing the pride or wounding the sensibilities of the Southern people. That proposal will never be forgotten by that people so long as the name of Charles Sumner lives in the memory of man. But, while it touched the heart of the South, and elicited her profound gratitude, her people would not have asked of the North such an act of self-renunciation.

Conscious that they themselves were animated by devotion to constitutional liberty, and that the brightest pages of history are replete with evidences of the depth and sincerity of that devotion, they cannot but cherish the recollections of sacrifices endured, the battle fought, and the victories won in defense of their hapless cause. And respecting, as all true and brave men must respect, the martial spirit with which the men of the North vindicated the integrity of the Union, and their devotion to the principles of human freedom, they do not ask, they do not wish the North to strike the mementos of her heroism and victory from either records or monuments or battle flags. They would rather that both sections should gather up the glories won by each section: not envious, but proud of each other, and regard them a common heritage of American valor.

Let us hope that future generations, when they remember the deeds of heroism and devotion done on both sides, will speak not of Northern prowess and Southern courage, but of the heroism, fortitude, and courage of Americans in a war of ideas; a war in which each section signalized its consecration to the principles, as each understood them, of American liberty and of the constitution received from their fathers.

It was my misfortune, perhaps my fault, personally never to have known this eminent philanthropist and statesman. The impulse was often strong upon me to go to him and offer him my hand, and my heart with it, and to express to him my thanks for his kind and considerate course toward the people with whom I am identified. If I did not yield to that impulse, it was because the thought occurred that other days were coming in which such a demonstration might be more opportune, and less liable to misconstruction. Suddenly, and without premonition, a day has come at last to which, for such a purpose, there is no tomorrow. My regret is therefore intensified by the thought that I failed to speak to him out of the fullness of my heart while there was yet time.

How often is it that death thus brings unavailingly back to our remembrance opportunities unimproved: in which generous overtures, prompted by the heart, remain unoffered; frank avowals which rose to the lips remain unspoken; and the injustice and wrong of bitter resentments remain unrepaired! Charles Sumner, in life, believed that all occasion for strife and distrust between the North and the South had passed away, and that there no longer remained any cause for continued estrangement between these two sections of our common country. Are there not many of us who believe the same thing? Is it not that the common sentiment—or if it is not, ought it not to be—of the great mass of our people, North and South? Bound to each other by a common constitution, destined to live together under a common government, forming unitedly but a single member of the great family of nations, shall we not now at last endeavor to grow *toward* each other once more in heart, as we are already indissolubly linked to each other in fortunes? Shall we not, over the honored remains of this great champion of human liberty, this feeling sympathizer with human sorrow, this earnest pleader for the exercise of human tenderness and charity, lay aside the concealments which serve only to perpetuate misunderstandings and distrust, and frankly confess that on both sides we most earnestly desire to be one; one not merely in community of language and literature and traditions and country; but more, and better than all that, one also in feeling and in heart? Am I mistaken in this?

Do the concealments of which I speak still cover animosities which neither time nor reflection nor the march of events have yet sufficed to subdue? I cannot believe it. Since I have been here I have watched with anxious scrutiny your sentiments as expressed not merely in public debate, but in the *abandon* of personal confidence. I know well the sentiments of these, my southern brothers, whose hearts are so infolded that the feeling of each is the feeling of all; and I see on both sides only the seeming of constraint, which each apparently hesitates to dismiss. The South—prostrate, exhausted, drained of her lifeblood, as well as of her material resources, yet still honorable and true—accepts the bitter award of the bloody arbitrament without reservation, resolutely determined to abide the result with chivalrous fidelity; yet, as if struck dumb by the magnitude of her reverses, she suffers in silence. The North, exultant in her triumph, and elated by success, still cherished, as we are assured, a heart full of magnanimous emotions toward her disarmed and discomfited antagonist; and yet, as if mastered by some mysterious spell, silencing her better impulses, her words and acts are the words and acts of suspicion and distrust.

Would that the spirit of the illustrious dead whom we lament to-day could speak from the grave to both parties to this deplorable discord in tones which should reach each and every heart throughout this broad territory: "My countrymen! *know* one another, and you will *love* one another."

Notes

INTRODUCTION. *"Voice" in Literature—Voices in Faulkner*

1. All cited passages in this paragraph are from "Barn Burning" (*CS* 3–25).
2. *FU* 21; see Millgate 21; and *LG* 215–16, 228–31 for other portrayals of Faulkner as a listener.
3. *FU* 233; see also J. Faulkner 158–59.
4. See also Sensibar's *The Origins of Faulkner's Art* for an extended analysis of why Faulkner failed as a poet.
5. Frost 111; Yeats 202; see also Donoghue 125–45.
6. This is especially true in Anglo-American criticism. See Polletta 373.
7. See Derrida, *Margins of Philosophy* 295.
8. See Genette, *Narrative Discourse* 212–62. Perhaps the ultimate version of voice as pure relationship cut off from intentional human origin is Guy Rosolato's "relative voice," a Voice (capitalized in Lacanian fashion) regarded as the primal oscillation between the opposites that comprise all discourse: "This relative voice, then, can be considered as the index of a series of oppositions through which the subject, in relation to discourse, accomplishes his movement of fading and return, his movement of pulsation" (206). These oppositions can be as physical as the "constitution of sound and voice" arising from the "tension and stiffness which the breath encounters in the vocal chords," or as abstract as the dialectic between fiction and myth into which the relative voice "inserts itself . . . revealing as it does so the close relation between religion and art" (208).
9. Matthews's introductory chapter ("How to Approach Language" 15–62) offers an excellent summary of Derridean thought in relation to Faulkner's language.
10. See the collection of essays, *Intertextuality in Faulkner* (Gresset and Polk).
11. In a book that appeared too late to be more than noted here, Warwick

Wadlington proposes another interesting variation on "voice": he rejects notions of text and reading as "silent" and finds literal voice in the reading aloud invited by Faulkner's "sonorous language." Wadlington focuses overtly on what I assume, that readers "perform" or "enact" the voices Faulkner's prose invokes. In this sense reading is not "silent," to be sure, though as I will discuss at various stages in the coming chapters, the problem of Faulkner's *writing* always confronts and contests such performance—there remain crucially unperformable qualities (and unvocalizable textual features) in the voices his texts generate.

CHAPTER ONE. *Phenomenal Voice*

1. Derrida, *Of Grammatology* 11–12. See especially Derrida's definition of presence (12) where he gives examples. See also Spivak's comment on Husserl (introduction to *Of Grammatology* liii).
2. *The Margins of Philosophy* 89. See Gregory Ulmer on Derrida's deconstruction of Hegel's semiotic value system (Ulmer 52).
3. Shattuck 26. See Hartman's discussion of voice's power to wound, in "Words and Wounds," *Saving the Text* 118–57.
4. Voice is, of course, a crucial feature of the liturgy; see Ihde 177.
5. Michel Gresset has demonstrated that the "gaze" is likewise a fundamental mode of intersubjectivity in Faulkner; see *Faulkner ou la fascination*.
6. Mortimer 37, 65–70. Hugh Ruppersburg also studies the relationship between sight and sound in Faulkner, analyzing "voice" and "eye" as differing points of view or perspectives offered the reader.
7. Fowler 103. For an excellent discussion of the problematic status of authorial presence, see Foucault, "What is an Author."
8. On the paean to the mule in *Flags*, see Guerard 220–221; and Stafford.
9. See Michel Gresset's discussion of the "dying fall" in Gresset, "Of Sailboats and Kites."
10. *FD* 138. See Matthews 52–53. See also Watson's discussion of letters in *Flags* (64–76).
11. See Magliola (passim) for an excellent consideration of "intentionality" in phenomenology and in literature.
12. *SO* 60. For other discussions of this passage, see Bleikasten, "Terror and Nausea: Bodies in *Sanctuary*" 27–29; and Polk, "The Space Between *Sanctuary*" 28–29.
13. Three excellent articles that deal with writing in *Pylon* are Bleikasten, "*Pylon*: Ou L'Enfer des signes"; Gresset, "Théorème"; and Pitavy, "Le Reporter: Tentation and derision de l'ecriture."

CHAPTER TWO. *Mimetic Voice*

1. See Genette's discussion of titles in *Seuils* 54–97.
2. There is even a self-description of him "lying": "How often have I lain beneath rain on a strange roof, thinking of home" (*AILD* 72; 76). For an argument that Darl is in fact the novel's controlling consciousness, see Ferrer. For other comments on the title of *As I Lay Dying*, see Sundquist 30; and Bleikasten, *Parcours de Faulkner* 177–78.
3. See Derrida, "The Double Session," in *Dissemination*, especially 186 (fn. 14) on the logic of Plato's overall concept of *mimesis*. See also Genette, *Narrative Discourse* 163–65; and "Frontiers of Narrative" 128–33.
4. See Genette's reconsideration of his ideas about represented speech in *Nouveau discours du récit* (34–39). There he uses the phrase "*(re)production du discours*" to suggest that the discourse is of course *produced* in fiction even while it seems to be *re*-produced (34).
5. Strauch, "De la littéralité" 175–78. Strauch argues elsewhere that to insist on a word-for-word echo as the only true reproduction is to confuse "literalness" with syntactical features (such as person and tense) that do not affect semantic content ("De quelques interprétations" 63–64).
6. Brian McHale argues that, in studying free indirect discourse, we should "bring the question of representation and illusionism to the forefront where it cannot be conjured away, by making categories of literary representation primary, and subordinating the syntactical categories to them" ("Free Indirect Discourse" 257). See also Banfield 248; and Chatman 167–69.
7. Page divides this conventional assumption of accuracy into three parts: (1) accuracy of dialogue; (2) expectation of actual speech; and (3) conflation into a single speech what was more plausibly uttered in many (28–29).
8. Abercrombie distinguishes between conversation, which cannot be recorded in writing, and "spoken prose," which can be: "writing is a device developed for recording prose, not conversation" (6). Randolph Quirk gives a nice example of a written version of an educated person's actual speech (rendered as literally as possible) in conversation: "He-seemed of course he had that kind of n er I I'm er i i er I i er er are you northern by any chance I was going to say that kind of northern—er-scepticism or at least questioning mind—which er-but of course he would mislead you with that he er he gave you the impression that he only er you know he gave you the impression that he was—sceptical and at times sceptical and nothing else————but I think he er—I think he appreciated the course there you know-from one or two things he said when I bumped into him" (108).
9. Page lists four "conventional accompaniments to speech in fictional dialogue":

attribution to speakers; gestural indicators (like stage directions); references to paralinguistic events such as tone, volume, and other features of "materiality"; and interpolated authorial commentary (26).

10. What I am calling "description" Genette would probably incorporate into "narrated" speech, part of his tripartite division of represented speech into "narrated," "transposed" (essentially indirect discourse), and "reported" speech (essentially direct discourse). See *Narrative Discourse* 170–73.

11. Banfield argues that one grammatical feature distinguishing colloquial narration from what she calls "narratorless narration" is some overt indication of the present time of enunciation. "Pure" narration, she claims, even in the first person has no such indicators (163–67). See also Genette's discussion of the timeless instant of narration in *Narrative Discourse* (223).

12. Genette discusses the diegetic-mimetic distinction under his concept of mood in narrative (*Narrative Discourse* 161–211). Strauch also insists that this duality is the starting point for any consideration of *style indirect libre*: "*Il convient d'abord de faire le départ entre l'énoncé produit spontanément par un locuteur . . . et l'énoncé dans lequel il se fait le rapporteur d'un discours d'autrui*" ("De quelques interpretations" 62).

13. McHale, for example, proposes several distinct variations within the direct-indirect continuum ("Free Indirect Discourse" 258–60).

14. Whether expressive features can be reproduced *only* in direct speech is much debated: contrast Banfield's first chapter (23–63) with Strauch, "De quelques interpretations." As I noted before, Genette and Strauch urge that we not take the notion of reproduction too literally; a writer can indirectly reproduce speech, and *style indirect libre* includes features of intonation. See Genette, *Nouveau discours du récit* 34; and Strauch, "De la littéralité." See also Banfield's first chapter (on direct and indirect speech); Chatman 199–200; and Page 30–31. Banfield rejects the implication of the word "mingling," that a distinct voice or speaker is heard along with a character's; she argues that true narrative is essentially "narratorless," and that a "dual voice" theory wrongly tries to account for narrative as if it were communication, when in grammatical fact the very nature of narration removes it from any possible communicative context. For counterviews see Strauch; Pascal; Culler; and especially McHale's "Unspeakable Sentences, Unnatural Acts." Banfield gives a lengthy account of the grammar of direct and indirect speech in her second chapter (65–109), but see Strauch's comments in "De quelques interpretations" (67–70).

15. See Wayne Booth's discussion of "The Ironist's Voice" in ch. 6 of *The Rhetoric of Irony*.

16. Charlotte Renner's description of discourse in *The Mansion* is apt, though her analysis does not sufficiently account for its effects: "*The Mansion* is not exactly a 'frame' narrative because the authorial account does not enclose or

subsume the discourse of other narrators. Instead, the narrative task seems to be shared fully with characters who contribute their own accounts to the composite text in such a way as to blur conventional boundaries between narrative writing and speaking, between authorial inscription and the transcription of narrator's discourse" (Renner 72).

17. I am adapting Hugh Kenner's nice phrase "Bloom-word," which he uses in discussing *Ulysses* (73). Bakhtin describes the dialogic interplay of the individual's "word" or "utterance" (also translated as "discourse") with the outer world of ideology as a "living dialectical synthesis . . . constantly taking place between the psyche and ideology, between the inner and outer. In each speech act, subjective experience perishes in the objective fact of the enunciated word-utterance, and the enunciated word is subjectified in the act of responsive understanding" (quoted from *Marxism and the Philosophy of Language*, in *The Dialogic Imagination* 433–34). See also Bakhtin's chapter on "Discourse in Dostoevsky," ch. 5 of *Problems of Dostoevsky's Poetics*.

18. Character-narrators employ mingled speech as well. Ratliff, as named colloquial narrator, brings Gavin Stevens's words to aid his own (*M* 62), and he describes Stevens as he suspects Montgomery Ward Snopes would describe the "meal-mouth sanctimonious Harvard- and European-educated lawyer that never even needed the excuse of his office and salaried job to meddle in anything providing it wasn't none of his business" (*M* 55).

19. The phrase "well-spoken narrator" is Graham Hough's, cited by Chatman (205), and refers to the convention that authorial narrators seldom employ colloquialisms on their own responsibility, outside of direct or mingled speech. The authorial-narrative voice conventionally serves as a standard idiom against which characters' more colloquial speech is measured.

20. There are many excellent discussions of Faulkner's black characters and of his attitudes toward race. See Davis; Jehlen; Jenkins; Grimwood (especially 223–99); Nilon; Snead; and Sundquist.

21. Cohen offers a classic example of a sentence that is phonetically "correct" in spelling but virtually unreadable until enunciated aloud: "The none tolled hymn she had scene a pare of bear feat in hour rheum" (83).

22. It is, I think, a weakness of Bridgman's book that he defines the colloquial style in a way that emphasizes the "laconic," and does not deal with more "expansive and opulent" styles typical of some Southern writers, though Bridgman in his introduction insists that such prose "shares the characteristics of the colloquial" (13).

23. An intriguing example of Faulkner's early (probably pre-1928) and extreme country-white dialect writing is a version of the horse auction story that later became "Spotted Horses" and, with much dialect deleted, part of *The Hamlet*. The typescript (entitled "As I Lay Dying") is written in dramatic form without any diegetic discourse, quotation marks, or speaker identification (except

separate paragraphing for each speech). The density of phonetic rendering and eye dialect is high ("cheer" for "chair," "sto'" for "store," etc.) and is employed with comic effect. The typescript is housed at the University of Virginia. See Blotner's notes on the fragment (*US* 689).

24. See Kenneth Lynn's extended discussion of the political significance of regional dialects in American literature; see also "Nineteenth-century Talk" in Bridgman. The most thorough summary of Faulkner's relation to Southwest Humor is Bungert; see also Inge; and Ross, "Jason Compson and Sut Lovingood."

25. As Davis points out (117–18), the black idiom in section 4 of *The Sound and the Fury* is far more pronounced than in section 1. Davis sees this as Faulkner's way of emphasizing and affirming the black experience in the fourth section: "Faulkner's use of a highly differentiated 'Negro' idiom . . . is his way of reinforcing his depiction of a Negro-centered world, and also of utilizing the resources of black speech in experimental fiction" (118).

26. There are country clowns too, of course, like Old Uncle Dick Bolivar in *The Hamlet* or the "slatern" woman at the jail in *Sanctuary*, who speak in excessive dialect. Wash Jones in "Wash" and *Absalom, Absalom!*, is a poor white who speaks heavy country dialect and who, like Rider, possesses considerable pride.

27. "The Bear Hunt" is a perfect example of a frame tale rendered as if it were mimicry performed on a stage. The frame narrator tells us that "Ratliff is telling this" and that he must "set the stage for Ratliff." He ends his introduction with "Now Ratliff tells about Lucius Provine and his hiccup." Then occurs a break in the text, a pause as if the mimic had turned away from his audience for a moment to assume the face and voice of another. Ratliff begins his "telling," but not in quotation marks, as if the original narrator has vanished behind the illusion of mimicry.

28. The same is true of women, who seldom narrate and who only in a few instances (Addie Bundren and Rosa Coldfield, for example) are permitted extensively articulated voice. But the underlying issues in the case of women are not related to transcription, for women's represented speech throughout Faulkner shows little formal variation from that of men. What women express, as well as what they experience and how they are regarded are always tied to their enforced status as "other" (see Weinstein); and as depicted characters they differ markedly from men. This is especially true of Caddy Compson, who is denied voice in *The Sound and the Fury*.

29. Other instances can be found in "Barn Burning" (*CS* 4), in an early story, "The Liar" (*New Orleans Sketches*), and in *Light in August*, when Hightower's black cook's stories are recorded in heavier dialect than other black speech in the novel.

30. Tull, MS. 12; final version 29–30. All references to the manuscript are to papers housed at the University of Virginia.

31. See Cohn's discussion of the "gnomic present—the tense used for timeless generalizations" in represented thought (Cohn 28).

32. Ferrer posits that Tull probably draws the outline of the coffin in the dust with his toe (3). But such an explanation tries too hard to recuperate the novel's shifting vocal registers for the sake of realistic representations. (Besides, Tull is in the Bundren house when he "reports" the coffin's shape [82].)

33. There may be a further modulation in Anse's first line of quoted dialogue: " 'If it was just up, we could drive across,' Anse says" (118). "Says" is used variously in the novel to represent either the correct present-tense form of the verb "to say" or as a common vernacular form of the past tense "said" (see Mac-Gowan's section, for example). Which it is here is unclear, perhaps deliberately so.

34. Faulkner revised this section to make it internally consistent by changing verbs ("says" and "begins") originally in present tense in the section's final paragraph so that they would match the past tense of the earlier, nonitalicized narrative, of which the final paragraph is a resumption (MS. 61; final version 144).

35. There is one apparent error in this section—in the last lines where a past-tense reference to seeing Darl is not in italics. This may have been an oversight in typing, because the manuscript (89) does indicate italics for these lines.

36. See Hemenway for a thematic analysis of this and other passages in which characters explore the nature of existence through the verb "to be."

37. Daniel Ferrer argues strongly and interestingly for reading *As I Lay Dying* as entirely generated within Darl's maddened psyche. Only such a reading explains certain unrealities such as Darl's clairvoyance and the similar content and wording of sections ostensibly narrated by different characters. Ferrer is still arguing from within the representational dilemma of expressive identity—in his thesis, all depends upon Darl's expressive identity—because he seeks to account for unreality by tracing all voice to one speaker. I argue for accepting the shared discourse as such, as an interrogation of the very convention that demands we find a single origin for similar mimetic voice.

38. See Franklin, generally; and Swiggart 61, 70.

39. Darl and Tull share other perceptions. For example, they both note how voices from inside the house come out of the air, borne on the draft (19, 29–30).

CHAPTER THREE. *Psychic Voice*

1. Genette is quick to point out the parallels between Cohn's categories and his own classification of narrative modes (*Nouveau discours du récit* 39–43).

2. Appropriate sounds can substitute for the sound of rain, such as the patterings of rat's feet in "Carcassonne," or the palm trees "murmuring beyond the bars" outside Harry Wilbourne's jail cell in *The Wild Palms* (322).

3. See Wilden's discussion (Lacan 200–204) of how "for Lacan, and I suggest also for Freud, psychic reality is primarily the intersubjective world of language" (200). He quotes Merleau-Ponty: "Thought has nothing 'interior' about it; it does not exist outside of the world and outside of words. What deceives us about it, what makes us believe in a thought which supposedly exists for itself before being expressed, are the thoughts which have already been constituted and expressed, which we can recall silently to ourselves, and by means of which we create the illusion of an interior life. But in fact this supposed silence echoes with spoken words; this interior life is an interior language" (203). See also Derrida, *Writing and Difference* 211.

4. *LG* 248. Hamblin cites this passage to argue that "Carcassonne"'s protagonist represents a poet struggling with inarticulateness (356–57).

5. See my discussion of "textual voice" in "Voice in Narrative Texts" (305–8). John Barth's term "printed voice" (*Lost in the Funhouse* ix) would do nicely, too, to label the effect of expressive print variations. Susan Lanser uses the phrase "textual voice" to denominate the author's presence we sense as ultimate public authority behind a printed work. Lanser does include in "textual voice" the physical contact between reader and book, by analogy to "tone of voice, gesture, voice quality [and any factors that] affect transmission . . . in oral discourse" (91).

6. The kind of interpretive difficulties that can result from attempts to define too strictly what italics *mean* can be seen in Diane L. Cox's discussion of italics in *As I Lay Dying*. Comparing the italics in that novel to those in *The Sound and the Fury* (and mistakenly claiming that Quentin's monologue "is cast predominantly in the present tense" [234]), Cox ties italics to "difference[s] in level or quality of consciousness when verb tense remains constant" (68). Even to equate italics to changes in consciousness not accompanied by changes in verb tense distorts their variable expressive force—and such equations seldom hold up, for four and arguably five of the thirteen instances of italics Cox cites do involve a change in verb tense.

7. François Pitavy sees these italicized portions as nearly always less colloquial, less in the character's own idiom than the quoted passages (with either single or double quotation marks), and he concludes that in these we find Faulkner's style (*Faulkner's* Light in August 67–70). Pitavy's distinction between a character's "voice" and Faulkner's "style" is not fully clear, partly because the italicized passages evince more colloquialisms than Pitavy allows, as when Byron Bunch thinks of Hightower "*Or maybe he has listened to it so much and so long that he dont even hear it anymore*" (75), and partly because the italicized passages vary greatly in stylistic features, sometimes favoring the colloquial, sometimes the more formal.

8. Exactly what physical oblivion Hightower fades into is not clear. Faulkner said that Hightower does not die (*FU* 75), and whether he literally dies "hardly matters," as Cleanth Brooks says (*Yoknapatawpha Country* 71). The imagery of

"a forgotten leaf" and "flotsam" do hint at a figurative death, and Hightower is at the chapter's end gone from the novel.

9. In typical play with textual voice, Faulkner calls attention to the parentheses by placing the end parenthesis of the Brownlee story at the beginning of the printed line:

> *Chrstms 1856 Spintrius*
>) took substance and even a sort of shadowy life . . .   (*GDM* 265)

10. Cohn argues, for example, that "despite [their] diversity, all interior monologues . . . conform to two principal tendencies: syntactical abbreviation and lexical opaqueness" (Cohn 94). While Faulkner's rhetoric shows some "lexical opaqueness" in pronoun references (the consistent use of "he" without a name for the central consciousness—usually Ike), it evinces the opposite of syntactical abbreviation, and even has excessive lexical cross-referencing. We will consider Faulkner's rhetoric further in chapter 4.

11. In an early version of "The Old People," narrated by Quentin Compson, it is the young protagonist's father who tells him what McCaslin tells Ike, that Sam Fathers had also shown him the phantom buck after he killed his first deer. See Blotner's note in *US* 691–92.

12. *LG* 225; see also *FU* 245–46. Myra Jehlen argues that rather than portray Ike ironically, Faulkner himself was confused about what Ike meant because, although Faulkner may have disagreed with Ike's response to racism, he nonetheless shared Ike's "vision of the New South" as a diminished place inhabited by racially amalgamated people (Jehlen 102–3). Elsewhere Jehlen writes, "Faulkner seems not quite certain whether Ike's refusal . . . constitutes renunciation or surrender" (123).

13. Matthews emphasizes the imaginary quality of the bear in this scene, that he is "present only as an absence," a result of Ike's desire to capture an "ever receding presence" (255). See also Zender's essay "Reading in 'The Bear.'"

14. I agree with Cohn's description of the monologues in *The Sound and the Fury* as "memory monologues," except that she places too much emphasis on the core day's events as *memories*, and thus becomes overly concerned with the "moment of locution" as a representational problem. See Cohn 183–84, 247–54.

15. Peter Swiggart also identifies narration as crucial to the Compson monologues, though he objects to its "unrealistic" nature (see Swiggart 61–74). Swiggart applies a standard of "objective" verisimilitude to voices that are a weave of varying modes in which conventional narration is but one strand. Over and over we have come upon ways in which Faulkner's texts are "unrealistic," abandoning literal or objective fact for larger goals of consciousness or theme. What seems to disturb the surface of objective reality can be better seen as Faulkner's interrogation (even parody) of the very notion of "objective reality" and his evocation of the "reality" of discourse in the form of voice. The Compson monologues are a case in point. If we were to assume that Faulkner is

representing either a purely internal stream-of-consciousness monologue or an objective narration, then the discovery of flaws in verisimilitude such as "disturbing transitions" and "unrealistic shifts from description to immediate statement" would be damning (the phrases are from Swiggart 70). But Faulkner's methods of generating voice always make "objectivity" problematic—and dependent on the play of discourse in his fiction rather than on fidelity to an external reality.

16. For a fuller treatment of Jason as a Southwest Humor narrator similar to G. W. Harris's Sut Lovingood, see Ross, "Jason Compson and Sut Lovingood."

17. For further discussion of the status of consciousness in relation to the subjectivity of speech, see Bakhtin, *Problems of Dostoevsky's Poetics* 290; and Derrida, *Margins of Philosophy* 288–90.

18. Maurice Blanchot describes in Kafka's fiction a "neuter" narrative voice that "tends to suspend the attributive structure of the language," that seems to come from nowhere, from no person (143). With Benjy, Faulkner has created, perhaps, a "neuter" narrative voice that retains the "attributive structure of the language."

19. In discussing the Quentin section, Carey Wall identifies three voices: an oral voice, which is properly punctuated and usually coherent; stream of consciousness, which is elliptical and usually unpunctuated; and the voice of Quentin's unconscious, printed in italics (377–78). I do not think we can make such rigid distinctions between oral, stream of consciousness, and unconscious discourse, since they flow and blend into one another. The notion of "oral" here is problematic in itself, since Quentin talks to no one as he narrates, and to base the distinction between levels of consciousness too much on italics is risky in Faulkner, as we have seen. Italics, for example, are not used exclusively for Quentin's deepest absorption in thought, nor for his most uncontrolled narration: he can quote even his father's words in a reasonably careful fashion: "*Father said it used to be a gentleman was known by his books; nowadays he is known by the ones he has not returned*" (92; 99).

20. MS. 70; *SF* Facsimile 72. Quentin's section begins on p. 34 of the manuscript (*SF* Facsimile 35). The six pages of the Caddy-Quentin conversation were originally numbered 34–40, but these are crossed out and replaced by, first, 43–49, then by 44–50, and finally by 70–76, their final position (*SF* Facsimile 72–78).

21. For an interesting defense of Jason's character, see Linda Wagner, "Jason Compson: The Demands of Honor."

22. This occurs in two other places: when Luster hunts in the branch for his quarter, the voices of the other blacks are not attributed but seem to come as disembodied sounds out of the air. When the golfers come down to the branch to find their ball, they are not identified as speakers until the caddie comes up to Luster and directly demands the ball. The same technique is used in "Barn Burning" (*CS* 3–4, 18).

23. Faulkner's care with such textual details as speaker identification and punctuation can be traced in the revisions he made in the manuscript of *The Sound and the Fury*. In the manuscript, all speakers, even strangers, are identified: "Can you ~~get~~ take him out of the house?" the man said. . . . "Better keep him there," the man said. (MS. 15; *SF* Facsimile 16). Faulkner also removed dialect spellings (retained in section 4 of the novel) such as "gwine" for "going" which, like the presence of question marks and commas (after dialogue followed by the speech tag) suggests that Faulkner perhaps originally conceived of even Benjy's section as a formally conventional first-person narration.

24. Linda Wagner describes one of Caddy's main functions as "that of creator and conveyor of language. Caddy attempts to create language for Benjy" ("Language and Act: Caddy Compson" 50).

25. Bleikasten, who sees "the entire first section [as] a 'trying to say' " (*Most Splendid Failure* 83), discusses this aspect of Benjy's monologue in the context of the close relations among creativity, sex, and death throughout Faulkner's fiction and career (67–89).

26. As Millgate (95) and Morrison (52) have pointed out, nearly all the references to "Father said" were added to the monologue during revision: as he made Quentin's narration less controlled, Faulkner also enhanced the importance of Mr Compson's words in Quentin's memory. For example, Mr Compson's comments on virginity as "a negative state and therefore contrary to nature" (143), were added after the manuscript version was written (MS. 53; *SF* Facsimile 55). In the manuscript Mr Compson speaks primarily in one scene, the debate with Quentin. In the final version Faulkner scattered Mr Compson's words throughout the monologue, so that they pervade Quentin's thoughts. One other minor change, in the debate itself, further suggests Faulkner's care in transforming reported conversations into psychic voice. The manuscript includes the word "said" with the speaker identifications, along with "father" to identify Mr Compson and a conventionally upper-case "I" for Quentin ("and I said . . . and father said" [MS. 86; *SF* Facsimile 88]).

27. Faulkner said it was "more passionate" not "to reduce her to telling what was going on" (*FU* 1). Faulkner's use of "passionate" instead of "compassionate" captures perfectly his love for her, his "heart's darling" (*FU* 40). See Bleikasten's discussion of Caddy's literal and symbolic role in Faulkner's creative psyche (*Most Splendid Failure* 43–66), and Matthews's comments on Caddy and the "space of writing" (20–22, 40–42).

28. The definition is phenomenologist Alexandre Kojeve's, quoted by Wilden in his commentary on Lacan (Lacan 193).

CHAPTER FOUR. *Oratorical Voice*

1. See the opening chapter of Logue and Dorgan for a discussion of assumptions about Southern oratory and demagoguery.

2. O'Faolain 354. William Van O'Connor mentions, in passing, the "Ciceronian periods of Southern oratory" as one source for Faulkner's style and rhetoric, but he does not develop this idea (342). See also Volpe (39–40), who discusses oratory in relation to Faulkner's style; and Kazin (350–61), who condemns Faulkner for excessive ornamentation.

3. Albert Guerard defends *A Fable* as a "Miltonic" novel precisely because it does share the high oratorical rhetoric he calls "Faulknerese" (229).

4. For excellent discussions of the history of Southern oratory see Braden, *Oratory in the Old South*; Braden, *Oratory in the New South*; and Logue and Dorgan. The nullification debate in South Carolina is discussed in Eubanks and in Christophersen.

5. Gunderson 112. See also Oliver (183) for more discussion of the importance of stump oratory to political success.

6. For other claims of differences between Southern and Northern discourse, see Tate 583–84. For discussion for and against the existence of a "genre of Southern oratory," see Braden's introductions to Braden, *Oratory in the Old South*, and Braden, *Oratory in the New South*; Braden, "The Emergence of the Concept of Southern Oratory"; Braden, "Southern Oratory Reconsidered: A Search for an Image"; Dickey; and Kearney.

7. The concept of discursive practice is also, of course, central to Michel Foucault's work; see especially *The Order of Things*.

8. William Faulkner's own public speeches show a strong tendency to appeal to shared assumptions, those "universal truths" he named in his Nobel Prize Acceptance Speech—"love and honor and pity and pride and compassion and sacrifice" (*ESPL* 120).

9. The example is Bourdieu's (11).

10. See Bakhtin's discussion of authoritative discourse as opposed to the "internally persuasive" (*The Dialogic Imagination* 342–45).

11. Francis Gaines makes such connotations explicit in referring to "the folk art of Southern oratory—the spread-eagle, flamboyant, ornate type of oratory, superfluous in verbiage and all but barren of thought" (4).

12. Gunderson describes an incident involving Cassius Marcellus Clay of Kentucky: "When sallying forth to champion Whiggery, Cassius Marcellus Clay of Kentucky, a more belligerent distant cousin of the more moderate Henry, carried a bowie knife and a brace of pistols. During oratorical festivities at Russell's Cave, Kentucky, a notorious brawler fired at him with a 'six-barrelled' pistol almost at arm's reach. Although struck by the shot, Clay unsheathed his bowie knife, cleaved his antagonist's skull, gouged out an eye, cut off an ear, and tossed his mangled body over a nearby cliff. Surprisingly, both lived to testify to the hazards of political speaking in the prewar South" (125–26).

13. Faulkner's narrating scenes in *Absalom, Absalom!* are often reminiscent of Conrad's in setting and mood, yet Conrad's are not "oratorical" largely be-

cause they do not involve relations of unequal authority. Marlow narrates to his equals, to fellow men of the sea, or to those empathetic with his adventures. He possesses the special knowledge of his experiences, of course, but he does not vie with his essentially passive listeners for discursive authority. See Ross, "Conrad's Influence on Faulkner's *Absalom, Absalom!*."

14. Said, *Beginnings* 86. See also Derrida's discussion of discourse and authority in *Dissemination* (especially 75–95).

15. Quentin Compson in *Absalom, Absalom!* and Ike McCaslin in *Go Down, Moses* are exceptions, for they are listeners who later take over the discourse.

16. Other examples, not assigned to characters, abound throughout Faulkner, especially in his later works. See, for example, the celebration of "Cotton" in *Requiem for a Nun* (226–27), or in *A Fable* see the superb oratorical sentence describing "Mama Bidet," the French general famous for knowing that "no army was better than its anus" (*FAB* 51–52).

17. See Reed's excellent discussion (151, 158) of the rhetorical effect figural density has in Faulkner.

18. Weathers argues that a series with two members creates "the aura of certainty, confidence, didacticism, and dogmatism," while a three-part series creates the effect of the "normal, the reasonable, the believable and the logical," and a four-part series suggests "the human, emotional, diffuse and inexplicable" (22). Such claims may fit the use of two-part series common in oratory, but it could be argued conversely that the common use of such compound pairs in oratory explains why Weathers finds them "dogmatic," etc. Faulkner's series do not follow Weathers's formulas, for most seem "confident" and "certain," regardless of how many members: "home and kin and all," or "man woman nigger or mule." Slatoff exhaustively describes Faulkner's penchant for oxymoron and polar oppositions, used, he argues, for the sake of the tension they create.

19. See Kartiganer for extended discussion of the form of Faulkner's novels. See also Reed's discussion of Faulkner's statements about fiction as being a matter of "craftsmanship, unity, and form" (Reed 1).

20. Lamar spoke in 1875 at Falkner's Station, named for William Faulkner's great-grandfather, W. C. Falkner (Murphy 151). Faulkner surely borrowed Lamar's name for Lucius Quintus Carothers McCaslin of *Go Down, Moses*. One coincidental verbal connection between Lamar and Faulkner, which probably has no empirical basis but is delightfully apt, is that Lamar's plantation twelve miles north of Oxford was named "Solitude." I only hope but do not believe that Faulkner had this in mind when he described his prose with "studbook style" phrases as "'by Southern Rhetoric out of Solitude' or 'Oratory out of Solitude'" (in *SL* 216; Cowley 78).

21. David Krause argues from Foucault's distinction between document and monument that in Bon's letter to Judith, Faulkner wants to create discourse

that is simultaneously document and monument. His analysis, however, is much more convincing as to the monumental qualities of Bon's letter. In discussing Mr Compson's reading of the letter, for example, Krause insists that Mr Compson wants to find in the letter some explanation for the events he knows have occurred. He wants to treat the letter as a document in hopes that it will reveal some truth of causation—perhaps in the form of an expression of Bon's motives. But the letter is better treated as Judith treats it, as a monument to Bon's memory. "[Mr Compson] expects Bon's letter to reveal its secrets to him, to tell him (in response to his pressing inquiries) what it thinks. But [it] does not reply; it remains unperturbed, 'shadowy inscrutable and serene'" (239). Krause argues less persuasively that the letter is documentary in that it permits us to read through its apparently opaque discourse to an implied "I-thou" relationship between Judith and Bon.

22. See Derrida's discussion (*Dissemination* 84–94) of the gods who are imaged as "engender[ing] through the mediation of the word." Derrida quotes Sauneron's description of "the initial god [who] had only to speak to create; and the beings and things evoked were born through his voice" (*Dissemination* 87; Sauneron 123). On Sutpen as father figure, see Irwin (generally) and Bleikasten, "Fathers in Faulkner" 140–43.

23. Rosa also describes her childhood's "stealth" and "creeping" as an attempt to *"rehearse [a] part as the faulty though eager amateur might steal wingward in some interim of the visible scene to hear the prompter's momentary voice"* (183; 147).

24. See, for example, Kartiganer 69–72.

25. See Sanae Tokizane's discussion of talking in *Absalom, Absalom!* as subservient not to an Overvoice but to writing (see especially 41–62).

26. Sutpen's decision to tell Henry is called his "last trump card" in his conversation with General Compson (341–42; 274).

27. Examples of other such figures are Aunt Jenny in *Flags in the Dust*, Rosa Millard in *The Unvanquished*, and Emily Grierson in "A Rose for Emily," all of whom possess an authority disproportionate to any social position except that of "Southern ladies" or "old undefeated spinster aunts," as Faulkner refers to them in the University of Virginia interviews (*FU* 254). He describes them in *Requiem for a Nun* as "the indomitable and undefeated, maiden progenitresses of spinster and childless descendants still capable of rising up and stalking out in the middle of *Gone with the Wind*" (256). He also said that "every young man should know one old woman . . . just to listen to" (*LG* 100).

28. Kauffman describes another form of traditionally public discourse in Rosa's story, the lover's, which creates the sense that her language is "at once intractable and enchanted" (189).

29. See Irwin 68–70 and 113–20; Matthews 134–42. But see Bleikasten's comment that Mr Compson is less a father than an alter ego for Quentin in *Absalom*. Bleikasten makes the valid point that in Faulkner the crucial confronta-

tion is generally between son and *forefather* rather than son and father ("Fathers in Faulkner" 126, 123).

30. Many critics have discussed Quentin as a listener. See, for example, Irwin 26; Ruppersburg 87–89; and Tokizane 48–55.

31. Some representative comments: *Absalom* "gets its chief effect as a novel from our sense that we are participating in its search for the truth" (Waggoner 169); *Absalom* is about "the nature of historical truth and . . . the problem of how we can 'know' the past" (C. Brooks, *Yoknapatawpha Country* 309); *Absalom* is "a virtual paean to the marvelous process of fictional creation" (Wittenberg 154); *Absalom* is a "supreme fiction . . . about the significance of fictions" (Kartiganer 69). One of the best overall discussions of narrative in *Absalom* is P. Brooks's chapter on the novel in *Reading for the Plot*. See also Young; and Matlock.

32. No convincing evidence for Sutpen's deduction that Bon is a Negro is offered other than his assertion, another instance of Sutpen's proclaiming "truth" into being. This is one of many factual uncertainties in the novel much discussed in the literature. See especially C. Brooks, *Yoknapatawpha Country* 436–38; and "The Narrative Structure of *Absalom, Absalom!*"

33. Sutpen's words invoke 2 Samuel 18:33, from which the novel's title comes: "O my son Absalom, my son, my son Absalom! Would God I had died for thee, O Absalom, my son, my son!" For a more complete discussion of the biblical parallels and their implications, see Ross, "Faulkner's *Absalom, Absalom!* and the David Story."

Works Cited

Abercrombie, David. *Studies in Phonetics and Linguistics*. London: Oxford University Press, 1965.

Aristotle. *Aristotle in 23 Volumes*. Loeb Classics. Cambridge, Mass.: Harvard University Press, 1973.

Austin, J. L. *How to Do Things with Words*. London: Oxford University Press, 1962.

Bakhtin, Mikhail. *The Dialogical Imagination*. Ed. Michael Holquist. Trans. Michael Holquist and Caryl Emerson. Austin: University of Texas Press, 1981.

———. *Problems of Dostoevsky's Poetics*. Trans. Caryl Emerson. Minneapolis: University of Minnesota Press, 1984.

———. *Speech Genres and Other Late Essays*. Ed. Caryl Emerson and Michael Holquist. Trans. Vern W. McGee. Austin: University of Texas Press, 1986.

Banfield, Ann. *Unspeakable Sentences: Narration and Representation in the Language of Fiction*. Boston: Routledge and Kegan Paul, 1982.

Barth, John. *Lost in the Funhouse: Fiction for Print, Tapes, and Live Voice*. New York: Doubleday, 1968.

Barthes, Roland. *The Pleasure of the Text*. Trans. Richard Miller. New York: Hill and Wang, 1975.

———. *S/Z*. Trans. Richard Miller. New York: Hill and Wang, 1974.

Beckett, Samuel. *Molloy*. Trans. Patrick Bowles. New York: Grove Press, 1959.

Benjamin, Walter. *Illuminations*. Ed. Hannah Arendt. New York: Schoeken, 1969.

Bickerton, Derek. "Modes of Interior Monologue: A Formal Definition." *Modern Language Quarterly* 28 (1967): 229–39.

Blair, Hugh. *Lectures on Rhetoric and Belles Lettres*. Ed. Harold F. Harding. 2 vols. London: 1783; Carbondale: Southern Illinois University Press, 1965.

Blanchard, Margaret. "The Rhetoric of Communion: Voice in *The Sound and the Fury*." *American Literature* 41 (1970): 555–65.

Blanchot, Maurice. *The Gaze of Orpheus and Other Literary Essays.* Trans. Lydia Davis. Barrytown: Station Hall, 1981.

Bleikasten, André. "Fathers in Faulkner." *The Fictional Father: Lacanian Readings of the Text.* Ed. Robert Con Davis. Amherst: University of Massachusetts Press, 1981. 115–46.

———. *Faulkner's* As I Lay Dying. Trans. Roger Little. Bloomington: Indiana University Press, 1973.

———. *The Most Splendid Failure: Faulkner's* The Sound and the Fury. Bloomington: Indiana University Press, 1976.

———. *Parcours de Faulkner.* Paris: Éditions Ophrys, 1982.

———. "*Pylon*: Ou L'Enfer des signes." *Études anglaises* 24 (1976): 437–47.

———. "Terror and Nausea: Bodies in *Sanctuary.*" *Faulkner Journal* 1 (1985): 17–29.

Blotner, Joseph. *Faulkner: A Biography.* 2 vols. New York: Random, 1974.

Booth, Wayne. *The Rhetoric of Fiction.* Chicago: University of Chicago Press, 1961.

———. *The Rhetoric of Irony.* Chicago: University of Chicago Press, 1974.

Bourdieu, Pierre. *Outline of a Theory of Practice.* Trans. Richard Nice. London: Cambridge University Press, 1977.

Braden, Waldo. "The Emergence of the Concept of Southern Oratory." *Southern Speech Journal* 26 (1961): 173–83.

———, ed. *Oratory in the New South.* Baton Rouge: Louisiana State University Press, 1979.

———, ed. *Oratory in the Old South: 1828–1860.* Baton Rouge: Louisiana State University Press, 1970.

———. "Repining Over an Irrevocable Past: The Ceremonial Orator in a Defeated Society, 1865–1900." *Oratory in the New South.* 8–37.

———. "Southern Oratory Reconsidered: A Search for an Image." *Southern Speech Journal* 29 (1964): 303–15.

———. "Three Southern Readers and Southern Oratory." *Southern Speech Journal* 32 (1966): 31–40.

Breitenbucher, Emile. Untitled Phi Beta Kappa speech. *Constitution* [Atlanta] 23 February 1900: 3.

Bridgman, Richard. *The Colloquial Style in America.* New York: Oxford University Press, 1966.

Brigance, William N. (vols. 1 and 2), and Marie K. Hochmuth (vol. 3), eds. *History and Criticism of American Public Address.* 3 vols. New York: McGraw, 1943, 1955.

Brooks, Cleanth. "The Narrative Structure of *Absalom, Absalom!.*" *Georgia Review* 29 (1975): 366–94.

———. *Toward Yoknapatawpha and Beyond.* New Haven: Yale University Press, 1978.

Works Cited

———. *William Faulkner: The Yoknapatawpha Country*. New Haven: Yale University Press, 1963.

Brooks, Peter. *Reading for the Plot: Design and Intention in Narrative*. New York: Knopf, 1984.

Brown, William Garrett. *The Lower South in American History*. New York, 1902.

Bungert, Hans. *William Faulkner und die humoristische Tradition des amerikanischen Südens*. Heidelberg: Carl Winter Universitätsverlag, 1971.

Burke, Kenneth. *A Rhetoric of Motives*. 1950. Berkeley: University of California Press, 1969.

Carothers, James B. *William Faulkner's Short Stories*. Ann Arbor: University of Michigan Research Press, 1985.

Carroll, David. *The Subject in Question: The Language of Theory and the Strategies of Fiction*. Chicago: University of Chicago Press, 1982.

Cash, W. J. *The Mind of the South*. New York: Knopf, 1941.

Chatman, Seymour. *Story and Discourse: Narrative Structure in Fiction and Film*. Ithaca: Cornell University Press, 1978.

Christopherson, Merrill G. "The Anti-Nullifiers." Braden, *Oratory in the Old South*. 73–103.

Cohen, William. "The Psychology of Reading." *New Literary History* 4 (1972): 75–90.

Cohn, Dorrit. *Transparent Minds: Narrative Modes for Presenting Consciousness in Fiction*. Princeton: Princeton University Press, 1978.

Conrad, Joseph. *Heart of Darkness*. Norton Critical Edition. Ed. Robert Kimbrough. New York: Norton, 1971.

Cowley, Malcolm. *The Faulkner-Cowley File: Letters and Memories, 1944–1962*. New York: Viking, 1966.

Cox, Diane L. *William Faulkner's* As I Lay Dying: *A Critical and Textual Study*. Diss. University of South Carolina, 1980. Ann Arbor: University of Michigan, 1980. 8119222.

Culler, Jonathan. "On Trope and Persuasion." *New Literary History* 9 (1978): 607–18.

Davis, Thadious M. *Faulkner's "Negro": Art and the Southern Context*. Baton Rouge: Louisiana State University Press, 1983.

De Man, Paul. *Allegories of Reading*. New Haven: Yale University Press, 1979.

Derrida, Jacques. *Dissemination*. Trans. Barbara Johnson. Chicago: University of Chicago Press, 1981.

———. *Margins of Philosophy*. Trans. Alan Bass. Chicago: University of Chicago Press, 1982.

———. *Of Grammatology*. Trans. Gayatri Chakravorty Spivak. Baltimore: Johns Hopkins University Press, 1976.

———. *Positions*. Trans. Alan Bass. Chicago: University of Chicago Press, 1981.

——. *Writing and Difference*. Trans. Alan Bass. Chicago: University of Chicago Press, 1978.

Dickey, Dallas. "Were They Ephemeral and Florid?" *Quarterly Journal of Speech* 32 (1946): 16–20.

——, and Donald C. Streeter. "Lucius Q. C. Lamar." Brigance and Hochmuth 3: 183–97.

Donoghue, Denis. "Yeats and the Living Voice." *The Ordinary Universe: Soundings in Modern Literature*. New York: Macmillan, 1968. 125–45.

Eco, Umberto. *A Theory of Semiotics*. Bloomington: Indiana University Press, 1976.

Eliot, George. *Daniel Deronda*. Vol. 8 of *Works*. Edinburgh: Blackwood, 1901.

Eliot, T. S. "The Three Voices of Poetry." *On Poetry and Poets*. New York: Farrar, 1957.

Erikson, Erik H. *Young Man Luther: A Study in Psychoanalysis and History*. New York: Norton, 1962.

Eubanks, Ralph T. "The Rhetoric of the Nullifiers." Braden, *Oratory in the Old South*. 19–72.

Falkner, Murry C. *The Falkners of Mississippi*. Baton Rouge: Louisiana State University Press, 1967.

Faulkner, John. *My Brother Bill: An Affectionate Reminiscence*. New York: Trident, 1963.

Ferrer, Daniel. "In omnis iam vocabuli mortem." Trans. Geoff Bennington. *Poétique* 44 (1980): 490–503.

Foucault, Michel. *The Archaeology of Knowledge*. Trans. A. M. Sheridan Smith. New York: Harper, 1972.

——. *The Order of Things: An Archaeology of the Human Sciences*. New York: Random, 1970.

——. "What is an Author." *Textual Strategies: Perspectives in Post-Structuralist Criticism*. Ed. Josué V. Harari. Ithaca: Cornell University Press, 1979. 141–60.

Fowler, Douglas. *Reading Nabokov*. Ithaca: Cornell University Press, 1974.

Fowles, John. "A Personal Note." *The Ebony Tower*. New York: New American Library, 1974.

Franklin, R. W. "Narrative Management in *As I Lay Dying*." *Modern Fiction Studies* 13 (1967): 57–65.

Friedman, Melvin. *Stream of Consciousness: A Study in Literary Method*. New Haven: Yale University Press, 1955.

Frost, Robert. *Selected Letters of Robert Frost*. Ed. Lawrence Thompson. New York: Holt, 1964.

Gaines, Francis Pendleton. *Southern Oratory: A Study in Idealism*. University: University of Alabama Press, 1946.

Genette, Gérard. "Frontiers of Narrative." *Figures of Literary Discourse*. New York: Columbia University Press, 1982.

Works Cited

———. *Narrative Discourse: An Essay in Method*. Ithaca: Cornell University Press, 1980.

———. *Nouveau discours du récit*. Paris: Éditions du seuil, 1983.

———. *Seuils*. Paris: Éditions du seuil, 1987.

Godden, Richard. "Call Me Nigger!: Race and Speech in Faulkner's *Light in August*." *Journal of American Studies* 14 (1980): 235–48.

Gold, Joseph. *William Faulkner: A Study in Humanism from Metaphor to Discourse*. Norman: University of Oklahoma Press, 1966.

Goody, Jack, and Ian Watt. "The Consequences of Literacy." *Literacy in Traditional Societies*. Ed. Jack Goody. Cambridge: Cambridge University Press, 1965.

Gresset, Michel. *Faulkner ou la fascination: poétique du regard*. Paris: Klincksieck, 1982.

———. "Of Sailboats and Kites: The 'Dying Fall' in Faulkner's *Sanctuary* and Beckett's *Murphy*." Gresset and Polk. 57–72.

———. "Théorème." *Recherches anglaises et américaines* 9 (1976): 73–94.

———, and Noel Polk, eds. *Intertextuality in Faulkner*. Jackson: University Press of Mississippi, 1985.

Grimwood, Michael. *Heart in Conflict: Faulkner's Struggles with Vocation*. Athens: University of Georgia Press, 1987.

Guerard, Albert. *The Triumph of the Novel: Dickens, Dostoevsky, Faulkner*. New York: Oxford University Press, 1976.

Gunderson, Robert G. "The Southern Whigs." Braden, *Oratory in the Old South*. 104–41.

Hagopian, John V. "Nihilism in Faulkner's *The Sound and the Fury*." *Modern Fiction Studies* 13 (1967): 45–55.

Hamblin, Robert W. "'Carcassonne': Faulkner's Allegory of Art and the Artist." *Southern Review* 15 (1979): 355–65.

Harris, George Washington. *Sut Lovingood's Yarns*. New York, 1867.

Hartman, Geoffrey H. *The Fate of Reading*. Chicago: University of Chicago Press, 1974.

———. *Saving the Text: Literature/Derrida/Philosophy*. Baltimore: Johns Hopkins University Press, 1981.

Heath, Stephen. *The Nouveau Roman: A Study in the Practice of Writing*. London: Elek, 1972.

Hegel, G. W. F. *Aesthetics*. Trans. T. M. Knox. New York: Oxford University Press, 1975.

Heilman, Robert B. "The Southern Temper." Rubin and Jacobs. 3–13.

Hemenway, Robert. "Enigmas of Being in *As I Lay Dying*." *Modern Fiction Studies* 16 (1970): 133–46.

Hergesheimer, Joseph. "The Pillar of Words." *Swords and Roses*. New York, 1928.

Hernadi, Paul. "Free Indirect Discourse and Related Techniques." *Beyond Genre: New Directions in Literary Classification*. Ithaca: Cornell University Press, 1972.

Hill, Benjamin H. "The Stars and Stripes." *History of Southern Oratory*. Ed. Thomas E. Watson. Vol. 9 of *The South in the Building of the Nation*. Ed. J. A. C. Chandler et al. 13 vols. Richmond, 1909–1913. 176–80.

Ihde, Don. *Listening and Voice: A Phenomenology of Sound*. Athens: Ohio University Press, 1976.

Ingarden, Roman. *The Cognition of the Literary Work of Art*. Trans. Ruth Ann Crowley and Kenneth R. Olson. Evanston: Northwestern University Press, 1973.

Inge, Thomas. "William Faulkner and George Washington Harris: In the Tradition of Southwestern Humor." *Tennessee Studies in Literature* 7 (1962): 47–59.

Irwin, John T. *Doubling and Incest/Repetition and Revenge: A Speculative Reading of Faulkner*. Baltimore: Johns Hopkins University Press, 1975.

Iser, Wolfgang. *The Implied Reader*. Baltimore: Johns Hopkins University Press, 1974.

Ives, Sumner. "Dialect Differentiation in the Stories of Joel Chandler Harris." *American Literature* 17 (1955): 88–96.

———. "A Theory of Literary Dialect." *Tulane Studies in English* 2 (1950): 137–82.

James, William. *Talks to Teachers on Psychology*. New York: Henry Holt, 1913.

Jehlen, Myra. *Class and Character in Faulkner's South*. New York: Columbia University Press, 1976.

Jenkins, Lee. *Faulkner and Black-White Relations: A Psychoanalytic Approach*. New York: Columbia University Press, 1981.

Josipovici, Gabriel. *The World and the Book*. Stanford: Stanford University Press, 1971.

Joyce, James. *Ulysses*. 1922. New York: Random, 1961.

Kartiganer, Donald M. *The Fragile Thread: The Meaning of Form in Faulkner's Fiction*. Amherst: University of Massachusetts Press, 1979.

Kauffman, Linda. "Devious Channels of Decorous Ordering: A Lover's Discourse in *Absalom, Absalom!*." *Modern Fiction Studies* 29 (1983): 183–200.

Kazin, Alfred. *On Native Grounds*. 1942. New York: Viking, 1956.

Kearney, Kevin E. "What's Southern about Southern Oratory?" *Southern Speech Journal* 32 (1966): 19–30.

Kenner, Hugh. *Joyce's Voices*. Berkeley: University of California Press, 1978.

Kierkegaard, Søren. *Either-Or*. Trans. D. F. Swenson and L. M. Swenson. Princeton: Princeton University Press, 1944.

Kinney, Arthur F. *Faulkner's Narrative Poetics: Style as Vision*. Amherst: University of Massachusetts Press, 1978.

Krause, David. "Reading Bon's Letter and Faulkner's *Absalom, Absalom!*." *PMLA* 99 (1984): 225–41.

Kristeva, Julia. *Desire in Language: A Semiotic Approach to Literature and Art*. New York: Columbia University Press, 1980.

Works Cited

Lacan, Jacques. *The Language of the Self: The Function of Language in Psychoanalysis*. Trans. and Commentary by Anthony Wilden. Baltimore: Johns Hopkins University Press, 1968.

Lanser, Susan Snaider. *The Narrative Act: Point of View in Prose Fiction*. Princeton: Princeton University Press, 1981.

Larsen, Eric. "The Barrier of Language: The Irony of Language in Faulkner." *Modern Fiction Studies* 13 (1967): 19–31.

Lilly, Paul R. "Caddy and Addie: Speakers of Faulkner's Impeccable Language." *Journal of Narrative Technique* 3 (1973): 170–82.

Linscott, Robert N. "Faulkner without Fanfare." *Esquire* 60 (July 1963): 36–40.

Logue, Cal M. "The Coercive Campaign Prophecy of Gene Talmadge, 1926–1946." Logue and Dorgan. 205–29.

———, and Howard Dorgan, eds. *The Oratory of Southern Demagogues*. Baton Rouge: Louisiana State University Press, 1981.

Lynn, Kenneth S. *Mark Twain and Southwest Humor*. Boston: Little, 1959.

McHale, Brian. "Free Indirect Discourse: A Survey of Recent Accounts." *PTL* 3 (1978): 249–87.

———. "Unspeakable Sentences, Unnatural Acts: Linguistics and Poetics Revisited." *Poetics Today* 4:1 (1983): 17–45.

McHaney, Thomas. "Faulkner Borrows from the Mississippi Guide." *Mississippi Quarterly* 19 (1966): 117.

Magliola, Robert R. *Phenomenology and Literature: An Introduction*. West Lafayette: Purdue University Press, 1977.

Matlock, James H. "Voices of Time: Narrative Structure in *Absalom, Absalom!*." *Southern Review* 15 (1979): 333–54.

Matthews, John T. *The Play of Faulkner's Language*. Ithaca: Cornell University Press, 1982.

Mayes, Edward. *Lucius Q. C. Lamar: His Life, Times, and Speeches*. Nashville, 1896.

Millgate, Michael. *The Achievement of William Faulkner*. New York: Random, 1966.

Milum, Richard A. "Faulkner's 'Carcassonne': The Dream and the Reality." *Studies in Short Fiction* 15 (1978): 133–38.

Minter, David. *William Faulkner: His Life and Work*. Baltimore: Johns Hopkins University Press, 1980.

Morgan, John T. (Senator from Alabama). Speech to Congress on the Gold Question. *Constitution* [Atlanta] 16 February 1900: 5.

Morris, Wesley. *Friday's Footprint: Structuralism and the Articulated Text*. Columbus: Ohio State University Press, 1979.

Morrison, Gail M. "The Composition of *The Sound and the Fury*." *William Faulkner's* The Sound and the Fury: *A Critical Casebook*. Ed. André Bleikasten. New York: Garland, 1982. 33–64.

Mortimer, Gail L. *Faulkner's Rhetoric of Loss: A Study in Perception and Meaning.* Austin: University of Texas Press, 1983.

Muravchik, Joshua. *New Republic* (16 and 23 July 1984): 34.

Murphy, James B. *L. Q. C. Lamar: Pragmatic Patriot.* Baton Rouge: Louisiana State University Press, 1973.

Nilon, Charles. *Faulkner and the Negro.* Boulder: University of Colorado Press, 1962.

O'Connor, William Van. "Rhetoric in Southern Writing: Faulkner." Utley. 342–46.

O'Faolain, Sean. "Faulkner's Stylistic Failings." Utley 352–53.

Oliver, Robert T. *History of Public Speaking in America.* Boston: Allyn and Bacon, 1965.

Ong, Walter. *The Presence of the Word.* New Haven: Yale University Press, 1967.

Page, Norman. *Speech in the English Novel.* New York: Longman, 1973.

Pascal, Roy. *The Dual Voice: Free Indirect Speech and Its Functions in the Nineteenth-Century European Novel.* Manchester: Manchester University Press, 1977.

Pei, Mario. *Glossary of Linguistic Terminology.* New York: Doubleday, 1966.

Pitavy, François. *Faulkner's* Light in August. Trans. Gillian E. Cook. Bloomington: Indiana University Press, 1973.

———. "Le Reporter: Tentation and derision de l'écriture." *Recherches anglaises et américaines* 9 (1976): 95–108.

Plato. *The Dialogues of Plato.* Trans. B. Jowett. New York: Random, 1937.

Polk, Noel. *Faulkner's* Requiem for a Nun. Bloomington: Indiana University Press, 1981.

———. "The Space Between *Sanctuary.*" Gresset and Polk. 16–35.

———. "William Faulkner's 'Carcassonne.'" *Studies in American Fiction* 12 (1984): 29–43.

Polletta, Gregory T. *Issues in Contemporary Literary Criticism.* Boston: Little, Brown, 1973.

Porter, Carolyn. *Seeing and Being: The Plight of the Participant Observer in Emerson, James, Adams, and Faulkner.* Middletown: Wesleyan University Press, 1981.

Pratt, Mary Louise. *Towards a Speech Act Theory of Literary Discourse.* Bloomington: Indiana University Press, 1977.

Quirk, Randolph. *The English Language and Images of Matter.* New York: Oxford University Press, 1972.

Rabkin, Eric. *Narrative Suspense.* Ann Arbor: University of Michigan Press, 1973.

Reed, Joseph. *Faulkner's Narrative.* New Haven: Yale University Press, 1973.

Renner, Charlotte. "Talking and Writing in Faulkner's Snopes Trilogy." *Southern Literary Journal* 15 (1982): 61–73.

Robertson, Joseph. *An Essay on Punctuation.* 1785. Ed. R. C. Alston. Menston, Eng.: Scholar, 1969.

Rosenberg, Bruce A. "The Oral Quality of Reverend Shegog's Sermon in William

Works Cited

Faulkner's *The Sound and the Fury.*" *Literatur in Wissenschaft und Unterricht* 2 (1969): 73–88.

Rosolato, Guy. "The Voice and the Literary Myth." *Structuralist Controversy: The Languages of Criticism and the Sciences of Man.* Ed. Richard Macksey and Eugenio Donato. Baltimore: Johns Hopkins University Press, 1970. 201–15.

Ross, Stephen M. "Conrad's Influence on Faulkner's *Absalom, Absalom!.*" *Studies in American Fiction* 2 (1974): 199–209.

———. "Faulkner's *Absalom, Absalom!* and the David Story: A Speculative Contemplation." *The David Myth in Western Literature.* Ed. Raymond-Jean Frontain and Jan Wojcik. West Lafayette: Purdue University Press, 1980. 136–55.

———. "Jason Compson and Sut Lovingood: Southwestern Humor as Stream of Consciousness." *Studies in the Novel* 8 (1976): 278–90.

———. "'Voice' in Narrative Texts: The Example of *As I Lay Dying.*" *PMLA* 94 (1979): 300–310.

Rubin, Louis D., Jr., and Robert D. Jacobs, eds. *Southern Renascence.* Baltimore: Johns Hopkins University Press, 1953.

Ruppersburg, Hugh M. *Voice and Eye in Faulkner's Fiction.* Athens: University of Georgia Press, 1983.

Said, Edward. *Beginnings: Intention and Method.* New York: Basic, 1975.

Sauneron, S. *Les Prêtres de l'ancienne Egypte.* Paris: Le Seuil, 1957.

Scholes, Robert, and Robert Kellogg. *The Nature of Narrative.* New York: Oxford University Press, 1966.

Segre, Cesare. "Persons and Voices in Literary Communication." *American Journal of Semiotics* 2 (1983): 89–97.

Sensibar, Judith L. *The Origins of Faulkner's Art.* Austin: University of Texas Press, 1984.

Shattuck, Roger. "The Devil's Dance." *New Republic* 26 (December 1983): 26–28.

Shelby, Annette. "Jeff Davis of Arkansas: 'Professional Man of the People.'" Logue and Dorgan. 13–46.

———. "The Southern Lady Becomes an Advocate." Braden, *Oratory in the New South.* 204–236.

Skei, Hans H. *William Faulkner: The Short Story Career.* Oslo: Universitetsforlaget, 1981.

Slatoff, Walter J. *Quest for Failure: A Study of William Faulkner.* Ithaca: Cornell University Press, 1960.

Snead, James A. *Figures of Division: William Faulkner's Major Novels.* New York: Metheun, 1987.

Stafford, William T. "'Some Homer of the Cotton Fields': Faulkner's Use of the Mule Early and Late (*Sartoris* and *The Reivers*)." *Papers on Language and Literature* 5 (1969): 190–96.

Strauch, Gérard. "De quelques interprétations récentes du style indirect libre." *RAMAN* 7 (1974): 40–73.

————. "De la 'littéralité' du discours rapporté." *RAMAN* 17 (1984): 159–182.

Strickland, William M. "James Kimble Vardaman: Manipulation through Myths in Mississippi." Logue and Dorgan. 67–84.

Sundquist, Eric J. *Faulkner: The House Divided*. Baltimore: Johns Hopkins University Press, 1983.

Swiggart, Peter. *The Art of Faulkner's Novels*. Austin: University of Texas Press, 1962.

Tate, Allen. *Essays of Four Decades*. Chicago: Swallow, 1968.

Taylor, Carole Ann. "*Light in August*: The Epistemology of Tragic Paradox." *Texas Studies in Literature and Language* 22 (1980): 48–68.

Thomas, Ota. "The Teaching of Rhetoric in the United States during the Classical Period of Education." Brigance and Hochmuth 1:193–210.

Thompson, Lawrence. *William Faulkner: An Introduction and Interpretation*. New York: Barnes, 1963.

Todorov, Tzvetan. *The Poetics of Prose*. Trans. Richard Howard. Ithaca: Cornell University Press, 1977.

Tokizane, Sanae. *Faulkner and/or Writing: On Absalom, Absalom!*. Tokyo: Liber, 1986.

Twain, Mark. *The Adventures of Huckleberry Finn*. 1885. New York: Bobbs-Merrill, 1967.

Ulmer, Gregory. *Applied Grammatology: Post(e)-Pedagogy from Jacques Derrida to Joseph Beuys*. Baltimore: Johns Hopkins University Press, 1985.

Utley, Francis Lee, Lynn Z. Bloom, and Arthur F. Kinney, eds. *Bear, Man, and God: Seven Approaches to William Faulkner's "The Bear."* New York: Random, 1964.

Vickery, Olga W. *The Novels of William Faulkner: A Critical Interpretation*. Baton Rouge: Louisiana University Press, 1959.

Volpe, Edmond L. *A Reader's Guide to William Faulkner*. New York: Noonday, 1964.

Wadlington, Warwick. *Reading Faulknerian Tragedy*. Ithaca: Cornell University Press, 1987.

Waggoner, Hyatt. *William Faulkner: From Jefferson to the World*. Lexington: University of Kentucky Press, 1959.

Wagner, Linda. "Jason Compson: The Demands of Honor." *Sewanee Review* 79 (1971): 554–75.

————. "Language and Act: Caddy Compson." *Southern Literary Journal* 14 (Spring 1982): 49–61.

Wall, Carey. "*The Sound and the Fury*: The Emotional Center." *Midwest Quarterly* 11 (1970): 371–87.

Watson, James G. *William Faulkner: Letters and Fictions*. Austin: University of Texas Press, 1987.